Process and Language

Process and Language

A Study of the *Mahābhāṣya* ad A1.3.1 *bhūvādayo dhātavaḥ*

HIDEYO OGAWA

Foreword by
GEORGE CARDONA

MOTILAL BANARSIDASS PUBLISHERS
PRIVATE LIMITED • DELHI

First Edition: Delhi, 2005

ISBN: 81-208-2951-4

MOTILAL BANARSIDASS
41 U.A. Bungalow Road, Jawahar Nagar, Delhi 110 007
8 Mahalaxmi Chamber, 22 Bhulabhai Desai Road, Mumbai 400 026
203 Royapettah High Road, Mylapore, Chennai 600 004
236, 9th Main III Block, Jayanagar, Bangalore 560 011
Sanas Plaza, 1302 Baji Rao Road, Pune 411 002
8 Camac Street, Kolkata 700 017
Ashok Rajpath, Patna 800 004
Chowk, Varanasi 221 001

Printed in India
BY JAINENDRA PRAKASH JAIN AT SHRI JAINENDRA PRESS,
A-45 NARAINA, PHASE-I, NEW DELHI 110 028
AND PUBLISHED BY NARENDRA PRAKASH JAIN FOR
MOTILAL BANARSIDASS PUBLISHERS PRIVATE LIMITED,
BUNGALOW ROAD, DELHI 110 007

To the memory of Nobuyuki Baba,
a dear student of mine,
who passed away
at the age of twenty-four
on August 3, 2001.

Table of contents

Foreword

Pāṇini had predecessors both in phonetics and phonology as well as in grammar, and he not only built upon the foundations established by these predecessors but also superceded them in major aspects. This is well known. One of the aspects of Pāṇini's departure from those to whom he succeeded is his increasing formalism. Thus, for example, there are general definitions of different kinds of compounds which are semantically based, depending on what they have as their primary significands: avyayībhāvas: the meaning associated with the first constitutent (पूर्वपदार्थप्रधानोऽव्ययीभावः), tatpuruṣa: the meaning of the second constituent (उत्तरपदार्थप्रधानस्तत्पुरुषः), bahuvrīhi: a meaning other than that of any constitutent (अन्यपदार्थप्रधानो बहुव्रीहिः), dvandva: the meanings of both constituents (उभयपदार्थप्रधानो द्वन्द्वः). Such classification is reflected in Kātyāyana's and Patañjali's comments on Pāṇinian sūtras, and commentators recognize that they are appropriate in general but are not fully adequate. Pāṇini's system is devoid of such general definitions for all compounds; instead, the class names *avyayībhāva, tatpuruṣa, dvandva,* and *bahuvrīhi* are assigned to compounds in accordance with the conditions under which they are formed, and, although Aṣṭādhyāyī 2.2.24: अनेकमन्यपदार्थे brings in a meaning other than that of the padas which enter into composition, the general rule assigning the class name *bahuvrīhi* to certain compounds simply says (Aṣṭādhyāyī 2.2.23: शेषो बहुव्रीहिः) that a compound that is residual with respect to those provided for by previous rules bears this name.

To be sure, pre-Pāṇinian scholars had already taken steps in this direction. Thus, for example, two prātiśākhyas which probably antedate Pāṇini in their cores—the Rgvedaprātiśākhya and the Taittirīyaprātiśākhya—clearly distinguish the terminology used in describing the production of sounds and in naming classes of sounds with respect to phonological operations. Nevertheless, at a stage reflected both in the Ṛgvedaprātiśākhya and in Yāska's Nirukta general semantic definitions of major word classes were accepted. According to the former (RPr. 12.18-19: तन्नाम येनाभिदधाति सत्त्वम् । तदाख्यातं येन भावं सधातु ।), a nominal form is one by means of which a speaker signifies a substance, a thing (सत्त्वम्=द्रव्यम् according to Uvaṭa); a verb form is one by means of which a speaker signifies an action (भावम् = क्रियाम् according to Uvaṭa) and which includes a verbal base (*sadhātu*). In a comparable manner, Yāska (Nirukta 1.1: तत्रैतन्नामाख्यातयोर्लक्षणं प्रदिशन्ति भावप्रधानमाख्यातं सत्त्वप्रधानानि नामानि ।) notes that the characteristics which define a verbal form and a nominal respectively are said to be as follows: the former has bhāva as its principal meaning, while nominal forms have substances as their principal meanings. In addition, Yāska remarks (Nirukta 1.1: तद्यत्रोभे भावप्रधाने भवतः ।) that where both such forms occur, they jointly have bhāva as the principal meaning; that is, the principal meaning signified by an utterance such as देवदत्तः पचति 'Devadatta is cooking' is the act of cooking. Yāska then proceeds (Nirukta 1.1: पूर्वापरीभूतं भावमाख्यातेनाचष्टे व्रजति पचतीत्युपक्रमप्रभृत्यपवर्गपर्यन्तम् मूर्तं सत्त्वभूतं सत्त्वनामभिर्व्रज्या पक्तिरिति ।) to contrast two aspects of bhāva which a speaker designates when using a finite verb form like *vrajati* 'goes, is going' or *pacati* 'cooks, is cooking' on the one hand and, on the other hand, a form of an abstract action noun, such as *vrajyā* (nom. sg.) 'going', *paktiḥ* 'cooking'. By means of a verb form, one signifies a bhāva whose defining characteristic is that it is sequential (*pūrvāparībhūtam*), starting from inception up to the termination of the act in question; by means of nominal forms, one signifies a bhāva which is embodied (*mūrtam*), has the characteristic of a thing (*sattvabhūtam*). Yāska ends his brief presentation (Nirukta 1.1: अद इति सत्त्वानामुपदेशः गौरश्वः पुरुषो हस्तीति । भवतीति भावस्यास्ते शेते व्रजति तिष्ठतीति ।) by noting that *adas* 'that' and the base *bhū* (*bhavati*) are the general referents through which one designates things and bhāvas, particular ones being referred to respectively by nominals like *go* (*gauḥ*)'ox, cow', *aśva* (*aśvaḥ*) 'horse', *hastin* (*hastī*) 'elephant' and verbs like *ās* (*āste*) 'be seated', *śī* (*śete*) 'lie, sleep', *vraj* (*vrajati*) 'go', and *sthā* (*tiṣṭhati*) 'come to a stop, be in place'.

That acts are brought together under the term bhāva and verb forms are referred to by *ākhyāta* could support the thesis that at one time such terminology fit within a system that operated with subjects and predicates such that a verb was considered a predicate which 'tells' (*ācaṣṭe*) something about a subject. This view could be buttressed with an appeal to the view which Yāska attributes to Vārṣyāyaṇi, according to whom (Nirukta 1.2: षड् भावविकारा भवन्तीति वार्ष्यायणिः जायतेऽस्ति विपरिणमते वर्धतेऽपक्षीयते विनश्यतीति ।) there are six varieties of bhāva: coming into being (*jāyate* 'is born, comes into being'), existing (*asti* 'is'), changing (*vipariṇamate* 'undergoes modification'), increasing (*vardhate* 'grows, increases'), diminishing (*apakṣīyate* 'diminishes'), and ceasing to be (*vinaśyati* 'perishes'). It is nevertheless patent from what Yāska himself says in Nirukta 1.1[1] that he considered the principal meaning of a sentence like देवदत्तः पचति to be the act of cooking and not a subject Devadatta of whom it is predicated that he is cooking.

The definition भावप्रधानमाख्यातम्—at times substituted by क्रियाप्रधानमाख्यातम्—continues to reverberate in later discussions, not only of grammarians like Patañjali and Bhartṛhari but others also. In Pāṇini's Aṣṭādhyāyī, however, one finds no such semantic definition, although Pāṇini does continue to use both *kriyā* and *bhāva* with reference to what verbal bases signify. Instead, Pāṇini assigns the class name *dhātu* to verbal bases by two sūtras, which deal respectively with primitive and derived bases: Aṣṭādhyāyī 1.3.1: भूवादयो धातवः and 3.1.32: सनाद्यन्ता धातवः. According to 1.3.1, items of the ordered set beginning with *bhū* are called *dhātu*. The bases in question are listed in one of the ancillaries to the Aṣṭādhyāyī proper, namely the dhātupāṭha. Aṣṭādhyāyī 3.1.32, on the other hand, presupposes rules introducing post-verbal affixes ***san*** (which serves predominantly to form desideratives), *yaṅ* (intensive suffix), ***ṇic*** (which serves to form causatives) as well as affixes such as ***kyac***, which serve to form denominative verbs;

---

[1] तद्यत्रोभे भावप्रधाने भवतः। पूर्वापरीभूतं भावमाख्यातेनाचष्टे व्रजति पचतीत्युपक्रमप्रभृत्यपवर्गपर्यन्तम् मूर्तं सत्त्वभूतं सत्त्वनामभिर्व्रज्या पक्तिरिति । This is the punctuation supported not only by the commentaries of Skanda-Maheśvara and Durga but also by testimonia such as Śabara on Jaimini Mīmāṃsāsūtra 1.1.5 (Ānandāśrama Sanskrit Series 97, fourth edition, Poona: 1976, vol. I, p. 56).

derivates ending in *san* and other affixes introduced by preceding sūtras are called *dhātu*.

The Mahābhāṣya on Aṣṭādhyāyī 1.3.1 contains a skillfully arranged discussion of topics related to units which should be called *dhātu*. The Bhāṣya begins with a discussion of why the sūtra has *bhūvādayaḥ* with *-ūv-*, and cites the first half of a ślokavārttika, stating that *-v-* is used for the sake of auspiciousness. Patañjali goes on immediately to take up the reason for Pāṇini stating *bhūvādayaḥ* using *-ādi-*, concluding that this shows there is a listing of bases outside the corpus of the Aṣṭādhyāyī sūtrapāṭha. This leads into Kātyāyana's first two vārttikas on Aṣṭādhyāyī 1.3.1, with a discussion of examples and arguments associated with them. In these vārttikas, Kātyāyana argues that if the class name *dhātu* is assigned through such a listing, two problems result that have to be resolved. First, the name could be assigned to items that are homophonous with ones listed in the dhātupāṭha but which should not be referred to by the name *dhātu* when this is used in rules stating operations which concern such units; for example, *vā* 'blow, go' should be a dhātu, but the particle *vā* 'or' should not. Secondly, one has also to specify what particular stretches of sounds in the list constitute individual units to be called *dhātu*; for example, it is necessary to provide that *bhū* ('be, become') and *edh* ('thrive') are separate units, that *bhvedh* is not a single unit. The problems thus brought up lead to the discussion of two alternative semantic definitions of units to be called *dhātu*: first that a dhātu is an element signifying an action viewed in such a manner that it is designated *kriyā* (क्रियावचनो धातुः); alternatively, that a dhātu is an element signifying an act, but now viewed in such a way that it is designated *bhāva* (भाववचनो धातुः). The rich and beautifully organized discussions surrounding these two possibilities involve Kātyāyana and Patañjali in an array of issues which continue to be objects of discussion throughout the subsequent Pāṇinian literature, from Bhartṛhari's Vākyapadīya down to Nāgeśa's various works.

In the present book, Professor Hideyo Ogawa has ably treated these discussions in the Mahābhāṣya and related works. He has produced a meticulously documented treatment of the texts, with penetrating comments and useful annotations. In addition, he has summarized and critically appraised earlier scholarship dealing with the topics he has studied. The result is, in my opinion, an outstanding piece of careful scholarship, which will take its place as a major contribution to our understanding of Pāṇini and the long tradition of renewed discussion which arose surrounding his Aṣṭādhyāyī. I commend him for his accomplishment and I hope that the scholarly community will give Professor Ogawa's work the favorable reception it deserves.

George Cardona
University of Pennsylvania

Preface

It has been nearly fifteen years since I adventured into a study of the *Mahābhāṣya* of Patañjali (2nd century B.C.) on the sūtra *bhūvādayo dhātavaḥ*, a grammatical rule formulated by Pāṇini (500 B.C.) in his *Aṣṭādhyāyī* (*A*1.3.1) and discussed by Kātyāyana (3rd century B.C.) in his vārttikas. It is a genuine pleasure to publish the present work as a result of years of laborious study.

I began my Pāṇinian studies with treatises on semantics and philosophy of grammar in the Pāṇinian tradition after Bhartṛhari (5th century), written by later Pāṇinīyas, i.e., Navya-Vaiyākaraṇas, such as Kauṇḍabhaṭṭa (17th century) and Nāgeśa (late 17th to 18th century). In the course of my study of them I felt it absolutely necessary to go back to the *Mahābhāṣya* where questions of general linguistic and philosophical import, which were the bases for later elaborations, were already treated fairly extensively.

As is well known, later Pāṇinīyas characterize a verbal cognition (*śābdabodha*) as *dhātvarthamukhyaviśeṣyakabodha* 'a cognition whose principal qualificand (*mukhyaviśeṣya*) is the meaning of a verb (*dhātvartha*)', while Naiyāyikas and Bhāṭṭa Mīmāṃsakas respectively define it as *prathamāntārthamukhyaviśeṣyakabodha* 'a cognition whose principal qualificand is the meaning of a nominative form (*prathamāntārtha*)' and as *ākhyātārthamukhya-viśeṣyakabodha* 'a cognition whose principal qualificand is the meaning of a verb ending (*ākhyātārtha*)'. In addition, Kauṇḍa-bhaṭṭa and Nāgeśa declare that a verb denotes an activity (*kriyā*, *vyāpāra*) and its result (*phala*), though, according to the former, a single verb has two denotative powers to convey them (*ubhaya-śakti*), and, according to the latter, a single verb has a single denotative power to convey an activity qualified by its result (*viśiṣṭaśakti*).

I had to face serious questions: What brings the later Pāṇinīyas to develop such a theory of a verbal cognition and to get such a view of the verb meaning? It was in the course of events that I went on to the *Mahābhāṣya* on *A*1.3.1 which was devoted to elaborating on the semantics of verbs. However, once you undertake the task of reading the text of the *Mahābhāṣya* on any sūtra, you will see that a proper understanding of it requires time and effort and that you have to make a painstaking disclosure of a hidden thought of Patañjali. I find a voice in the *Mahābhāṣyapradīpa* or simply the *Pradīpa*, the commentary on the *Mahābhāṣya* by Kaiyaṭa (early 11th century), to express what was in my mind at the time I started reading the text:

bhāṣyābdhiḥ kvātigambhīraḥ kvāhaṃ mandamatis tataḥ /
chātrāṇām upahāsyatvaṃ yāsyāmi piśunātmanām //
(*Pradīpa* [maṅgala 6])
"What comparison is there between the Bhāṣya, deep ocean that it is, and me, who am slow-witted. Therefore, I will be exposed to the ridicule of pupils who by nature find fault with what their teachers say."

Kaiyaṭa confessed that the *Mahābhāṣya* was so deep that he was afraid of not fully comprehending it. He continued to say:

tathāpi haribaddhena sāreṇa granthasetunā /
kramamāṇaḥ śanaiḥ pāraṃ tasya prāptāsmi paṅguvat //
(*Pradīpa* [maṅgala 7])
"But even so, I will reach the further side of the ocean, crossing slowly, like a lame man, that excellent bridge in the form of a treatise which has been constructed by Bhartṛhari."

The commentary on the *Mahābhāṣya* written by Bhartṛhari, which Kaiyaṭa expresses metaphorically as a bridge to cross to the further side of the ocean of the *Mahābhāṣya*, is the *Mahābhāṣyaṭīkā* or the *Mahābhāṣyadīpikā*, whose preserved text, beginning with a lacuna and ending with the seventh āhnika, does not cover the text on *A*1.3.1. The fact that the text requires us to read between the lines reflects its depth. For acquiring a deeper understanding of the text, as Kaiyaṭa resorted to the above-mentioned commentary, so I resorted to the *Vākyapadīya* of the same author, the major text on semantics and philosophy of grammar in the Pāṇinian school. It is beyond question that the *Vākyapadīya* also in great part constitutes a commentary on the *Mahābhāṣya*. The study of the *Vākyapadīya* also deservedly cost much time and effort.

I have taken this exposition of the argument developed by Patañjali in his Bhāṣya on *A*1.3.1 as far as I can. Readers of the present work will judge for themselves to what extent I have been successful. Regardless of what the reader's judgement is, I must say that I feel relieved to bring this project to an end.

I would like to discharge a debt of gratitude to my teachers by presenting this work:

The late Professor Atsushi Uno, from whom I learned Sanskrit and who initiated me into the Navya-Nyāya system so that I could deal with Navya-Naiyāyikas' treatises on semantics such as the *Vyutpattivāda* of Gadādhara (17th century).

Professor Nobuhiko Kobayashi, who introduced the world of Pāṇinian grammar to me by his classes in Pāṇini's grammar where I could for the first time read a kaumudī ('moonlight') work, the *Laghusiddhāntakaumudī* of Varadarāja (17th century), and the *Mahābhāṣya* on *A*2.1.55.

Professor Shoryu Katsura, under whom I studied Buddhist logic and whose lectures on meta-rules (*paribhāṣā*) with the major kaumudī work, the *Siddhāntakaumudī*, struck me.

Professor Saroja Bhate, under whose guidance I pursued the study of Pāṇini's grammar in Poona from 1982 to 1983 and with whose help I could read through the *Siddhāntakaumudī*.

The late Pt. K. A. Sivaramakrishna Sastri, a traditional Pandit with a scholarly knowledge of the various traditional branches of learning, to whom I am profoundly indebted for two years of instruction in Pāṇini's grammar and whom I asked to help me with several texts, including the *Vaiyākaraṇabhūṣaṇasāra* of Kauṇḍabhaṭṭa and the *Paramalaghumañjūṣā* of Nāgeśa.

Professor George Cardona, to whom also I am deeply indebted for his encouragement to continue this work on the *Mahābhāṣya* and who was generous enough with his time to read the Kriyāsamuddeśa of the *Vākyapadīya* with me.

Special thanks are due to Professor Tom Tillemans, Lausanne University, for giving me a chance to be intent on carrying out the present work in Lausanne and also to Professor Katsura for making arrangements for me to stay there for this purpose.

I am also happy to acknowledge the help of friends who read and commented on drafts of this work: Yoshichika Honda, Yoshie Kobayashi, Koji Ezaki, Yohei Kawajiri, Suguru Ishimura, and Sayaka Nakano.

Finally, it is my special pleasure to thank Professor Brendan S. Gillon, Professor Shin Fujinaga, Dr. Masato Kobayashi, Dr. Mithilesh Chaturvedi, Dr. Kanshi Ram, and Mr. Narendra Prakash Jain for their helpful suggestions in publishing the present work.

Hiroshima, December 31, 2003 Hideyo Ogawa

References and abbreviations

A: Pāṇini's *Aṣṭādhyāyī*.

BM: Vāsudeva Dīkṣita's *Bālamanoramā*. See Giridhara Śarmā Caturveda and Parameśvarānanda Śarmā Bhāskara [1958-61].

BŚIŚ: Nāgeśa's *Bṛhacchabdenduśekhara*. See Sitaram Shastri [1960].

Darpaṇa: Harivallabha's *Darpaṇa*. See Pañcholi [1969].

JS: Jaimini's *Mīmāṃsāsūtra*. See Abhyankar/Joshi [1976].

Kāśikāvṛtti: Vāmana and Jayāditya's *Kāśikāvṛtti*. See (1) Miśra [1985] and (2) Aryendra Sharma, Khanderao Deshpande, and D. G. Padhye [1969-70].

LŚIŚ: Nāgeśa's *Laghuśabdenduśekhara*. See Nene [1987].

MBh: Patañjali's *Vyākaraṇamahābhāṣya*. See (1) Vedavrata [1962–63], (2) Kielhorn [1980-85] = Abhyankar [1962-72], and (3) the Nirnaya-Sagar edition (Joshi (Jośi) [1942, 1945, 1951], Kudāla [1912], Raghunātha (Kāśinātha) Śāstrī and Śivadatta D. Kudāla [1937], Śivadatta D. Kudāla and Raghunātha Śāstrī [1935]).

MBhD I: Bhartṛhari's *Mahābhāṣyadīpikā*. See Bronkhorst [1987].

MBhD III: Bhartṛhari's *Mahābhāṣyadīpikā*. See Palsule [1985].

Nirukta: Yāska's *Nirukta*. See Sarup [1927a].

Niruktavṛtti: Durga's *Niruktavṛtti*. See Bhadkamkar [1985].

Niruktabhāṣyaṭīkā: *Niruktabhāṣyaṭīkā* of Skandasvāmin and Maheśvara. See Sarup [1927b; 1935].

Nyāsa: Jinendrabuddhi's *Nyāsa*. See Miśra [1985].

Nyāyāgamānusāriṇī: Siṃhasūri's *Nyāyāgamānusāriṇī*. See Jambūvijaya [1966-88].

Padamañjarī: Haradatta's *Padamañjarī*. See Miśra [1985].

Paddhati: Vṛṣabhadeva's *Paddhati*. See Subramania Iyer [1966].

PIŚ: Nāgeśa's *Paribhāṣenduśekhara*. See Abhyankar [1962].

Pradīpa: Kaiyaṭa's *Pradīpa*. See Vedavrata [1962–63].

Prakāśa: Helārāja's *Prakāśa*. See Subramania Iyer [1963, 1973].

Puṇyarāja: See Subramania Iyer [1983].

Ṛgvedaprātiśākhya: Śaunaka's *Ṛgvedaprātiśākhya*. See Tripāṭhī [1986].

ŚK: Bhaṭṭoji Dīkṣita's *Śabdakaustubha*. See Nene [1929], [1933], and Vindhyeśvarī Prasāda Dvivedī [1917].

SK: Bhaṭṭoji Dīkṣita's *Vaiyākaraṇasiddhāntakaumudī*. See Giridhara Śarmā Caturveda and Parameśvarānanda Śarmā Bhāskara [1958-61].

ŚS: *Śivasūtra*. Pāṇini's *akṣarasamāmnāya*.

TV: Kumārila Bhaṭṭa's *Tantravārttika*. In: Abhyankar and Joshi [1976].

Uddyota: Nāgeśa's *Uddyota*. See Vedavrata [1962–63].

US: *Uṇādisūtra*. (1) Aufrecht [1859]. (2) In Bhaṭṭoji Dīkṣita's *Vaiyākaraṇasiddhāntakaumudī*. See Giridhara Śarmā Caturveda and Parameśvarānanda Śarmā Bhāskara [1958-61].

VBhS: Kauṇḍabhaṭṭa's *Vaiyākaraṇabhūṣaṇasāra*. See Pañcholi [1969].

VP: Bhartṛhari's *Vākyapadīya*. See Rau, Subramania Iyer.

Vṛtti: *Vākyapadīya Vṛtti*. See Subramania Iyer [1966, 1983].

VSK: Bhaṭṭoji Dīkṣita's *Vaiyākaraṇasiddhāntakārikā*. In: Pañcholi [1969].

VSLM: Nāgeśa's *Vaiyākaraṇasiddhāntalaghumañjūṣā*. See Bhāṇḍāri [1925].

VSM: Nāgeśa's *Vaiyākaraṇasiddhāntamañjūṣā*. See (1) Śukla [1977] and (2) Kapil Dev Shastri [1985].

On references and notation

References of the text of the *Mahābhāṣya* are to volumes, pages, and lines of Kielhorn [1980–85] = Abhyankar [1962–72]. Note that the text is not necessarily given as in this edition, especially regarding punctuation.

References of the texts of the *Pradīpa* and the *Uddyota* are to volumes and pages of Vedavrata [1962–63].

References to kārikās of the *Vākyapadīya* are made according to Rau [1977], so that kārikā numbers are given according to his edition.

I use bold face italics in order to indicate markers (*it, anubandha*; *A*1.3.2-8), which are unconditionally deleted (*A*1.3.9). Markers also serve to form abbreviations that refer to members of ordered groups (*A*1.1.71); for example, *ti**ṅ*** is an abbreviatory term which refer to verb endings, consisting of the verbal ending *ti* with the marker ***ṅ***.

In general, I follow the most widely accepted system for transliterating Devanāgarī. Except where the topics under discussion call for marking accents and a Vedic passage is cited, Sanskrit items are unmarked for accentuation.

Introduction

The keynote of the *Mahābhāṣya* on *A*1.3.1

0.1. Basic to Pāṇini's derivational system

In Pāṇini's derivational system, by means of which utterances (*vākya*) and their components are accounted for, items assigned the name *dhātu* 'verb, root' rank as core elements of utterances that are actually usable and serve as a starting point of the derivation of such utterances. In order to illustrate this, let us consider the following simple sentence:

devadatta odanaṃ pacati 'Devadatta is cooking rice-gruel'.

This sentence is derived from the following posited string.

devadatta-s odana-am pac-L

In Pāṇini's system, the nominals *devadatta* 'the person called *Devadatta*' and *odana* 'rice-gruel' are termed *prātipadika* 'nominal base' (*A*1.2.45), the affixes *-s* (***su***) and *-am* are nominal endings referred to by the term *sup* (*A*4.1.2; 1.1.71), the verb *pac* is termed *dhātu* (*A*1.3.1), and the L-affixes are abstract verb endings subsequently replaced by finite endings or participial affixes. The following sūtras involved in the derivation of the sentence under consideration will have only to be taken up here.

[1] *A*3.1.91 *dhātoḥ* //
[2] *A*3.2.123 *vartamāne laṭ* //
[3] *A*3.4.69 *laḥ karmaṇi ca bhāve cākarmakebhyaḥ* //
[4] *A*3.4.78 *tiptasjhisipthasthamibvasmastātāṃjhathāsāthāṃdhvamiḍvahimahiṅ* //
[5] *A*1.3.78 *śeṣāt kartari parasmaipadam* //
[6] *A*1.4.108 *śeṣe prathamaḥ* //
[7] *A*1.4.22 *dvyekayor dvivacanaikavacane* //
[8] *A*3.1.68 *kartari śap* //
[9] *A*4.1.2 *svaujasamauṭchaṣṭābhyāmbhisṅebhyāmbhyasṅasibhyāmbhyasṅasosāmṅyossup* //
[10] *A* 2.3.1 *anabhihite* //

[11] A2.3.2 *karmaṇi dvitīyā* //
[12] A2.3.18 *kartṛkaraṇayos tṛtīyā* //
[13] A2.3.46 *prātipadikārthaliṅgaparimāṇavacanamātre prathamā* //

0.1.1. [1] *A*3.1.91 heads a group of rules which introduce affixes that occur with units called *dhātu*. [2] *A*3.2.123, a rule of the section headed by [1] *A*3.1.91, provides for the L-affix *laṭ* to be introduced after verbs (*dhātu*) under a condition of a specific time reference: if the act denoted by a verb is referred to the present time (*vartamāna*). In the situation conveyed by the sentence in question, the time reference of the act signified by the verb *pac*, the act of cooking, is present, so that we have the following sequence:

pac + *laṭ* (DHĀTU + L)

According to [3] *A*3.4.69, any L-affix follows a verb when an agent (*kartṛ*), an object (*karman*), or the mere act signified by the verb (*bhāva*) is to be signified. In the present case, an L-affix is introduced to denote an agent with respect to the act signified by the verb *pac*.

[4] *A*3.4.78 simply allows a series of basic verb endings possibly to substitute for an L-affix. The actual ending is to be selected by application of restrictive rules specifying what particular endings occur under different conditions.

First, a choice is made between the sets of endings called *ātmanepada* and *parasmaipada*. The verb *pac* is taught in the dhātupāṭha with a svarita vowel marker *à* (***ḍupacàṣ***), so that it takes ātmanepada affixes (*taṅ*; from *ta* to *mahiṅ*) signifying an agent if the agent in question cooks something for himself (A1.3.72). The sentence at hand is used to speak of Devadatta cooking rice for someone else, so that parasmaipada endings (from *ti**p*** to *mas*) are selected to replace L-affixes signifying an agent by [5] *A*1.3.78.

Within the parasmaipada and ātmanepada sets of endings, a selection is next made among the triplets called *prathama*, *madhyama*, and *uttama* (A1.4.101), the personal endings. Here, according to [6] *A*1.4.108, prathama endings are chosen. For the conditions given in preceding sūtras are not met that a form of the second person pronoun *yuṣmad* or the first person pronoun *asmad* that is coreferential (*samānādhikaraṇe*) with an L-affix in a derivation could be used as a cooccurring word (*upapade*), even if it is not actually used (*sthāniny api*). The cooccuring word with which the L-affix of the present sentence is coreferential is the item *devadatta.*

Once a choice has been made among prathama, madhyama, and uttama endings, one finally selects an ekavacana, dvivacana, or bahuvacana ending (A 1.4.102). The choice depends on the number of things signified. In the present case, there is one thing to serve as agent, so that according to [7] *A*1.4.22 an ekavacana ending is chosen.

This is how the agentive ending is selected for the present sentence. The selected ending is the parasmaipada prathama ekavacana affix *ti* (*ti**p***). It is after the L-affix is replaced in this manner by the ending *ti* that [8] *A*3.1.68 comes into play; the rule states that the suffix ***śap*** occurs after a verb which is followed by a sārvadhātuka denoting an agent. The ending *ti* is called *sārvadhātuka* (*A*3.4.113), denoting an agent. Thus we have the form *pacati.*

0.1.2. In [9] *A*4.1.2 the basic nominal endings (*su**p***) are given. Sūtras such as [11] *A*2.3.2, [12] *A*2.3.18, and [13] *A*2.3.46 provide for the occurrence of particular triplets of these endings under specified conditions. According to [11] *A*2.3.2, after a nominal base, the second triplet of endings (*dvitīyā*)—that is, accusative endings—is introduced if an object is to be denoted; [12] *A*2.3.18 provides that the third triplet of endings (instrumental endings) occurs with a nominal base if either an agent or instrument (*karaṇa*) is to be denoted; and, according to [13] *A*2.3.46, the first triplet of endings (nominative endings) is introduced after a nominal base when there is to be signified nothing more (*-mātre*) than a base meaning (*prātipadikārtha*) and a gender (*liṅga*), a measure (*parimāṇa*), or a number (*vacana*). Which ending of each triplet is selected for a given derivation is determined by the number of things designated, in accordance with A1.4.21–22: here in the given sentence, by [7] *A*1.4.22 ekavacana endings occur.

But when we apply [11] *A*2.3.2 to introduce the second triplet of endings after a nominal base, we have to take into consideration [10] *A*2.3.1, under the heading of which [11] *A*2.3.2 comes and which provides that nominal endings occur on condition that given kārakas are to be signified if they are not otherwise signified (*anabhihita*). Now in the given sentence the L-affix and endings that replace it, which can denote either of the kārakas, an agent and an object, by [3] *A*3.4.69, denote an agent and not an object, so that [12] *A*2.3.18 is not applicable since an agent is denoted by the verb ending *-ti* and [13] *A*2.3.46 applies instead; and, [11] *A*2.3.2 does apply, for an object is not denoted by the verb ending. Thus the prathamā ekavacana *s* (***su***) occurs after the nominal base *devadatta* and the dvitīyā ekavacana *am* after the nominal base *odana.*[1]

0.1.3. What we can see from these things is that in Pāṇini's derivational system sentences such as *devadatta odanaṃ pacati* is derived from the following string in the very initial stage:

PRĀTIPADIKA + ***sup*** DHĀTU + L

What is more, by [6] *A*1.4.108 and [10] *A*2.3.1, it is clearly shown that the formation of a syntactic unit (*pada*) like the finite verb form *pacati* or that of a syntactic unit such as the nominal form *devadattaḥ* (*devadatta-s*) is sentence-conditioned, namely that the syntactic units DHĀTU + L and PRĀTIPADIKA + ***sup***, components of an utterance, should be syntactically and semantically related to each other in order for them to be derived: In Pāṇini's derivational system syntactic units that terminate in nominal (***sup***) and verbal (***tiṅ***) endings are called *pada* (*A*1.4.14); after items called *prātipadika* (*A*1.2.45–46) occur nominal endings

[1] With the application of phonological rules *devadatta* and *odanam* in the given sentence are respectively derivable from *devadatta-a* and *odana-am*: *devadatta-s* → *devadatta-R* (*A*8.2.66) → *devadatta-y* (*A*8.3.17) → *devadatta* (*A*8.3.19); *odana-am* → *odanam* (*A*6.1.107) → *odanaṃ* (*A*8.3.23).

(*A*4.1.2). And besides, by [10] *A*2.3.1, it is also plainly shown that in Pāṇini's system the denotation of kārakas by nominal endings is subordinate to their expression by verbal affixes. From the principle that the denotation of kārakas by verbal endings takes precedence over the denotation of kārakas by nominal endings is derived that the principal meaning of any sentence is a verb meaning in view of Pāṇini's derivational procedure.

0.1.4. In order to derive utterances of the type *devadatta odanaṃ pacati* (*devadatta-s odana-am pac-**laṭ***), we start with the string PRĀTIPADIKA + ***sup*** DHĀTU + L. As shown, within this string we cannot begin first on the derivation of the syntactic unit PRĀTIPADIKA + ***sup*** but on that of the syntactic unit DHĀTU + L which is derived by introducing an L-affix to be replaced by basic verb endings after an item called *dhātu*.

Thus, from a viewpoint of Pāṇini's derivational system, items called *dhātu* are placed at a starting point of the sentence derivation, and, as is like the other side of the same coin, from a semantic point of view, one can accordingly grasp a verb meaning, an act denoted by an item called *dhātu*, as the core of a sentential meaning.[2]

0.2. The class name *dhātu*

0.2.1. Pāṇini formulates two rules that assign the class name *dhātu* to certain items: *A*1.3.1 *bhūvādayo dhātavaḥ* and *A*3.1.32 *sanādyantā dhātavaḥ*. The first of these sūtras provides that items of the ordered set that begins with *bhū* 'be, be born', listed in the dhātupāṭha, have the class name *dhātu*. The second sūtra provides that derivates which end in the affixes ***san*** etc., introduced

[2] There are two views concerning the word formation in Pāṇini's derivational system: *padasaṃskārapakṣa* and *vākyasaṃskārapakṣa* depending upon whether the boundary of the word formation is a syntactic item or a sentence. On the former view words such as *devadatta-s* and *pac-a-ti* are derived individually, whereas on the latter view the derivational procedure involves syntactic units as related to each other in a sentence. [6] *A*1.4.108 and [10] *A*2.3.1 conclusively show that Pāṇini's derivational system is in principle founded on the *vākyasaṃskārapakṣa*. For further details of these two views, see Joshi/Roodbergen [1980: Introduction].

by preceding rules (*A*3.1.5–31), are called *dhātu*. For example, the verb *pac* (***ḍupacàṣ***) is recited in the dhātupāṭha, so that it has the class name by *A*1.3.1; the derivate *pāci* (*pac*-***ṇic***), in which the causative affix ***ṇic*** is introduced after the verb *pac* according to *A*3.1.26, is called *dhātu* by *A*3.1.32. *A*1.3.1 concerns primitive verbal bases and *A*3.1.32 derived verbal bases, in short.

0.2.2. In this connection it has to be noted that we do not have to make a distinction between these verbal bases from a semantic point of view. As we shall see later, in his Bhāṣya on *A*3.1.19 Patañjali observes that items such as *putrīya* 'desire a son for oneself', a derived verbal base ending in the affix ***kyac*** (*A*3.1.19), denote by nature actions (*kriyāvacanatā ca gamyate*), just like primitive verbal bases such as *pac*.[3] It is an item which is called *dhātu*, according to him, that the property of being an item which denotes an action (*kriyāvacanatā*) should be attributed to. And also, in the very same Bhāṣya he justifies from the viewpoint of Pāṇini's derivational system that such derived verbal bases denote actions.

Items termed *dhātu* are subject to operations stated in the sūtras headed by *A*3.1.91 *dhātoḥ*. Consider the utterance *devā namasyitavyāḥ* 'the deities are to be revered', wherein after the derived verbal base *namasya* (*A*3.1.19, the nominal base *namas* 'obeisance' + ***kyac***; 'worship') the kṛt affix *tavya* occurs by *A*3.4.70 under the heading of *A*3.1.91 which provides that the affix *tavya*, called *kṛtya* also (*A*3.1.96), occurs if an object or a mere act is to be signified. In the present sentence the affix *tavya* signifies an object. Regarding the derivation of the sentence in question Patañjali argues:

> *MBh* ad *A*3.1.19 (II.27.9–12): *sādhane tavyadādayo vidhīyante, sādhanaṃ ca kriyāyāḥ / kriyābhāvāt sādhanābhāvaḥ / sādhanābhāvāt satyām api dhātusaṃjñāyāṃ tavyadādayo na syuḥ / paśyati tv ācāryaḥ—kriyāvacanāḥ kyajādaya iti / tataḥ sanādyantā dhātava iti dhātusaṃjñāṃ śāsti /*

---

[3] See Section 5 [5.2.3.2].

"[In utterances such as *devā namasyitavyāḥ*] affixes like *tavyat* are introduced [after bases called *dhātu*] when a sādhana[4] [an object here] is to be signified. And [something is] a sādhana in relation to an action. Because there is no action, there is no sādhana. It would follow from the absence of a sādhana that even if a certain item has the name *dhātu*, there do not occur affixes like *tavyat* after that item. But the teacher [Pāṇini] sees that items ending in affixes such as ***kyac*** denote actions, so that he teaches that the name *dhātu* [is assigned to such items] by formulating the sūtra *sanādyantā dhātavaḥ.*"

What Patañjali means to say here is clear. On the assumption that a sādhana such as an object and an action are mutually related, if an action were absent which is to be brought to accomplishment, a sādhana would be absent which is a means for bringing the action to accomplishment. Now in *namasyitavyāḥ* in which the kṛt affix *tavya* occurs after the derived verb *namasya* to denote an object in relation to the significand of the item *namasya*, if the meaning signified by the item *namasya* were not an action, then the occurrence of the affix *tavya* after that item could not be justified. But we do have the derivate *namasyitavyāḥ*. This will show that the meaning signified by the derived verb *namasya* is nothing but an action. According to Patañjali, thus, in formulating *A*3.1.32 using the term *dhātu*, Pāṇini presupposes that items terminating in affixes such as ***kyac*** denote actions. For *A*3.1.32 allows such items to have the name *dhātu* and thereby lets them be subject to operations provided for in the sūtras under the heading of *A*3.1.91, the conditions for which are characterized by the relation between sādhana and action.

---

[4]The term *sādhana* 'means' is synonymous in this context with kāraka, referring to what plays the role of a factor in the activity. See Section 1.

In *A*3.1.96 Pāṇini distinguishes between *tavyat* and *tavya*. The former has the marker *t* which is unconditionally deleted. Thus *A*3.1.96 concerns two elements *tavya*. An affix generally has high pitch on its first vowel according to *A*3.1.3 and an affix marked with *t* has a svarita vowel according to *A*6.1.185, so that one has, for example, both *namasyitávya* and *namasyitavyà*.

All of this amounts to saying: Patañjali considers that Pāṇini applies the term *dhātu* to items which denote actions and that those items are classified into two categories: underived and derived—the former and latter items are respectively covered by *A*1.3.1 and *A*3.1.32, in both of which the term *dhātu* is used. Viewed in this light, therefore, Pāṇini's derivational system, it is reasonable to say, corroborates the idea that primitive and derived verbal bases have a common semantic character, as far as both classes of verbal bases are equally given the name *dhātu*.[5]

0.3. Bhartṛhari's definition of the term *kriyā*

We are now sure that in Pāṇini's derivational system items which he calls *dhātu* serve as a starting point of the derivation of utterances. As has been suggested by the Bhāṣya just quoted above, Pāṇinīyas like Patañjali unequivocally speak of the meanings of such items or *dhātvarthas* 'verb meanings' as *kriyā* 'act, action'.[6]

---

[5] In Bhartṛhari's opinion, there are two categories of items which denote actions: the items which are not unanalyzable into smaller units and those which are subject to analysis. With reference to the latter, he states as follows. *VP*3.14.76: *arthasyānugamaṃ kaṃcid dṛṣṭvaiva parikalpitam / padaṃ vākye pade dhātur dhātau bhāgaś ca muṇḍivat //* ("It is after seeing a certain form of continued presence of meaning that a syntactic unit is posited in a sentence, a verb in a syntactic unit, and a part in a verb as in *muṇḍi*.") *A*3.1.21 provides that the affix ***ṇic*** follows the nominal base *muṇḍa* 'bald' to form the denominative *muṇḍi* 'shave the head'. Pāṇini derives the complex unit *muṇḍi* from the posited components *muṇḍa* and ***ṇic***, which shows that from the verb *muṇḍi* the putative parts are extracted. In addition, when a part like *muṇḍa* is extracted from a verb such as *muṇḍi*, the part is not its real constituent. Insofar as the verb *muṇḍi* is regarded as an indivisible unit, its meaning is also indivisible. Taking *putrīyati* 'desires a son for himself' for example, Bhartṛhari states as follows. *VP*3.14.70: *putrīyatau na putro 'sti viśeṣecchā tu tādṛśī / vinaiva putrānugamād yā putre vyavatiṣṭhate /* ("There is no part like *putra* in the item *putrīya*. One understands from that item a specific desire such that relates to a son and not a mere son.") Although one abstracts the elements *putrīya* and *ti* from *putrīyati* and further does the elements *putra* 'a son' and ***kyac*** from *putrīya*, one understands from the item *putrīya* as an indivisible meaning the act of desiring a son for oneself. On Pāṇinīyas' linguistic analysis, see Section 3 [3.2.3].

[6] On Patañjali's exposition of a verb meaning as an action, see Section

0.3.1. *sādhyatvenābhidhīyate*

Bhartṛhari is the first Pāṇinīya to formulate the definition which specifies what is meant by the term *kriyā* in Pāṇini's grammar, that is, to give its technical definition (*śāstrīyalakṣaṇa*).[7] In VP3.8.1 he states:

> VP3.8.1: *yāvat siddham asiddhaṃ vā sādhyatvenābhidhīyate / āśritakramarūpatvāt tat kriyeti pratīyate //*
> "Whether it has or has not been brought to accomplishment, whatever is denoted as something yet to be brought to accomplishment because it assumes sequence is what one understands by the word *kriyā* [in grammar]."[8]

In the situation where one would use *apākṣīt* '. . . has cooked' the act of cooking has already been brought to accomplishment. Both in the situation where one would use *pacati* '. . . is cooking'

---

1 [1.4] and Section 5 [5.3.2].

[7] Helārāja introduces VP3.8.1 by saying as follows. *Prakāśa* on VP3.8.1: *idānīṃ sādhyāpekṣatvāt sādhanasya sādhanānantaram uddiṣṭāyāḥ kriyāyāḥ śāstrīyaṃ lakṣaṇam āha /* ("Since a sādhana requires [lit. 'expects'] what is to be accomplished by it (*sādhya*), an action (*kriyā*) [which is something to be accomplished] is taken up after examining the sādhana. Now [Bhartṛhari] states its technical definition.") According to Helārāja, the definition of the term *kriyā* Bhartṛhari is going to give in the kārikā is of a technical character.

[8] The phrase *āśritakramarūpatvāt* (pāda c) in this kārikā can be taken as stating the reason why a denotatum as thus characterized is called *kriyā*. This line of interpretation is given by Nāgeśa. *VSLM*545: *āśriteti yogapradarśanaṃ kriyate avayavānāṃ krameṇotpattyā / ata evāśritakramarūpā kriyā . . . /* ("By the phrase *āśrita* . . . is shown an etymological meaning (*yoga*) [of the word *kriyā*]. What is brought about through its components occurring in a sequence is called *kriyā*. For this very reason that which is called *kriyā* is something that assumes the form of sequence.") According to Nāgeśa, the kārikā in question is interpreted as follows: "Whether it has or has not been brought to accomplishment, whatever is denoted as something yet to be brought to accomplishment is what one understands by the word *kriyā* since the word *kriyā* [etymologically] means something that assumes the form of sequence." See also *VSM*45, where Nāgeśa says: *kriyate avayavānāṃ krameṇotpattyā krameṇotpādyate iti kriyety arthaḥ*.

Nāgeśa's reading of the present kārikā pāda d is different from Rau's. Nāgeśa reads: *sā kriyety abhidhīyate*, which is also supported by Haradatta. See the *Padamañjarī* on the *Kāśikāvṛtti* ad A1.3.1.

and in the one in which one would use *pakṣyati* '. . . will cook', the act in question has not been brought to accomplishment yet, because in the former it has been begun and not yet terminated and in the latter it has not been begun yet. However, an essential feature of what is understood to be an action (*kriyā*), as Bhartṛhari sketches out, is that, irrespective of such actual state of affairs, it has sequence (*krama*) and is accordingly spoken of as something that is brought to accomplishment (*sādhyatvenābhidhīyate*). For Bhartṛhari, the defining feature of an action is thus being denoted as something that is to be brought to accomplishment.

0.3.2. *apoddhārapadārtha*

Now there is another point to be noted in this connection. As said, Bhartṛhari intends to define a kind of technical *kriyā* in the kārikā cited above. To ignore the fact that the term *kriyā* he tries to define therein is the one employed in grammar and of a technical value is to miss the fundamental point of the semantics with which he deals in the third kāṇḍa of the *Vākyapadīya*. For Bhartṛhari, meanings (*artha*) such as *kriyā* characterized as *dhātvartha* are originally those which are abstracted from the meaning of a larger linguistic unit (*apoddhārapadārtha* 'meaning gotten through extraction').[9] As an utterance, which is viewed as the

---

[9]In *VP*1.24 Bhartṛhari uses the word *apoddhārapadārtha* as standing in contrast to *sthitalakṣaṇa*[*-artha*]. See the present section, fn. 14. In his *Paddhati* on this kārikā Vṛṣabha explains the former as follows. *Paddhati* on *VP*1.24: *padyate anenārtha iti padam, na pāribhāṣikam, tasyārthāḥ padārthāḥ, apoddhriyante ity apoddhārāḥ padārthāś ceti, apoddhṛtānāṃ vā padānām arthāḥ, apoddhāreṇa parikalpitā vā arthāḥ iti śākapārthivādiḥ / apoddhārasambandhino veti ṣaṣṭhīsamāsaḥ / apoddhāro vibhāgaḥ* / To begin with, the word *pada* here is not a technical term such as the one provided for by *A*1.4.14 *suptiṅantaṃ padam* which refers to a syntactic unit but that through which a meaning is reached, i.e., understood (*padyate 'nenārthaḥ*), a meaningful unit. Thus the word *padārtha* means 'a meaning of a meaningful linguistic item'. The word *apoddhāra*, glossed with the word *vibhāga* 'partition, separation', may signify either what is abstracted (*apoddhriyata iti*; *apoddhṛta*) or the act of abstracting, abstraction. Hence the word *apoddhārapadārthāḥ* is interpreted in four ways: 1) those which are abstracted and which are meanings of meaningful items (*apoddhārāḥ padārthāś ca*); 2) meanings of the meaningfull items which are abstracted (*apoddhṛtānāṃ padānām*

unit of communication and as, being impartite, a single indivisible whole, is analyzed into words as syntactic units (*pada*), which in turn are analyzed into smaller units such as bases (*prakṛti*) and affixes (*pratyaya*), for the sake of grammatical description, so also is a meaning of the utterance, which is equally impartite, analyzed into word meanings, from which are abstracted further the meanings of the smaller units, for the sake of grammatical description. In the following kārikās Bhartṛhari sets forth a basic framework for his own semantics of such smaller units:

> *VP*3.4.1–2: *saṃsargarūpāt saṃbhūtāḥ saṃvidrūpād apoddhṛtāḥ / śāstre vibhaktā vākyārthāt prakṛtipratyayārthavat // nimittabhūtāḥ sādhutve śāstrād anumitātmakāḥ / kecit padārthā vakṣyante saṃkṣepeṇa yathāgamam //*
>
> "Word meanings (*padārtha*) are abstracted (*apoddhṛta*) from a sentence meaning (*vākyārtha*) through the cognition consisting in [abstraction] (*saṃvidrūpa*); those word meanings are united (*sambhūta*) in the sentence meaning and the latter is in essence a fusion (*saṃsargarūpa*) of [its putative partial meanings].
>
> Those abstracted word meanings [united in a sentence meaning] are discriminated from one another in a grammar (*śāstre vibhaktāḥ*) [according to domains for rules to apply in].
>
> The way in which partial meanings of a sentence meaning are posited as word meanings is the same as that in which the constituent meanings of a meaning of a syntactic unit (*pada*) are posited as base and affix meanings. [The abstraction (*apoddhāra*) works for positing meanings of smaller units.]
>
> They [i.e., abstracted word meanings] serve as a means for explaining correct speech forms (*nimittabhūta*).

---

arthāḥ); 3) meanings postulated through abstraction (*apoddhāreṇa parikalpitā arthāḥ*); 4) meaningful items' meanings related to abstraction (*apoddhārasambandhinaḥ padārthāḥ*). Here I take the third interpretation. It may be noted in passing that Vṛṣabha explicates the word *sthitalakṣaṇa*[-*artha*] as follows. *Paddhati* on *VP*1.24: *sthitaṃ lakṣaṇam eṣām, svarūpasyāpracyuteḥ /* Meanings defined as *sthitalakṣaṇa* are those which have a fixed character on account of not being deprived of their essence. They are, in other words, what is beyond conceptualizations.

> Of such word meanings, those whose essence is inferred from grammar (*śāstrād anumitātmakāḥ*) will be succinctly explained according to tradition (*yathāgamam*)."

Here Bhartṛhari characterizes meanings such as *kriyā* as those which are abstracted from the meaning of a sentence and as serving to account for correct speech. Moreover, he adds that the essence of those abstracted meanings is to be inferred from a grammar.[10]

What we can recognize from these things, therefore, is the following:

The *kriyā* Bhartṛhari takes up here in *VP*3.8.1 can be described as an abstracted meaning the term for which is conventionally

---

[10]The word meanings Bhartṛhari declares to be explained in his *Vākyapadīya* are the ones which are discussed in samuddeśas from the Bhūyodravyasamuddeśa to the Liṅgasamuddeśa: *dravya* (substance), *guṇa* (quality), *diś* (direction), *sādhana* (means), *kriyā* (action), *kāla* (time), *puruṣa* (person), *saṅkhyā* (number), *upagraha* (diathesis), *liṅga* (gender). Concerning the word *padārtha* 'word meaning' used by Bhartṛhari in the present kārikā, Helārāja gives the following explanation. *Prakāśa* on *VP*3.4.1-2: *padārthā iti / yady api saṃsṛṣṭānām eva sarvathābhāvas tathāpy apoddhṛtāḥ / athaikaikasya padasya guṇapradhānabhūtā bahavo 'rthāḥ / tad yathākhyātasya kriyākālasādhanasaṅkhyāpuruṣopagrahāḥ, nāmapadasyāpi dravyaliṅgasaṅkhyāsādhanāni kriyā kāla ityādi / padavācyatvena vā padārthatopapattiḥ / kevalānāṃ pacatyādipadavācyatvābhāvāt /* According to Helārāja, what is meant by the term *pada* 'word' here is a finite verb form (*ākhyāta*) and a nominal form (*nāman*) and hence a syntactic unit. Therefore, the word *padārtha* may mean 'meanings of a single word such as a finite verb form', since such a single word conveys many meanings (*artha*) such as an action, time, and so on, of which one meaning is principal and the rest are subordinate to it; alternatively, 'what is understood from such a single word', since meanings conveyed by it are understood from it as constituting a complex meaning.

We must consider that when abstracted from a sentence meaning, the meaning of an action has to be understood as forming a part of a complex meaning conveyed by a finite verb form; and, when abstracted from a word meaning, such a complex meaning conveyed by the finite verb form, it has to be understood to be the meaning of the base (*prakṛti*) of the finite verb form. That is to say, at the stage of its abstraction from a sentence meaning, an action is understood as related to other meanings which constitute a word meaning, and at the stage of its abstraction from the word meaning, it is understood as a separate meaning.

used in grammar for the sake of explaining correct speech forms and hence whose characteristics are to be known from the grammar.

And further, let us note the following statement:

> *Vṛtti* on *VP*1.24: *tathaiva cāpravibhāge śabdātmani kāryārthaṃ anvayavyatirekābhyāṃ rūpasamanugamakalpanayā samudāyād apoddhṛtānāṃ śabdānām abhidheyatvenāśrīyate / so 'yam apoddhārapadārthaḥ śāstravyavahāram anupatati, śāstravyavahārasadṛśaṃ ca laukikaṃ bhedavyavahāram /*
>
> "In the very same manner, with reference to a linguistic item as an impartite whole, its putative components are abstracted from it, for the purpose of grammatical description, on the grounds that the linguistic item is assumed to be accompanied by different forms constituting it through reasoning from *anvaya* and *vyatireka.*[11] And in this case, it is admitted that a certain abstracted meaning is conveyed by a certain abstracted item. The abstracted meanings in question enter into grammatical talk and a variety of everyday talk resembling the grammatical talk."

In everyday speech also one understands that sentences such as *devadattaḥ pacati* 'Devadatta is cooking' speak of an agent, an action, and so on. But this does not detract in the least from the fact that an action is an abstracted meaning. In everyday speech one speaks of it, under the influence of grammar, as if it were a distinct object.[12]

In this connection it is to be noted in passing that Helārāja mentions the Bhāṣya on *A*1.3.1 as that in which an action is characterized.

> *Prakāśa* on *VP*3.4.1–2: *kriyāpi bhūvādivārttike bhāṣye pūrvāparībhūtā sādhyasvabhāvānumānagamyā lakṣitā /*
>
> "[Not only are word meanings such as a substance characterized in grammar.] An action is also characterized in the Bhāṣya to

---

[11] On the reasoning from *anvaya* and *vyatireka* for abstraction of smaller units from a larger unit, see Section 3 [3.2.3].

[12] *Paddhati* on *VP*1.24: *yo 'yaṃ loke pravibhāgaḥ ayaṃ kartā aparā kriyā, yady avyavartana ity ayam api śāstranirūḍhatvāt tatsadṛśo bhavati /*

> the Vārttika on A1.3.1 as something whose component actions take place in a sequence, which is in essence what is to be brought to accomplishment, and which is to be known through inference."

The question of how Patañjali views an action is the key subject of the present work, so that it shall be discussed in detail.

In his grammar Pāṇini makes statements using two sorts of terms: *akṛtrima* terms, namely those whose meanings are well known from common usage (e.g., *paśu* 'animal' in A1.2.73), and, *kṛtrima* terms, or artificial terms such as *bha* in A1.4.18. Unlike artificial terms such as *bha*, which are used only in grammar, the term *kriyā* is certainly used both in everyday speech and in grammar, but in grammar it is used in a technical sense, even different from the sense in which it is used in other schools of thought, though what is meant by the term *kriyā* is nothing more than the meaning abstracted from a sentential meaning, regardless of in what value the term is used.[13]

0.3.3. *yathāgamam*

The term *kriyā* defined in *VP*3.8.1 has a technical value and the essential feature of what is signified by that term is known on the basis of grammar. Having got this point firmly established, let us turn to another point.

0.3.3.1. Note Bhartṛhari's declaration in *VP*3.4.1–2 of the principle on which he deals with word meanings. By saying *yathāgamam* 'according to tradition' he declares there that in describing abstracted meanings which serve as a means for grammatical description he bases himself on a long tradition of usage and grammar. This principle of traditionalism naturally applies to his definition of an action in his *VP*3.8.1. Thus we have to assume that he

---

[13] In the everyday world (*loka*), what is called *kriyā* is commonly accepted as something that consists in physical movement (*parispanda*, *parispandana*). In the Vaiśeṣika school also *kriyā* is defined as such. *Prakāśa* on *VP*3.8.1: *kiṃ ca parispandasvabhāvā loke kriyā prasiddhā / . . . kaṇādadarśane caikā kriyānekatra na bhavet / tīrthikāntaradarśanaṃ ceha nāśrīyate / ata eva parispandalakṣaṇa eva vyāpāro na kriyā /*

describes an action there following tradition and that his description of an action in his *VP*3.8.1 is deeply rooted in the tradition.

One must note that his position as a 'traditionalist' is declared not only here but also in the kārikās (*VP*1.24–26) where he outlines the eight topics (*aṣṭaka*) to be covered in his *Vākyapadīya*, in which the abstracted word meaning (*apoddhārapadārtha*) is included.[14] After mentioning the eight topics at issue, he says in *VP*1.26 as follows:

> *VP*1.26: *te liṅgaiś ca svaśabdaiś ca śāstre 'sminn upavarṇitāḥ / smṛtyartham anugamyante kecid eva yathāgamam /*
> "Those eight topics are described in this grammar both through indirect indications and direct statements. Only those particular topics are followed according to tradition (*yathāgamam*) in order to hand down them (*smṛtyartham*)."

It is evident that what Bhartṛhari says here conforms with what he states in *VP*3.4.2 in that he declares that he will present the subjects which have already been described in grammar, according to tradition, that is, without intruding his own theory into them.[15] Thus his basic position on the eight topics he covers in his *Vākyapadīya* turns out to be that he confines himself to presenting them as they are accepted in tradition.

---

[14]The eight topics Bhartṛhari deals with in his *Vākyapadīya* are: two kinds of meanings: *apoddhārapadārtha* 'meaning gotten through extraction' and *sthitalakṣaṇo 'rthaḥ* 'meaning whose character is fixed', two types of linguistic units: *anvākhyeyaḥ śabdaḥ* 'linguistic unit that is to be explained' and *pratipādakaḥ śabdaḥ* 'linguistic unit which serves to convey the former', two kinds of relations: *kāryakāraṇabhāva* 'causal relation' and *yogyatā*, i.e., a relation such that a certain linguistic unit is capable of conveying a certain meaning and a certain meaning is capable of being conveyed by a certain linguistic item, two kinds of results: the comprehension of meaning (*pratyaya*) and the acquisition of merit (*dharma*). *VP*1.24-25: *apoddhārapadārthā ye ye cārthāḥ sthitalakṣaṇāḥ / anvākhyeyāś ca ye śabdā ye cāpi pratipādakāḥ // kāryakāraṇabhāvena yogyabhāvena ca sthitāḥ / dharme ye pratyaye cāṅgaṃ saṃbandhāḥ sādhvasādhuṣu //*

[15]Vṛṣabha appropriately explains: By the phrase *yathāgamam* Bhartṛhari means to say that he presents the eight topics not as those which he invents (*utprekṣayā*) but as those which accord with tradition. *Paddhati* on *VP*1.26: *yathāgamam iti / notprekṣayā api tv āgamānusāreṇeti /*

0.3.3.2. Then what does Bhartṛhari mean by 'tradition' (*āgama*)? By definition 'tradition' is the teaching uninterruptedly transmitted from generation to generation (*pāramparyeṇāvicchinna upadeśaḥ*); and there are two types of tradition: that which is characterized as *śruti* (the revealed lore) and that which is characterized as *smṛti* (man-made lore).[16]

The phrase *yathāgamam* in *VP*3.4.2 is explained by Helārāja as follows:

> *Prakāśa* on *VP*3.4.2: *yathāgamam iti / yādṛśo vaiyākaraṇānām āgamas tam anullaṅghya vyākhyātṝṇām upadeśapāramparyānatikrameṇa yasya padārthasya yasmin anvākhyāne 'ṅgabhāvaḥ sa kathyata ity arthaḥ /*
>
> "What is meant by the passage *yathāgamam* is this: Without transgressing such tradition as has been handed down by grammarians, that is, without being against the successive teaching of [grammarians] who explain [correct speech forms] (*vyākhyātṛ*), that word meaning which has the property of being a means for their explanation [of correct linguistic forms] is described."[17]

Obviously Helārāja refers to grammatical tradition by *āgama*. To be sure, there are different grammatical traditions and Pāṇini is not the first to describe the usage of the śiṣṭas (*śiṣṭa*, lit. 'the cultured'), having the predecessors in the field of grammar and being merely one among the śiṣṭas who composed a *smṛti*, a work which hands down a memorialized tradition that is determined by the uninterrupted tradition of usage by śiṣṭas.[18] It is said in *VP*1.43 as follows:

> *VP*1.43: *tasmād akṛtakaṃ śāstraṃ smṛtiṃ ca sanibandhanām / āśrityārabhyate śiṣṭaiḥ sādhutvaviṣayā smṛtiḥ //*

---

[16]Of the *āgama* Bhartṛhari gives the following description: *MBhD* I.3.3: *āgamaḥ khalv api / pāramparyeṇāvicchinna upadeśa āgamaḥ / śrutilakṣaṇaḥ smṛtilakṣaṇaś ca /*

[17]I do not follow the punctuation . . . *anullaṅghya / vyākhyātṝṇām* . . . given by Iyer [1963], but the one by Raghunātha Śarmā [1979].

[18]See Section 8 [8.6.2.1] for an account of the notion of śiṣṭa.

"Śiṣṭas [like Pāṇini] have undertaken grammatical teaching (*smṛti*) whose object is the correctness of speech, basing themselves on the teaching (*śāstra*) that has no author [i.e., the Veda] and *smṛti* based on it."

But, within the tradition of Pāṇini's grammar, not only is Pāṇini characterized as *smartṛ* 'one who composes a *smṛti* or memorializes the tradition of usage', but Kātyāyana and Patañjali are also so characterized. Pāṇini, Kātyāyana, and Patañjali, whom in a group later tradition calls the three sages (*trimuni*, *munitraya*) of grammar, are regarded as siṣṭas and hence may well be said to be *smartṛs*, since for Bhartṛhari the term *śiṣṭa* applies to those who have an insight into the true nature of things (*VP*1.171: *svabhāva-jña*; *VP*3.13.21: *bhāvatattvadṛś*), so that his notion of śiṣṭa covers both an élite of model speakers and grammarians like Pāṇini.

Thus, if we take what has been said into consideration, it follows that the tradition on which Bhartṛhari declares himself based is in direct reference to the grammatical tradition established by Pāṇini, Kātyāyana, and Patañjali.[19] And if we look at Bhartṛhari's definition of the term *kriyā* in *VP*3.8.1 from this angle, we can say with fair certainty that he describes an action, which is nothing but a meaning abstracted from a meaning of a larger unit, as it is accepted in Pāṇinian grammatical tradition.

0.4. The aim of the present work

As has already been shown, in Pāṇini's derivational system, an item called *dhātu* is placed at a starting point of the sentence derivation and its meaning, an action, is accordingly viewed as forming the core of a sentence meaning. The tradition of Pāṇini's grammar provides a framework for Bhartṛhari to work within. This being so, when Bhartrhari describes an action: what is denoted

---

[19] Unlike Pānini and Patañjali, Kātyāyana is not explicitly called *smartṛ*. But when Bhartṛhari calls Patañjali both as *ādiśiṣṭa* 'the foremost of the śiṣṭas' and as *smartṛ*, he implies to say that the three sages are equally *smartṛs* as well as *śiṣṭas*. *MBhD* III.18: *asya ca smartā bhāṣyakāraḥ / ayaṃ cādiśiṣṭaḥ /*

Vṛṣabha glosses the words *tair eva śiṣṭair* in *Vṛtti* on *VP*1.23 with *pāṇinyādibhiḥ*. In *MBhD* I.8.2 Bhartṛhari calls Pāṇini *smartṛ*.

by a verb as something to be brought to accomplishment is an action (*sādhyatvenābhidhīyate*), he has to follow Pāṇinian grammatical tradition. As Helārāja states, the source from which Bhartṛhari's conception of an action is derived is Patañjali's *Mahābhāṣya* on *A*1.3.1. If we wish to trace the notion of an action as expressed by Bhartṛhari to its original source, it is imperative to make clear the semantics of verbs, the study of meanings of verbs (*dhātvartha*), developed by Patañjali therein. Moreover, Patañjali is a Pāṇinīya or a student of Pāṇini's grammar. In this respect it is unquestionable that his semantics of verbs also has to be rooted in Pāṇini's grammar.

The present work is intended as a comprehensive and detailed study of the *Mahābhāṣya* on *A*1.3.1. It was not without reason that I introduced Bhartṛhari's definition of an action in *VP*3.8.1 here. As shall be seen later, what is characteristic of the *Mahābhāṣya* on *A*1.3.1 is the semantics of verbs established by Patañjali with refinement. *VP*3.8.1, so to speak, strikes the keynote of the *Mahābhāṣya* in question. Therefore, in the present work, I will investigate the *Mahābhāṣya* on *A*1.3.1, placing it as marking an important link in the chain of the development of the semantics of verbs from Pāṇini to Bhartṛhari.

Granted that the *Mahābhāṣya* on *A*1.3.1 can be considered to be chiefly concerned with the semantics of verbs, Patañjali's semantics of verbs is incidental to the main issue: How *A*1.3.1 is to be interpreted? In this respect one must not forget that the semantics of verbs is closely connected with a matter of a semantic definition of the term *dhātu*. In addition, in discussing a definition of the term *dhātu*, Patañjali follows up two extremes of its definition, formal and semantic. This will also help us know characteristic features of his semantics of verbs.

0.5. The framing of the present work

The present work consists of ten sections and two appendixes.

Section 1 attempts to show how Pāṇini views a verb meaning in his grammar, finding a clue to the question in his kāraka theory.

Section 2 surveys traditional interpretations of *A*1.3.1 with special emphasis on the ones by the *Kāśikāvṛtti* and the *Siddhānta-kaumudī.*

Section 3 analyzes the arguments brought forward in Kātyāyana's vārttikas on *A*1.3.1.

Section 4 is divided into four parts: Part 1 deals with the Bhāṣya on vārttikas 1–2 in which Kātyāyana discusses the dhātupāṭha-based definition of the term *dhātu*; Part 2 is concerned with the Bhāṣya in which Patañjali in accordance with vārttikas 3–7 considers a semantic definition of the term *dhātu* with special reference to a *kriyā*-based definition; Part 3 treats the Bhāṣya on another semantic definition of the term *dhātu*, a *bhāva*-based definition, whose related problems Kātyāyana addresses in his vārttikas 8–11; Part 4 is devoted to the Bhāṣya in which, arguing against Kātyāyana who emphasizes the need for the dhātupāṭha in his vārttikas 12–13, Patañjali carries his semantic definition to such an extreme that he has to deny the absolute necessity of having the dhātupāṭha in Pāṇini's grammar.[20]

Section 5 handles the question of how Kātyāyana and Patañjali conceive of *kriyā* and *bhāva* which are posited as verb meanings.

Section 6 deals with Patañjali's demonstration, meant for making the *kriyā*-based definition equivalent to the *bhāva*-based definition, that the meaning of the verb *as* is an action.

Section 7 takes up Patañjali's interpretations of *A*1.3.1 as a semantic definition of the term *dhātu* without alloy and as both indicating the dhātupāṭha and furnishing a semantic definition.

Section 8 discusses the question of what brings Patañjali to denying the functions Kātyāyana claims the dhātupāṭha to discharge on the condition that a semantic definition of the term *dhātu* is given.

Section 9 provides a roundup of Patañjali's interpretations of *A*1.3.1 to make it clear how the original dhātupāṭha determines his two extremes of approach to *A*1.3.1

Section 10 is meant for a brief review of the Pāṇinian semantics of verbs, from Pāṇini's to Bhartṛhari's.

[20] For what I call 'dhātupāṭha-based definition', '*kriyā*-based definition', and '*bhāva*-based definition', see Section 3.

Two appendixes follow.

Appendix 1 gives a survey of previous researches on the *Mahābhāṣya* ad *A*1.3.1.

Appendix 2 furnishes an analyzed text of the *Mahābhāṣya* on *A*1.3.1.

As this organization of the work shows, I gave first a thorough analysis of the arguments presented by Kātyāyana and Patañjali under A1.3.1 and then argued the essential points brought out thereby. As a result, my method of presentation and argument required that materials be repeated on several occasions. I am afraid lest readers should say that I have been repetitious. It is hoped that this is sufficiently offset by the accomplishment I have achieved.

The present book intends to give us a complete and wholly unvarnished account of the points made by Kātyāyana in his vārttikas on *A*1.3.1 and by Patañjali in his Bhāṣya thereupon. It is my hope that this work will make some contribution to Pāṇinian studies.

Section 1

Pāṇini's views of *dhātvartha*: *sādhya* and *kriyā*

1.1. *sādhakatama*

It is well known that in his derivational system Pāṇini operates with syntactico-semantic categories called *kāraka*. There are seven kāraka categories: *kartṛ* 'agent', *karman* 'object', *karaṇa* 'instrument', *sampradāna* 'recipient', *apādāna* 'point of departure', *adhikaraṇa* 'locus', and *hetu* 'incitor' as a subcategory of *kartṛ*.[1] These category names are assigned to factors participating in actions by sūtras headed by the following sūtra:

*A*1.4.23 *kārake* //

This rule provides that subsequent rules apply with respect to kārakas. Of the above-mentioned kāraka names, Pāṇini defined the category name *karaṇa* by one of such rules as follows:

*A*1.4.42 *sādhakatamaṃ karaṇam* //
"That kāraka which most serves to bring about an act (*sādhakatama*) is called *karaṇa*."

The derivate *sādhakatama* is formed by introducing the superlative suffix *tamap* to the base *sādhaka*. In addition, the derivate *sādhaka* is formed from the derived verb *sādhi* (*sidh*/*sādh* 'be accomplished' + ***ṇic***; *A*3.1.26) with the kṛt affix ***ṇvul*** (*A*3.1.133), meaning 'that which accomplishes something'.[2]

---

[1] The *kartṛ* class includes a subcategory called *hetu*: a kāraka which functions as causal agent. Pāṇini, it is to be noted, recognizes six categories to which entities that function as kārakas are assigned by giving them class names *kartṛ* and so on.

[2] *Padamañjarī* on *Kāśikāvṛtti* ad *A*1.4.42: *ṣidhū saṃrāddhau ity asya hetumaṇṇyantasya sidhyater apāralaukike ity ātve rādha sādha saṃsiddhau ity asya vā ṇyantasya sādhakaśabdaḥ / kriyātmakaś cārthaḥ / prayojyaḥ kartā, sidhyataḥ sādhyavato vā kriyātmano 'rthasya prayojakatamaṃ sādhakatamam /* According to Haradatta, the verb from which *sādhaka* is derived is either *ṣidhū*/*ṣidhú* (IV.83) or *sādhá* (V.17) followed by the causative affix ***ṇic***; the verb *ṣidhū* (or *ṣidhú*) occurs in the meaning 'be accomplished' (*saṃrāddhi*) and the verb *sādhá* in the meaning 'be completed' (*sáṃsiddhi*), as the dhātupāṭha teaches it.

The following sūtra provides for the occurrence of the superlative suffix *tamap*:

*A*5.3.55 *atiśāyane tamabiṣṭhanau* //

According to this sūtra, the suffixes ***tamap*** and *iṣṭhan* follow a nominal base on condition that excellence (*atiśāyana*) is to be conveyed. For example, when all these men are rich (*āḍhya*); of these, he is exceedingly rich or most rich, he is spoken of as *āḍhyatama.* Similarly, of the kārakas, which are all *sādhakas*,[3] the kāraka that accomplishes best of all, or more correctly, that whose function of serving to bring about an act is the most effective compared to functions other kārakas have, is spoken of as *sādhakatama*. Evidently Pāṇini's use of the superlative *sādhakatama* presupposes that all kārakas are *sādhakas*.

I.	*ṣidhū̃* → *sidh*	(*A*6.1.64, 1.3.9)
	(*sidh* + ***ṇic***) + ***ṇvul***	(*A*3.1.26, 3.1.133)
	(*sedh* + *i*) + ***ṇvul***	(*A*7.3.86, 1.3.9)
	(*sādh* + *i*) + ***ṇvul***	(*A*6.1.49)
	sādh + ϕ + ***ṇvul***	(*A*6.4.51)
	sādhaka	(*A*1.3.9, 7.1.1)
II.	*sādhá̃* → *sādh*	(*A*1.3.9)
	(*sādh* + ***ṇic***) + ***ṇvul***	
	sādhaka	

*A*6.1.49 *sidhyater apāralaukike* provides that the guṇa vowel *e* which replaces *i* of the verb *sidh* is replaced by *ā* when an affix with the marker *ṇ* follows the verb, on condition that what is accomplished has nothing to do with things of the next world (*apāralaukike*). If an action (*kriyā*) is treated as a thing of this world, the verb *sidh* which signifies the act of being accomplished the action has is subject to this operation.

The causative affix ***ṇic*** introduced after *sidh*/*sādh* indicates that the term *sādhakatama* denotes what most serves to cause an action, which as an agent and a causee (*prayojya*) is involved in the act of being accomplished or completed, to be accomplished or completed. This is how the term *sādhakatama* signifies what most contributes to the accomplishment of an action.

[3] In his Bhāṣya on *A*1.4.42 (I.331.12) Patañjali states: *sarvāṇi hi kārakāṇi sādhakāni* / Based upon Pāṇini's identification of *kāraka* with *sādhaka*, Kātyāyana and Patañjali make an attempt to define the term *kāraka* as follows. *MBh* on *vt.* 1 ad *A*1.4.23 (I.323.8–9): *sādhakaṃ nirvartakaṃ kārakasaṃjñam bhavatīti vaktavyam* / ("The formulation is to be made that what brings about [an act] (*sādhaka*) or what brings [an act] to a completion (*nirvartaka*) is called *kāraka*.")

In this connection what Bhartṛhari says of the comparative and superlative is worth a mention in passing. Consider the following kārikās:

*VP*3.5.6: *sarvaṃ ca sarvato 'vaśyaṃ niyamena prakṛṣyate* / *saṃsargiṇā nimittena nikṛṣṭenādhikena vā* //
"Anything necessarily exceeds any other things [of the same class to which it belongs] exclusively on the basis of that with which it is connected (*saṃsargin*), whether the basis for the excellence may be superiority or inferiority itself."
*VP*3.5.8: *savyāpāro guṇas tasmāt svaprakarṣanibandhanaḥ* / *dravyātmānaṃ bhinatty eva svaprakarṣaṃ niveśayan* //
"Therefore, on the basis of its own excellence, committing the excellence of its own to a *dravya* ('substance'), what is understood to be a *guṇa* ('quality') because of carrying out the activity [of differentiating] differentiates the *dravya* itself [which is related to it from other *dravyas* of the same class]."

In order to exclude a certain thing from other things of the same class it belongs to, one has to resort to the excellence in its relatum which functions as what differentiates it from the things of a different class. Let us take up the example of the superlative *pācakatama* 'best cook'. What is spoken of as *pācaka* is a person engaged in the act of cooking. So the act of cooking in this case differentiates the person from other persons who are not engaged in that act. Suppose that there are three or more cooks here. If one intends to convey that a certain cook is the best of them, one uses the superlative *pācakatama* resorting to the excellence in the act of cooking, so that the cook referred to by the word *pācakatama* is differentiated from other cooks.

In the case of the use of the superlative *sādhakatama*, what is treated as a *guṇa* is nothing but the meaning of the causative verb *sādhi* (*sidh*/*sādh* + *ṇic*) or the action of accomplishing.[4]

[4]The terms *dravya* and *guṇa* here are technically defined by Bhartṛhari in his *VP*3.4.3 and *VP*3.5.1, respectively: in brief, whatever is intended to be conveyed as something differentiated from others is a *dravya* and whatever serves to differentiate a *dravya* from others is a *guṇa*. We need not go into details here.

The kāraka which is characterized as *sādhakatama* is an instrument (*karaṇa*). And the excellence in the act of accomplishing which the instrument performs consists in its being most immediately connected with the accomplishment of a main action. In the situation conveyed by the utterance *devadatta odanaṃ kāṣṭhaiḥ pacati* 'Devadatta is cooking rice-gruel with firewood', Devadatta, the rice-gruel, and the fire-wood function respectively as agent, object, and instrument with respect to the main act, the action of cooking. All these are kārakas and hence *sādhakas*. Of them the fire-wood is considered to be *sādhakatama* because of its excellence in the act of accomplishing the action of cooking.[5]

1.2. The term *sādhana* as a *sambandhiśabda* 'relative term'

The term *sādhaka* refers to what brings something to accomplishment. Then, in correlation to it, what is the thing to be brought to accomplishment by it (*sādhya*)? For considering this question it will be useful to adduce a passage from the *Mahābhāṣya*. Concerning the use of the word *sādhana* (*sidh*/*sādh* (*ṣidhū́* (*ṣidhú*)/*sādhá*) + ***lyuṭ***; *A*3.3.117) 'that by which something is brought to accomplishment', which is also used by Pāṇinīyas to refer to a kāraka, Patañjali states:

> *MBh* ad *A*3.1.19 (II.27.13–17): *sādhanam iti sambandhiśabdo 'yam / sambandhiśabdāś ca punar evamātmakā yad uta sambandhinam ākṣipanti / tad yathā mātari vartitavyam, pitari śuśruṣitavyam iti / na cocyate svasyāṃ mātari svasmin vā pitarīti / sambandhāc caitad gamyate yā yasya mātā yaś ca yasya piteti / evam ihāpi sambandhād etad gamyate yasya dhātor yat sādhanam iti /*
>
> "The word *sādhana* is a relative term (*sambandhiśabda*). And relative terms have as their nature that they imply something related to them (*sambandhinam ākṣipanti*). For example, one says *mātari vartitavyam* '[You] should follow the mother', *pitari śuśruṣitavyam* '[You] should obey the father' and not *svasyāṃ*

---

[5] In *VP*3.7.90 Bhartṛhari states: *kriyāyāḥ pariniṣpattir yadvyāpārād anantaram / vivakṣyate yadā tatra karaṇatvaṃ tadā smṛtam //* A thing is spoken of as instrument when its component activity is viewed as immediately preceding the accomplishment of an action.

mātari [*vartitavyam*] '[You] should follow [your] own mother' nor *svasmin pitari* [*śuśruṣitavyam*] '[You] should obey [your] own father'. And, on the basis of relation, one understands whose mother is meant by the word *mātṛ* and whose father is meant by the word *pitṛ* (*yā yasya mātā yaś ca yasya pitā*). In the same manner, in the present case also, on the basis of relation, one understands which verb [meaning] the thing meant by the term *sādhana* in question is related to (*yasya dhātor yat sādhanam*)."

To begin with, let us note Patañjali's description of the term *sādhana* as a relative term (*sambandhiśabda*). A relative term is an item which implies (*ākṣipanti*; *ākṣepa*) what its meaning is in relation to and, according to Bhartṛhari, the one which always is used with its own meaning in expectancy for its relatum.[6] Now what is the thing meant by the term *sādhana* related to and what does the term *sādhana* imply when used? Patañjali clearly states that it is a verb meaning. What is spoken of as *sādhana* does have a relation (*sambandha*) to a verb meaning and hence, on the basis of the relation, the term *sādhana* can imply the verb meaning and is also used in expectancy for it. It suffices, for the present, to note these points here. As said above, what is spoken of as *sādhana* is a means for bringing something to accomplishment. In the context where the thing meant by the word *sādhana* is said to have a relation to a verb meaning, it is the verb meaning which turns out to be what is to be brought to accomplishment (*sādhya*) by means of that thing.

Needless to say, the term *sādhana* is synonymous in this context with the term *kāraka*. Since kārakas are ancillaries to an action, a verb meaning, the principal significand, it is licit to call them *sādhana*. Therefore, what is true for the term *sādhana* is true for the term *sādhaka*. That is to say, the thing referred to by the term *sādhaka* has a relation to a verb meaning and expects the latter as what is to be brought to accomplishment, just as a mother,

---

[6] *VP*3.14.48ab: *sambandhiśabdaḥ sāpekṣo nityaṃ sarvaḥ prayujyate* / *Prakāśa* on *VP*3.14.48: *iha kecic chabdāḥ svārtham itarāpekṣaṃ nāntarīyakam abhidadhānāḥ sambandhiśabdāḥ kathyante* /

being a producer (*janaka*), has a relation to her son and expects him as the produced (*janya*).[7] Thus, if we take into account Patañjali's present Bhāṣya in this way, there is no doubt that when Pāṇini calls kārakas *sādhakas*, he regards verb meanings as being in correlation to them and hence as what are to be brought to accomplishment by them. Pāṇini did assume that there holds the accomplisher-accomplished relation, *sādhyasādhanabhāva* or *sādhyasādhakabhāva*, between kāraka and verb meaning.

1.3. Pāṇini's characterization of a verb meaning as *sādhya*

Consider the following utterances:

A. *devadattaḥ sthālyāṃ kāṣṭhair odanaṃ pacati* /
'Devadatta is cooking rice-gruel in a pot with firewood'.
B. *devadatto 'sti* /
'Devadatta is'.

With reference to A, one can easily imagine that the action of cooking signified by the verb *pac* is something that is to be brought to accomplishment. Here the person called *Devadatta*, the pot (*sthālī*), the rice-gruel (*odana*), and the firewood (*kāṣṭha*) serve respectively as agent, locus, object, and instrument. Concerning B, however, one may well feel it difficult to say that being, which is denoted by the verb *as* in *asti*, is also something to be brought to accomplishment in the same sense as the act of cooking. For utterance B presupposes the established existence of Devadatta. Still, in Pāṇini's grammar the following sūtra compels us to understand the meaning of the verb *as* as what is to be brought to accomplishment.

A3.4.69 *laḥ karmaṇi ca bhāve cākarmakebhyaḥ* //

This sūtra provides that after a verb L-affixes, which are subsequently replaced by finite endings or participial affixes, are introduced if an agent or an object is to be denoted; if, however, the action denoted is objectless, they are introduced to denote an

---

[7] *Prakāśa* on *VP*3.3.31cd: . . . *iyam asya putrasya māteti janyajanakabhāvaḥ* . . . /

activity itself (*bhāva*) or an agent.[8] According to this sūtra, a verb ending which follows any verb—irrespective of the question whether the verb comes under the *kṛ*-class or the *as*-class: this distinction came to puzzle Kātyāyana and Patañjali, as we shall see later—may signify a specific kāraka, that is, an agent. And this clearly shows that any verb meaning requires an agent, which brings Pāṇinīyas such as Helārāja to saying from a semantic point of view that there is not any action, verb meaning, without an agent.[9] As said, what functions as kāraka is what brings an act to accomplishment (*sādhaka*). An agent is a *sādhaka.* This being the case, thus, the following is revealed by Pāṇini's analysis of finite verb forms such that any verb is followed by a verb ending to signify an agent:

For Pāṇini, whatever is denoted by a verb is characterized as something to be brought to accomplishment.

In B the person called *Devadatta* functions as agent. This being so, the meaning of the verb *as* in question has to be regarded as what is to be brought to accomplishment in correlation to Devadatta as agent.

At this point, let us recall that Bhartṛhari defines an action which is nothing but a verb meaning as what is denoted as something to be brought to accomplishment. Apart from his introduction of the aspect of denotation (*abhidhāna*), which will be discussed in detail,[10] we can be fairly certain that the characterization of a

---

[8] See Introduction [0.1.1].

[9] *Prakāśa* on *VP*3.7.102: *akartṛkāyāḥ kriyāyā abhāvāt* / Pāṇini defines the name *kartṛ* by *A*1.4.54 *svatantraḥ kartā*, according to which the kāraka that is called *kartṛ* is that which is spoken of as an independent participant in comparison with other participants in an act. Be it the case that there is no act without an agent, Pāṇini's definition of the name *kartṛ* is not made from that angle. Clearly, on the assumption that an agent, being a kāraka, is connected with an act, Pāṇini intends to differentiate it from other kārakas in the sūtra. Pāṇini's correlating an agent with other kārakas finds Patañjali's concise explanation of the independence which characterizes an agent as follows. *MBh* ad *A* 1.4.23 (I.326.10): *yat sarveṣu sādhaneṣu sannihiteṣu kartā pravartayitā bhavati* / An agent is an independent and principal kāraka in that it sets other kārakas into play.

[10] See Section 5 [5.2.3.2].

verb meaning as something to be brought to accomplishment has already been well prepared by Pāṇini, if we take into consideration the semantics which Pāṇini assumes so as to have utterances in his derivational system.[11]

1.4. *kriyā* as what is brought into being

What is more, it is suggestive that in formulating *A*1.4.23 *kārake* Pāṇini uses the term *kāraka* to refer to what brings a thing signified by a verb to accomplishment. The term *kāraka* is a derivate which is formed from the verb *kṛ* 'do, make' (***ḍukṛñ***) with the kṛt affix ***ṇvul*** (*A*3.1.133). According to Patañjali, the term *kāraka* is a technical term whose etymological meaning is retained (*anvarthasaṃjñā*), so that it means 'that which brings about something'.[12] We have already seen that it is verb meanings that are characterized as those which are brought to accomplishment by kārakas. Therefore, we may refer to the verb meanings in correlation to kārakas by using derivates of the verb *kṛ*. Pāṇini's derivational system indeed allows the term *kriyā* to be among the forms derived from the verb *kṛ* used in the sense of what is brought to accomplishment.

---

[11] Cardona [1997: par. 228] has already pointed out that Pāṇini conceives of a verb meaning as *sādhya*. Cardona says as follows: "On the other hand, Pāṇini does consider that any verb denotes something that is brought to accomplishment in time. The term *kāraka*, which Pāṇini uses without defining (**A**1.4.23 [**214**]), refers to something that directly contributes to an act's being accomplished. Any kāraka, then, is properly termed *sādhaka* 'that which accomplishes'. In **A**1.4.42, Pāṇini uses the superlative *sādhakatamam* in order to exclude from the karaṇa category kārakas that are not the immediate means of accomplishing an act. Similarly, Pāṇini uses the superlative *īpsitatamam* 'most sought to be reached, obtained' in **A**1.4.49 to exclude other goals from the karman category. However, a given act may have more than one karaṇa or karman taking part in it."

Cardona penetrates what Pāṇini considers a verb meaning to be in this way. He brings in the notion of time (*kāla*) also to characterize the verb meaning as conceived of by Pāṇini. As shall be seen later (see Section 4, Part 4 [4.8.2.2]; Section 6 [6.3]), Pāṇinīyas such as Patañjali and Bhartṛhari mention the association of a verb meaning with time as one of the features the verb meaning has.

[12] *MBh* ad *A*1.4.23 (I.324.9): *karotīti kārakam* / This paraphrase of the term *kāraka* shows that the term *kāraka* is an agent noun.

In the *Padamañjarī* on A3.3.100 is given the derivation of the term *kriyā*,[13] which can be explained in two ways.

1)	*kṛ + śa + ṭāp*	(A3.3.100, 4.1.4)
	kṛ + yak + a + ā	(A3.1.67)
	kri + ya + a + ā	(A7.4.28)
	kriya + ā	(A6.1.97)
	kriyā	(A6.1.101)
2)	*kṛ + śa + ṭāp*	(A3.3.100, 4.1.4)
	kri + a + ā	
	kriy + a + ā	(A6.4.77)
	kriyā	(A6.1.101)

A3.3.100 *kṛñaḥ śaś ca* provides that on condition that the meaning 'feminine' is to be conveyed, if an act in the abstract (*bhāva*) or a kāraka other than an agent is to be signified, the kṛt affix *śa* occurs with the verb *kṛ*. By A3.4.113 the affix *śa* is called *sārvadhātuka* since it has the marker *ś* (*śit*). Therefore, if an act in the abstract or an object is to be conveyed by the affix *śa*, A3.1.67 applies here which states that the vikaraṇa *yak* follows any verb that occurs with a sārvadhātuka affix which has been introduced to convey an act or an object. Accordingly in derivation 1) the resulting form *kriyā* signifies either the mere act, in the abstract, of bringing about something (*bhāvasādhana*) or that which is brought about (*karmasādhana*).[14] To make in passing a

[13] *Padamañjarī* on A3.3.100: *śakāraḥ sārvadhātukasaṃjñārthaḥ, tatra yadā bhāvakarmaṇoḥ śas tadā sārvadhātuke yak, riṅ śayaglinkṣu iti riṅādeśaḥ, anyatra śakāra eva parato riṅādeśaḥ, aci śnudhātu ityādineyaṅ* / See Introduction fn. 8, where Nāgeśa's etymological explanation of the term *kriyā* in *VP*3.8.1 is found: *kriyate avayavānāṃ krameṇotpattyā*. According to Nāgeśa, the term *kriyā* means 'what is brought about'.

[14] According to Pāṇinīyas, a certain item that ends in a kṛt affix which is introduced to a base to convey an abstract act (*bhāva*) is called *bhāvasādhana*, or an item formed by adding an affix to denote *bhāva* to a base, while an item that ends in a kṛt affix denoting an object (*karman*) is called *karmasādhana*, or an item formed with a kṛt affix to denote an object. Needless to say, this is said of items ending in kṛt affixes to signify meanings other than *bhāva* and *karman*. We may have items called *kartṛsādhana*, *karaṇasādhana*, and so on.

remark about the form *kriyā* in derivation 2), it may denote kārakas other than an agent and an object with respect to the act of bringing about something.

Thus clearly Pāṇini allows the form *kriyā* to signify what is brought to accomplishment. It is reasonable to say, therefore, that when by the term *kāraka* Pāṇini speaks of what brings about a thing denoted by a verb, he has in mind that the thing meant by the verb is properly called *kriyā.* For Pāṇini, the term *kāraka* is a relative term, used in correlation to the term *kriyā.* This is endorsed not only by the fact that later Pāṇinīyas hold that it is *kriyā* which is connected with a kāraka (*kriyākārakayor abhisambandhaḥ*) but also by their description of the verb meaning as *kriyā* (*kaḥ punar dhātvarthaḥ, kriyā*).[15]

In this connection it will be of use to cite the following passage from the *Uddyota*:

> *Uddyota* on *MBh* ad *A*1.4.23 (II.379): *nanu karotīty asya niṣpādayatīty arthaḥ / evaṃ ca niṣpādakatve labdhe 'pi kriyānirvartakam ity arthālābhaḥ . . . / kriyāyā eva śabdena sādhyatvapratīter nirvartakārthe kārakaśabde sambandhyākāṅkṣāyāṃ saiva sambadhyate /*
>
> "[Objection] The word *karoti* '. . . brings about' [in the paraphrase *karotīti kārakam*] means '. . . produces' (*niṣpādayati*). And such being the case, even if one obtains the understanding that what is spoken of as *karoti* is something which produces, one cannot obtain the understanding that the word *karoti* means 'what produces an action' (*kriyānirvartaka*). . . .
>
> [Answer] It is nothing but an action that is understood from a word as something to be brought to accomplishment. Therefore, when the term *kāraka* refers to what brings something to completion (*nirvartaka*), and its relatum is expected (*sambandhyākāṅkṣāyām*), the very action is connected with it."

This statement of Nāgeśa's accords exactly with the Bhāṣya on

---

[15] *MBh* ad *A*2.1.1 (I.356.13): *kriyākārakayor abhisambandhasya . . . / MBh* ad *A*3.2.84 (II.111.4–5), 3.2.115 (II.120.7–8), 5.1.118 (II.365.3): *kaḥ punar dhātvarthaḥ, kriyā /*

*A*3.1.19 quoted above. It is only an action (*kriyā*) as a verb meaning that is denoted as something to be brought to accomplishment. The term *kāraka* signifies what brings something to accomplishment and hence the referent of that term expects its relatum as what is brought to accomplishment by it. It follows, consequently, that when the term *kāraka* is used, what is connected with its referent is the very action as a verb meaning.

1.5. We have seen how Pāṇini viewes verb meanings. Reflection on his use of the terms *sādhaka* and *kāraka* so far examined will make clear the following:

> Pāṇini assumes that a verb meaning is something characterized as *kriyā* in correlation to kārakas[16] and describes semantically the verb meaning as something yet to be brought to accomplishment in correlation to sādhakas.

[16] This point is argued by Deshpande [1991: 468-470] also.

Section 2

Traditional interpretations of *A*1.3.1 *bhūvādayo dhātavaḥ*

2.0. Before entering into an investigation of the question of what verbs signify, the question committed to Patañjali in his Bhāṣya on *A*1.3.1, it is necessary to see what rule *A*1.3.1 is and how Kātyāyana and Patañjali discuss the sūtra in question. In this section the first question shall be dealt with to make clear how *A*1.3.1 is traditionally interpreted on the basis of the *Kāśikāvṛtti* and the *Siddhāntakaumudī* and in the following two sections the second question shall be taken up to examine the arguments the Pāṇinīyas develop under the sūtra.

2.1. *A*1.3.1 as a saṃjñāsūtra

As has already been said, *A*1.3.1 is a saṃjñāsūtra or a definitional rule by which the class name (*saṃjñā*) *dhātu* is assigned to relevant items and the convention regarding the use of the term *dhātu* is established. One may notice that the present sūtra contains only the nominative plural forms *bhūvādayaḥ* (*bhūvādi-jas*), *dhātavaḥ* (*dhātu-jas*). According to Patañjali, in formulating saṃjñāsūtras Pāṇini simply follows the conventions of normal Sanskrit usage; in normal Sanskrit usage, for the name-giving the linkage is established between the object named and the name itself, by means of using the utterance in which the term for the named and the one for the name are coreferential with each other (*sāmānādhikaraṇya*) and hence they end in nominal endings of the like kind (*ekavibhaktitva*), as in *ayaṃ devadattaḥ* 'He is "Devadatta"'. Here, therefore, we have no difficulty in accepting *A*1.3.1 as a saṃjñāsūtra.[1] As a matter of fact, there is no disagreement among

---

[1] *MBh* ad *A*1.1.1 (I.39.22–23): *idaṃ khalv api bhūyaḥ sāmānādhikaraṇyam ekavibhaktitvaṃ ca'/ dvayos caitad bhavati / kayoḥ / viśeṣaṇaviśeṣyayor vā saṃjñāsaṃjñinor vā /* In his *Vṛtti* on *VP*1.68 Bhartṛhari explains a name-giving sentence of this type as follows: *svarūpādhyāropacikīrṣāyāṃ bāhyeṣv arthātmasu śabdārthānāṃ svarūpeṇādhiṣṭhānabhūtenārthavattvāt prathamā vidhīyate, so 'yam iti ca saṃjñinā śaktyavacchedalakṣaṇaḥ sambandho niyamyate /* ("When one intends to superimpose a linguistic item's own form on objects other than a form

Pāṇinīyas as to a character of the present sūtra, namely that it is a saṃjñāsūtra.

2.2. *vyākhyāna* of *A* 1.3.1

Although Pāṇinīyas agree that *A* 1.3.1 is a saṃjñāsūtra, however, its interpretation by them is another story. With regard to this sūtra, it is indeed difficult to expect a uniform interpretation of the same tone from them.

In the Paspasā, Patañjali states that for arriving at a proper understanding of correct speech from sūtras their explanations (*vyākhyāna*) are also necessary. There are two types of explanations: that which consists of an analysis of a sūtra into its components, suppletion of items necessary to the understanding of the

---

[understood from the term for the named] (*bāhyeṣu*), the linguistic item which denotes itself becomes meaningful (*arthavat*) on account of its own form being a basis for applying it, so that an ending of the first triplet (*prathamā*), a nominative ending, is introduced after it. And through establishing the [name-named] relationship in such a way that this is that (*so 'yam*), the relation of the name with the named, which is characterized as the delimitation of the denotative capacity of the item serving as name, is restricted." Note: I have translated with singular forms under the assumption that *śabdārthānām* and so on are plural forms whose alternants are generic singulars, according to *A* 1.2.58.) In the case of *bhūvādayo dhātavaḥ*, the form of the item *dhātu* is superimposed on what are denoted by the item *bhūvādi*, such as *bhū*, and thereby the identity between them are established, so that one can obtain the name-named relationship between them.

In addition to a name-giving sentence, there is another type of sentence of the same structure. According to Patañjali, it is a sentence such as *nīlam utpalam* 'a blue lotus', in which the term for the qualifier (*viśeṣaṇa*), '*nīla*', and the one for the qualificand (*viśeṣya*), '*utpala*', are used appositionally. See the following kārikā of the *Vākyapadīya*. *VP*3.14.21: *sāmānādhikaraṇyaṃ ca śabdayoḥ kaiścid iṣyate / viśeṣaṇaviśeṣyatvaṃ saṃjñāsaṃjñitvam eva ca //* (Iyer, Raghunātha: *eva vā* instead of *eva ca*.) This kārikā will be again taken up in Section 4, Part 2, fn. 20.

One has to note that there is another type of utterance meant for establishing the name-named relationship. That is the utterance in which a genitive form is used. Genitive endings refer to unspecified relations so that they can convey the relationship in question. As an instance *A*1.1.17 *uñaḥ* can be given. The sūtra is interpreted as *uñaḥ pragṛhyam* (*uñaḥ*, gen. sg.; *pragṛhyam*, nom. sg.), providing that the nipāta *u* (*uñ*) is called *pragṛhya*. See *VP*3.3.3: *asyāyaṃ vācako vācya iti ṣaṣṭhyā pratīyate / yogaḥ śabdārthayos tattvam apy ato vyapadiśyate //*

sūtra (*vākyādhyāhāra*), citation of examples (*udāharaṇa*) and counterexamples (*pratyudāharaṇa*) illustrating how the sūtra operates;[2] and that which consists of the following six factors: a separation of constituent units of a sūtra (*padaccheda*), a mention of the meanings of the constituent units (*padārthokti*), an analysis of a constituent unit into its components (*vigraha*), the construction of the sūtra as a sentence (*vākyayojanā*), raising objections (*ākṣepa*), and answering the objections (*samādhāna*).[3] The type of explanation one finds in the vārttikas and in the *Mahābhāṣya* is precisely the latter and one might consider that style of explanation as in essence assuming an aspect of an argumentation about a sūtra, so that it is not so easy to get the idea in a straightforward way of how exactly *A*1.3.1 is to be interpreted on the basis of the vārttikas and the Bhāṣya upon the sūtra at issue. Therefore, let us first see how *A*1.3.1 is interpreted in the tradition of Pāṇini's grammar, based upon the *Kāśikāvṛtti* and the *Siddhāntakaumudī* both of which follow the former way of explaining sūtras.

2.3. *Kāśikāvṛtti* ad *A*1.3.1

2.3.1. The *Kāśikāvṛtti* interprets the sūtra under consideration as follows:

bhū ityevamādayaḥ śabdāḥ kriyāvacanā dhātusaṃjñā bhavanti/ bhū bhavati / edha edhate / spardha spardhate /

dhātuśabdaḥ pūrvācāryasaṃjñā / te ca kriyāvacanānāṃ saṃjñāṃ kṛtavantaḥ / tad ihāpi pūrvācāryasaṃjñāśrayaṇāt kriyāvācināṃ eva bhūvādīnāṃ dhātusaṃjñā vidhīyate /

bhūvādīnāṃ vakāro 'yaṃ maṅgalārthaḥ prayujyate /
bhuvo vārthaṃ vadantīti bhvarthā vā vādayaḥ smṛtāḥ //
dhātupradeśāḥ—dhātoḥ ityevamādayaḥ /

---

[2] *MBh* (Paspaśā) [I.11.20–23]: *na hi sūtrata eva śabdān pratipadyante / kiṃ tarhi / vyākhyānataś ca / nanu ca tad eva sūtraṃ vigṛhītaṃ vyākhyānaṃ bhavati / na kevalāni carcāpadāni vyākhyānaṃ vṛddhiḥ āt aij iti / kiṃ tarhi / udāharaṇaṃ pratyudāharaṇaṃ vākyādhyāhāra ity etatsamuditaṃ vyākhyānaṃ bhavati /* See Cardona [1980: 243].

[3] Kielhorn [1874: 2 (fn. 1)]: *padacchedaḥ padārthoktir vigraho vākyayojanā / ākṣepo 'tha samādhānaṃ vyākhyānaṃ ṣaḍvidhaṃ matam //*

"Items of the set beginning with an item such as *bhū*, denoting actions (*kriyā*), are called *dhātu*.

bhū (*bhū́*) 'be, be born' – *bhavati* '. . . is, is born'
edha (*édha*) 'thrive' – *edhate* '. . . thrives'
spardha (*spárdha*) 'contend' – *spardhate* '. . . contends'

[The above-mentioned items are called *dhātu* by A1.3.1. They are subject to particular operations provided for by rules headed by A3.1.91. In addition, they are subject to particular operations according to their accentuations of base vowels and markers attached to them.][4]

The term *dhātu* is a borrowing from the terminology of earlier teachers (*pūrvācāryasaṃjñā*).[5] And they assigned the term [*dhātu*] to items denoting actions. Therefore, in this [grammar of Pāṇini's] also, it is provided by Pāṇini that items are called *dhātu* if they belong to the set beginning with *bhū*,[6] and they denote actions, since he resorts to the terminology of earlier teachers.

[Tradition says that A1.3.1 admits of different interpretations, as is shown by the following ślokavārttika.]

bhūvādīnāṃ vakāro 'yaṃ maṅgalārthaḥ prayujyate /
bhuvo vārthaṃ vadantīti bhvarthā vā vādayaḥ smṛtāḥ //

---

[4] On accentuations of base vowels and markers pertaining to verbs recited in the dhātupāṭha, see Section 3 [3.2.6].

[5] When the word *dhātu* is used in its non-technical sense, it means 'a basic element of something'.

In connection with the terminology for a verb, it must be recalled here that the term *dhātu* is used in the *Ṛgvedaprātiśākhya*, which shows less influence of Pāṇinian methodology than the other prātiśākhyas (Cardona [1980: n. 428). *Ṛgvedaprātiśākhya* 12.19: *tad ākhyātaṃ yena bhāvaṃ sadhātu //* ("A verb form is that by means of which *bhāva* is denoted and which includes a verbal base (*sadhātu*).") According to Uvaṭa, the term *bhāva* here means an action (*kriyā*).

[6] We have to note that the *Kāśikāvṛtti* reads *bhūvādīnāṃ dhātusaṃjñā* instead of *bhvādīnāṃ dhātusaṃjñā*. Here the *Kāśikāvṛtti* presupposes that the form *bhūvādi* is a ready-made form (*nipātana*) with the augment *-v-* to *bhū* or to *ādi*, which accords with the interpretation of *bhūvādi* set forth in the first half of the ślokavārttika cited here; the first half of the ślokavārttika at hand is cited in the Bhāṣya on A1.3.1 also.

Rules in which the term *dhātu* is mentioned are *A*3.1.91 *dhātoḥ* and others."

2.3.2. ślokavārttika

The *Kāśikāvṛtti* cites the ślokavārttika to show that *A*1.3.1 has given rise to most diverse interpretations in the Pāṇinian tradition, apart from an interpretation the *Kāśikāvṛtti* itself gives it.

The ślokavārttika presented here demands an independent inquiry because commentators give different interpretations to it, especially with reference to the last half of it; we do not see any difference between their interpretations of the first half of it. Interestingly Patañjali cites only the first half of the present ślokavārttika, leaving out of consideration the second half of it. What the last line of the ślokavārttika tells, as is interpreted by the commentators, does not exactly accord with certain possible interpretations of *A*1.3.1 given by Patañjali, which shall be shown later.[7]

2.3.2.1. *Nyāsa* on the ślokavārttika

Let us first take up the interpretation of the ślokavārttika given in the *Nyāsa*.

1) [First alternative]

The sound *-v-* of the word *bhūvādayaḥ* ((*bhū-v-ādi*)-*jas*) is used for the sake of auspiciousness (*maṅgalārthaḥ*) [so that the *bhūvādayaḥ* is a bahuvrīhi, meaning 'those the first item of which is *bhū*'].

2) [Second alternative]

Signifiers (*vādi*), which, being spoken of as *bhvartha* (*bhū-artha*) because of (*iti*) denoting (*vadanti*) the meaning of the verb *bhū* (*bhuvo 'rtham*), denote *bhū* [i.e., an action in general (*kriyāsāmānya*)], are intended [to be understood as the named] (*smṛtāḥ*).[8]

---

[7] See Section 7 [7.4].

[8] *Nyāsa* on *Kāśikāvṛtti* ad *A*1.3.1: *atha vā bhūvādaya ity atra nirdeśe nāyam ādiśabdasya prayogaḥ, nāpi maṅgalārthasya vakārasya / kiṃ tarhi vādiśabdasyauṇādikasya / vadantīti vādayaḥ, vācakā ity arthaḥ / vader dhātoḥ vasivapiyajirājivrajisadihanivāśivādivāribhya iñ iti kartarīñpratyayaḥ / yady api vādīti sūtre ṇyantasyopādānam, tathāpi bahula-*

3) [Third alternative]

Items of the *vā*-type (*vādi*; *vā* 'go, strike' [II. 41],[9] which, being spoken of as *bhvartha* (*bhū-artha*) because of (*iti*) denoting (*vadanti*) the meaning of the verb *bhū* (*bhuvo 'rtham*), denote *bhū* [i.e., an action in general (*kriyāsāmānya*)], are intended [to be understood as the named] (*smṛtāḥ*).[10]

Concerning the first interpretation that the sound -*v*- of the word *bhūvādayaḥ* is used for the sake of auspiciousness, the *Nyāsa* explains that the sequence *bhū-v-ādi* reflects an archaic linguistic phenomenon that semivowels appear after *i*, *u* when dissimilar vowels follow (*yaṇvyavadhāna*).[11] What has to be noticed here,

---

vacanād aṇyantād api bhavati /

bhvarthā iti / *teṣām vādīnāṃ idaṃ viśeṣaṇam, bhavanaṃ bhūḥ, sampadāditvād bhāve kvip* / *bhavater arthaḥ kriyāsāmānyam* / *bhūr artho yeṣāṃ te bhvarthāḥ* / *kasmāt punas te bhvarthāḥ* / *bhuvo vārthaṃ vadantīti* / *itikaraṇo hetau—yasmād bhuvo dhātor arthaṃ vadanty abhidadhati tasmāt te bhvarthāḥ* / *evaṃvidhā vādayo vācakāḥ śabdā bhavatyarthābhidhāyina itīha sūtre saṃjñinaḥ smṛtāḥ abhimatāḥ abhipretā ity arthaḥ* / (Note: I have corrected the punctuation *nāpi maṅgalārthasya vakārasya, kiṃ tarhi* / *vādiśabdasyauṇādikasya* given by Miśra [1985]. *kiṃ tarhi* here is better taken as an adversative conjunction than as 'what then?', so that the sentence including the present passage might mean: 'Alternatively, in this mention of the word *bhūvādayaḥ* the word *ādi* is not used in this way, nor is the sound -*v*- meant for auspiciousness; but on the contrary, the derivate *vādi* with the uṇādi affix ***iñ*** is used.' See Cardona [1998].) Here in the *Nyāsa* it is simply stated that the verb *bhū* signifies an action in general (*kriyāsāmānya*). The derivation of the form *bhū* in question is accounted for by *vt.* 9 ad *A*3.3.108: *sampadādibhyaḥ kvip*. As shall be shown in Section 5, the question of what the verb *bhū* means is absolutely crucial to Patañjali's interpretation of *A*1.3.1 as a semantic definition of the term *dhātu*.

[9] In the dhātupāṭha as handed down to us, the item *vā* is the forty-first entry of the subgroup *adādigaṇa*.

[10] *Nyāsa* on *Kāśikāvṛtti* ad *A*1.3.1: *atha vā—ādiśabdasyaivātra vā gatigandhanayoḥ ity asmāt parasya prayogaḥ* / *vā ādi yeṣāṃ te vādayaḥ* / *ādiśabdaḥ prakāravācī, vāprakārā ity arthaḥ* / *prakāras tu sādṛśyam, tat punaḥ kriyātmakatayā, yad āha—bhvarthā iti* / *bhvarthatā tu bhuvo 'rthaṃ vadatīti hetoḥ* / *evaṃvidhā vāprakārakāḥ śabdā iha sūtre saṃjñinaḥ smṛtāḥ* /

[11] *Nyāsa* on *Kāśikāvṛtti* ad *A*1.3.1: *yathā vede triyambakaṃ yajāmahe ity atra yakārasya dṛṣṭaprayojanaṃ nāstīty adṛṣṭārtho dharmārtha eva pāṭhas tasya, tathehāpi vakārasya* / As one has *triyambaka* 'three-eyed'

however, is that even if the occurrence of the sound *-v-* in that sequence may be explained in this way, no rule of the *Aṣṭādhyāyī* accounts for it.

In the *Nyāsa*'s second interpretation, the sequence *bhūvādi* is segmented into two elements: *bhū* and *vādi*. The term *bhū*, derived from the verb *bhū* with the kṛt affix ***kvip*** used to signify the mere act in the abstract (*bhāva*) by *A*3.3.94, refers to a meaning of the verb *bhū*, which is taken as an action in general (*kriyāsāmānya*).[12] And the word *vādi* is interpreted as a derivate formed from the verb *vad* 'articulate, utter' by adding the uṇādi affix ***iñ***, meaning 'that which denotes something'.[13] Thus these two items are combined to form a genitive tatpuruṣa by *A*2.3.50.[14] Consequently, the word *bhūvādi* means, according to this interpretation, 'a signifier (*vādi*) of *bhū*', in other words, an item which signifies an action in general. An etymological explanation of the compound *bhūvādi* is shown by saying *bhuvo vārthaṃ vadantīti*, which means 'items are called *bhūvādi* since they denote a meaning of the verb *bhū*'.

In the third interpretation, the word *vādi* in the compound *bhūvādi* is taken differently from the one in the second interpretation, although the same rule (*A*2.3.50) applies for the formation of that compound (*bhuvo vādayaḥ*). That is, the sequence *vādi* is analyzed into *vā* and *ādi*. The word *vā* refers to the verb *vā* 'go, strike' and the word *ādi* here means *prakāra* ('type, sort'), or similarity (*sādṛśya*).[15] These words are combined so as to form the bahuvrīhi compound *vādi*, which compound means 'a group

---

instead of *tryambaka*, so can one have *bhūvādi* instead of *bhvādi*. See Palsule [1957: 138–139; fn. 59].

[12] One should note that the kṛt affix ***kvip*** is simply deleted according to *A*6.1.67.

[13] *US*4.124: *vasivapiyajirājivrajisadihanivāśivādivāribhya iñ //* See also Section 7, fn. 9.

[14] See the *Nyāsa* on the interpretation of *bhuvo vādayaḥ* in the ślokavārttika. *Nyāsa* on *Kāśikāvṛtti* ad *A*1.3.1: *asminn api vyākhyāne bhūvādayaḥ iti ṣaṣṭhīsamāso 'yam / ṣaṣṭhī ca vācyavācakasambandhalakṣaṇā veditavyā /*

[15] On the use of the word *ādi* in the sense of *prakāra*, see Section 7 [7.3].

of items which are like the item *vā*', or a set of items which are similar to the item *vā* in that they signify the meaning of the verb *bhū* (*bhvarthā*), an action (*kriyā*). As a consequence of it, the compound *bhūvādi* refers to a group of *vā*-like items which signifies *bhū* or an action in general.

To sum up the interpretations given in the *Nyāsa*:

1) Items of the set beginning with *bhū*, recited in the dhātupāṭha, are called *dhātu*.

2) Signifiers (*vādi*) of *bhū* or an action in general are called *dhātu*.

3) A set of *vā*-like items which signifies *bhū* or an action in general is called *dhātu*.

2.3.2.2. *Padamañjarī* on the ślokavārttika

According to the *Padamañjarī*, the present ślokavārttika is interpreted in the following manner:

1) [First alternative]

The sound -*v*- of the word *bhūvādayaḥ* ((*bhū-v-ādi*)-*jas*) is used for the sake of auspiciousness (*maṅgalārthaḥ*) [so that the *bhūvādayaḥ* is a bahuvrīhi, meaning 'those the first item of which is *bhū*'].

2) [Second alternative]

By the word *bhūvādayaḥ* are meant those items which denote the meaning of the verb *bhū* [i.e., an action in general] (*bhuvo vārthaṃ vadantīti*).[16]

3) [Third alternative]

Two sets of items that denote *bhū* [i.e., an action in general] are intended [to be understood as the named] (*bhvarthā vā vādayaḥ smṛtāḥ*): a set of items which precede or are recited prior to *vā* (*vādayaḥ*) and items of the set which begins with *vā* (*vādayaḥ*).[17]

---

[16] *Padamañjarī* on *Kāśikāvṛtti* ad A1.3.1: *prakārāntaram āha—bhuvo vārthaṃ vadantīti / bhuvo dhātor arthaṃ vadantīti vā, bhūvādaya iti nirdeśa ity arthaḥ / arthakathanaṃ caitad / vyutpattis tu bhavanaṃ bhūḥ, kriyāsāmānyabhuvaṃ vadantīty auṇādiko 'yam, vasivapiyajirājivrajisadihanivāśivādivāribhya iñ iti kartari vadeḥ iñ pratyayaḥ /*

[17] *Padamañjarī* on *Kāśikāvṛtti* ad A1.3.1: *tṛtīyaṃ prakāram āha—bhva-*

What the *Padamañjarī* adds to the *Nyāsa* on the first interpretation is a grammatical description of the bahuvrīhi compound *bhūvādi*. According to the *Padamañjarī*, the form *bhūvādi* with the augment -*v*- is not an item which obtains by rule and hence is given as a ready-made form, so that it is accepted as correct by *A*6.3.109.[18]

The second interpretation given by the *Padamañjarī* is the same as the one given by the *Nyāsa*.

The third interpretation is complicated by considering that the item *vādayaḥ* in the compound *bhū-vādayaḥ* formed by *A*2.2.8[19] is a single remainder (*ekaśeṣa*; *A*1.2.64) of a series of items of the same form *vādayaś ca vādayaś ca*.

We have two types of *vādayaḥ*. One is *vādi* as a bahuvrīhi compound formed from *vā* and *ādi*, signifying 'items of the set whose first member is *vā*'. In this case the word *ādi* is used in the sense of *vyavasthā* ('arrangement'). The other as a tatpuruṣa, signifying 'items that occur prior to *vā*' and hence referring to items of the set beginning with *bhū* and ending with an item occurring immediately before *vā* (*yā*; II. 40).[20] As said, the item *vādayaḥ* is a single remainder of these two compounds.[21] Thus the present interpretation leads us to take the sūtra in question as

rthā vā vādayaḥ smṛtā iti / bhavanaṃ bhūḥ, so 'rtho yeṣāṃ te bhvarthāḥ, evambhūtā vādayo vātra saṃjñinaḥ smṛtā ity arthaḥ / kim idaṃ vādaya iti / vā gatigandhanayoḥ vā ādir yeṣāṃ te vādayaḥ, vā gati ity ārabhyā curādisamāpteḥ / tathā ca bhvādayo vādayaḥ bhūprabhṛtaya ā vā gatigandhanayoḥ ity asmād /

[18] *Padamañjarī* on *Kāśikāvṛtti* ad *A*1.3.1: *lakṣaṇenāprāpto nipātyata ity arthaḥ / . . . / bahuvrīhes tu bhūvādiśabdasya pṛṣodarāditvāt sādhutvam / A*6.3.109 provides that items of the type *pṛṣodara* 'spotted-belly' are accepted as taught. The items in question are treated as derived elements and their derivation involves deletion (*lopa*), augmenting (*āgama*), and sound replacement (*vikāra*), but Pāṇini does not state these operations explicitly for them in the *Aṣṭādhyāyī*. See also Section 8 [8.6.2.1].

[19] *Padamañjarī* on *Kāśikāvṛtti* ad *A*1.3.1: *tato bhuvo vādaya iti vācyavācakasambandhe śeṣaṣaṣṭhīsamāsaḥ /*

[20] The item *yā* is the fortieth entry of the subgroup *adādigaṇa*. See the present section, fn. 9.

[21] It is to be noted in passing that what remains of a bahuvrīhi and a tatpuruṣa compounds is the former according to *vt*. 23 ad *A*1.2.64: *svarabhinnānāṃ yasyottarasvaravidhiḥ*.

follows: A set of items preceding *vā* and items of the set beginning with *vā* are called *dhātu* if they signify *bhū* or an action in general.

In short, according to the *Padamañjarī*, *A*1.3.1 is interpreted as follows:

1) Items of the set beginning with *bhū*, recited in the dhātupāṭha, are called *dhātu*.
2) Signifiers (*vādi*) of *bhū* or an action in general are called *dhātu*.
3) A set of items preceding *vā* and items of the set beginning with *vā* are called *dhātu* if they signify *bhū* or an action in general.

2.3.3. Interpretation of *A*1.3.1 by the *Kāśikāvṛtti*

We have seen that the third interpretation of the word *bhūvādayaḥ* in the ślokavārttika is taken differently by the *Nyāsa* and the *Padamañjarī*. But the important thing to note here is that the ślokavārttika as interpreted by them shows that *A*1.3.1 can be interpreted in three different ways: as a purely formal definition, based upon the dhātupāṭha; as a semantic definition; and, in a combined way, as a formal and semantic definition, based upon the dhātupāṭha with the semantic condition. The interpretation of *A*1.3.1 the ślokavārttika in question gives here shall be again taken up later in connection with the question how Patañjali interprets the sūtra.[22]

---

[22]Palsule [1957: 136] says: "The author of the Ślokavārttikas has explained the word bhūvādayo in three different ways, thus: (1) *bhūvādayo* = *bhū* + *v* + *ādayo*, 'bhū and the following (verbs listed in the dhātup.)', the letter *v* being meant only for the sake of the maṅgala (in the middle of the work); (2) *bhūvādayo* = *bhū* + *vādayaḥ* (*bhuvo vādayaḥ*) '(words) expressive (*vādayaḥ*) of action (*bhū*)'; here *bhū* is taken as an abstract noun in the sense of *bhavana* = *kriyā* and *vādi* an agent noun from √*vad* 'speak, express'. (3) *bhūvādayo* = *bhū* + *vā* + *ādayaḥ* '(verbs) beginning with *vā* and having the nature of *bhū* (i.e., which are expressive of action)'; here *ādi* is taken to be connected with both *bhū* and *vā*, meaning *prakāra* when going with *bhū*, and *vyavasthā* with *vā*." Against the third interpretation as understood by him an objection can be raised. He holds that in the third interpretation of *bhūvādayo* in the ślokavārttika a double reading of *ādi* is made, remarking in his footnote (55): "and

The interpretation of A1.3.1 made by the *Kāśikāvṛtti* was this:

> Items of the set beginning with an item such as *bhū*, denoting actions (*kriyā*), are called *dhātu*.

It is clear that the *Kāśikāvṛtti* takes the term *bhūvādayaḥ* as referring to the items recited in the dhātupāṭha, leaving the question of how to explain the form *bhūvādayaḥ* to the ślokavārttika and adopting implicitly the first interpretation given by it. Apart from that, we notice here that the *Kāśikāvṛtti* presupposes that the definition of the term *dhātu* requires a semantic condition such that a certain item is called *dhātu* only if it signifies an action, and considers that such a semantic condition is obtained through Pāṇini's grammatical terminology. According to the *Kāśikāvṛtti*, in using the term *dhātu* in this sūtra Pāṇini simply follows the terminology of earlier teachers who have applied it to items that denote actions. The latter point is supported neither by any of the interpretations given by the ślokavārttika nor by those of Patañjali.

2.4. *Siddhāntakaumudī* on A1.3.1

The *Siddhāntakaumudī* presents the following interpretation of the sūtra under consideration:

> *kriyāvācino bhvādayo dhātusaṃjñāḥ syuḥ* |
> "Items of the set beginning with *bhū* are to be called *dhātu* if they denote actions."

Note that Bhaṭṭoji Dīkṣita characterizes items to be called *dhātu*

---

(3) the Bhāṣya also understands the last quarter as containing a third interpretation, since its explanation *vā ityevamādayo bhū ityevaṃprakārāḥ* (got by a double interpretation of the word *ādi*) is evidently a paraphrase of *vādayaḥ* and *bhvarthāḥ* in the Vārttika." As has been seen, however, there is no evidence given in the ślokavārttika that *bhūvādayo* admits of a double interpretation of *ādi*. Concerning the third interpretation of *bhūvādayo*, both the *Nyāsa* and the *Padamañjarī* take it as the ṣaṣṭhī compound which is analyzable as *bhuvo vādayaḥ*, though they interpret *vādayaḥ* in this compound differently. In this case the word *bhvarthāḥ* in the ślokavārttika explains that the ṣaṣṭhī ending of *bhuvo* (*bhū-ṅas*) denotes a denotative relation (*vācyavācakasambandha*). See the present section, fn. 14.

as denoting actions and as belonging to the set beginning with *bhū*. Unlike the *Kāśikāvṛtti* he gets these characterizations from the wording *bhūvādayaḥ* in the sūtra itself. And, as is clear from commentaries on the *Siddhāntakaumudī*, this interpretation of *A*1.3.1 is based upon one of the interpretations of *A*1.3.1 given by Patañjali, which shall be discussed later in Section 7.[23] Importantly the *Siddhāntakaumudī* also takes it for granted that the same semantic condition as the *Kāśikāvṛtti* puts, is necessary for the definition of the term *dhātu*.

2.5. Features of the traditional interpretations of *A*1.3.1

The *Kāśikāvṛtti* and the *Siddhāntakaumudī* introduce a semantic condition into their interpretations of it so that one can avoid the difficulties which would result if one were given a definition of the term *dhātu* based solely upon the dhātupāṭha. The combination of the dhātupāṭha and the meaning condition is what they consider to be essential for the definition of the term *dhātu*. In addition, they refer to items recited in the dhātupāṭha as those of the set beginning with *bhū* and do not involve the item *vā* in the reference to the dhātupāṭha as the third interpretation in the ślokavārttika does.

It is highly important to note that none of them propose that *A*1.3.1 should merely be interpreted in such a way that items of the set beginning with *bhū* are called *dhātu*. The reasons for their giving up interpreting the sūtra in that way are those which have already been presented by Kātyāyana and Patañjali.[24] In this sense we may say that the framework within which the authors of the *Kāśikāvṛtti* and the *Siddhāntakaumudī* have to interpret the sūtra has already been established by Kātyāyana and Patañjali.

As shall be seen, Kātyāyana, who is not explicit about how

---

[23] *BM* on *SK*18: *bhūś ca vāś ca bhūvau / ādiś ca ādiś ca ādī / prathama ādiśabdaḥ prabhṛtivacanaḥ, dvitīyas tu prakāravacanaḥ / bhūvau ādī yeṣāṃ te bhūvādayaḥ / bhūprabhṛtayo vāsadṛśāś ca ye, te dhātusaṃjñakā ity arthaḥ / vādhātusādṛśyaṃ ca kriyāvācakatvena /*

[24] See Section 3 [3.2.1] and Section 4, Part 1 [4.1; 4.2].

one should read *A*1.3.1, is aware that the dhātupāṭha-based definition of the term *dhātu* and its semantic definition each have their own limits but acknowledges the authority of the dhātupāṭha as an ancillary text to the *Aṣṭādhyāyī*. On the other hand, Patañjali who is faithful in the performance of his duty to offer interpretations of the sūtra indeed suggests reading it as a combination of the indication of the dhātupāṭha and a semantic definition—one of such interpretations of the sūtra is found in the *Siddhāntakaumudī*—but, discussing the validity of the dhātupāṭha and proposing its elimination, approaches *A*1.3.1 from a different angle: How far is it possible to do without the dhātupāṭha, namely to define semantically the term *dhātu*? Patañjali's approach to the sūtra in this line cannot be accepted by Pāṇinīyas after Patañjali, since for them the dhātupāṭha is a text established as an essential constituent of Pāṇini's grammar.

Section 3

Vārttikas ad *A*1.3.1 *bhūvādayo dhātavaḥ*

3.0. Vārttikas under four heads

In his Bhāṣya on *A*1.3.1, which contains the first half of a ślokavārttika also,[1] Patañjali cites and discusses thirteen vārttikas of Kātyāyana. The vārttikas of Kātyāyana are grouped under four main heads in accordance with key subjects he deals with.

1. Formal definition of the term *dhātu*: dhātupāṭha-based definition
2. Semantic definition of the term *dhātu*: *kriyāvacano dhātuḥ* (*kriyā*-based definition)
3. Semantic definition of the term *dhātu*: *bhāvavacano dhātuḥ* (*bhāva*-based definition)
4. Roles to be played by the dhātupāṭha

Let us first take an overall look at the vārttikas, and then give a clear picture of them.

3.1. A perusal of the vārttikas

Under *A*1.3.1 Kātyāyana composed his vārttikas as follows:

I. Formal definition of the term *dhātu*: dhātupāṭha-based definition

1.1. First difficulty entailed:

Vt. 1: *pāṭhena dhātusaṃjñāyāṃ samānaśabdapratiṣedhaḥ* //
"If the class name *dhātu* is assigned to items by virtue of their being recited in the dhātupāṭha (*pāṭhena dhātusaṃjñā*), then one has to deny the name to certain items which are homophonous with elements listed in the dhātupāṭha (*samānaśabda*)."[2]

[1] The ślokavārttika is cited in full in the *Kāśikāvṛtti*, which reads as follows: *bhūvādīnāṃ vakāro 'yaṃ maṅgalārthaḥ prayujyate / bhuvo vārthaṃ vadantīti bhvarthā vā vādayaḥ smṛtāḥ //* On the interpretation of this ślokavārttika, see Section 2 [2.3.2].

[2] Although it does not always refer to the dhātupāṭha, the word *pāṭha* in the present vārttika refers to the dhātupāṭha. Neither Kātyāyana nor Patañjali uses the term *dhātupāṭha;* instead, Kātyāyana uses the expres-

1.2. Second difficulty entailed:

Vt. 2: *parimāṇagrahaṇaṃ ca* //

"In addition, it is necessary to specify that such and such a particular stretch (*parimāṇa*) constitutes a given unit."

II. Semantic definition of the term *dhātu*: *kriyāvacano dhātuḥ* (*kriyā*-based definition)

2.1. Third difficulty entailed:

Vt. 3: *kriyāvacana upasargapratyayapratiṣedhaḥ* //

"If the name *dhātu* applies to an item which signifies an action, then one must state a prohibition denying the name to a preverb-verb complex and a verb-affix complex."[3]

Vt. 4: *saṅghātenārthagateḥ* //

"For one understands meanings by means of such complexes (*saṅghāta*)."[4]

---

sion *bhūvādipāṭha* for referring to the text of the dhātupāṭha. The word *pāṭha* means not only 'reciting' but also can refer to a text in which items are recited. According to Patañjali, the term *pāṭha* in *vt.* 1 may refer either to the sūtrapāṭha (the sūtra text, the *Aṣṭādhyāyī*) or to the dhātupāṭha. By considering Pāṇini's use of the bahuvrīhi compound with *-ādi*, the word *pāṭha* here is determined to refer to the reciting of elements listed in the dhātupāṭha and to the text in which items to be named *dhātu* are listed. On Patañjali's justification of the present vārttika *pāṭhena saṃjñāyām* intending the dhātupāṭha-based definition, see Section 4, Part 1 [4.1].

[3] According to Nāgeśa, by the phrase *upasargapratyayayoḥ* in the present vārttika is meant a verb which is qualified by a preverb (*upasarga*) and the one which is qualified by an affix. *Uddyota* on *MBh* ad *A*1.3.1 (II.182): *upasargapratyayayor ity asya tadviśiṣṭayor ity artha iti bhāvaḥ* /

[4] In his eighth vārttika on *A*1.2.45, Kātyāyana states that in the case of nominal forms also a real meaning conveyer in actual usage is a nominal base-affix complex and not a nominal base itself, since the nominal base is not used alone. *Vt.* 8 ad *A* 1.2.45: *na vā pratyayena nityasambandhāt kevalasyāprayogaḥ* // ("Or rather, [the difficulty] does not arise. Since a base is always connected with an affix, the former is not used alone.")

In connection with a preverb-verb complex, it will be useful to quote the following kārikā of the *Vākyapadīya*, which says that in actual usage a preverb is used inseparably from a verb. *VP*2.180: *aḍādīnāṃ vyavasthārthaṃ pṛthaktvena prakalpanam / dhātūpasargayoḥ śāstre dhā-*

2.2. Fourth difficulty entailed:

Vt. 5: *astibhavatividyatīnāṃ ca'dhātutvam* //
"In addition, it is imperative to state that *as* 'be', *bhū* 'be', and *vid* 'exist' are called *dhātu*."

2.3. Removal of difficulty 3 (a verb-affix complex):

Vt. 6: *pratyayārthasyāvyatirekāt prakṛtyantareṣu, dhātoś cārthābhedāt pratyayāntareṣu, siddhan tv anvayavyatirekābhyām* //
"Because meanings of affixes do not differ (*avyatireka*) when there are different bases [with different meanings, [we assume that what denotes an action is a verb and not a verb-affix complex]; or (*ca*)[5] because meanings of verbs do not differ (*abheda*) when there are different affixes [with different meanings], [we assume so].

But [the assignment of certain particular meanings to a base and an affix is] established on the basis of the reasoning from concurrent presence (*anvaya*) and absence (*vyatireka*)."

2.4. Removal of difficulty 3 (a preverb-verb complex):

Vt. 7: *kriyāviśeṣaka upasargaḥ* //
"A preverb denotes a meaning which qualifies an action."[6]

---

tur eva tu tādṛśaḥ // ("In grammar, items called *dhātu* and items called *upasarga* are assumed to be separated from each other for the purpose of establishing grammatical operations such as the proper positioning of the augment *aṭ* [A6.4.71]. However, in actual usage, such [a complex of a preverb and a verb] is an item to be called *dhātu* [i.e., an item which denotes an action]").

[5] For a reason that the particle *ca* here is taken in a disjunctive sense, see Section 4, Part 2 [4.5.2; fn. 37].

[6] The same view is expressed by the *Ṛgvedaprātiśākhya* 12.25ab: *kriyāvācakam ākhyātam upasargo viśeṣakṛt*, which also states: a verbal form (*ākhyāta*) denotes an action and the meaning of a preverb qualifies the action.

In Pāṇini's system, A1.4.59 *upasargāḥ kriyāyoge* provides that *pra* and the other items of the *prādi*-gaṇa are called *upasarga* when they are linked to verbs.

III. Semantic definition of the term *dhātu*: *bhāvavacano dhātuḥ* (*bhāva*-based definition)

3.1. Fifth difficulty entailed:

Vt. 8: *bhāvavacane tadarthapratyayapratiṣedhaḥ* //
"If a verb is defined as denoting *bhāva*, one must state a prohibition to prevent the term *dhātu* from applying to an affix which signifies that *bhāva.*[7]"

3.2. Sixth difficulty entailed:

Vt. 9: *itaretarāśrayaṃ ca pratyaye bhāvavacanatvaṃ tasmāc ca pratyayaḥ* //
"And also, if an item which denotes *bhāva* is termed *dhātu*, then operations become mutually dependent (*itaretarāśraya*). That is to say, when there is an affix, the base after which the affix is introduced is understood to denote *bhāva;* on the other hand, the affix is to be introduced after the base which is understood to denote *bhāva.*"

3.3. Removal of difficulty 6:

Vt. 10: *siddhaṃ tu nityaśabdatvād anāśritya bhāvavacanatvaṃ pratyayaḥ* //
"But [the desired end, namely that one has the understanding of the base as denoting *bhāva* and the occurrence of the affix after the base without resorting to each other, is] established. For speech is eternal (*nitya*).[8] And, given that speech is eternal, an affix occurs without depending upon the property of denoting *bhāva* [which characterizes a single whole unit, a base-affix complex]."

---

[7] I will not put the term *bhāva* into English, since it has such a multiplicity of meaning that no proper English equivalent for it can be found. For the meaning of the term *bhāva*, see Section 5.

[8] For Pāṇinīyas' concept of *nitya*, see Section 8, foot-notes 39, 51.

3.4. Removal of difficulty 5:

Vt. 11: *prathamabhāvagrahaṇaṃ ca* //

"In addition, the suggested definition *bhāvavacano dhātuḥ* should be revised as *prathamabhāvacacano dhātuḥ.*"

IV. Roles to be played by the dhātupāṭha

4.1. Roles of dhātupāṭha 1:

Vt. 12: *bhūvādipāṭhaḥ prātipadikāṇapayatyādinivṛttyarthaḥ* //

"The text in which items of the set beginning with *bhū* are recited serves to prevent the name *dhātu* from applying to nominal bases and [corruptions] such as *āṇapi*- 'order, command'."

4.2. Roles of dhātupāṭha 2:

Vt. 13: *svarānubandhajñāpanāya ca* //

"And also, items of the set beginning with *bhū* should be recited in order to make known the distinctive accentuations of base vowels (*svara*) and markers (*anubandha*)."

3.2. Expositions on the vārttikas

Each of the four heads shall be sketched out in the following.

3.2.1. Vārttika I

3.2.1.1. Under Vārttika I, Kātyāyana presupposes that *A* 1.3.1 is a saṃjñāsūtra that assigns the class name *dhātu* to items which are recited in the dhātupāṭha, a text external to the *Aṣṭādhyāyī*. According to Patañjali, the sound *-v-* in *bhūvādayaḥ* is used for the sake of auspiciousness as is argued by the first half of the ślokavārttika: *bhūvādīnām vakāro 'yaṃ maṅgalārthaḥ prayujyate*[9] and Pāṇini's use of the item *ādi* indicates that there is a text in

---

[9] *MBh* ad *A* 1.3.1 (I.253.2–4): *kuto 'yaṃ vakāraḥ / yadi tāvat saṃhitayā nirdeśaḥ kriyate bhvādaya iti bhavitavyam / athāsaṃhitayā bhū ādaya iti bhavitavyam / ata uttaraṃ paṭhati—bhūvādīnāṃ vakāro, 'yaṃ maṅgalārthaḥ prayujyate /* But for the sound *-v-* here in the compound formed from *bhū* and *ādi*, we might have had a choice between *bhvādayaḥ* with sandhi modification and *bhū ādayaḥ* without sandhi modification.

which items like *bhū* are listed and that the text is outside of the *Aṣṭādhyāyī*.[10] Thus here A1.3.1 is interpreted as follows:

> Items of the set beginning with *bhū*, recited in the dhātupāṭha, are called *dhātu* (*pāṭhena dhātusaṃjñā*).

In his vārttikas 1–2, Kātyāyana points out difficulties involved in this definition.[11]

3.2.1.2. First, in his first vārttika, Kātyāyana says that a prohibition has to be laid on the application of the term *dhātu* to items which are homophonous with items recited in the dhātupāṭha. For example, the particle *vā* 'or' should not be called *dhātu*, but this name should apply to *vā* 'go, strike'; what is recited in the dhātupāṭha is the latter *vā*. It is evident that the dhātupāṭha-based definition, where we have only to take into account the fact of the item *vā* being recited therein, leads to the undesired result that an item homophonous with it, a non-verb, has the name *dhātu*.

3.2.1.3. What Kātyāyana says in his second vārttika is particularly significant. Under the dhātupāṭha-based definition of the term *dhātu*, what we are expected to understand from the dhātupāṭha are mere forms (*rūpa*) or sequences of uttered sounds of items recited in the dhātupāṭha and not the items as distinct meaningful

---

[10] For Patañjali's interpretation that in the sound sequence *bhūvādayaḥ* the augment *-v-*, either to *bhū* or to *ādi*, is added, see Section 4 [4.1.1].

[11] Bronkhorst [1981], who is an upholder of the view that the original dhātupāṭha associated with the *Aṣṭādhyāyī* includes meaning entries, suggests reading vārttikas 1–2 as follows: "Owing to the Dhātupāṭha, [utterances] of the same sound-pattern [as verbal roots] are prevented from [assuming] the designation 'root'; and the measure [of the individual roots] is known." His interpretation of these two vārttikas are totally untenable, as has already been pointed out by Cardona [1984; 1999b: 140–145]. For the vārttikas at issue as interpreted by Bronkhorst could not be properly placed in the whole argument brought forward by Kātyāyana in his vārttikas on A1.3.1. We have to note that, as shall be shown in this section, Kātyāyana brings the contrast between formal and semantic definitions into clear relief. The formal definition is the dhātupāṭha-based definition such that items of the set beginning with *bhū*, recited in the dhātupāṭha, are called *dhātu*. In this type of definition, according to Kātyāyana, no semantic considerations are invoked.

units. And this is suggested by the term *samānaśabda* 'homophonous linguistic item' employed by Kātyāyana in his first vārttika, which is glossed as *samānaśruti* 'that which is of an equal phonetic form' by Kaiyaṭa.[12] Now, as Cardona [1984; 1997: par. 133] pointed out, while the dhātupāṭha as handed down by commentators has the arthapāṭha (gloss, meaning entry), the one as known to earliest Pāṇinīyas such as Kātyāyana and Patañjali does not contain it, which shall be demonstrated in another section.[13] In the dhātupāṭha as known to Kātyāyana, items that are to have the name *dhātu* are supposed to be recited in the following manner:

*bhū́ édh***a** *spárdh***a** . . .

Here we need not care about the accentuations of base vowels of these items (high-pitched *udātta* vowels *ū́*, *é*, *á*) and markers attached to them (vocalic marker *a*) for a theoretical reason.[14] According to Patañjali, it is to be stated, if one adopts the dhātupāṭha-based definition, that the sequence *bhū* constitutes a single element called *dhātu* and not the sequence *bhvedha*; without the specification of segments one cannot decide what segment is to be called *dhātu*. This difficulty evidently arises from the premise that in the dhātupāṭha-based definition proposed, any semantic considerations are left aside. For, the segmentation of a sequence of sounds into smaller sound-sequences has for its occasion meanings conveyed by it, which is taken for granted by Kātyāyana who theorizes the *anvaya-vyatireka* method for segmentation.[15] Therefore, without semantic information, nothing except a specific mention of a given extent can prevent one from assuming the

[12] According to Bhartṛhari, different linguistic items are assumed to be identical with each other by virtue of their equality in form (*tulyarūpa*). *VP*3.7.57: *bhede 'pi tulyarūpatvād ekatvaparikalpanā* / Helārāja also states that linguistic items are determined to be identical with each other because of their having an equal form (*rūpasāmya*) when they have an equal phonetic form (*tulyaśruti*). *Prakāśa* on *VP*3.14.484: *tulyaśrutitvād rūpasāmyād ekatvam avasāya* / See Section 4, Part 1, fn. 37 and Ogawa [2002].

[13] See Section 4 [4.2] and Section 8 [8.7].

[14] See Section 4 [4.2.2].

[15] See the present section [3.2.3].

sequence of sounds *bhū edha*, resulting in *bhvedha* with sandhi modification, to be called *dhātu*.

3.2.2. Vārttika II (1)

3.2.2.1. Under Vārttika I problems related to a formal definition of the term *dhātu*, the dhātupāṭha-based definition, have been discussed. Under Vārttika II is taken up an alternative definition, a semantic definition of a *kriyā*-based definition. The *kriyā*-based definition is put in this way:

> An item which denotes an action (*kriyā*) is called *dhātu* (*kriyā-vacano dhātuḥ*).

This semantic definition is proposed in order to overcome objections raised in *vts.* 1–2. Given the *kriyā*-based definition, the particle *vā* which is homophonous with the item *vā* listed in the dhātupāṭha is not called *dhātu* for the reason that it does not denote an action; and, the sequence *bhvedha* is not eligible for having the name *dhātu* for the very same reason.

However, the *kriyā*-based definition also leads to difficulties.

3.2.2.2. The first difficulty, which is pointed out in *vt.* 3, is this:

What we observe in actual usage is the following. Items to be called *dhātu* are used, always accompanied by affixes (*pratyaya*) and sometimes, as the case may be, preceded by preverbs (*upasarga*). They are not used alone. As in *vt.* 4 Kātyāyana states, in accordance with this, meanings of the items in question, namely, actions, are understood from complexes (*saṅghāta*) including bases with preverbs and affixes, as in *pacati* '. . . is cooking' where a base-affix complex is used; and as in *prapacati* 'cooks excellently' where a preverb-verb-affix complex is used. Thus if we take such actual usage into account, the *kriyā*-based definition will allow a verb-affix complex and a preverb-verb complex to be called *dhātu*, so that a prohibition should be made saying that neither a verb-affix complex nor a preverb-verb-affix complex is called *dhātu*.

In this connection the following has to be noted. I have already stated that Pāṇini's derivational system is aimed at accounting for the sentence associated with a sentence meaning which is the unit of actual communication and that words and word meanings are abstracted from such sentences. Here in his vārttika 4, however, Kātyāyana asserts that one understands the meaning in question, an action, from syntactic units (*pada*) such as *pacati* and *prapacati* in actual usage. This can be explained by considering the feature of Pāṇini's derivational system that the derivation of syntactic units necessarily entails that of a sentence composed of them. It is precisely because of this feature that Kātyāyana is allowed here to treat syntactic units such as *pacati* and *prapacati* as linguistic units to be explained (*anvākhyeyaśabda*).[16]

3.2.2.3. In the fifth vārttika is pointed out one of the essential problems Patañjali meets in Kātyāyana's argumentation on *A* 1.3.1. Kātyāyana says that, if the *kriyā*-based definition were given, then an additional statement would have to be made that items such as *as*, *bhū*, and *vid*, items conveying the meaning 'be', are called *dhātu*. According to Patañjali, the verb *pac* 'cook' is known to denote an action on the basis of what is found in actual usage, such as *kiṃ karoti—pacati* 'What is he doing?—He is cooking'; but it is unlikely that one finds in actual usage a set of utterances of the type *kiṃ karoti—asti* 'What is he doing?—He is'. As a consequence of the observation of actual usage it is difficult to know items conveying the meaning 'be' to denote actions, so that they would not be allowed to have the name *dhātu*.[17]

3.2.3. Vārttika II (2)

3.2.3.1. In *vt.* 3 Kātyāyana has pointed out that if one adopts the *kriyā*-based definition one has to state prohibition on the application of the term *dhātu* to a verb-affix complex and a preverb-verb complex. *Vt.* 6 treats a verb-affix complex. Let us consider the

---

[16] See Introduction [0.1] and Introduction, fn. 14.

[17] *MBh* on *vt.* 5 ad *A*1.3.1 (I.255.2–4): *astibhavatividyatīnāṃ ca dhātusaṃjñā vaktavyā / yathā hi bhavatā karotinā pacādīnāṃ sāmānādhikaraṇyaṃ nidarśitaṃ na tathāstyādīnāṃ nidarśyate / na hi bhavati—kiṃ karoti, astīti /* See also Section 4, Part 4 [4.8.4].

case in which first *pacati* '. . . is cooking' is uttered and then *paṭhati* '. . . is reciting' is uttered. In this case we observe that while a base is changed, the meaning of an affix remains constant. In addition, let us think of the case in which *paktiḥ*, *pacanam*, and then *pākaḥ* are uttered; the item *pakti* is a feminine derivate formed by *A*3.3.94 (*pac* + ***ktin***), the item *pacana* a neuter action noun by *A*3.3.115 (*pac* + ***lyuṭ***). and the item *pāka* a masculine action noun by *A*3.3.18 (*pac* + ***ghañ***). Here we observe that while an affix is changed, the meaning of the base, a verb, remains constant: all three share the meaning of cooking viewed in the abstract and differ only in that each is associated with a different gender.[18]

What Kātyāyana means to say is as follows:

In his *Vākyapadīya*, Bhartṛhari states the following kārikā based upon the Bhāṣya on *ŚS*5: *hayavaraṭ* in which Patañjali discusses the question of whether sounds (*varṇa*) are meaningful (*arthavat*):[19]

> *VP*2.169: *na kūpasūpayūpānām anvayo 'rthasya dṛśyate / ato 'rthāntaravācitvaṃ saṅghātasyaiva gamyate //*
>
> "When *kūpa* 'well', *sūpa* 'soup', and then *yūpa* 'sacrificial post' are uttered, it is not observed that a certain meaning remains constant. For this reason, we understand that the property of being what conveys a different meaning (*arthāntaravāci-*

---

[18] *MBh* ad *A*1.3.1 (I.255.9–10): *paktiḥ pacanaṃ pāka iti / pratyayārtho 'nyaś cānyaś ca bhavati prakṛtyarthaḥ sa eva /* Instead of Kielhorn's reading *paktā pacanam pāka iti*, I have adopted the reading *paktiḥ pacanaṃ pāka iti* which is given in the Rohatak edition and the Nirṇayasāgara Press edition. Nāgeśa comments on this Bhāṣya as follows. *Uddyota* on *MBh* ad *A*1.3.1 (II.183): *anyaś ceti / liṅgabhedād ity arthaḥ /*

Even if we followed Kielhorn's reading, of course, the same could be said. When *paktā* (*pac* + ***tṛc***; *A*3.1.133) 'one who cooks', *pacanam* (*pac* + ***lyuṭ***; *A*3.3.117) 'that with which something is cooked', and then *pākaḥ* (*pac* + ***ghañ***; *A*3.3.18) 'the act of cooking' are uttered, we observe that an affix is changed, while a meaning of the base remains constant.

[19] *MBh* on *vt.* 15 ad *ŚS*5 (I.32.7–10): *idaṃ khalv api bhavatā varṇānām arthavattāṃ bruvatā sādhīyo 'narthakatvaṃ dyotitam / yo hi manyate yaḥ kūpe kūpārthaḥ sa kakārasya, yaḥ sūpe sūpārthaḥ sa sakārasya, yo yūpe yūpārthaḥ sa yakārasyeti / ūpaśabdas tv asyānarthakaḥ syāt /*

tva) is attributed precisely to complexes such as *kūpa* [and not to their components, the sounds *k*, *s*, *y*]."

The point Bhartṛhari makes is this: With reference to the set of sequences of sounds *kūpa*, *sūpa*, *yūpa*, we observe that although *ūpa* recurs, there is no constant meaning associated with this,[20] so that we have to consider that meaning difference is attributed to complexes such as *kūpa*. According to Bhartṛhari, thus, if it is not observed, with respect to a certain set of sequences of sounds like that of *kūpa*, *sūpa*, *yūpa*, that when a certain element remains constant and others are changed, there is a certain meaning that remains constant, then meaning difference should be attributed to a complex including these elements. Now what we observe with reference to a verb-affix complex, according to Kātyāyana, is just contrary to this. *pacati-paṭhati/pakti-pacana-pāka*: one can attribute meaning differences to distinct elements. However if a meaning does not remain constant while a certain element remains constant and others are changed, as in *kūpa* 'well'-*sūpa* 'soup'-*yūpa* 'sacrificial post', one has to attribute meaning difference to a complex including these elements. Such is not the case with the verb-affix complex. Therefore, it is proper to say that a verb-affix complex is not called *dhātu* in that what is responsible for denoting an action is its component and not the complex itself.

3.2.3.2. Now that it has been established that what is responsible for conveying the act is not a verb-affix complex itself, another question arises: How should one establish meaning assignment such that this meaning is attributed to the base and this meaning to the affix? Kātyāyana presents the method of the meaning assignment, the reasoning from *anvaya* and *vyatireka*. This method has been thoroughly studied by Cardona who is the first scholar

---

[20]Nāgeśa puts this point clearly and concisely. *Uddyota* on *MBh* ad *SS* 5 (I.106): *varṇānām arthavattve ūpaśabdasya triṣv anvayād arthānvayaḥ syān na ca dṛśyate* . . . / ("[In *kūpa*, *sūpa*, *yūpa*,] if it were the case that the sounds [*k*, *s*, *y*] are meaningful, there would have to be a constant meaning associated with the item *ūpa* because that item remains constant in the three items at issue. But this is not observed. . . .")

to give much attention to this linguistic analysis procedure.[21] According to Cardona, the *anvaya-vyatireka* method is formulated as follows: If *x* occurs consequent on the occurrence of *y*; and, if *y* is absent, *x* does not occur—on condition that both obtain, one concludes that *x* is related to *y*. Accordingly, by means of this method, one can properly establish that an action, understood from the verb-affix complex in question, is the meaning of the verb.[22]

3.2.3.3. The seventh vārttika deals with a preverb-verb complex. The principle which applies in the case of verb-affix complexes applies here also. When *pacati* is uttered, the action of cooking is understood. And when *prapacati* 'cooks excellently' is uttered, the act of cooking which is qualified by excellence is understood. Let us take *pacati* as a zero (preverb)-verb complex. It is obvious that meaning difference here cannot be attributed to the preverb-verb complex. Moreover, if we apply the method of meaning assignment here, we will properly understand that the action in question is related to the verb; its qualifier is related to the preverb.[23]

---

[21]See Cardona [1997: sec. 4]. The *anvaya-vyatireka* method works on the assumption that one linguistic item corresponds to one meaning. Patañjali points out that there are cases in which more than one item denotes one and the same meaning and in which a single item conveys more than one meaning. If such were true of *pacati*, one could not properly do the meaning assignment to the constituent items of it. On Patañjali's treatment of this matter, see Section 4, Part 2 [4.4].

[22]With clear insight Cardona [1981] says that the reasoning from *anvaya* and *vyatireka* is used as a method for discovering a relation. The reasoning is regularly employed when establishing that one thing is the cause of another. If the following both: *when x occurs, y occurs* and *when x is absent, y is absent* hold between *x* and *y*, then *x* is considered to be a cause of *y*. It goes without saying that the relation in question is a causal relation (*kāryakāraṇabhāva*) between the utterance of linguistic items and the understanding of their meanings. See Introduction, fn. 14 also. From the hearer's point of view a given linguistic item is the cause of the hearer's understanding a meaning associated with it; from the speaker's point of view a given meaning is the cause of the speaker's use of a linguistic item associated with it. On the latter point, see also Section 4, Part 2 [4.3.2.2.2.2].

[23]In the case of the preverb-verb complex, the assignment of a meaning to a verb is complicated by the fact that there are found three kinds of

In this connection it is to be noted in passing that in stating his sixth vārttika Kātyāyana uses the particle *ca* 'and' as *pratyayārthasyāvyatirekāt prakṛtyantareṣu, dhātoś cārthābhedāt pratyayāntareṣu.* The particle *ca* there has the value of *vā* 'or', so that when either of these conditions is met, one can consider that the meaning difference is attributed to the complex verb + affix. As shall be seen later in Section 4 (Part 2 [4.5]), in some of the preverb-verb complexes, as in *adhyeti* '. . . remembers' for example, both of similar conditions cannot be met. It is because of this that Kātyāyana had to formulate the conditions for the meaning assignment by using *ca* in the sense of *vā*. Consequently, in order to apply the sixth vārttika to the case of preverb-verb complexes also, we have to read it as follows:

> Because meanings of verbs do not differ when there are different preverbs with different meanings, we assume that what denotes an action is a verb and not a preverb-verb complex; or, because meanings of preverbs do not differ when there are different verbs with different meanings, we assume so.

3.2.4. Vārttika III (1)

3.2.4.1. In Vārttika III Kātyāyana discusses problems pertaining to the second of the alternative semantic definitions of the term *dhātu*, that is, a *bhāva*-based definition. The *bhāva*-based definition is as follows:

> An item which denotes *bhāva* is called *dhātu* (*bhāvavacano dhātuḥ*).

In *vt*. 5 an objection has been raised: If the *kriyā*-based definition is given, one has to make an additional statement that such items as *as* which convey the meaning 'be' are called *dhātu*. It is in order to overcome this objection that Kātyāyana proposes the *bhāva*-based definition, under which of course come not only items such as *as* but also ones like *pac*.

---

combinations of a preverb and a verb. See Section 4, Part 2 [4.5] for details.

3.2.4.2. *Vt.* 8 points out: If the *bhāva*-based definition were provided, it would undesiredly follow that affixes such as *-e* (*liṭ* → *ta* → *eś*; *A*3.4.81) in *śiśye* 'slept' (3sg. pfct.),[24] which *A*3.4.69 *laḥ karmaṇi ca bhāve cākarmakebhyaḥ* provides for to be introduced after verbs when *bhāva* is to be signified, are called *dhātu*. The following has to be noted here: When in his eighth vārttika he states: *bhāvavacane tadarthapratyayapratiṣedhaḥ*, Kātyāyana assumes that *bhāva* as a verb meaning, that is, the one referred to by the term *bhāva* of the *bhāva*-based definition under consideration, is identical with *bhāva* as a meaning of a verb ending, namely the one mentioned by Pāṇini in *A*3.4.69. This is not simply a matter of terminology.

As is well known, Pāṇinīyas such as Patañjali distinguish between *tiṅabhihitabhāva* ('*bhāva* which is denoted by a verb ending') and *kṛdabhihitabhāva* ('*bhāva* which is denoted by a kṛt affix'); the former is called *ābhyantarabhāva* ('internal *bhāva*') and hence the meaning of a verbal base itself (*svārtha*), while the latter is called *bāhyabhāva* ('external *bhāva*'), being the act in the abstract.[25] Here the *bhāva* which an affix like *-e* in *śiśye*

---

[24] The finite verb form *śiśye* may occur in utterances such as *devadattena śiśye* 'Devadatta slept'. The derivation of *śiśye* can be shown as follows:

śī (*śīṅ*) + *liṭ*	(*A*3.2.115; 3.4.69)
śī + *ta*	(*A*3.4.78; 1.3.12; 1.3.13; 1.4.22; 1.4.108)
śī + *eś*	(*A*3.4.81)
śī + *śī* + *e*	(*A*1.1.59; 6.1.8)
śi + *śī* + *e*	(*A*7.4.60; 7.4.59)
śi + *śy* + *e*	(*A*6.4.82)
śiśye	

[25] For the distinction between two varieties of *bhāva*, see Cardona [1997: par. 297]. In his Bhāṣya on *A*3.4.67 (II.177.18–21) Patañjali states: *tad eva tarhi prayojanam—svārthe mā bhūvann iti / nanu coktaṃ yam icchati svārthe āha tam—bhāve ghañ bhavatīti / anyaḥ sa bhāvo bāhyaḥ prakṛtyārthāt / anenedānīm ābhyantare bhāve syuḥ, tatra mā bhūvann iti kartṛgrahaṇam / kaḥ punar etayor bhāvayor viśeṣaḥ / ukto bhāvabhedo bhāṣye /* and in his Bhāṣya on *A*3.1.67 (II.57.7–16): *asti khalv api viśeṣaḥ kṛdabhihitasya bhāvasya tiṅabhihitasya ca / kṛdabhihito bhāvo dravyavad bhavati / kim idaṃ dravyavad iti / dravyaṃ kriyayā samavāyaṃ gacchati / kaṃ samavāyaṃ *[gacchati] / dravyaṃ kriyābhinirvṛttau sādhanatvam upaiti / tadvac cāsya bhāvasya kṛdabhihitasya bhavati—pāko vartata iti / kriyāvan na bhavati / kim idaṃ kriyāvad iti / kriyā*

signifies is nothing but the former and therefore such an affix is one which conveys a meaning that the base with which the affix

---

kriyayā samavāyaṃ na gacchati—pacati paṭhatīti / tadvac cāsya kṛdabhihitasya na bhavati—pāko vartata iti / asti khalv api viśeṣaḥ kṛdabhihitasya bhāvasya tiṅabhihitasya ca / tiṅabhihitena bhāvena kālapuruṣopagrahā abhivyajyante, kṛdabhihitena punar na vyajyante / asti khalv api viśeṣaḥ kṛdabhihitasya bhāvasya tiṅabhihitasya ca / tiṅabhihito bhāvaḥ kartrā saṃprayujyate, kṛdabhihitaḥ punar na saṃprayujyate. (Note: *Kielhorn's edition lacks *gacchati*.) What is called *tiṅabhihitabhāva* or *ābhyantarabhāva* is distinguished from what is called *kṛdabhihitabhāva* or *bāhyabhāva* in the following points: The latter behaves like a substance (*dravyavat*) so that it is connected with gender (*liṅga*) and number (*saṅkhyā*) and functions as a sādhana; the former manifests time (*kāla*), person (*puruṣa*), and diathesis (*upagraha*); the former has to be connected with an agent. It may be mentioned in passing that *upagraha* has to do with the differences associated with the contrast between ātmanepada and parasmaipada affixes.

On the *ābhyantarabhāva and bāhyabhāva* Bhartṛhari has the following kārikā. *VP*3.8.59: *vanaṃ vṛkṣā iti yathā bhedābhedavyapāśrayāt / arthātmā bhidyate bhāve sa bāhyābhyantare kramaḥ //* The point made is that a forest, which is a conglomerate of trees, can be viewed as an undifferentiated whole, but one can also refer to the component trees as distinct units, so that one can say both *vanam* 'forest' and *vṛkṣāḥ* 'trees'. Similarly, a verb meaning, an action, has two facets: it can be viewed as an act being carried out, brought to accomplishment, or as an abstract whole. The former, spoken of as *ābhyantarabhāva*, is understood as a single entity undifferentiated by gender or number, and whatever number differences one has in forms like *pacati* (3rd sg. pres.), *pacataḥ* (3rd du. pres.), *pacanti* (3rd pl. pres.) depend on the participants involved, not on the single action signified by the base *pac*. On the other hand, the abstract action signified by *pākaḥ* (nom. sg. masc.), *pākau* (nom. du. masc.), *pākāḥ* (nom. pl. masc.) or *paktiḥ* (nom. sg. fem.) and so on, spoken of as *bāhyabhāva*, has inherent number and gender differentiation.

Note that Patañjali speaks of a *kriyā* or a *bhāva* as being singular. *MBh* ad *A*1.2.64 (I.233.11-12): *yadi tarhy ekā kriyā dvivacanabahuvacanāni na sidhyanti / pacataḥ pacanti / naitāni kriyāpekṣāṇi / kiṃ tarhi sādhanāpekṣāṇi /* (for the punctuation regarding *kiṃ tarhi* see Section 2, fn. 8); *MBh* ad *A*3.1.67 (II.56.18): *bhāvaḥ punar eka eva /* As said, an act signified by a verbal base has no connection with number. When the act is spoken of as being singular, the singular number is an unmarked singular, the kind of singular which Bhartṛhari calls *abhedaikatvasaṅkhyā* or a singular of non-distinction among all numbers. See *Pradīpa* on *MBh* ad *A*3.1.67 (III.142): *bhedābhāvalakṣaṇam abhedaikatvaṃ bhāvasya, na tv ekatvasaṅkhyākhyātavācyasya bhāvasyāsti /*; *VP*3.14.99.

occurs conveys (*svārthika*).[26] In this sense, the *bhāva*-based definition allows one to call *dhātu* an affix which denotes *bhāva*. It is to be noted, therefore, that the *kriyā*-based definition also will allow one to do so, since such an affix is considered to convey a meaning of the base after which the affix is introduced.[27]

Thus, in this way, the *bhāva*-based definition leads to the undesired result that an affix which is introduced to signify *bhāva* according to *A*3.4.69 has the name *dhātu*, so that one has to make a prohibition saying that such an affix is not called *dhātu*.[28]

3.2.4.3. What Kātyāyana points out in his ninth vārttika is as follows:

Let us take a view of Pāṇini's derivational system, in which a procedure is followed such that affixes are introduced to given items on certain conditions. In this system, unless a verb-affix complex is formed by letting an affix be introduced to a base which is to be called *dhātu*, there is no united whole to be found from which the base and the affix are abstracted. In this case, it is obviously impossible to assign the particular meaning *bhāva* to the base entitled to the name *dhātu* through reasoning from *anvaya* and *vyatireka*. This amounts to saying that without the occurrence of an affix after a base signifying *bhāva* one cannot

---

[26] An affix Pāṇinīyas call *svārthika* is said not to differ from a base followed by the affix in their meanings. *MBh* ad *A*1.1.28 (I.89.23): *svārthikāḥ pratyayāḥ prakṛtito 'viśiṣṭā bhavanti* /

[27] This is why Patañjali can say that a difficulty remaining unsolved in connection with the *kriyā*-based definition is only the one pointed out in *vt*. 5. *MBh* ad *A*1.3.1 (I.258.7–8): *iha ya eva bhāvavacane dhātau doṣās ta eva kriyāvacane 'pi / tatra ta eva parihārāḥ / tatredam aparihṛtam—astibhavatividyatīnāṃ dhātutvam iti* / According to Patañjali, what is argued about in *vts*. 8–11 with reference to the *bhāva*-based definition is also true of the *kriyā*-based definition; as one has the revised *bhāva*-based definition, so also can one have the revised *kriyā*-based definition *prathamakriyāvacano dhātuḥ* 'an item which first denotes an action is called *dhātu*'. See this section [3.2.6].

[28] *A*3.4.70 states that kṛtya affixes, *kta*, and affixes with the meaning of ***khal*** (*A*3.3.126) occur only when an object and *bhāva*, explicitly given in *A*3.4.69, are to be signified. Thus in *kartavya* 'to be made', when the affix *tavya*(***t***) denotes *bhāva*, it could be undesiredly called *dhātu*. See Section 8 [8.3.3.2].

understand that the base in question denotes *bhāva* (*pratyaye bhāvavacanatvam*). Unless the name *dhātu* is given to the base, on the other hand, the grammatical operations are not allowed to apply which introduce the affix to the base (*tasmāt pratyayaḥ*). In this case, consequently, one cannot have the whole unit, the base-affix complex, through derivation.

Plainly what one finds in the above-described situation is that the occurrence of an affix after a base and the understanding of the base as denoting *bhāva* become mutually dependent (*itaretarāśraya*).

3.2.5. Vārttika III (2)

3.2.5.1. In *vts.* 8–9 Kātyāyana, assuming that the *bhāva*-based definition has a broad domain that includes the whole domain of the *kriyā*-based definition, has pointed out that the *bhāva*-based definition involves the fault of the over-application of the term *dhātu* to verbal endings and that of the mutual dependence between the occurrence of an affix after a base and the understanding of the base as denoting *bhāva*.

3.2.5.2. In his tenth vārttika Kātyāyana tries to avoid the fault of the mutual dependence between the occurrence of an affix and the understanding of the base as denoting *bhāva*. What is to be noted is that Kātyāyana there is speaking of linguistic units at different levels. Speech units are existent prior to grammatical analysis (*nitya*). Recall that in his very first vārttika Kātyāyana declared that words, their meanings, and the relation between them are all considered to be given things.[29] In real communication linguistic items function as single units with complex meanings. The property of denoting *bhāva* is in reality to be attributed to such single units. However, for the purpose of grammatical description, from a single whole unit with a complex meaning component linguistic items like a base and an affix with component meanings are abstracted through analysis: the reasoning from

---

[29] *Vt.* 1 (Paspaśā): *siddhe śabdārthasambandhe lokataḥ arthaprayukte śabdaprayoge śāstreṇa dharmaniyamaḥ yathā laukikavaidikeṣu* // See Section 8 [8.6.2.2; 8.7.1.3].

anvaya and *vyatireka*. It is only on the basis of such abstraction that one may say that the occurrence of an affix depends upon a base's property of denoting *bhāva* (*bhāvavacanatva*).[30] Thus the property which occasions an affix to occur should be a fictitiously posited one, since the base and its meanings are elements abstracted as such from a complex unit. Mutual dependence of the kind discussed here occurs only on the view that speech is produced or generated by grammar (*kāryapakṣa*).[31]

3.2.5.3. In *vt.* 8 Kātyāyana has pointed out the need for making a prohibition saying that an affix to denote *bhāva* specified in *A* 3.4.69 should not be called *dhātu*. To wave aside this objection, Kātyāyana states the eleventh vārttika. In *śiśye*, if the proposal of the revision of the definition is accepted, one can prevent the term *dhātu* from applying to the affix *-e* since the definition as reformulated is such that an item which first (*prathama*) denotes *bhāva* is called *dhātu*. The *bhāva* which is denoted by the affix *-e* has already been denoted by the base *śī* itself (*abhihita*).

3.2.6. Vārttika IV

3.2.6.1. As said above, in his eleventh vārttika, Kātyāyana proposed the revision of the *bhāva*-based definition. The revised definition was as follows:

> An item which first denotes *bhāva* is called *dhātu* (*prathamabhāvavacano dhātuḥ*).

We will see that this is the semantic definition of the term *dhātu* which is finally accepted by Kātyāyana, if we take it into consideration that he considers the *bhāva*-based definition of the

---

[30]Such a property as causes an affix to occur is a meaning that is fictitiously posited, through analysis, as denoted by a base. Kaiyaṭa, commenting on *vt.* 10, states: *anāśrityeti / pāramārthikaṃ nāśrīyate, parikalpitaṃ tv āśrīyata eva / tattvato hi śabdāntarāṇy evārthāntareṣu prayujyante /* The meaning *bhāva* which is attributed to a verb is nothing but an *apoddhārapadārtha*. See Introduction [0.3.2].

[31]Mutual dependence as pointed out here which might be considered to take place in grammatical procedure and its solution on the basis of *śabdanityatva* 'eternity of linguistic items' are patternized in the *Mahābhāṣya*. See *vt.* 8 on *A* 1.1.1 and *MBh* thereon.

term *dhātu* to cover any item that is properly to be called *dhātu*. Now the question arises: What roles on earth should the dhātupāṭha play? For, if the term *dhātu* can be semantically defined in this way, then there will be left no room for the dhātupāṭha to take part in for defining the term in question. Vārttika IV deals with this question.

3.2.6.2. In his twelfth and thirteenth vārttikas Kātyāyana states that, even if one were given a semantic definition to specify what items are to be called *dhātu*, it would still be necessary to list verbs in the dhātupāṭha for the following reasons:

1) To prevent the name *dhātu* from applying to nominal bases (*prātipadikanivṛttyartha*). [*Vt.* 12]

2) To prevent the name *dhātu* from applying to corruptions like *āṇapi-* (*āṇapayatyādinivṛttyartha*).[32] [*Vt.* 12]

3) To make known accentuations of base vowels (*svarajñāpanāya*). [*Vt.* 13]

4) To make known markers (*anubandhajñāpanāya*). [*Vt.* 13]

3.2.6.3. The revision suggested in *vt.* 11 does not allow the name *dhātu* to apply to affixes which denote *bhāva* as has already been denoted by bases. However, there are other items that denote *bhāva* as denoted by items properly to be called *dhātu*. They are certain nominal bases and certain corruptions like *āṇapi-*, although neither Kātyāyana nor Patañjali specifies what these nominal bases are.[33] As far as they denote *bhāva*, we cannot avoid their coming under the given definition. This is why Kātyāyana establishes that one of the roles the dhātupāṭha plays is to exclude them from the *dhātu* class.

[32] Items such as *āṇapi-* are indeed corruptions, but note that Patañjali does not use the term *apabhraṃśa* 'corruption' for them here in his Bhāṣya on *vt.* 12. Nāgeśa uses the terms *prākṛta* and *apabhraṃśa* to refer to items such as *āṇavi-* 'command'. *Uddyota* on *MBh* ad A1.3.1 (II.175): *ājñāpayatītyarthe āṇavayatīti prākṛtam / apabhraṃśānām api svātantryeṇaiva bodhakatvāṅgīkārād eṣāṃ kriyāvācitvaṃ bodhyam /*

[33] See Section 8 [8.3].

3.2.6.4. As is well known, in addition, verbs recited in the dhātupāṭha have markers, which Pāṇini calls *it*[34] and Pāṇinīyas also call *anubandha* and which are unconditionally dropped,[35] and their base vowels are pronounced with distinct pitches.[36] Markers added to verbs and particular accentuations of base vowels serve to show that verbs are connected with particular operations. Thus, *bhū́* 'be', *édha* 'thrive', *dhvánsu* 'perish', *lúncá* 'tear away', *údjhá* 'abandon', *nṛ́tī́* 'dance' have high-pitched base vowels (*udātta*), and all but the first have vocalic markers attached to them: low-pitched (*anudātta*) *a*, *u* and high-pitched *á*, *ī́*. The base vowels of *adá* 'eat', *haná* 'kill', *hu* 'pour oblations', *ñibhī* 'be afraid', *bhrasjà* 'fry', *ṣuñ* 'press juice', and *sṛjá* 'let loose' are low-pitched; *hu* has no appended marker, but *ñibhī* and *ṣuñ* are marked with *ñi* and *ñ*, *bhrasjà* with the *svarita* vowel *à*, the others with high-pitched *á*. It goes without saying that without resorting to the dhātupāṭha one cannot know with reference to verbs either their accentuations of base vowels or their markers.

3.3. Survey of the vārttikas on A1.3.1

Points Kātyāyana made in his vārttikas on *A*1.3.1 can be summarized as follows:

Kātyāyana discusses the following points:

1) A formal definition of the term *dhātu* in which one depends purely upon the dhātupāṭha without presupposing a meaning aspect of an item to be called *dhātu*, and problems involved in the definition. [*Vts*. 1–2]

The definition, as it is explained by Patañjali, is that items of the set beginning with *bhū*, recited in the dhātupāṭha, are called *dhātu*.

2) An alternative semantic definition of the term *dhātu* and problems ensuing under the definition. [*Vts*. 3–13 (3, 5, 8, 11)]

---

[34] *A*1.3.2–8. Vocalic markers are called *it* according to *A*1.3.2. They were originally nasalized (*anunāsika*). See Section 9 [9.6] also.
[35] *A*1.3.9.
[36] See Section 8 [8.5] for details.

Two semantic definitions are suggested: *kriyā*-based and *bhāva*-based definitions.

kriyā-based definition: An item which signifies an action (*kriyā*) is called *dhātu*. [*Vt*. 3]

bhāva-based definition: An item which signifies *bhāva* is called *dhātu*. [*Vt*. 8]

3) An application of the semantic definitions to linguistic items and its related problems: A distinction is drawn between linguistic units posited for the grammatical procedure and those which occur within the realm of actual communication. [*Vts*. 4, 6, 7, 9, 10] Whichever semantic definition of the term *dhātu* be chosen, this point can be made as far as linguistic items are viewed at two levels: at the level of actual communication and at that of grammatical analysis.

4) Functions to be carried out by the dhātupāṭha under the condition that a semantic definition is given. [*Vts*. 12–13]

What Kātyāyana did under *A* 1.3.1 is nothing more than to indicate the directions in which the term *dhātu* is defined and to point out the problems involved in the proposed definitions of the term *dhātu*. As can be seen easily, Kātyāyana assumes that what is considered to be a more precise, satisfactory definition of the term *dhātu* is the *bhāva*-based definition with a modification: *prathamabhāvavacano dhātuḥ* (*vt*. 8). He does not suggest any solution to the problems involved in the dhātupāṭha-based definition of the term *dhātu* and a problem unique to the *kriyā*-based definition of the term *dhātu*, the problem that the definition cannot allow *as* and others to be called *dhātu*, remains unsolved.

However, in connection with his semantic definitions, we should notice that, according to him, the application of any semantic definition presupposes the abstraction of items to be called *dhātu* from finite verb forms through the analysis on the basis of the reasoning from *anvaya* and *vyatireka*.

What is more, the point to observe in Kātyāyana's discussion concerning *A* 1.3.1 is that he maintains a conservative attitude toward the dhātupāṭha: even if the revised *bhāva*-based definition were provided, the dhātupāṭha would still be necessary not only to complement such a semantic definition but also to establish Pāṇini's derivational system. As shall be seen in Section 8, Patañjali will have to question, from a point of view of his theory of semantics and grammar, such an attitude of Kātyāyana toward the dhātupāṭha.

Section 4

Part 1: Bhāṣya on vārttikas 1–2 (dhātupāṭha-based definition)

4.0. *Mahābhāṣya* on *A* 1.3.1

Important points found in the arguments by Patañjali shall be elaborated in the following. The outline of the argumentation of the *Mahābhāṣya* on *A* 1.3.1 shall be given in a synopsis.[1]

I have divided the vārttikas on the sūtra into four heads. Therefore, for convenience of exposition, I will also divide the Bhāṣya under consideration in four in conformity with the division of the vārttikas. Accordingly this section consists of the following four parts:

Part 1: Bhāṣya on vārttikas 1–2 (dhātupāṭha-based definition)
Part 2: Bhāṣya on vārttikas 3–7 (*kriyā*-based definition)
Part 3: Bhāṣya on vārttikas 8–11 (*bhāva*-based definition)
Part 4: Bhāṣya on vārttikas 12–13 (roles of the dhātupāṭha)

Note that, in the course of the explication of the Bhāṣya, Patañjali's mere glosses of vārttikas will not be taken up.

4.1. On vārttika 1

4.1.1. Preliminaries

Before entering into the discussion on the first vārttika in which Kātyāyana presupposes that *A* 1.3.1 is the dhātupāṭha-based definition of the term *dhātu*, Patañjali had two tasks to carry out: that is,

1) The task of justifying that Kātyāyana, in stating his first vārttika: *pāṭhena dhātusaṃjñāyām*, means the dhātupāṭha by the word *pāṭha*;

2) As a consequence of it, the task of making clear how it is possible to take *A* 1.3.1 itself as the dhātupāṭha-based definition.

4.1.1.1. In order to refer to groups of items both in the dhātupāṭha and in the gaṇapāṭha, Pāṇini uses bahuvrīhi compounds of a

---

[1] See Appendix 2.

particular kind (*tadguṇasaṃvijñāna*), with *ādi*, such as *cādi* (*A*1.4.57 *cādayo 'sattve*) and *sarvādi* (*A*1.1.27 *sarvādīni sarvanāmāni*). They refer to groups that include the elements denoted by the first members of the bahuvrīhi compounds.[2] And besides, the word *ādi* which forms the last member of a bahuvrīhi compound that refer to members of an ordered set is the one used with reference to *vyavasthā* (arrangement) and not the one used in the sense of *prakāra* ('kind, sort'; similarity), so that from such a bahuvrīhi compound one understands that a given element denoted by its first member is the first of the ordered group. If the word *ādi* were taken as used in the sense of *prakāra*, the bahuvrīhi compound would refer to a group of items that are like the element denoted by its first member.[3]

Now turning to the item *bhūvādayaḥ* used in *A*1.3.1, when one wishes to take the derivate *bhūvādayaḥ* as a compound of a *bahuvrīhi* type with *ādi*, one faces a difficulty. That is, if a compound is formed from the words *bhū* and *ādi*, then the form of the resulting compound should be either *bhvādayaḥ* or *bhū*

[2] *MBh* ad *A*1.1.27 (I.86.2–8): *sarvādīnīti ko 'yaṃ samāsaḥ / bahuvrīhir ity āha / ko 'sya vigrahaḥ / sarvaśabda ādir yeṣāṃ tānīmānīti / yady evaṃ sarvaśabdasya sarvanāmasaṃjñā na prāpnoti / kiṃ kāraṇam / anyapadārthatvād bahuvrīheḥ / bahuvrīhir ayam anyapadārthe vartate / tena yad anyat sarvaśabdāt tasya sarvanāmasaṃjñā prāpnoti / tad yathā citragur ānīyatām ity ukte yasya tā gāvo bhavanti sa ānīyate, na gāvaḥ / naiṣa doṣaḥ / bhavati hi bahuvrīhau tadguṇasaṃvijñānam api / tad yathā citravāsasam ānaya, lohitoṣṇīṣā ṛtvijaḥ pracarantīti tadguṇa ānīyate, tadguṇāś ca pracaranti /* This kind of bahuvrīhi compound with *-ādi* is comparable to the compound *citravāsas* 'bright-garb, a person whose garment is bright'. When the utterance *citravāsasam ānaya* 'Bring the man with the bright garb' is used, one understands that the man's garment comes along with him. In this case not only the person characterized by the property (*guṇa*), the garment, but also the garment gets involved in the activity spoken of. On the other hand, in the utterance *citragur ānīyatām* 'Spotted-cow should be brought', one understands that a man who has spotted cows is asked to be brought, and not that the man is asked to be brought along with such cows. See Cardona [1997: par. 208].

[3] On these two sorts of use of the word *ādi*, see Section 7 [7.3]. Note that Patañjali knows the use of the word *ādi* in other senses: in the sense of *avayava* 'part' and in that of *sāmīpya* 'vicinity'. See *MBh* ad *A*6.4.161 (III.231.4–6).

ādayaḥ and not *bhūvādayaḥ* with the element *-v-*.[4] Thus Patañjali had to explain the occurrence of the element *-v-* in *bhūvādayaḥ*. In order to do this, he cited the first half of the ślokavārttika: *bhūvādīnāṃ vakāro 'yaṃ maṅgalārthaḥ prayujyate*, which has been given in Section 2 in connection with the interpretation of the present sūtra by the *Kāśikāvṛtti*. According to the ślokavārttika, the form *bhūvādayaḥ* is a bahuvrīhi formed from *bhū* and *ādi* containing the augment *-v-*; the sound *-v-* is for the sake of auspiciousness.[5] If we accept this interpretation, we have to be concerned with a matter of the composition of Pāṇini's work, the *Aṣṭādhyāyī*. Thus Patañjali states:

> *MBh* ad *A*1.3.1 (I.253.5–7): *māṅgalika ācāryo mahataḥ śāstraughasya maṅgalārthaṃ vakāram āgamaṃ prayuṅkte* /

---

[4] Kaiyaṭa remarks that in proposing the possibility of the sequence *bhū ādayaḥ* Patañjali takes a purely hypothetical case (*abhyupagamyavāda*), since, in syntactic units (*pada*) such as the compound *bhū* + *ādi* followed by nominal endings, elements are not pronounced in no close junction. *Pradīpa* on *MBh* ad *A*1.3.1 (II.173): *athāsaṃhitayeti* / *abhyupagamyavādo 'yam* / *na tv ekasmin pade 'saṃhitāsti* / *saṃhitaikapade nityeti vacanāt* / Nāgeśa cites the following kārikā (the source unknown): *saṃhitaikapade nityā nityā dhātūpasargayoḥ* / *nityā samāse vākye tu sā vivakṣām apekṣate* //

[5] As said in Section 2 [2.3.2], the resultant form *bhūvādi* of compounding *bhū* and *ādi* is not accounted for by any rule of the *Aṣṭādhyāyī*, so that it has to be understood as a ready-made form (*nipātana*). *Pradīpa* on *MBh* ad *A*1.3.1 (II.173): *ata eva nipātanād āgamarūpo 'tra vakāraḥ kṛtaḥ* / In addition, this form cannot be incorrect because the sequence *-ū-v-ā-* is not observed in everyday speech. For such linguistic phenomenon is commonly established among grammarians. *Pradīpa* on *MBh* ad *A*1.3.1 (II.173): *na cāyam asādhuḥ, vaiyākaraṇanikāye prasiddhatvāt* /

According to Kaiyaṭa, just as obtaining a newly born thing (*apūrva*) like curds (*dadhi*) is a sign of auspiciousness in daily life, similarly the augment *-v-* also serves to indicate auspiciousness; or, in consequence of the sound *-v-* intervening between *bhū* and *ādi*, the item *bhū* subject to no sandhi modification reminds us of the *mahāvyāhṛtis* 'great utterances' (*bhūr bhuvaḥ svaḥ*) which indicate auspiciousness. *Pradīpa* on *MBh* ad *A*1.3.1 (II.174): *apūrvasya hi lābho dadhyāder loke maṅgalaṃ sūcayati* / *tathehāpy āgamo vakāro maṅgalārthaḥ saṃpadyate* / *atha vā sati vakāre 'vikṛte bhūśabde uccāryamāṇe mahāvyāhṛtismaraṇaṃ maṅgalaṃ bhavatīti pāramparyeṇa vakāro maṅgalārthaḥ saṃpadyate* /

> *maṅgalādīni maṅgalamadhyāni maṅgalāntāni hi śāstrāṇi prathante vīrapuruṣāṇi ca bhavanty āyuṣmatpuruṣāṇi cādhyetāraś ca maṅgalayuktā yathā syur iti* /
>
> "The teacher [Pāṇini] employs here the augment *-v-* for the purpose of auspiciousness of the great multitude of śāstras (grammatical rules). The corpus of grammatical rules which has the auspicious sign at the beginning, in the middle, and at the end prevails and those who have studied it become heroes and long-lived. The augment *-v-* is used so that students of the *Aṣṭādhyāyī* may be endowed with auspiciousness."[6]

According to Jinendrabuddhi, the word *vṛddhi* 'growth' in *A*1.1.1, the sound *-v-* in the present sūtra, and the word *udaya* 'rise' in *A*8.4.67 are used by Pāṇini for the sake of auspiciousness.[7]

What is interesting in this connection is that Patañjali does not cite the second half of the ślokavārttika anywhere else in his Bhāṣya on this sūtra. This problem will be taken up later.[8]

4.1.1.2. Pāṇini, as said above, refers to groups of items in the dhātupāṭha using a bahuvrīhi compound with *ādi*. But how can we know that a set of items listed in the dhātupāṭha are referred to by the compound *bhūvādayaḥ*? This was another question Patañjali had to answer.[9]

Patañjali supposes the following cases:

Case.1: items to be called *dhātu* are recited in *A*1.3.1 itself.

---

[6] In his Bhāṣya on *A*1.1.1 (I.40.5–9) Patañjali states the same thing regarding Pāṇini's use of the word *vṛddhi* in the sūtra: *katham vṛddhir ād aij iti / etad ekam ācāryasya maṅgalārtham mṛṣyatām / māṅgalika ācāryo mahataḥ śāstraughasya maṅgalārtham vṛddhiśabdam āditaḥ prayuṅkte / maṅgalādīni hi śāstrāṇi prathante vīrapuruṣakāṇi ca bhavanty āyuṣmatpuruṣakāṇi cādhyetāraś ca vṛddhiyuktā yathā syur iti.*/

[7] *Nyāsa* on *Kāśikāvṛtti* ad *A*1.3.1: *iha cādau vṛddhiśabdo maṅgalam, madhye cāyaṃ vakāraḥ, ante ca svaritodayam ity udayaśabdaḥ* /

[8] See Section 7 [7.4].

[9] *MBh* ad *A*1.3.1 (I.253.7–11): *athādigrahaṇaṃ kimartham / yadi tāvat paṭhyante nārtha ādigrahaṇena / anyatrāpi hy ayaṃ paṭhann ādigrahaṇaṃ na karoti / kvānyatra / mṛḍamṛdagudhakuṣakliśavadavasaḥ ktveti / atha na paṭhyante natarām artha ādigrahaṇena / na hy apaṭhitāḥ śakyā ādigrahaṇena viśeṣayitum* / See Cardona [1984: 79–80].

Case 2: they are not recited in any texts.

We have to note that items to be called *dhātu* are recited not only in the dhātupāṭha but also in sūtras of the *Aṣṭādhyāyī*. Consider the first case. According to Patañjali, if items called *dhātu* were recited in A1.3.1 itself, there would be no use of employing the word *ādi* therein. For, as in A1.2.7 *mṛḍamṛdagudhakuṣakliśavadavasaḥ ktvā* where Pāṇini mentions items called *dhātu* such as *mṛḍ* 'be gracious' as items pertaining to a certain operation, he would have only to list items to be called *dhātu* there without using the word *ādi*. On the other hand, if the second case held, it would be beyond discussion that the use of the word *ādi* in A1.3.1 serves no purpose. For it is unreasonable that the bahuvrīhi compound with *-ādi* in question could refer to a group of items which are not listed at all.[10]

In this connection it is to be noted that in order to refer to items recited in sūtras of the *Aṣṭādhyāyī*, Pāṇini does not use a compound with the term *ādi* which is used with reference to *vyavasthā*: In some he makes an explicit mention of items as in A1.2.7, and in others a reference to items by using demonstratives as in A4.1.174 *te tadrājāḥ* 'those are called *tadrāja*'. Of course, Pāṇini could have formulated A1.3.1 as *te dhātavaḥ* 'those are called *dhātu*' after listing *bhū* and others in preceding sūtras, which procedure he did not adopt in reality.[11]

All these considerations will lead one to reach the following conclusion: Insofar as the bahuvrīhi compound with *-ādi* (*vyavasthā-ādi*) is used, items of the ordered set are recited in a certain text and the text is outside the corpus of sūtras, the

---

[10] According to Kaiyaṭa, case 1 leads to the result that the purpose of using the word *ādi* is otherwise achieved (*gatārthatva*) and case 2 to the result that no relation is grasped between the bahuvrīhi compound with *ādi* and its referent (*asambaddhatva*). If there is a text in which items to be called *dhātu* are listed, then one can avoid the fault of the latter; and, if the text is external to the *Aṣṭādhyāyī*, then one can avoid the fault of the former

[11] This is pointed out by Kaiyaṭa. *Pradīpa* on *MBh* ad A1.3.1 (II.174–75): *bhūvādīn paṭhitvā te dhātavaḥ iti vaktavyam, yathā te tadrājā iti* /

Aṣṭādhyāyī.[12] Patañjali explicitly states: By using the bahuvrīhi compound *bhūvādayaḥ* in the present sūtra, Pāṇini suggests that there indeed is a text in which *bhū* and others are recited, a text external to the corpus of sūtras of the *Aṣṭādhyāyī*; the text is the dhātupāṭha.

> *MBh* ad *A*1.3.1 (I.253.11–12): *evaṃ tarhi siddhe sati yad ādi-grahaṇaṃ karoti, taj jñāpayaty ācāryo 'sti ca pāṭho bāhyaś ca sūtrād iti / kim etasya jñāpane prayojanam / pāṭhena dhātu-saṃjñety etad upapannaṃ bhavati /*
> "If so, then the following is suggested by the fact that Pāṇini mentions the word *ādi* in his sūtra in spite of the reference to a group of items recited in the sūtrapāṭha being established without using that word: There is a text in which *bhū* etc. are recited, a text external to the sūtrapāṭha.
> [Question] What is the purpose of suggesting this?
> [Answer] In order to suggest that it is justified that *A*1.3.1 allows the name *dhātu* to apply to items listed in the dhātupāṭha (*pāṭhena dhātusaṃjñā*)."[13]

This is how Patañjali makes clear that Kātyāyana presupposes

---

[12] According to Kaiyaṭa, in addition to the dhātupāṭha and sūtras of the *Aṣṭādhyāyī*, there are other places where verbs are recited: vārttikas, the Bhāṣya, and the gaṇapāṭha. *Pradīpa* on *MBh* ad *A*1.3.1 (II.175): *tatra sūtravārttikabhāṣyagaṇeṣu ye paṭhyante te 'pi sūtrakārādiprāmāṇyād dhātutvenāśrayaṇīyāḥ /* Nāgeśa explains that *A*3.1.29 mentions the verb *ṛt* 'go'; Kātyāyana mentions verbs such as *culump* 'swing' in his vārttika on *A*3.1.35 (the vārttika is not found in the *Mahābhāṣya*; see the *Kāśikāvṛtti* on the same sūtra); a group of verbs, beginning with *kaṇḍūñ* 'scratch', are listed in the gaṇapāṭha. It is interesting to note in this connection that Nāgeśa points out the possibility that there might have taken place omission of certain entries from the dhātupāṭha (*pāṭha-bhraṃśa*). *Uddyota* on *MBh* ad *A*1.3.1 (II.175): *tena ca pūrvaṃ dhā-tupāṭhe paṭhitānām idānīṃ pāṭhabhraṃśo 'numīyate /*

[13] It goes without saying that if the word *ādi* in the bahuvrīhi compound *bhūvādayaḥ* were the one used in the sense of *prakāra*, Pāṇini's use of such a compound could not indicate the presence of the dhātupāṭha. For, in that case, it would refer to a set of items that are similar to *bhū* and not to items of the ordered set beginning with *bhū*. What we obtain by taking the word *ādi* in the compound *bhūvādayaḥ* as *prakāra-ādi* is a kind of semantic definition. See Section 7 [7.3].

that items are recited in a text external to the corpus of sūtras of the *Aṣṭādhyāyī* when he introduces his first vārttika by saying *pāṭhena dhātusaṃjñāyām* and establishes that *A*1.3.1 is properly interpreted as the dhātupāṭha-based definition.

4.1.1.3. In this connection it is interesting to note Kaiyaṭa's explanation for Pāṇini's use of the bahuvrīhi compound *bhūvādayaḥ* with the word *ādi* to refer to items of the ordered set beginning with *bhū*.

> *Pradīpa* on *MBh* ad *A*1.3.1 (II.175): *ye dhātupāṭhe paṭhitās teṣām eva dhātusaṃjñā / teṣāṃ ca pāṭho nopalakṣaṇārthaḥ, api tu iyattāpratipādanārthaḥ / tatra yadi kriyāvācī dhātur ity etal lakṣaṇaṃ kriyeta tarhi āṇavayati vaṭṭayatītyādīnām api dhātusaṃjñā syāt / atha sūtrapaṭhitānām anantaraṃ te dhātava ity ucyeta tadā tatrāpaṭhitānāṃ na syāt / tasmād bhūvādaya ity uktam /*
>
> "Only the items recited in the dhātupāṭha are called *dhātu*. And they are not recited there to provide illustrations but to make known that the assignment of the term *dhātu* is restricted to these items recited therein. Concerning that assignment, if a definition of the term *dhātu* were formulated such that an item which denotes an action is called *dhātu*, [corruptions] such as *āṇavi-* 'command' and *vaṭṭi-* 'cause to occur' would also have the name *dhātu*. On the other hand, if a sūtra were formulated as *te dhātavaḥ* 'those items are called *dhātu*' after reciting them in preceding sūtras, only the items recited there would have the name *dhātu*. For these reasons Pāṇini stated that items of the set beginning with *bhū* are called *dhātu*."

According to Kaiyaṭa, the formulation of the present sūtra by using the bahuvrīhi compound *bhūvādayaḥ* with *ādi* has the following advantages:

1) By means of making the sūtra the dhātupāṭha-based definition, it has the advantage of preventing the term *dhātu* from applying to corruptions.

2) By virtue of making the text in which items to be called

dhātu are recited external to the corpus of sūtras, it has the advantage of avoiding the restriction of the assignment of the term *dhātu* to items recited in sūtras.

The first advantage is pointed out in comparison with a semantic definition of the term *dhātu* by taking Kātyāyana's twelfth vārttika into consideration and the second in view of another way of referring to items that is adopted by Pāṇini himself. It is to be noted that of these advantages Kaiyaṭa claims the first one can be cited within the framework formed by Kātyāyana[14] and that Pāṇini seems to have intended something else in formulating the present sūtra in the above-described way.[15]

4.1.2. Limits of the dhātupāṭha-based definition

What has been said above is all Patañjali had to do to establish how to interpret *A* 1.3.1 as the dhātupāṭha-based definition. After establishing in this manner that the present sūtra is the dhātupāṭha-based definition, he goes on to examine that definition following Kātyāyana.

Concerning the dhātupāṭha-based definition, Kātyāyana pointed out in his first vārttika the difficulty of the over-application of the term *dhātu* to items homophonous with the ones listed in the dhātupāṭha. In his Bhāṣya on this vārttika, Patañjali attempts to solve the difficulty. What is important to note here is that he finally shows that one can by no means get around the difficulty at issue. By doing so, it is obvious, Patañjali intends to say that in order to make a definition of the term *dhātu* satisfactory a semantic aspect of items to be given the name *dhātu* should be brought in the definition.

Next, how Patañjali treats the difficulty under consideration and finally comes to make clear the limitations of the dhātupāṭha-based definition shall be shown.

---

[14] See Section 4, Part 4 [4.8.1].

[15] See Section 9 [9.5].

4.1.2.1. In connection with *vt.* 1, Patañjali discusses five instances.

1) The undesired occurrence of kṛt affixes such as *tavyat* after nominal bases homophonous with items recited in the dhātupāṭha. The introduction of the kṛt affix *tavyat* to items called *dhātu* is provided for by *A*3.1.96 headed by *A*3.1.91 *dhātoḥ*. Following Kaiyaṭa, I will explain what Patañjali means.[16]

Consider the utterance *divaṃ paśya* 'Look at the heaven'. In this instance the nominal ending of the second triplet *am* is introduced after the nominal base *div* 'heaven' by *A*2.3.2 which provides that nominal endings of the second triplet occur after a nominal if an object is to be signified. The object denoted by the nominal ending *am* in *divam* is with respect to the act of seeing signified by the verb *dṛś* in *paśya.*[17] Now by *A*3.1.96 kṛt affixes such as *tavyat* follow verbs, items called *dhātu*, and by *A*3.4.70 their occurrence is conditioned by the denotation of an object. Therefore, if the nominal base *div* were called *dhātu*, just as the nominal affix occurs after the nominal base *div* to denote an object with respect to the act of seeing signified by the verb *dṛś*, so also could the kṛt affix *tavyat* occur after the item *div* which has the name *dhātu* to denote an object with respect to the act of seeing signified by the verb *dṛś*, so that one could have **div-tavya* (*-sup*) *paśya*.

2) The undesired application of *A*6.4.140 to the item *yā* 'whom' (acc. pl. fem.; *yad* + *ṭāp* + *śas*) in the string *yāḥ paśya* 'Look at [the women] whom . . . '. According to *A*6.4.140, which provides that the *-ā* of a presuffixal base called *bha* (*A*1.4.18), being a part of a verb, is deleted, the *-ā* of *yā* (*ya-a* + *ā*; *A*7.2.102: *ya* + *ā*; *A*6.1.97: *yā*; *A*6.1.101) would be deleted before *śas* (acc. pl.) so that one would have **y-as*, since this *yā*

[16] *Pradīpa* on *MBh* ad *A*1.3.1 (II.176): *yathaiva divaṃ paśyeti bāhya-kriyāpekṣe karmaṇi dvitīyā bhavati, evaṃ tavyadādayo 'pi syur ity arthaḥ* /

[17] By *A*7.3.78 *paśya* replaces *dṛś* before a suffix marked with *ś*: *dṛś(ir)* + *loṭ* → *dṛś* + *sip* → *dṛś* + *śap* + *sip* (*A*3.1.68) → *paśya* + *a* + *si* → *paśya* + *si* (*A*6.1.97) → *paśya* + *hi* (*A*3.4.87) → *paśya* + *ϕ* (*A*6.4.105) → *paśya*.

has the name *dhātu* because of its homophony with the item *yā* 'go' recited in the dhātupāṭha.

3) The undesired consequence that the particle (*nipāta*) *vā* 'or' cannot be called *pada* (*A*1.4.14) for the reason that the particle *vā* with the name *dhātu*—the item *vā* 'go, strike' is listed in the dhātupāṭha—is not called *prātipadika* (*A*1.2.45) and hence takes no nominal ending (*A*4.1.2) subsequently deleted (*A*2.4.82). If the particle *vā* were not called *pada*, for example, then *A*8.1.28 could not apply to a finite verb form following it so that we would have . . . *vā́ khā́ñjati* (*khañjati* 'walks lame') instead of . . . *vā́ khañjati*. For the sūtra provides that a pada with a verb ending has no high-pitched vowel if it follows a pada that does not end in a verb ending.

4) The undesired application of *A*6.4.77 at the stage *trasnu* + *au* (nom. du.) in deriving *trasnū* 'two men fearful of something'. The nominal base *trasnu* 'fearful' is derived from the verb *tras* 'fear' by adding the kṛt affix ***knu*** by *A*3.2.140. *A*6.4.77 provides that before a vowel, ***iyaṅ*** and ***uvaṅ***, respectively, replace final *i*- and *u*-vowels of presuffixal bases called *aṅga* (*A*1.4.13) with the suffix *śnu*, bases that are verbs, and *bhrū* 'blow'. If the affix *nu* (***knu***) in the item *trasnu* were called *dhātu* on account of its homophony with the item *nu* (*ṇú*) 'praise' recited in the dhātupāṭha, we would have **trasnuvau*. We have to note that Pāṇini posits some verbs with *ṣ* and *ṇ* which are unconditionally replaced respectively by *s* and *n* (*A*6.1.64–65).

5) The undesired result that the primitive nominal base *div* 'heaven' cannot be called *prātipadika* and hence nominal endings are not allowed to occur after it. The homophony of the nominal base *div* and the item *div* (*dívú*) 'play, gamble' listed in the dhātupāṭha provokes this consequence.

These are the undesired consequences Patañjali assumes might follow from the dhātupāṭha-based definition. He succeeded in getting around all of them except the last. His ways of solving the first four difficulties are as follows:

1) From a viewpoint of Pāṇini's kāraka theory, the kṛt affix

tavyat which signifies sādhana or kāraka (an object in the present case) cannot occur after a nominal base which does not denote an action, even if the nominal base is called *dhātu*.[18] The reason for the undesired string **div-tavya* (*-sup*) *paśya* ensuing lies in seeing no difference between the acts, objects with respect to which are denoted by the nominal affix *am* and the kṛt affix *tavyat* respectively. An object to be signified by the ending *am* is in correlation to the act of seeing denoted by the verb *dṛś* in *paśya* (*bāhyakriyā*, external act), whereas an object to be signified by the kṛt affix *tavyat* should be in correlation to the act denoted by the base to which it is introduced (*antaraṅgadhātu-vācyakriyā*, internal act).[19]

2) With reference to the second instance, Patañjali resorts to a reformulation of *A*6.4.140 that Kātyāyana has suggested: *āto anāpaḥ*. The suggested reformulation states that the *-ā* of *bha* stems is deleted if it is other than the feminine suffixes *āp* (*ṭāp*, *ḍāp*, *cāp*). Therefore, the *-ā* of *yā* in *yāḥ paśya* would not be deleted even if the feminine relative pronoun *yā* were called *dhātu*.[20]

3) Patañjali suggests making an additional statement that an

[18] *MBh* ad *A*1.3.1 (I.253.16–19): *dhātor iti tavyadādīnām utpattiḥ prasajyeta / naiṣa doṣaḥ / sādhane tavyadādayo vidhīyante sādhanaṃ ca kriyāyāḥ / kriyābhāvāt sādhanābhāvaḥ / sādhanābhāvāt satyām api dhātusaṃjñāyāṃ tavyadādayo na bhaviṣyanti /* See also Introduction [0.2.2].

[19] *Pradīpa* on *MBh* ad *A*1.3.1 (II.176): *antaraṅgadhātuvācyakriyāpekṣe sādhane tavyadādayaḥ sāvakāśā bāhyakriyāpekṣe sādhane notpadyante ity arthaḥ /* Kaiyaṭa adds that *svārthika* affixes—affixes to be introduced when meanings of bases with which they occur are to be signified—such as *tumun* provided for by *A*3.4.65 inevitably take place after nominal bases that have the name *dhātu*. Their occurrence is not semantically conditioned, so that, even if bases to which they are introduced do not denote actions, they are allowed to occur after those bases by virtue of the bases being called *dhātu*. In order to avoid such a consequence one has to resort to the *anabhidhāna* principle. *Pradīpa* on *MBh* ad *A*1.3.1 (II.176): *yo 'pi śakadhṛṣeti svārthikas tumun so 'py anabhidhānān na bhaviṣyati /* On this principle, see Section 8 [8.6.2.1].

[20] *MBh* ad *A*1.3.1 (I.253.19–20): *iha tarhi yāḥ paśya āto dhātor iti lopaḥ prasajyeta / naiṣa doṣaḥ / anāpa ity evaṃ saḥ /*

item called *nipāta* has the name *prātipadika* (*nipātaḥ prātipadikam*), which itself is a reformulation of vārttika 12 on A1.2.45: *nipātasyānarthakasya prātipadikatvam* 'items called *nipāta* which have no meanings have the name *prātipadika*'. What this additional statement provides for applies in the domain other than that in which A1.2.45 applies, so that even if the particle *vā* were called *dhātu*, it would have the name *prātipadika*, since the exclusion of items called *dhātu* (*adhātuḥ*) in A1.2.45 does not extend to the particle because of A1.2.45 applying only to meaningful items.[21]

4) Concerning the string *trasnu* + *au*, Patañjali considers that Pāṇini's mentioning *śnu* in A6.4.77 indicates that A6.4.77 does not apply to items ending in affixes in general. The item *trasnu* is a derivate that terminates in the kṛt affix ***knu***.[22]

4.1.2.2. As said, with respect to the fifth difficulty which the undesired application of the name *dhātu* to the nominal base *div* entails, Patañjali fails to get around it. The arguments Patañjali brought forward are rather complicated.[23]

---

[21] *MBh* ad A1.3.1 (I.253.20–23): *asya tarhi vāśabdasya nipātasyādhātur iti prātipadikasaṃjñāyāḥ pratiṣedhaḥ prasajyeta / aprātipadikatvāt svādyutpattir na syāt / naiṣa doṣaḥ / nipātasyānarthakasya prātipadikatvaṃ coditaṃ tatrānarthakagrahaṇaṃ na kariṣyate, nipātaḥ prātipadikam ity eva /* It is to be noted that items called *nipāta* are regarded as meaningless in that they do not have meanings denoted by them (*abhidheyārtha*). They are meaningful in that they function as cosignifiers with meaning to be manifested by them (*dyotyārtha*). No further details need be discussed here.

[22] *MBh* ad A1.3.1 (I.253.23–254.3): *iha tarhi trasū iti aciśnudhātubhruvāṃ yvor iyaṅuvaṅāv ity uvaṅādeśaḥ prasajyeta / naiṣa doṣaḥ / ācāryapravṛttir jñāpayati na pratyayasyovaṅādeśo bhavatīti, yad ayaṃ tatra śnugrahaṇaṃ karoti /*

[23] Relevant passages shall be quoted with numbering as a matter of convenience. *MBh* ad A1.3.1 (I.254.3–9): (1) *asya tarhi divśabdasyādhātur iti prātipadikasaṃjñāyāḥ pratiṣedhaḥ prasajyeta / aprātipadikatvāt svādyutpattir na syāt /* (2) *naiṣa doṣaḥ / ācāryapravṛttir jñāpayaty utpadyante divśabdāt svādaya iti, yad ayaṃ divaḥ sāv auttvaṃ śāsti /* (3) *naitad asti jñāpakam / asti hy anyad etasya vacane prayojanam / kim / divśabdo yat prātipadikaṃ tadartham etat syāt—akṣadyūr iti /* (4) *na vā atreṣyate /* (5) *aniṣṭaṃ ca prāpnotīṣṭaṃ ca na sidhyati /* (6) *evaṃ tarhi—ananubandhakagrahaṇe na sānubandhakasyety evam etasya na*

(1) It has been argued that if the nominal base *div* were called *dhātu* because of its being homophonous with the item *div* recited in the dhātupāṭha, nominal endings could not occur after the nominal base *div* since the exclusion of verbs by *A*1.2.45 *arthavad adhātur apratyayaḥ prātipadikam* disallows the application of the term *prātipadika* to it.

(2) A solution is proposed: Although *adhātuḥ* of *A*1.2.45 excludes a verb from having the class name *prātipadika*, the sūtra *A*7.1.84 *diva aut* shows that a nominal ending follows *div* 'heaven', even if this underived element is eligible for the label *dhātu* because of a homophonous *div* being listed in the dhātupāṭha. For the sūtra provides for replacing the *-v* of *div* by *au* (*aut*) before the nominative ending ***su*** to derive *dyauḥ* (*div* + ***su*** → *di-au* + *s* → *dyau* + *s* → *dyauḥ*), which would be purposeless unless *div* could be followed by this nominal ending.

(3) *A*7.1.84 does not serve to make this known. It would if there were no other purpose, but there is: the replacement would now be intended for the *-v* of *div* that is a prātipadika by *A*1.2.46 *kṛttaddhitasāmāsāś ca*, that is, for *-div* which is a derivate formed with ***kvip*** by *A*3.2.76 after the verbal base *div* (***kvip*** → ϕ by *A*6.1.67). By the principle stated in the paribhāṣā (*PIŚ*28): *kṛdgrahaṇe gatikārakapūrvasyāpi grahaṇam*, the kṛdanta *div* (i.e., the item *div* which ends in the kṛt affix ***kvip***) referred to in *A*7.1.84 includes reference also to *akṣadiv-* 'one who plays with dice'.[24] Accordingly, one can let the replacement apply in *akṣadiv-s*, to derive **akṣadyauḥ*.

(4) This objection is rebutted: It is known from usage that the replacement in question should not apply here. Instead, one should allow for *akṣadyūḥ*, with the *-v* of *-div* replaced by ***ūṭh*** according to *A*6.4.19.[25] The application of *A*7.1.84 here is blocked

---

bhaviṣyati / (7) *evam apy ananubandhako divśabdo nāstīti kṛtvā sānubandhakasya grahaṇaṃ vijñāsyate* /

[24] This paribhāṣā teaches that when a kṛdanta is mentioned in a sūtra, the kṛdanta preceded by a gati (*A*1.4.60-79) or by an item denoting a kāraka is also understood. In the case of *akṣadiv*, the term *akṣa* signifies dice which are classed as *karaṇa* (*A* 1.4.42) and *karman* (*A*1.4.43).

[25] In ((*akṣadiv*)-ϕ)*s*, the replacement conditioned by ***kvip***, provided for

just on the basis of the *anabhidhāna* principle: the resultant derivate is grammatically correct but not attestable in usage.[26]

This implies that Pāṇini must have intended the item *div* in *A*7.1.84 to be the underived nominal base *div* 'heaven'. Consequently, if this *div* were called *dhātu*, *A*7.1.84 would become purposeless. Therefore the formulation of *A*7.1.84 does indicate that a nominal ending follows the underived form *div* even if this form is eligible for the label *dhātu*.

(5) Another objection is raised: From a viewpoint of *lakṣaṇaika-cakṣuṣkas* or those whose eyes are solely fixed on the rules of grammar,[27] however, a result that is undesirable (*aniṣṭa*), namely **akṣadyauḥ*, obtains and what is desireble (*iṣṭa*), namely *akṣadyūḥ*, does not suceed in applying. *A*7.1.84, being intended for the derived prātipadika *div* which ends in the kṛt affix ***kvip***,[28] has as its purpose to derive **akṣadyauḥ*, even if this derivate is undesirable.[29]

This naturally implies that the second argument stated above falls to the ground.

(6) A solution is offered: In order to decide which *div*, of the

---

by *A*6.4.19, is internally conditioned, hence takes precedence over the replacement conditioned by the ending ***su***, provided for by *A*7.1.84. *Nyāsa* on *A*7.1.84: *akṣadyūr iti akṣair dīvyatīti kvipi kṛte tadāśraye cāntaraṅgatvāt cchvoḥ śūḍ anunāsike ca iti ūṭh* /

[26] See the present section, fn. 19.

[27] See Section 8 [8.7.1.3].

[28] On this assumption, Kātyāyana in his first vārttika on *A*7.1.84 (*diva auttve dhātupratiṣedhaḥ*) states prohibition on the application of *A*7.1.84 to verbs. Note that an item ending in ***kvip*** has the status of being a verb. *Pradīpa* on *MBh* ad *A*7.1.70 (V.62): *kvibantā dhātutvaṃ na jahati* . . . /

[29] *Uddyota* on *MBh* ad *A*1.3.1 (II.178): *aprayogasya lakṣaṇaika-cakṣuṣkair durjñeyatayā cāritārthyasambhāvanāsattvād* . . . *yady apīṣṭaṃ na sidhyati tathāpy aniṣṭaprāptyartham eva śāstraṃ syāt* / *tathā ca viparīta eveṣṭāniṣṭavibhāgaḥ syād* . . . / The form *akṣadyauḥ* obtains because, even after the replacement by ***ūṭh*** has applied to *akṣadiv*-; by the paribhāṣā (*PS*37): *ekadeśavikṛtam ananyavat* which states the principle that an item modified in part is treated as not being different from the original item, *-dyū* has the status *-div-*.

underived and the derived, *A*7.1.84 is intended for, one might resort to the following paribhāṣā:

PIŚ 81: *niranubandhakagrahaṇe na sānubandhakasya* //
"When an item without a marker is mentioned in a sūtra, the item does not refer to an item with a marker."

In *A*7.1.84 the item *div* without a marker, an underived prātipadika, is mentioned, so that it does not refer to the verb *div* which has the marker *ú* (*dívú*). Accordingly, on the basis of the present paribhāṣā, *A*7.1.84 does not apply to the *-v* of the derived prātipadika *div*, which is an item ending in the kṛt affix ***kvip*** and hence has the status of being a dhātu.[30]

Thus the above-mentioned second argument stands up since it is established that the sūtra at issue is intended for the underived prātipadika *div*.

(7) An objection is entered: However, there is the restriction on the application of the paribhāṣā just mentioned: The paribhāṣā is taken into consideration only if two items with and without a marker are both possibly subject to the operation provided for by the sūtra in question. With respect to *A*7.1.84, needless to say, one should take account of the present paribhāṣā when the *-v* of the underived prātipadika *div* and that of the verb *div* can both be subject to the replacement provided for by the sūtra. But what if the underived prātipadika *div* which has no marker were called *dhātu* because of a homophonous *div* being listed in the dhātupāṭha? In this case, there would be no possibility of the *-v* of this underived prātipadika *div* being subject to the replacement since the *div* in question could not be followed by the nominal ending ***su*** because of its not being given the class name *prātipadika* by *A*1.2.45. Accordingly, one has to say that, under the assumption that the

[30] *MBh* on *vt.* 2 ad *A*4.1.15 (II.208.6-8): *ananubandhakagrahaṇe hi sānubandhakasya grahaṇaṃ na bhavatīty eṣā paribhāṣā kartavyā / kāny etasyāḥ paribhāṣāyāḥ prayojanāni / tavyagrahaṇe tavyadgrahaṇaṃ mā bhūt / divgrahaṇe divugrahaṇaṃ mā bhūt /* *Kāśikāvṛtti* on *A*7.1.84: *div iti prātipadikam asti niranubandhakam / dhātus tu sānubandhakaḥ, sa iha na gṛhyate—akṣadyūḥ /* On the point that an item which terminates in the kṛd affix ***kvip*** does not lose the status of being a verb, see fn. 28 in this section.

underived prātipadika *div* which has no marker is called *dhātu*, there is no chance of the paribhāṣā at issue being considered with reference to *A*7.1.84.[31]

This indicates that the solution suggested in (6) should be abandoned under the assumption that the underived prātipadika *div*, without a marker, is eligible for the class name *dhātu* on account of its being homophonous with the verb *div* recited in the dhātupāṭha. If one could not come up with the solution, as a matter of course, one could not avoid **akṣadyauḥ* which would result if *A*7.1.84 were taken as being intended for the kṛdanta *div*. One cannot argue, under the same assumption, that the sūtra in question is not intended for the kṛdanta *div* but for the underived prātipadika *div*. For, if so, then the sūtra would become purposeless because it cannot apply in the latter *div*; this *div* is no longer eligible for the name *prātipadika* under the assumption accepted here. Accordingly, insofar as the prohibition is not made saying that non-verbs which are homophonous with items listed in the dhātupāṭha are not called *dhātu*, one has to assume that by the term *div* in *A*7.1.84 is meant the one with a marker, that is, the verb *div*, just on the contrary to what the paribhāṣā teaches. Naturally, it follows from this that one cannot avoid the undesired form **akṣadyauḥ* resulting from the operation provided for by *A*7.1.84. Thus, in order to avoid such an undesirable result, the prohibition stated above would have to be made.

In connection with Patañjali's argument about this *div* issue, we must pay close attention to the fact that he consistently maintains, to develop the argument, that the relevant sūtra *A*7.1.84 should be interpreted solely from a viewpoint of *lakṣanaikacakṣuṣkas*. Which forms a striking contrast with the fact that he is to introduce the notion of the respect for the usage of the śiṣṭas (*śiṣṭaprayoga*) to deal with a semantic definition of the term *dhātu*.[32]

---

[31] *Pradīpa* on *MBh* ad *A*1.3.1 (II.178): *adhātur iti prātipadikasaṃjñāniṣedhān niranubandhakāt sor asambhavaḥ, ubhayasambhave cāsyāḥ paribhāṣāyā upasthānaṃ nānyathā* /

[32] See Section 8.

4.1.2.3. Now we have arrived at the conclusion: If the name *dhātu* were assigned to items by virtue of their being recited in the dhātupāṭha, we would have to lay a prohibition saying that items which are homophonous with items recited in the dhātupāṭha are not called *dhātu*. Clearly, this shows that the dhātupāṭha-based definition has a fatal defect, which would entail grammatically serious difficulty; and, moreover, that, as far as any semantic aspect is not introduced to define the term *dhātu*, one cannot escape such a difficulty.[33] The latter point of course is linked with accepting the alternative, semantic definitions of the term *dhātu*.

Strictly speaking, as Cardona [1984: 82] pointed out, we cannot establish that, for example, the feminine relative pronoun *yā* is truly homophonous with the verb *yā*. For, while the verb *yā* is recited with a low-pitched base vowel, the feminine relative pronoun *yā* has a high-pitched vowel. This point also must be born in mind, since such an intentional neglect of accentuations is a matter of great significance to be considered in connection with the question of whether semantic considerations are invoked in the dhātupāṭha-based definition as accepted by Kātyāyana and Patañjali.[34]

4.2. On *vt.* 2

It has been stated by Kātyāyana in his second vārttika that if the dhātupāṭha-based definition is accepted, a specific mention of the extent of each unit to be called *dhātu* has to be made. To this difficulty, Patañjali pursues no solution at all. Therefore, we

---

[33] According to Nāgeśa, Patañjali on the second vārttika does not explain that in his second vārttika Kātyāyana employs the word *ca* 'and' in the sense of *tarhi* 'then', because Patañjali considers that the over-application of the term *dhātu* to homophonous non-verbs cannot be avoided by any means. Nāgeśa's idea is that if the difficulty in question could have been avoided, Kātyāyana would have had to raise another objection from a different angle. *Uddyota* on *MBh* ad *A*1.3.1 (II.178): *tad evaṃ samānaśabdātiprasaṅgaḥ sthitaḥ / ata eva parimāṇagrahaṇaṃ ceti cakāras tarhyarthe bhagavatā na vyākhyātaḥ /*

[34] In the case of the undesired application of *A* 6.4.77 at the stage *trasnu* + *au*, the shape of the affix *nu* (***knu***) is different from that of the verb *nu* which is listed as *ṇú* in the dhātupāṭha.

may say that the difficulty pointed out here furnishes a good reason for leaving the dhātupāṭha-based definition for semantic definitions.

As is well known, the second vārttika in question and the Bhāṣya thereon are deeply concerned with the question whether the original dhātupāṭha associated with the *Aṣṭādhyāyī* included meaning entries (*arthapāṭha*).[35] Here we shall also discuss the question in detail.

4.2.1. **bhvedha*: arthapāṭha in the dhātupāṭha

Patañjali gives the following explanation of the vārttika under consideration:

MBh ad A1.3.1 (I.254.11–12): *parimāṇagrahaṇaṃ ca kartavyam / iyān avadhir dhātusaṃjño bhavatīti vaktavyam / kuto hy etad bhūśabdo dhātusaṃjño bhaviṣyati na punar bhvedhaśabda*[36] *iti /*

---

[35] See Cardona [1999b: 140–145].

[36] I have adopted the reading *bhvedha* following the Nirṇayasāgara Press edition[1.2] instead of *bhvedh* adopted in Kielhorn's edition and the Rohatak edition. Patañjali here talks about a mere sequence of sounds of an item given in the dhātupāṭha. That is, he expects a string of entries in the text of the dhātupāṭha, such as *bhū́* and *edha*, to be understood as mere sound-sequences, as in the case where, when a certain text written in a foreign language which one cannot understand is recited, a sentence used in the text can but be taken as a mere array of sound-sequences. As shall be hereafter clearly shown, this is a theoretical consequence of the assumption which underlies the proposal of the dhātupāṭha-based definition of the term *dhātu*, that in the proposed dhātupāṭha-based definition no semantic considerations should be invoked, nor should verbal features associated with these be considered.

One may notice that Patañjali could be referring to the items which might have the name *dhātu* given to them, and these could include *bhvedh* (not *bhvedha*); he is not necessarily citing from the dhātupāṭha as such. In this case what he means by the present Bhāṣya would be as follows: The verbs *bhū* and *edh* are both listed in the dhātupāṭha, their base vowels being accented and the latter having a vocalic marker attached to it; if they were not taken as two separate meaningful units on account of their meanings being not taken into consideration, on what grounds could one say that *bhū* is a dhātu and not *bhvedh*? However, I find it difficult to accept this interpretation, assuming that the argument at issue on the proposed dhātupāṭha-based definition has to do with the question of how a string of entries in the dhātupāṭha are to be understood

"In addition, a specific mention of the extent of each unit to be called *dhātu* must be made. It is to be stated that such and such a particular stretch of sounds is called *dhātu*. For, on what grounds should it be the case that a sequence of sounds like *bhū* will be called *dhātu* and not a sequence of sounds such as *bhvedha*?"

Patañjali points out that if the dhātupāṭha-based definition were provided, it would follow that the segment *bhvedha* which cannot in reality have a claim to be called *dhātu* is called so. The reason that Patañjali had to raise such a possibility of the segment *bhvedha* being called *dhātu* is clear from the following premises which Patañjali probably assumed in discussing the second vārttika. There are two premises to be considered behind his argument here.

4.2.2. No semantic considerations

4.2.2.1. First, with reference to items to be called *dhātu* by the dhātupāṭha-based definition, one may not take any of their semantic aspects into consideration. For, insofar as the dhātupāṭha-based definition is regarded by Kātyāyana and Patañjali as an alternative to semantic definitions, we must think that they sharply distinguish between formal and semantic approaches to the question of how to define the term *dhātu*.

In Pāṇini's grammar, what is termed *dhātu* is a meaningful unit (*arthavat*). Consider the following sūtra, which defines the term *prātipadika* (nominal base).

A1.2.45 *arthavad adhātur apratyayaḥ prātipadikam* //

This sūtra provides that a meaningful element (*arthavat*) other than a verb (*adhātuḥ*), an affix, or an item that ends in an affix

---

when the text is recited. A specific mention of the extent of each unit has to be made with reference to an array of sound-sequences in this manner: A stretch whose last element is *ū*, that is, *bhū*, is a dhātu (*iyān avadhir dhātusaṃjño bhavati*), which amounts to saying that it must be specified that an item which begins with *bh* and which ends with *ū* is a dhātu, that an item which begins with *e* and which ends with *dh* is a dhātu, and so on.

(apratyayaḥ) is called *prātipadika.* Here the exclusion of items called *dhātu* from the class whose members are meaningful units is made.[37] This clearly shows that items called *dhātu* are supposed to be meaningful units.

Now, utterances are segmented into a sequence of successive sounds or complexes of sounds. As has been seen in the previous section, the method of segmentation was already known to Kātyāyana. That is the reasoning from *anvaya* and *vyatireka* (*vt.* 6). How were items recited in the dhātupāṭha posited as verbs? From a theoretical point of view, we will have to say that in abstracting the segment *pac* from *pacati*, for example, the segmentation has for its occasion the distinct meanings of the segments *pac* and *ati.* Without a meaning corresponding to a linguistic unit, we cannot abstract the unit from a more comprehensive one that contains it. Certainly, therefore, those recited items were posited as distinct meaningful units by the method of segmentation. The discreteness of items recited in the dhātupāṭha other than those of different forms with the same meaning, thus, obviously presupposes that of their meanings. However, as a logical consequence from the context, we are not allowed to assume with respect to the dhātupāṭha-based definition under discussion that there are given items as distinct meaningful units in the dhātupāṭha, so that we have to posit complexes of sounds as a mere sequence of successive sounds, such as *bhvedha.*

4.2.2.2. Let us look at this situation from another angle. Consider A1.1.27 *sarvādīni sarvanāmāni.* According to this sūtra, items of the class beginning with *sarva* 'all' have the class name *sarvanāman.* In the gaṇapāṭha we find the following sequence of items recited in association with the present sūtra:

sarva viśva ubha ubhaya . . .

---

[37] As is stated by Bhartṛhari, there are three meanings understood from an uttered linguistic item: its own form (*svarūpa*), an external thing, and a speaker's intention. Here it is purposeless to say that items recited in the dhātupāṭha are meaningful because of their denoting their own forms. *VP*3.3.1: *jñānaṃ prayoktur bāhyo 'rthaḥ svarūpaṃ ca pratīyate / śabdair uccaritais teṣāṃ saṃbandhaḥ samavasthitaḥ //*

The same is true of this case. That is, unless we assume that items such as *sarva* are given as distinct meaningful units, on what grounds should it be the case that the speech segment *sarva* will be called *sarvanāman* and not the segment **sarvaviśva*? In this case, however, there is no doubt that the presupposition that items such as *sarva* are distinct meaningful units entirely prevents the term *sarvanāman* from applying to the sequence *sarvaviśva*. Therefore, it is clear that Patañjali's positing the sequence *bhvedha* is based on the implicit assumption that items such as *bhū* recited in the dhātupāṭha cannot be taken as distinct meaningful units because from a theoretical point of view any semantic aspect of an item to be called *dhātu* should not be introduced here.

This is also suggested by the following remark of Kaiyaṭa:

> *Pradīpa* on *MBh* ad *A* 1.3.1 (II.179): *evaṃ sati samānaśabdānāṃ pratiṣedho na vaktavyo nāpi parimāṇagrahaṇam / na hi bhvedhaśabdasamudāyaḥ kriyāvācī /*
>
> "If so [i.e., if an alternative semantic definition such as *kriyāvacano dhātuḥ* were given], the prohibition on the application of the name *dhātu* to items homophonous with items recited in the dhātupāṭha would not need to be stated. Nor would the specific mention of the extent need to be made. For, it is not the case that the entire sequence *bhvedha* conveys an action (*kriyā*)."

Kaiyaṭa states that if the *kriyā*-based definition were accepted, the entire segment *bhvedha* would not be called *dhātu* for the reason that it does not denote an action even if its components *bhū* and *edh* denote respective actions. This implies that in order for *bhvedha* to be called *dhātu* by the dhātupāṭha-based definition it is unnecessary to take its semantic aspect into consideration; to put it in a general way, that semantic considerations are never invoked in such a dhātupāṭha-based definition as Kātyāyana and Patañjali consider to be an alternative to semantic definitions.

4.2.3. No verbal features considered

As said in Section 3 [3.2.6], verbs are recited in the dhātupāṭha with metalinguistic features. They have markers and their base vowels are pronounced with distinct pitches.[38]

The second premise which Patañjali assumes in his Bhāṣya on *vt.* 2 is that one should not take the accentuations of base vowels and the markers into consideration. For items whose base vowels are pronounced with distinct pitches and which have markers appended to them are supposed to be individual units, since the accentuations of base vowels and the markers serve to differentiate verbs for particular grammatical operations. For example, *vídá* 'know' and *vida* 'be' are distinguished from each other: one *vid* ('know') is marked with a high-pitched vowel *á* and its base vowel is high-pitched; the other *vid* ('be') is marked with a low-pitched vowel *a* and its base vowel is low-pitched. Thus these features given to verbs presuppose the individuality or distinctness of verbs. The specified features should not be obscured. But how to get such individuality of verbs? This question again drives us to the fundamental question of how to posit the verbs through the analysis of given linguistic items in actual use. As shown, the abstraction of items called *dhātu* from a given sequence of sounds is based upon semantic considerations. Therefore it naturally follows that if we take such features of verbs into account, we cannot have the sequence *bhvedha*. On the contrary, as far as verbs are recited in the dhātupāṭha with metalinguistic features, they have to be treated as distinct meaningful units in themselves. Instead of the arthapāṭha, the metalinguistically featuring of the verbs listed in the dhātupāṭha bears up the fact that they are distinct meaningful units, in short. In Pāṇini's grammar, items listed in the dhātupāṭha are not those which have been presented there merely for the sake of showing their own forms (*svarūpa*) but those which have been strategically posited presupposing

---

[38] In addition, some verbs such as *ṣidhū́* and *ṇú* are listed with *ṣ* and *ṇ* and some verbs such as *lúncá* are listed with word-interior sequences like *-nc-*. The verb initials *ṣ* and *ṇ* are unconditionally replaced respectively by *s* and *n* (*A*6.1.64, 65).

that they are distinct meaningful units. In this sense, therefore, there is no room for the arthapāṭha in the original dhātupāṭha.

4.2.4. Viewed in this light, when we are not asked to take into account any semantic aspect with reference to a given sequence of sounds like *bhvedha*, it is natural that we should resort to statements which specify segmented items. Moreover, from the above we are now certain that Patañjali's assumption that there may be the possibility of the sequence *bhvedha* being called *dhātu* is purely hypothetical and theoretical. It is highly important to note in this context that in his thirteenth vārttika Kātyāyana asserts that the dhātupāṭha serves to make known with regard to verbs their accentuations of base vowels and markers. Naturally, here Patañjali (probably Kātyāyana too) assumes that verbs listed in the dhātupāṭha are recited in such a way as to obscure those verbal features, with a clear conception of them.

4.2.5. Roles of arthapāṭha

In the dhātupāṭha as transmitted by commentators, verbs are accompanied by the arthapāṭha. For example, the first entry is *bhū sattāyām* '*bhū* occurs in the meaning "being"'. Then, provided that the dhātupāṭha includes the arthapāṭha, what functions does it carry out? Let us next discuss this question.

4.2.5.1. *paricchedaka* and *niyāmaka*

Now consider the following statement made by Kaiyaṭa. Concerning the arthapāṭha, Kaiyaṭa says as follows:

> *Pradīpa* on *MBh* ad *A*1.3.1 (II.178–79): *na cārthapāṭhaḥ paricchedakaḥ, tasyāpāṇinīyatvāt / abhiyuktair upalakṣaṇatayopāttatvāt, anekārthadarśanād arthasya niyāmakatvābhāvāt /*
> "And the mention of meanings in the dhātupāṭha (*arthapāṭha*) does not serve to demarcate a stretch of a given extent, since it is not Pāṇinian. For they have been stated by the learned as example meanings, implying others, because verbs are seen to have more than a single meaning.[39] Therefore meanings given

[39] Nāgeśa reports that meaning entries were added by post-Pāṇinian grammarians, foremost among them Bhīmasena. *Uddyota* on *MBh* ad *A*1.3.1 (178): *abhiyuktair iti / bhīmasenenety aitihyam /* See also the

in the dhātupāṭha do not serve to make a restriction such that given items are called *dhātu* only if they are used to denote meanings specified in the dhātupāṭha. Consequently we cannot solve the difficulties pointed out here by resorting to the arthapāṭha."

The most important remark he made that the arthapāṭha is not Pāṇinian will be examined later. From this statement of Kaiyaṭa's we see that the arthapāṭha is considered to have two functions: the function of demarcating a stretch of a given extent (*paricchedaka*) and that of restricting meanings in order to convey which verbs are used (*niyāmaka*).

4.2.5.2. To begin with, we have to note that the arthapāṭha cannot discharge its demarcating function simply because it comes in between two items. Given the sequence *bhū sattāyām edha*, if no semantic considerations are provoked, we will only have the segment *bhūsattāyām* instead of *bhvedha.*[40] Therefore, we have to admit that the arthapāṭha serves for one to understand a given item to denote a particular meaning so that one may take the item as a distinct meaningful unit. To put it another way, with the arthapāṭha *sattāyām* we understand that the given item *bhū* signifies being (*sattā*) and thereby take it as a distinct meaningful unit, for example. It is only in this sense that the arthapāṭha is said to demarcate a stretch of an extent.

Then what about its restricting function? For instance, the verb *vā* is given with its meanings 'go, strike' in the dhātupāṭha as known to us (*vā gatigandhanayoḥ*). This means that the verb *vā* is called *dhātu* only in the sense of 'go, strike', so that its corresponding homophonous nominal form *vā* cannot have the name *dhātu* since the latter does not convey those senses. However,

---

present section [4.2.6.4.1]. Bhaṭṭoji Dīkṣita also makes a remark to the same effect.

[40] In this connection it is interesting to note that if a sequence of sounds such as *bhūsattāyām* is taken as an *anukaraṇaśabda* (an imitative word) there is no harm in treating it as a distinct unit. An item characterized as an *anukaraṇaśabda* is meaningful with respect to its own form. See A5.2.59 *matau chaḥ sūktasāmnoḥ*.

if you think of the restricting function in this manner, then the verb *vā* which signifies meanings other than specified ones will result in not being called *dhātu*. Verbs are seen to have more than a single meaning (*anekārtha*).[41] It is for this reason that the arthapāṭha has to be considered to serve to show illustrative examples (*upalakṣaṇārtha*).

Thus, if the dhātupāṭha had the arthapāṭha, it would have to be assumed that, the arthapāṭha serves to solve the difficulty pointed out in *vt.* 1 by means of its restricting function and to solve the second difficulty in *vt.* 2 by virtue of its demarcating function, though Kaiyaṭa denies the former function for the reason that the original dhātupāṭha contains no arthapāṭha, and the latter for the reason that a verb is polysemous.

4.2.6. The original dhātupāṭha without arthapāṭha

We come now to the point at which it is necessary to deal with the question whether the original dhātupāṭha contained the arthapāṭha.

4.2.6.1. It is beyond question that when the dhātupāṭha, a text external to the *Aṣṭādhyāyī*, is referred to by the bahuvrīhi compound with the word *ādi* used with reference to *vyavasthā*, one is expected to know what items are to be called *dhātu* from that text, the dhātupāṭha. Therefore, the second vārttika should be related to the question of how the dhātupāṭha was composed. We may assume the following two cases:

Case 1:

bhū (*bhū́*)	+	*ϕ*
edha (*édh**a***)	+	*ϕ*
spardha (*spárdh**a***)	+	*ϕ*

Case 2:

bhū	+	*sattāyām*
edha	+	*vṛddhau*
spardha	+	*saṃgharṣe*

[41] See Section 4, Part 2 [4.5.3.2].

In case 1:

1) If one understands, aware of markers and accentuations of base vowels, given items such as *bhū* as distinct meaningful items, just as items like *sarva* given in the *sarvādigaṇa*, then there is no need for segmentation and therefore the sequence *bhvedha* is unlikely to be called *dhātu*. Needless to say, the meaningfulness of these item is with respect to meanings other than their own forms.

2) On the other hand, if one does not understand them as distinct meaningful units, or if one merely accepts them as their own forms, then the specification of segments is asked for to assign the name *dhātu* to distinct segments. This situation is conceivable when any semantic considerations are cast aside and naturally where one is supposed to be unconscious of markers and accentuations of base vowels. To be brief, therefore, the situation is comparable to that in which a mere beginner of Sanskrit is asked abruptly to read a longer complex compound. A teacher will help his student to split it into its components. Similarly one has to specify that *bhū* is a unit, *edh* is another unit, and that the complex *bhvedha* is not a unit, in this way.

In case 2:

In this case, each item listed in the dhātupāṭha is understood as having its own particular meaning by virtue of the arthapāṭha, because one is taught that *bhū* occurs in the meaning 'being', that *edh*, with the vocalic marker *a*, occurs in the meaning 'thrive', and so forth. Here there is no possibility at all of the sequence *bhvedha* being called *dhātu*, since the dhātupāṭha with the arthapāṭha prevents us from understanding items recited there to be meaningless; *bhvedha* is meaningless.

The examination of these two cases clearly shows that Kātyāyana and Patañjali here presuppose that the dhātupāṭha has no arthapāṭha. Case 1–2) is precisely the situation assumed by them. The importance of the fact that Kātyāyana and Patañjali draw a sharp distinction between formal and semantic definitions of the term *dhātu* cannot be overemphasized.

4.2.6.2. *A*1.3.1 and *A*1.4.57

As shall be seen later in Section 7, Patañjali tries to propose a definition of the term *dhātu* into which are integrated formal and semantic aspects of items to be assigned the name *dhātu*. For him, *A*1.3.1 can be a definitional rule such that both the reference to the members of a certain set and the specification of a semantic condition for the assignment of a certain term are made. According to which side of these one lays a stress upon, one may have its different interpretations. If one wishes to stress the former side, then one will have the following:

> 1) An item listed in the dhātupāṭha is called *dhātu* only if it conveys an action/*bhāva*.

And, if one intends to stress the latter, then one will have the following:

> 2) An item which denotes an action/*bhāva* is called *dhātu* if it is listed in the dhātupāṭha.

Although the context where Patañjali proposes interpreting the sūtra as containing both sides presupposes interpretation 2), it is natural that the sūtra in question should allow one to have interpretation 1) from another perspective. What we have to do here is to take note of this interpretation 1).

Let us suppose that the sūtra in question has a structure such that an item listed in the dhātupāṭha is called *dhātu* only if it conveys an action/*bhāva*. We already have a sūtra of a similar type. Consider the following sūtra:

> A1.4.57 *cādayo 'sattve* //

This sūtra provides that items of the set beginning with *ca* 'and' (*cādigaṇa*) are assigned the name *nipāta* 'particle' on condition that they are not used with reference to a substance (*sattva*). The *cādigaṇa* runs as follows:

> *ca vā ha . . . paśu . . . ātaḥ* /

Now we find the item *paśu* listed here. If items such as *ca* were called *nipāta* merely by virtue of being listed in the gaṇa, it would follow that the item *paśu*, recited there, which conveys the sense of '*samyak*' ('well') and that of cattle, animal as well, has the name *nipāta* in the latter sense also, so that one should have *paśu vai puruṣaḥ* instead of *paśur vai puruṣaḥ* 'Indeed, the man is an animal' by *A* 1.1.37. 2.4.82. In order to avoid that, a meaning condition 'on condition that they are not used with reference to a substance' is stated here. First of all, therefore, there is nothing peculiar in introducing a semantic condition into a definitional rule for avoiding its over-application to undesirable items which are not specified in the gaṇa.

*A*1.3.1 interpreted as containing a meaning condition is likened to this sūtra.

paśu	*sattva*/*asattva*
items listed in the dhātupāṭha	*kriyā*/*akriyā* (*bhāva*/*abhāva*)

Consider *A* 1.4.57 just quoted above. In that sūtra Pāṇini made a restriction on the meaning condition by saying *asattve* 'on condition that they are not used with reference to a substance'. Suppose that the items of the set beginning with *ca* (*cādigaṇa*) are recited accompanied by their specific meanings, as **paśu samyagarthe* '*paśu* occurs in the sense of "*samyak*"', for example. That would make the meaning condition purposeless. For, if the item *paśu* were accompanied by the item for its meaning in the *cādigaṇa*, one would understand that the item *paśu* is called *nipāta* when it is used to convey the sense of *samyak*, and not to convey a substance. Therefore, it is obvious that in formulating *A*1.4.57 Pāṇini presupposes that the set *cādigaṇa* has no meaning entry, so that he can introduce the meaning condition there.

In the same vein, the fact that Pāninīyas like Patañjali try to introduce a semantic condition into the definition of the term *dhātu* in one way or another proves undoubtedly that the dhātupāṭha has no meaning entry. Evidently, if the original dhātupāṭha had the entry *vā gatigandhanayoḥ*, it would become purposeless to set a meaning condition such that, on condition that it denotes an action/*bhāva*, the item *vā* is called *dhātu*. Thus, from one of

Patañjali's interpretations of *A*1.3.1 the original dhātupāṭha is clearly shown to have no arthapāṭha. The same is true of traditional interpretations of *A*1.3.1 which agree, as the ślokavārttika tells us, that a semantic aspect of items to be called *dhātu* should also be considered.

4.2.6.3. The dhātupāṭha known to Kātyāyana and Patañjali

As has been seen in Section 3, Kātyāyana had the alternative of a formal definition, the dhātupāṭha-based definition, or semantic definitions, the *kriyā*-based and *bhāva*-based definitions. Given that the original dhātupāṭha has the arthapāṭha, how could one explain Kātyāyana's approach to the question how to define the term *dhātu* at hand? If the arthapāṭha had been given in the dhātupāṭha, he could not have pointed out such difficulties as he did in his first and second vārttikas and he need not have resorted to semantic definitions in order to get around those difficulties. He had simply to say: If the arthapāṭha is taken into consideration, there will not arise such difficulties as pointed out in *vts.* 1–2. And further, as suggested above, Patañjali tries to read semantic definitions directly into *A*1.3.1. Thus, either of Kātyāyana's approach to the question stated above or Patañjali's approach to the question how to interpret *A*1.3.1 does not reflect the presence of the arthapāṭha in the dhātupāṭha.

We may, therefore, reasonably conclude: It is pretty certain that the dhātupāṭha in the form known to earliest Pāṇinīyas such as Kātyāyana and Patañjali did not contain the arthapāṭha. Kātyāyana and Patañjali attempted to pursue the possibility to semantically define *dhātu*. Their attempts best show that the dhātupāṭha as known to them contained no arthapāṭha.[42] Accordingly,

---

[42] I do not share the opinion of Bronkhorst [1981: 354] who says, "(1) The oldest works of the Pāṇinian school—i.e. Pāṇini's *Aṣṭādhyāyī* and Dhp., Kātyāyana's vārttikas, and Patañjali's *Mahābhāṣya*—contain no clear and unambiguous evidence that the original Dhp. contained no meaning entries." As far as the vārttikas and the Bhāṣya on *A*1.3.1 are concerned, they contain a clear and unambiguous evidence that the dhātupāṭha as known to Kātyāyana and Patañjali has no meaning entries.

Cardona [1984: 83] is more convincing on this matter when he says: "In sum, in the dhātupāṭha originally adopted by Pāṇini bases must

it is a valid assumption that the original dhātupāṭha was in the following form:

bhū́ édha spárdha . . .

Moreover, as shall be seen later,[43] the reason for the fact that the arthapāṭha entered the original dhātupāṭha might be explained by the loss of the nasalization of vocalic markers provided for by *A*1.3.2 *upadeśe 'j anunāsika it* and that of distinct accents in the tradition of Pāṇinian recitation. The loss of features of verbs listed in the dhātupāṭha required the substitutes for them. What replaced the verbal features was the arthapāṭha. Meanings given through the arthapāṭha are also considered to characterize the listed verbs. Thus one must say that the entry of the arthapāṭha into the dhātupāṭha does have something to do with the delegation of the authority with respect to accents and nasalization to *pratijñā* 'declaration', that is, the acceptance of them according to what authoritative teachers have said earlier.

4.2.6.4. Bhaṭṭoji Dīkṣita and Nāgeśa on the arthapāṭha

In concluding the present part, let us see what the later Pāṇinīyas, Bhaṭṭoji Dīkṣita and Nāgeśa, say about the arthapāṭha. They are known to differ in opinion as to the arthapāṭha. Observations on their views about it will confirm what I have said of the original dhātupāṭha.

4.2.6.4.1. We have the following statement by Bhaṭṭoji Dīkṣita.

ŚK on *A*1.3.1: *na ca yā prāpaṇe ityādyarthanirdeśo niyāmakaḥ / tasyāpāṇinīyatvāt / bhīmasenādayo hy arthaṃ nirdidiśur iti smaryate / pāṇinis tu bhvedha ityādy apāṭhīd iti bhāṣyavārttikayoḥ spaṣṭam /*

"And, the mention of the meaning (*arthanirdeśa*) such as *prāpaṇe* 'in the meaning "reaching"' in *yā prāpaṇe* ('*yā* occurs in the

---

have been recited without sandhi modifications: *bhū́ édhA spárdhA* and so on. Of course, such a list clearly shows the extent of each base, with its markers." See also Cardona [1997: par. 133]. On this assumption, *A*1.3.1 is to be interpreted as the dhātupāṭha-based definition. See Section 9 [9.3].

43 See Section 9.

meaning "reaching"'; *yā* 'go') does not function as what restricts the item *yā* in its meaning in such a way that it is called *dhātu* only when occurring in the given meaning. For, such mention of the meaning is not Pāṇinian. Tradition says that the learned like Bhīmasena assigned meanings to items listed in the dhātupāṭha. Kātyāyana's and Patañjali's statements make it clear that the way Pāṇini recited those items was *bhvedha* and so on."

Regarding the arthapāṭha, Bhaṭṭoji Dīkṣita holds the same view as Kaiyaṭa. The latter's view has already been shown.[44] The important point to note is what Bhaṭṭoji Dīkṣita says about the way Pāṇini listed verbs in the dhātupāṭha.

pāṇinis tu bhvedha ityādy apāṭhīd . . . /

According to Bhaṭṭoji Dīkṣita, in the dhātupāṭha Kātyāyana and Patañjali knew one had simply *bhvedha* and so on, without intervening glosses. We have to note that, when he states this, Bhaṭṭoji Dīkṣita intends to imply that the original dhātupāṭha had no arthapāṭha and not to say that items listed in the dhātupāṭha were recited with sandhi modification. This will not disallow assuming the original recitation of verbs in the dhātupāṭha to be *bhū́ édha spárdha* and so on.

4.2.6.4.2. Nāgeśa, on the other hand, expounds quite another view. He states as follows:

LŚIŚ II.460 (SK2232 [A8.4.18]: *sattādyarthanirdeśaś copalakṣaṇam*): *arthanirdeśaś ceti / bhū sattāyām ityādir abhiyuktakṛta ity arthaḥ / sa ca kriyāvācitvabodhārtha iti bhāvaḥ / pāṇinis tu kāṃś cid artharahitān paṭhati, kāṃś cid arthasahitān / ata eva bhūvādisūtre parimāṇagrahaṇaṃ kartavyam / kuto hy etat, bhūśabdo dhātusaṃjño bhaviṣyati na punar bhvedhaśabdaḥ iti bhāṣye uktam / cuṭū iti sūtre yad ayam iritaḥ kāṃś cin numanuṣaktān paṭhati, ubundir niśāmane, skandir gatiśoṣaṇayor iti / tena neritām ididvidhiḥ iti bhāṣye uktam / tathā namovariva iti sūtre bhāṣye uktam—kaḥ khalv api*

---

[44] See the present section [4.2.5.1].

pacādīnāṃ kriyāvacanatve yatnaṃ karotīti / atha khalv apy ācāryaś citrayati kvacid ekaṃ kvacin na iti / upalakṣaṇam iti / anekārthā api dhātavo bhavanti iti bhāṣyam atra mānam / tac ca prayogānusāreṇaiva, na tv amaryādam / bhāṣyasthāpiśabdāt / evañ ca sedhater gatau iti sūtre gatau ity upādānāt ṣidha gatyām ity arthanirdeśo 'pāṇinīya iti bodhyam /

I will not render this passage; instead, I will explicate the points Nāgeśa makes.

To begin with, as Nāgeśa argues, the arthapāṭha in the dhātupāṭha as handed down to us is provided by the learned in order to show that items listed in the dhātupāṭha denote actions (*kriyāvācitvabodhārthaḥ*). However, this does not necessarily mean, what is important, that Pāṇini recited all the items without glosses in the dhātupāṭha. According to Nāgeśa, Pāṇini's way of reciting verbs in the dhātupāṭha is as follows:

pāṇinis tu kāṃś cid artharahitān paṭhati, kāṃś cid arthasahitān /

"Pāṇini recites some items unaccompanied by meaning entries and others accompanied by them."

Evidence for this is assembled by Nāgeśa from the *Mahābhāṣya.*

1) The Bhāṣya on vārttika 2 to *A*1.3.1 shows that some items were recited in the dhātupāṭha unaccompanied by meaning entries.[45]

2) The Bhāṣya on *A*1.3.7 indicates that some verbs were recited therein accompanied by meaning entries. In the Bhāṣya in question Patañjali states that Pāṇini recites verbs marked with the marker *ir* with the augment *n* (***num***) and gives the following examples: *ubundir niśāmane* (*bund* 'perceive'), *skandir gatiśoṣaṇayoḥ* (*skand* 'jump, dry'). Patañjali's citations are in accord with the way of listing verbs and their meanings in the later version of the dhātupāṭha.

3) The Bhāṣya on *A*3.1.19 tells that Pāṇini is not consistent in teaching meanings for items posited in grammar; in some cases meanings of items such as *pac* are supposed to be understood

---

[45] See the present section [4.2].

from their actual use so that those meanings are not taught by Pāṇini, in consequence of which they are not shown as meaning entries in the dhātupāṭha.

There is another interesting point to note. Nāgeśa points out that there is a case where a form used to show a meaning of a verb in a sūtra is different from that of the meaning entry of the verb in the dhātupāṭha. For example, while we have the sūtra *sedhater gatau* (*A*8.2.113), we have *ṣidha gatyām* in the later version of the dhātupāṭha. In this case the meaning entry *gatyām* has to be considered to have been added by non-Pāṇinian grammarians.[46]

What is to be noted is that Nāgeśa considers that Pāṇini does not make the mention of the meaning for all the verbs in the dhātupāṭha. According to him, it is not possible that the arthapāṭha universally serves to make items listed in the dhātupāṭha meaningful in that they denote actions. That is why the cases have to be admitted where Pāṇini recites items unaccompanied by meaning entries and where the difficulty pointed out in vārttika 2 results.[47]

In the arguments presented by Nāgeśa two points are to be noted. First, he assumes that in the dhātupāṭha as known to Patañjali verbs were not given as meaningful units and that the verbs recited therein could not be understood as meaningful without meaning entries. Secondly, it is quite likely that the locative forms *niśāmane*, *gatiśoṣaṇayoḥ* in the Bhāṣya on *A*3.1.19 adduced as evidence that in some cases Pāṇini recited verbs accompanied by meaning entries were later glosses which made their way into

---

[46] In the passage quoted here Nāgeśa explains that the arthapāṭha serves to show illustrative examples (*upalakṣaṇa*) by resorting to Patañjali's statement *anekārthā api dhātavo bhavanti* (*MBh* ad *A*8.2.48 [III.480.22], see Section 4, Part 2 [4.5.3.2]). In this context Nāgeśa takes the statement as indicating that items listed in the dhātupāṭha are called *dhātu* even if they denote meanings other than those specified therein, though there is a limitation such that the assignment of meanings to the items has to be made in accordance with usage.

[47] *Uddyota* on *MBh* ad *A*1.3.1 (II.178–79): *arthanirdeśasya vyabhicaritatvenāprayojakatvād vyavasthāpakatvābhāvena parimāṇagrahaṇam api kāryam iti bhāvaḥ* /

the text of the *Mahābhāṣya*.[48] Whatever the case may be, my point is that in the original dhātupāṭha verbs were given as distinct meaningful units and that their meaningfulness, as a given, is not conditional upon the arthapāṭha.

---

[48] Liebich [1930: 246-247]: "Dhātupāṭha-Zitate finden sich an einer einzigen Stelle: I, 264 *ubundir niśāmane / skandir gatiśoṣaṇayoḥ.* Aber auch hier zeigt die nähere Prüfung, daß es sich nicht um eine Lücke im Text handelt, die von einem Späteren ausgefüllt wurde, denn die sehr gute Handschrift E liest: *u[bu]ndir niśāmane skandir iti.* Dies zeigt uns, daß *niśāmane* eine Randglosse ist, die zur Verdeutlichung hinzugefügt wurde, später in den Text geriet und noch später auch das *gatiśoṣaṇayoḥ* nach sich zog. Die Stelle lautete also ursprünglich *ubundir skandir iti.*" See Cardona [1976/1980: 163].

Section 4

Part 2: Bhāṣya on vārttikas 3–7 (*kriyā*-based definition)

4.3. On *vt.* 3

4.3.1. Preliminaries

In his third vārttika Kātyāyana introduced the *kriyā*-based definition of the term *dhātu* as an alternative to its dhātupāṭha-based definition for the purpose of clearing away the difficulties involved in the latter definition. To be sure, if we introduce a semantic aspect of an item that is to have the name *dhātu* by means of adopting the *kriyā*-based definition instead of the dhātupāṭha-based definition, we do not have to make a specific mention of a stretch given in the dhātupāṭha. For, as Kaiyaṭa states, the segment *bhvedha* which would be possibly called *dhātu* under the given definition does not denote an action.[1] However, in order to make the *kriyā*-based definition of the term *dhātu* effective against the over-application of the term *dhātu* to non-verbs homophonous with items recited in the dhātupāṭha, the distinction should first have been established between action (*kriyā*) and non-action at a semantic level in such a way that an item such as *yā* (the feminine relative form) is not called *dhātu* precisely because of its denoting what is other than an action which is considered to be denoted by the verb *yā* listed in the dhātupāṭha. Granted that the term *dhātu* is defined as an item which denotes an action, if we do not know what an action is like and that there is an entity spoken of as an action separately from a substance (*dravya*) which is considered to be the meaning of a nominal base and which Patañjali places in juxtaposition with an action in this context, the definition newly proposed will not work.

In addition, in this case, even if the *kriyā*-based definition were provided, items such as *pac* could not be called *dhātu* if

[1] See Section 4 [4.2.2.2].

they were not known as denoting actions. The way of understanding items such as *pac* to convey such a meaning as an action will also have to be established.

Thus, as a preliminary to the discussion on the problems involved in the *kriyā*-based definition, Patañjali has to deal with the following:

1) Epistemological and ontological problems pertaining to an action;
2) The question of how to establish that the verb *pac* signifies an action.

4.3.2. An action—what is it and how is it known?

4.3.2.1. Explaining words with words

It is interesting that Patañjali, in answering the question of what an action is, did so in the first place by way of mentioning words synonymous with the term *kriyā* in the following order: *īhā*, *ceṣṭā*, and *vyāpāra*.[2]

According to Kaiyaṭa, the terms *īhā* and *ceṣṭā* are respectively used in everyday usage specifically to signify mental and physical acts; they have in common that they are particular activities (*vyāpāraviśeṣa*), so that they are used in grammar to signify an activity (*vyāpāra*).[3] The significance of the fact that an action

---

[2] *MBh* ad A1.3.1 (I.254.13–14): *kā punaḥ kriyā / īhā / kā punar īhā / ceṣṭā / kā punaś ceṣṭā / vyāpāraḥ /*

[3] *Pradīpa* on *MBh* ad A1.3.1 (II.179): *īhāceṣṭāśabdayor anyatra vyāpāraviśeṣavacanatve 'pi iha vyāpāramātravacanatvaṃ boddhavyam /* Nāgeśa properly notes that *icchā* is a mental activity, wishing, while *ceṣṭā* is a physical activity involving movement of the body. *Uddyota* on *MBh* ad A1.3.1 (II.179): *mānasavyāpāra icchārūpehā / . . . kāyaparispandaś ceṣṭā /* As Kaiyaṭa notes, although *īhā* and *ceṣṭā* elsewhere signify distinct activities, they are used in the present context with reference to activity in general (*vyāpāramātra*).

In the Paspaśā Patañjali makes the following statement during a discussion of what it is precisely that one calls *śabda* ('linguistic item'). *MBh* (Paspaśā) [I.1.7–8]: *yat tarhi tad iṅgitaṃ ceṣṭitaṃ nimiṣitaṃ sa śabdaḥ / nety āha / kriyā nāma sā /* ("Then that which one knows as a gesture (*iṅgita*), a physical activity (*ceṣṭita*), or the winking of the eye (*nimiṣita*) is a *śabda*. No, he says. That is an action (*kriyā*).") Here Patañjali calls a gesture and the others actions. According to Kaiyaṭa,

(*kriyā*) is equated with an activity (*vyāpāra*) is appreciated in Patañjali's view of an action as being of a causal value. When the term *kriyā* is glossed with the term *vyāpāra* and what is meant by the former is regarded as the meaning of the verb *kṛ*, what is assumed to be an action in this context consists in nothing but *phalānukūlavyāpāra* 'an activity to lead to a result' as later Pāṇinīyas like Nāgeśa hold,[4] which will be dealt with later in Section 5.

The reason that in reply to the query as to what an action is Patañjali had to explain words with words is clear: He meant to show that one cannot point out an action visually: In a specific situation where a certain finite verb form is used, all that one sees is a substance and one cannot see an entity called an action anywhere. Thus we have to say: Patañjali's way of answering the query in question implies beyond doubt his view that an action is beyond perception and therefore one cannot establish at a perceptual level the distinction between substance and action (*dravyavyatireka*).[5]

---

the gesture, the physical activity, and the winking of the eye are respectively characterized as a physical activity which one does to indicate one's intention (*abhiprāyasya sūcakaḥ śarīravyāpāraḥ*), bodily movement (*kāyaparispanda*), and an activity of the eye (*akṣivyāpāra*).

[4] Nāgeśa, for instance, declares that an activity, including conscious effort (*yatna*), which leads to a result, is a verb meaning, that is, an action. *VSLM*531: *tatra phalānukūlo yatnasahito vyāpāro dhātvarthaḥ iti siddhāntaḥ* /

[5] *MBh* ad *A*1.3.1 (I.254.14–15): *sarvathā bhavāñ chabdenaiva śabdān ācaṣṭe na kiṃcid arthajātaṃ nidarśayaty evaṃjātīyikā kriyeti* / The point made by Patañjali here is explained by Kaiyaṭa as follows. *Pradīpa* on *MBh* ad *A*1.3.1 (II.179): *yāvad dravyavyatirekeṇa kriyāsadbhāve pramāṇaṃ noktaṃ tāvat paryāyopādānamātreṇa tasyāḥ svarūpaṃ na niścīyate* / According to Kaiyaṭa, as long as one is not told of a means of knowing that an action is existent separately from a substance which is perceptible, one cannot determine its distinction from a substance simply through synonyms for the term *kriyā* being taught. In the same line he explains Patañjali's intention in putting the question: *kā punaḥ kriyā* (see the present section, fn. 2), saying that the question is brought up by one who would not think of an action as existent separately from a substance. *Pradīpa* on *MBh* ad *A*1.3.1 (II.179): *dravyavyatirekeṇa tasyāḥ sattām asambhāvayataḥ praśnaḥ* /

4.3.2.2. Ontological and Epistemological description of action

The imperceptibility of an action has been suggested. Patañjali goes on to state it explicitly showing its reason and to undertake an ontological and epistemological description of the action.

4.3.2.2.1. First, Patañjali declares that an action is absolutely imperceptible.

> *MBh* ad *A*1.3.1 (I.254.15–17): *kriyā nāmeyam atyantāparidṛṣṭā / aśakyā kriyā piṇḍībhūtā nidarśayitum, yathā garbho nirluṭhitaḥ / sāsāv anumānagamyā /*
> "What is called *kriyā* is absolutely not visible (*atyantāparidṛṣṭā*). It, being a mass (*piṇḍībhūtā*), cannot be pointed out visually like a foetus that has come out of the womb. That which is at issue [i.e., the action] can only be known through inference (*anumānagamyā*)."[6]

An action is beyond perception and hence can only be known through inference. The reason for its non-perceptibility lies in its assuming the form of a mass.[7] That is, an action as signified by

---

[6]Kaiyaṭa comments that there is also a reading *garbho 'nirluṭhitaḥ*, which means that an action is not visible as a foetus still in the womb cannot be shown visually. *Pradīpa* on *MBh* ad *A*1.3.1 (II.180): *garbho 'nirluṭhita iti / yathā kukṣistho garbho 'pratyakṣas tathā kriyety arthaḥ / atha vā yathā nirluṭhito nirgataḥ kukṣer garbhaḥ pratyakṣo naivaṃ kriyeti vaidharmyeṇa dṛṣṭāntaḥ /* See Cardona [1991: 453, fn. 47] for further details.

[7]Kaiyaṭa notes that the very contrary is the case with atoms (*paramāṇu*), which in a mass become perceptible. *Pradīpa* on *MBh* ad *A*1.3.1 (II.180): *yathā paramāṇavaḥ piṇḍībhūtā upalabhyante na kevalāḥ, evaṃ piṇḍībhāvāt kriyā na pratyakṣā /* It must be noted that the Nirṇayasāgara Press edition (1st, 2nd) has the variant reading of this *Pradīpa* passage: *yathā paramāṇavaḥ piṇḍībhūtā upalabhyante na kevalāḥ, evaṃ piṇḍībhāvābhāvāt kriyā na pratyakṣā.* Under this reading, an action is considered to be imperceptible because it does not assume the form of a mass in the same manner as do atoms which, forming a mass and not separately, are perceived. See *Uddyota* on *MBh* ad *A*1.3.1 (II.179): *tatra nidarśanasyāśakyatve hetum āha—ākhyāteti / tatrāpratyakṣatve hetur anekāvayavarūpatvam, tac ca ghaṭādiṣu vyabhicaritam ataḥ—sadasad iti /; Uddyota* on *MBh* ad *A*1.3.1 (II.180): *nanu yadi piṇḍībhūtā kriyā, kuto nidarśayitum na śakyety ata āha—yatheti /* A pot is a

a verb, being a composite of component actions which take place in a sequence in time (*pūrvāparībhūtāvayavā, bhūtabhaviṣyad-vartamānasadasadanekāvayavasamūharūpā*), cannot be known through perception whose object is solely something existent (*sadvastuviṣayendriyagrāhyā na bhavati*).[8] That an action as signified by a verb takes the form of such a complex means that the action is viewed as in process (*sādhyamānāvasthā*), which shall be touched on in Section 5 [5.2.4].

4.3.2.2.2. Patañjali presents three sorts of inference,[9] though he does not explicitly formulate them but simply hints at logical reasons on which they are based. There are three logical reasons hinted at, of which one serves to infer the distinction between action and substance; and, all the rest are adduced for the inference of action as such.[10]

---

composite of atoms and an action is also a composite of atomic actions. There is, however, indeed the difference between the former and the latter. The atoms which constitute the pot coexist with one another, while the atomic actions which constitute the action do not coexist with one another since they occur in a temporal sequence.

[8] According to Bhartṛhari, the constituent moments of action which make up the composite act have no sooner arisen than they pass, so that they do not come into relation with sense-organs whose range of operation is limited to existent objects. *VP*3.8.6: *kramāt sadasatāṃ teṣām ātmano na samūhinām / sadvastuviṣayair yānti saṃbandhaṃ cakṣurādibhiḥ //* Following Bhartṛhari, Kaiyaṭa explains the present Bhāṣya as follows. *Pradīpa* on *MBh* ad *A*1.3.1 (II.179–80): *ākhyātapadavācyā pūrvā-parībhūtāvayavā sādhyamānāvasthā bhūtabhaviṣyadvartamānasadasa-danekāvayavasamūharūpā sadvastuviṣayendriyagrāhyā na bhavati /*

[9] Patañjali introduces the discussion about the inference of an action by saying: *ko 'sāv anumānaḥ*. Note that he uses the nominative singular masculine form *anumānaḥ*. Kaiyaṭa explains the form in question in two ways: *anu-mā* + ***lyuṭ*** (*karaṇa*; *A*3.3.113, 117); *anu-mān* + ***ghañ*** (*bhāva*; *A*3.3.18). *Pradīpa* on *MBh* ad *A*1.3.1 (II.180–81): *yo bhāve **lyuṭ** sa napuṃsakaḥ, anyatra tv abhidheyavaśād aniyataliṅgaḥ / atha vā manyater ghañy anumāna iti rūpam /* Nāgeśa adopts the first alternative. We may justify *anumānaḥ* by taking it as meaning 'a reason (*hetuḥ*) for inferring an action'.

[10] *Uddyota* on *MBh* ad *A*1.3.1 (II.180): *nanv anumāpakaliṅgapraśne kārakasamavadhānakālikapacatyādivyavahāravyatirekaprayojakavyati-rekapratiyogitvarūpaṃ lakṣaṇam uktaṃ na tu liṅgam ity atas tad api sūcitam ity āha—yasminn iti / itarabhedasādhane lakṣaṇasyaiva liṅgatve*

4.3.2.2.2.1. INFERENCE 1: Establishment of the distinction between action and substance

> *MBh* ad *A*1.3.1 (I.254.17–18): *iha sarveṣu sādhaneṣu saṃnihiteṣu kadācit pacatīty etad bhavati, kadācin na bhavati* /
> "On condition that all participants in an action (sādhanas) are present, sometimes one rightly says *pacati* ('he is cooking'), and sometimes one does not have this."

It is to be noted, first of all, that the word *sādhana* here refers to a substance (*dravya*) which functions as kāraka and not to its quality (*guṇa*) of being a kāraka, such as *adhikaraṇatva* 'the quality of being a locus'; the quality is nothing but what Bhartṛhari calls *sāmārthya* or *śakti* ('power, capacity').[11] Patañjali is quite aware that a means for bringing an action to accomplishment

---

'pi liṅgāntarasūcanam idam / According to Nāgeśa, an action has as its essential characteristic (*lakṣaṇa*) that it can be absent when all kārakas that can bring it to accomplishment are present, so that it cannot lead to a verbal expression such as *pacati*. On this characteristic of an action, see the next subsection on INFERENCE 1. The point Nāgeśa makes is this: Even if this characteristic of an action can be a reason (*liṅga*, 'inferential mark') for inferring the distinction between action and substance as in INFERENCE 1, it does not serve as a reason for inferring an action. That is why by saying *yasmin* [INFERENCE 2] Patañjali introduces a reason for inferring an action as such, the alternative to which he introduces by saying *yayā* [INFERENCE 3].

[11] In his Bhāṣya on *A* 1.4.23 (I.326.11–13: *na hi kārakam ity anenādhikaraṇatvam uktam adhikaraṇam iti vā kārakatvam / ubhau cānyonyaviśeṣakau bhavataḥ / katham / ekadravyasamavāyitvāt* /) Patañjali states that in the situation conveyed by the utterance *sthālyāṃ pacati* the pot (*sthālī*) has the property of being a locus (*adhikaraṇatva*) and in his Bhāṣya on *vt.* 6 ad *A*1.3.1 (see the present section [4.4.1]) he assumes the property of being an agent (*kartṛtva*) to be a meaning of a verbal affix. Bhartṛhari sets forth the following kārikā. *VP*3.7.1: *svāśraye samavetānāṃ tadvad evāśrayāntare / kriyāṇām abhiniṣpattau sāmarthyaṃ sādhanaṃ viduḥ* // According to Bhartṛhari, grammatical tradition says that a capacity for bringing an act to accomplishment is a sādhana; the capacity abides in the same locus as the act in the case of an agent and an object and in a different locus in the case of other kārakas.

(sādhana) is considered either as a substance or as its quality according to cases.[12]

Now take for example the situation expressed by the utterance *devadattas taṇḍulān edhaiḥ sthālyāṃ pacati* 'Devadatta is cooking rice in a pot with firewood'. Without being set into play by Devadatta, substances such as rice cannot function as respective kārakas; Devadatta in turn has to be set into play by external factors such as a desire to obtain a certain result; otherwise he could not function as agent.[13] Therefore, on condition that all substance-sādhanas are present, whether one can say *pacati* or not depends upon whether or not the agent Devadatta is set into play to participate in bringing the action of cooking to accomplishment.

What is intended to be known from this inference? Let the observation made by Patañjali be in order. In this case one may reason as follows.

If the action which is denoted by *pacati* were not distinct from substance-sādhanas which serve as means for bringing it to accomplishment, one might say *pacati* whenever these are present. But this is not the case. Therefore the action, which is denoted by *pacati*, has to be distinct from substance-sādhanas in question.[14]

---

[12] In his Bhāṣya on *A*2.3.1 (I.442.20) Patañjali shows that we have the alternative of substance and quality concerning the question what sādhana is (*kiṃ punar dravyaṃ sādhanam āhosvid guṇaḥ*) and remarks that it is proper to consider the latter to be a sādhana (I.442.22: *kiṃ punaḥ sādhanaṃ nyāyyam / guṇa ity āha*). On the other hand, in his Bhāṣya on *A*5.3.55 (II.414.5) he states that a substance is a sādhana (*sādhanaṃ vai dravyam*). There is no need to go into details here.

[13] *MBh* ad *A*1.4.23 (I.326.10): *yat sarveṣu sādhaneṣu sannihiteṣu kartā pravartayitā bhavati* / *VP*3.7.101a: *prāg anyataḥ śaktilābhāt* / To use Bhartṛhari's term, an agent from whom the capacity of functioning as agent is drawn out by external factors draws out the capacities of functioning as other kārakas from other substance-sādhanas. See Ogawa [2000b].

[14] Explaining the Bhāṣya at issue, Helārāja says the same thing. *Prakāśa* on *VP*3.8.1: *anvayavyatirekābhyāṃ pacatyādiśabdavācyā kriyā dravyāt kārakaśaktiyuktād anyā / tathā hi—audāsīnyāvasthāyāṃ satsv api sādhaneṣu pacatītyādiprakhyopākhyayor abhāvād arthāntaraviṣayatvaṃ tayoḥ / tad yathā ghaṭasannidhāne 'nutpadyamānānāṃ pākajānām agnisaṃyogāpekṣitvam . . . kādācitkaḥ prakhyāviśeṣo hetuḥ kriyāyā*

The establishment of the distinction of an action from substance-sādhanas involved in the action—known through the inference of the kind stated above—is very significant for the *kriyā*-based definition of the term *dhātu*, as I have already pointed out. Even if the *kriyā*-based definition were given, if an action were not known as distinct from a substance, then one could not avoid the given definition applying to items which denote substances, so that the definition in question could not prevent nominal bases, which are homophonous with verbs listed in the dhātupāṭha and which denote substances, from being called *dhātu*.

4.3.2.2.2.2. INFERENCE 2: Inference of an action from the use of a verb form like *pacati*

> *MBh* ad *A*1.3.1 (I.254.18–19): *yasmin saṃnihite pacatīty etad bhavati sā nūnaṃ kriyā* /
>
> "That, as a consequence of whose being one rightly says *pacati*, is an action."[15]

From a speaker's point of view, Patañjali recognizes that the

---

vyatireke 'bhihitaḥ / ("On the basis of the presence (*anvaya*) and absence (*vyatireka*) of the utterance *pacati* under the specified condition, it is established that an action which is denoted by that utterance is distinct from a substance endowed with the capacity of functioning as kāraka. To explain: a cognition (*prakhyā*) and expression (*upākhyā*) such as 'someone is cooking' (*pacati*) occurs with reference to something other than substance-sādhanas because they are absent even if the substance-sādhanas are present. For example, on condition that a pot is present, its [color] produced by heat expects its conjunction with fire. . . . [In this way] a specific cognition that occasionally takes place (*kādācitkaḥ prakhyāviśeṣaḥ*) is stated as a reason (*hetu*) for the distinction (*vyatireka*) of an action from a substance.") Thus, Helārāja and Nāgeśa are unanimous that Patañjali in the present Bhāṣya explicitly states the reason for inferring the distinction between action and substance.

[15] According to Kaiyaṭa, there are two different readings: 1) *yasmin saṃnihite pacatīty etad bhavati sā nūnaṃ kriyā* (adopted by the Nirṇayasāgara Press edition); 2) *yasmin sādhane saṃnihite pacatīty etad bhavati sā nūnaṃ kriyā* (adopted by Kielhorn's edition and the Rohatak edition). In the latter reading, what is meant is as follows: That, as a consequence of whose being one rightly says *pacati* with reference to a particular substance-sādhana, e.g., Devadatta, is an action. Whichever reading is adopted makes no difference to what Patañjali intends to say here. I follow the reading by the Nirṇayasāgara Press

utterance of linguistic items is conditioned by the desire to convey their meanings (*arthanimittaka eva śabdaḥ*).[16] This inference presupposes that in order to use the verb form *pacati* with reference to Devadatta, Devadatta should be involved in bringing the act of cooking to accomplishment. We will see that the inference under consideration seems not to be valid since one can use *pacati*, irrespective of the actual existence of the action at issue, whether or not the action is actually being performed. This is comparable to the case where someone perceives erroneously water (*jala*) in a situation in which only a mirage (*mṛgatṛṣṇikā*) is present in the visual field.[17] Thus Patañjali has to put forward the inference of the following type.

4.3.2.2.2.3. INFERENCE 3: Inference of an action from a spatial movement

MBh ad *A*1.3.1 (I.254.19): *yayā devadatta iha bhūtvā pāṭaliputre bhavati sā nūnaṃ kriyā* /

---

edition.

[16] *MBh* ad *A*1.1.46 (I.114.14). Commenting on the Bhāṣya: *arthanimittaka eva śabdaḥ*, Kaiyaṭa states as follows. *Pradīpa* on *MBh* ad *A*1.1.46 (I.351): *artha eva śabdasya prayojakas tatpratipādanāya śabdaprayogaḥ* / *aprayogāc cānumīyate—nūnam artha evātra prayojako nāsti śabdaprayogaṃ yaḥ prayuñjīta* . . . / It is a meaning that causes one to utter a linguistic item since one employs the linguistic item in order to convey the meaning. On this assumption, if the linguistic item in question is not used, one reasons as follows: Assuredly, there is no meaning which causes one to utter a linguistic item; if there had been, one would have employed the linguistic item. Nāgeśa explains the present inference as follows. *Uddyota* on *Pradīpa* to *MBh* ad *A*1.1.46 (I.351): *kāryābhāvena kāraṇābhāvo 'numīyate* / *yathā nadīpūrābhāvenoparideśe vṛṣṭyabhāva iti bhāvaḥ* / According to Nāgeśa, the inference from the absence of the linguistic item to that of the meaning is the kind of inference through which one knows the absence of a cause (*kāraṇābhāva*) from the absence of an effect (*kāryābhāva*), as one knows the absence of rain upstream from the absence of the swollen river downstream. Note that a causal relation obtains between a linguistic item and its meaning both from the speaker's point of view and from the hearer's point of view. See also Introduction, fn. 14 and Section 3, fn. 22.

[17] *Pradīpa* on *MBh* ad *A*1.3.1 (II.181): *mṛgatṛṣṇikāviṣayajalajñānavat pacatīty etad asatyaviṣayam eva jñānam* /

> "That, on account of which someone like Devadatta is first in one place and then in another place, is an action."

As INFERENCE 2 is established on the basis of a causal relation (*kāryakāraṇabhāva*), so is INFERENCE 3 also. One may say that a result such as reaching another place does not occur without its cause being present. Devadatta's movement from the spot A to B is conditioned by the action of going, so that when one observes his movement one can infer that action as its cause.[18]

4.3.2.2.3. In the manner stated above, Patañjali has fulfilled the first preliminary to the discussion on the *kriyā*-based definition. He has made clear the following points:

In the first place, what Pāṇinīyas speak of as an action is absolutely beyond perception. In the second place, the action as denoted by a verb is assumed to be distinct from a substance. Furthermore, from an epistemological point of view, an action, being considered to be a cause of a certain effect, is inferred from the effect the action has brought about.

In the above-described manner Patañjali has established that although an action is beyond perception, it can be known through inference and that it is distinct from a substance. Now Patañjali moves on to go through the second preliminary.

---

[18] *Pradīpa* on *MBh* ad *A*1.3.1 (II.181): *deśāntaraprāptilakṣaṇena kāryeṇābādhitena kriyākhyaṃ kāraṇam anumīyate* / We will face the question of how one can grasp the invariable concomitance between action and its result on the assumption that actions are not perceptible. On this question, see Ogawa [1995]. According to Kaiyaṭa, while the composite action which is denoted by a verb is beyond perception (*apratyakṣa*), each action-moment is perceptible; one uses *pacati* on the basis of mentally unifying these action-moments; and moreover, it is by its intrinsic denotative nature that a verb does not denote an action-moment. *Pradīpa* on *MBh* ad *A*1.3.1 (II.181): *dhātuvācyasya samūhasya yugapadasaṃnidhānād apratyakṣatve 'py ekaikasya tu kṣaṇasya pratyakṣatve buddhyā tān kṣaṇān saṃkalayya pacatīti prayujyate / yadāpy ekasmin kṣaṇe pacatīti prayogas tadā tatra samūharūpāropaṇam / śabdaśaktisvabhāvāc caikaḥ kṣaṇo naiva dhātuvācyaḥ /*

4.3.3. Establishment of the denotation of an action by *pac*

The second preliminary Patañjali has to fulfill to the discussion on the *kriyā*-based definition is to establish how one can understand that items like *pac* denote actions.

As said, Patañjali finds in the usage of the question-and-answer of the type *kiṃ karoti—pacati* the reason for items such as *pac* being known to denote actions. In the semantic structure on which *kiṃ karoti—pacati* is based, one has to recognize the relation of concurrence (*sāmānādhikaraṇya*) between the meanings of the verbs *kṛ* and *pac*.[19] According to Kaiyaṭa, the relation in question consists in the relation of universal and particular (*sāmānyaviśeṣabhāva*), since the action of cooking which is denoted by *pac* can be said to be a particular action (*kriyāviśeṣa*).[20]

---

[19] See Section 3 [3.2.2].

[20] *Pradīpa* on *MBh* ad *A*1.3.1 (II.182): *sāmānyaviśeṣabhāvena sāmānādhikaraṇyāt kriyāviśeṣavacanāḥ pacādayaḥ pratīyanta ity arthaḥ /* We have to note that Nāgeśa advises one not to take the present *sāmānādhikaraṇya* as a relation such that two items between which the relation obtains refer to one and the same object, that is, coreferentiality. *Uddyota* on *MBh* ad *A*1.3.1 (II.181): *ekārthabodhakatvaṃ sāmānādhikaraṇyaṃ na prakṛte /* See also Section 5, fn. 12. On the notion of *sāmānādhikaraṇya* as held by Pāṇinīyas, see *VP*3.14.20–21, which go as follows: *dravyātmānas trayas tasmād buddhau nānā vyavasthitāḥ / āśrayāśrayidharmeṇety ayaṃ pūrvebhya āgamaḥ // sāmānādhikaraṇyaṃ ca śabdayoḥ kaiścid iṣyate / viśeṣaṇaviśeṣyatvaṃ saṃjñāsaṃjñitvam eva ca //* ("Therefore, the tradition which has come down from the ancients says the following: Three elements that are not distinct from a single substance, [say, in the case of *nīlam utpalam* 'a blue lotus', a substance as something blue, a substance as a lotus, and a substance as a blue lotus] appear to the mind separately; [in this case the substance is analyzed into] a locus (*āśraya*) and the properties that abide in the locus (*āśrayidharma*) [say, the quality blue color and the generic property lotus-ness]. Some accept that the relation of *sāmānādhikaraṇya* obtains between words only and so do that of qualifier and qualificand and that of name and the named, and that the latter relations consist in the former.") According to Helārāja, Bhartṛhari here speaks of two sorts of *sāmānādhikaraṇya*: one between meanings (*arthayoḥ sāmānādhikaraṇyam*) and the other between words (*śabdayoḥ sāmānādhikaraṇyam*). The former *sāmānādhikaraṇya* is characterized by the fact that one and the same substance is understood as having different aspects and the latter by the fact that one and the same substance is referred to by different words (*samānābhidheyatva*). See also Section 2, fn. 1. In the present case it is obvious that a certain

In this connection it will be useful to present here Patañjali's observation on the use of the question *kiṃ karoti*.

> *MBh* ad *A*5.3.66 (II.418.16-18): *kathaṃ punar jñāyate kriyāpradhānam ākhyātaṃ bhavati dravyapradhānaṃ nāmeti / yat kriyāṃ pṛṣṭas.tiṅācaṣṭe—kiṃ devadattaḥ karoti, pacatīti / dravyaṃ pṛṣṭaḥ kṛtācaṣṭe—kataro devadattaḥ, yaḥ kārako hāraka iti /*
>
> "[Question] But how do we know that a verbal form has an action as its principal meaning, while a nominal form has a substance as its principal meaning?
> [Answer] Because someone asked about an action states it with a term ending in a verb ending, as in *kiṃ devadattaḥ karoti—pacati* 'What is Devadatta doing?—He is cooking', while someone asked about a substance states it with a term ending in a kṛt affix, as in *kataro devadattaḥ—yaḥ kārakaḥ/yo hārakaḥ* 'Which is Devadatta?—The man who is doing the act/The man who is doing the act of taking away (a thief)'."[21]

Commenting on this Bhāṣya, Kaiyaṭa states as follows:

> *Pradīpa* on *MBh* ad *A*5.3.66 (IV.218–19): *karotir atra kriyāsāmānyavacanaḥ / tatra viśeṣaparijñānāya kiṃśabdaḥ kriyāviśeṣaṇaṃ pravartate, kriyāviśeṣaṇatvāc ca kim ity etad dvitīyāntaṃ napuṃsakaṃ ca / prakaraṇādivaśāc ca kriyāpraśnāvagatiḥ / guṇadravyaviṣayasyāpi praśnasya sambhavāt—vāyakaḥ kiṃ śuklaṃ vastraṃ karoty atha kṛṣṇam, tathā kiṃ śāṭakaṃ karoty atha prāvārakam iti /*
>
> "The verb *kṛ* used in the question *kiṃ karoti* denotes actions in general (*kriyāsāmānya*). There in the question the word *kim* is employed as an adverb (*kriyāviśeṣaṇa*) with the intention of knowing a specific action (*viśeṣaparijñāna*). And the word *kim* here, being an adverb, is an item which ends in a second

---

agent is understood as performing an act, the act of cooking, and the act in the form of the action of cooking, with the result that the agent is analyzed as a locus of both actions in general and a particular action.

[21] *kāraka*: *kṛ* + *ṇvul*, *hāraka*: *hṛ* + *ṇvul* (*A*3.1.133).

triplet ending (accusative ending) and which is used as a neuter.[22] In addition, it is by the force of the context and others that one understands the question to be about an action. For, using the utterance *kiṃ karoti*, one can also ask about a quality or a substance, as in *vāyakaḥ kiṃ śuklaṃ vastraṃ karoty atha kṛṣṇam* 'What color cloth is the weaver making, white or black?' and *vāyakaḥ kiṃ śāṭakaṃ karoty atha prāvārakam* 'What is the weaver making, a petticoat or a mantle?'"

According to Kaiyaṭa, when the question *kiṃ karoti* is addressed about an action, the word *kim* functions as adverb, so that one may understand the utterance of the question to mean 'What kind of action is he performing?'. Therefore to the question at hand one has to reply in such a way as to specify what action he is producing. Thus it follows that the verb *pac* in the answer *pacati* to such a question denotes a specific action (*kriyāviśeṣa*).

4.4. On *vt.* 6

4.4.1. Kātyāyana, in his sixth vārttika, stated that the abstraction of bases and affixes in syntactic units and the assignment of particular constituent meanings to the bases and affixes are established by the method of analysis: reasoning from *anvaya* and *vyatireka.* Patañjali explains the vārttika as follows:

When first *pacati* '. . . cooks' and then *paṭhati* '. . . recites' are uttered, we observe that *pac* disappears, *paṭh* appears, and *ati* remains constant; the meaning of the act of softening (*viklitti*) disappears, the meaning of the act of reciting appears, both the meanings, the property of being an agent (*kartṛtva*) and singularity (*ekatva*), remain constant. On the basis of this observation we may reason that the meaning which disappears is related to the item which disappears, the meaning which appears to the item which appears, the meaning which remains constant to the item

[22] We have the paribhāṣā: *kriyāviśeṣaṇānāṃ karmatvaṃ napuṃsakaliṅgatā ca.* See *Paribhāṣāsaṃgraha*, Sīradeva 54; Haribhāskara 56. What serves as a qualifier of an action is eligible for being classed as *karman* (object), so that by A2.3.2 *karmaṇi dvitīyā* the second triplet of nominal endings occurs after an item which denotes such a qualifier.

which remains constant. The positive and negative relations are respectively called *anvaya* and *vyatireka*.[23]

4.4.2. Here in the Bhāṣya on the present vārttika also, Patañjali develops the same argument as he did with reference to nominal forms in the Bhāṣya on the ninth vārttika to *A*1.2.45.

What Patañjali points out in the first place is the limits of the *anvaya-vyatireka* method. According to him, the reasoning from *anvaya* and *vyatireka* does not work either in the domain of synonyms or in that of homonyms. For example, the words *indra, śakra, puruhūta* are synonymous with one another, all denoting Indra (*bahavo hi śabdā ekārthā bhavanti*); the word *akṣa* is a homonym, being of a single form and with two or more meanings: 'axis', 'cart', 'die', and so on (*ekaś ca śabdo bahvarthaḥ*). It is clear that, in the former, even when the word *indra* is absent, the understanding of its meaning arises from the others (*vyatirekavyabhicāra* 'deviation in *vyatireka*'); and, in the latter,

[23] *MBh* ad *A* 1.3.1 (I.255.13–20): *iha pacatīty ukte kaścic chabdaḥ śrūyate pacchabdaś cakārāntaḥ, atiśabdaś ca pratyayaḥ / artho 'pi kaścid gamyate viklittiḥ kartṛtvam ekatvaṃ ca /*

paṭhatīty ukte kaścic chabdo hīyate, kaścid upajāyate, kaścid anvayī / pacchabdo hīyate, paṭhśabda upajāyate, atiśabdo 'nvayī / artho 'pi kaścid dhīyate, kaścid upajāyate, kaścid anvayī / viklittir hīyate, paṭhikriyopajāyate, kartṛtvaṃ caikatvaṃ cānvayī /

te manyāmahe—yaḥ śabdo hīyate tasyāsāv artho yo 'rtho hīyate, yaḥ śabda upajāyate tasyāsāv artho yo 'rtha upajāyate, yaḥ śabdo 'nvayī tasyāsāv artho yo 'rtho 'nvayī / We have to note that Patañjali treats the item *ati* in *pacati* as an affix; the *ati* is analyzable further into the affixes ***śap*** and ***tip***. Kaiyaṭa explains that this is because Patañjali's chief concern at the moment is the base or because he just follows the grammatical analysis of early teachers. *Pradīpa* on *MBh* ad *A*1.3.1 (II.183–84): *atiśabdaś ceti / yady apy ayaṃ pratyayasamudāyaḥ, tathāpi prakṛtibhāgāvabodhaparatvāt pratyayabhāgaparyālocane 'nādarād evam uktam / atha vā pūrvācāryaiḥ kaiścid atiḥ pratyayatvena kalpita iti tadapekṣayaitad uktam /*

According to Bhartṛhari, linguistic items used for grammatical description in grammar (*pratipādakaśabda*) can differ from grammatical system to system. They are conceptually posited through abstraction. In his *Vṛtti* on *VP*1.26 he states: *padasya cānvākhyeyatvam abhyupagamya bhū bhūti ati ityevamādayaḥ śabdāntarasamudāyapratipattihetavaḥ parikaliptāḥ pratipādakāḥ śabdā upādīyante /* See also Section 3 [3.2.3].

when the word *akṣa* is present, the understanding of an intended meaning may not arise (*anvayavyabhicāra* 'deviation in *anvaya*').[24] Consider the following sequence of utterances:

pacati (*pac-ati*)
paṭhati (*paṭh-ati*)
pacati (*pac-ati*).

If the items *pac* and *paṭh* were synonymous with each other, the act of softening which is assumed to be the meaning of the item *pac* would be understood not only when the item *pac* is used but also when the item *paṭh* is uttered. On the other hand, if the item *pac* were a homonym, a meaning other than the act of softening could be understood when it is repeated. This is also said of the affix *ati*. Obviously, Patañjali considers that the meaning assignment based on the reasoning from *anvaya* and *vyatireka* presupposes that a linguistic item and its meaning should be in one to one correspondence.[25]

In the second place, however, he takes up the following question: While admitting that the *anvaya-vyatireka* method for the meaning assignment works in the domain of finite verb forms, for what reason should it be the case that this meaning, say, the act of cooking, is attributed to a base such as *pac* and this meaning, say, the property of being an agent (*kartṛtva*), to an affix such as *ati* and not that the meanings in question are both attributed either to the base or to the affix?[26] One may reason that the base

---

[24] *MBh* ad A1.3.1 (I.255.20–22): *viṣama upanyāsaḥ / bahavo hi śabdā ekārthā bhavanti / tad yathā—indraḥ śakraḥ puruhūtaḥ purandaraḥ / kanduḥ koṣṭhaḥ kusūla iti / ekaś ca śabdo bahvarthaḥ / tad yathā—akṣāḥ pādā māṣā iti / ataḥ kim / na sādhīyo 'rthavattā siddhā bhavati /* In his commentary on *MBh* ad A1.2.45 Nāgeśa states as follows. *Uddyota* on *MBh* ad A1.2.45 (II.78): *evaṃ cākṣādiśabde tasmin śabde saty eva tadarthāpratīter arthāntarapratīteḥ, paryāyasthale tasmin śabde 'saty api tadarthapratītes cedṛśāv anvayavyatirekāv anirṇāyakāv iti bhāvaḥ /*

[25] *Pradīpa* on *MBh* ad A1.2.45 (II.78): *yady ekaḥ śabda ekasminn arthe niyataḥ syāt tata etad yujyate vaktum /*

[26] *MBh* ad A1.3.1 (I.255.23–24): *nāpi brūmo 'rthavattā na sidhyatīti / varṇitā hy arthavattānvayavyatirekābhyām eva / tatra kuta etad ayaṃ prakṛtyartho 'yaṃ pratyayārtha iti, na punaḥ prakṛtir evobhāv arthau brūyāt pratyaya eva vā /*

denotes a set of meanings, the act of cooking and the property of being an agent, while the affix manifests them (*dyotaka*), namely that such a set of meanings is manifested by the affix to belong to the base; to the contrary, one may reason that the affix denotes such a set of meanings, while the base manifests them, namely that such a set of meanings is manifested by the base to belong to the affix.[27]

He answers this question in the following manner: If we accepted that a single base has both of the meanings or that a single affix has both of them, the base or the affix would have to be regarded as a *sāmānyaśabda* 'generic term', which for the specification of its own meaning requires an item denoting something specific (*viśeṣa*) and a context (*prakaraṇa*). For example, the *guṇavacana* ('quality-word') *śukla* 'a white thing' is used to refer to a white ox, a white horse, or whatever else may be white. In this sense it may be called a *sāmānyaśabda*.[28] In order to specify what white thing is meant by the word *śukla* the word *go* is mentioned as in

---

[27] *Pradīpa* on *MBh* ad *A*1.2.45 (II.79): *prakṛtiḥ sarvān arthān abhidadhāti, dyotikās tu vibhaktaya iti siddhaivārthavattā / pratyaya eveti / tataś ca prakṛter arthavattā na sidhyatīti tadavastho doṣa ity arthaḥ /* In this case, we may say that when a certain linguistic item is present, a certain meaning is manifested; and, when the linguistic item is absent, the meaning is not manifested. For the notion of *dyotaka*, see the present section [4.5.4]. Note that the meaningfulness (*arthavattā*) of a base or an affix is considered here with respect to their meanings to be denoted (*abhidheyārtha*) and not to their meanings to be manifested (*dyotyārtha*). On this assumption, of course, if a base were taken as what denotes its meanings and an affix following the base as a manifester of the meanings, one could not establish the meaningfulness of the affix. See Section 4, Part 1, fn. 21. As shall be seen, the *anvaya-vyatireka* method works well in establishing a relation between a preverb and its meaning. Preverbs are regarded as *dyotakas*. In his comments on *vt.* 7 ad *A*1.3.1, Nāgeśa explicitly states that one can establish by the *anvaya-vyatireka* method that preverbs manifest qualifiers of actions denoted by verbs. *Uddyota* on *vt.* 7 ad *A*1.3.1: *yathānvayavyatirekābhyāṃ pratyayo 'rthabodhakas tathā tābhyām eva kriyāviseṣadyotaka upasargaḥ. kriyāvācī dhātur eva . . . /*

[28] See *MBh* ad *A*2.1.1 (I.363.19–22): *bhavati hi guṇābhidhāne guṇinaḥ sampratyayaḥ / tad yathā śuklaḥ kṛṣṇa iti / viṣama upanyāsaḥ / sāmānyaśabdā eta evaṃ syuḥ / sāmanyaśabdāś ca nāntareṇa viśeṣaṃ prakaraṇaṃ vā viśeṣeṣv avatiṣṭhante /*

śuklo gauḥ 'the white ox' so that one may understand the white thing to be the ox. In the same way, the logical hypothesis that the base *pac* or the affix *ati* be used to refer both to the act of cooking and to the property of being an agent leads us to conclude that such conditions have to be met in order to specify which of them is meant by the base or the affix.[29] But let the word *śukla* refer to a specific thing such as a white ox and not to other white things. In that case, there will be no need for the specification of its own meaning. This is said of the present case. Patañjali states:

> *MBh* ad A1.3.1 (I.255.26–256.2): *yatas tu khalu niyogataḥ pacatīty ukte svabhāvataḥ kasmiṃś cid viśeṣe pacatiśabdo vartate 'to manyāmahe—neme sāmānyaśabdā iti / na cet sāmānyaśabdāḥ prakṛtiḥ prakṛtyarthe vartate, pratyayaḥ pratyayārthe /*
> "Indeed, however, it is necessarily the case that when the word *pacati* is uttered, the verb *pac* denotes a certain specific thing according to its 'own nature' (*svabhāvataḥ*).[30] For this reason, we think that these [i.e., the base and the affix] are not *sāmānyaśabdas*. If they are not *sāmānyaśabdas*, it is established that the base denotes its own meaning and the affix denotes its own meaning."

In conclusion, considering their 'own nature' neither the base *pac* nor the affix *ati* can be taken as a *sāmānyaśabda*. They respectively denote by nature their own specific meanings and hence it does not hold that a single base conveys both the meanings, the act of softening and the property of being an agent, or that a single affix conveys both of them. Therefore, it is proper to say that by the method of reasoning from *anvaya* and *vyatireka* the base and the affix are established respectively as denoting their

[29] *MBh* ad A1.3.1 (I.255.25–26): *sāmānyaśabdā eta evaṃ syuḥ / sāmānyaśabdāś ca nāntareṇa prakaraṇaṃ viśeṣaṃ vā viśeṣeṣv avatiṣṭhante /*

[30] Here Patañjali introduces the notion of the 'own nature' (*svabhāva*). The 'own nature' is nothing but a linguistic item's intrinsic denotative nature and what forms a core of Patañjali's semantics. On this point, see Section 5 [5.2.3].

own specific meanings, the action of cooking and the property of being an agent.

Let us note that in his arguments on the application of the *anvaya-vyatireka* method to finite verb forms such as *pacati* Patañjali eliminates the possibility of bases or affixes being synonyms for other bases or affixes, and homonyms, and further *sāmānya-śabdas*.

4.5. On *vt.* 7

In connection with the *kriyā*-based definition the third vārttika of Kātyāyana pointed out the difficulty that, under the given definition, with reference to both a verb-affix complex and a preverb-verb complex, one has to deny them to be called *dhātu*. The sixth vārttika dealt with the verb-affix complex. The aim of the seventh vārttika is to offer a solution to the difficulty at issue concerning the preverb-verb complex.

In the present vārttika Kātyāyana says that preverbs denote qualifiers of actions and not the actions themselves, which he tacitly accepted is established by the method of reasoning from *anvaya* and *vyatireka*. By saying so, Kātyāyana wishes to imply that a meaning supposed to be in reference to a preverb is not an action itself but its qualifier, so that the term *dhātu* is applied neither to a preverb nor to such a complex item.

Under this vārttika Patañjali carefully examines the cases in which verbs are used with preverbs. He takes up three types of instances: *prapacati* '. . . cooks exceedingly', *adhyeti* '. . . remembers' or *adhīte* '. . . studies the Veda',[31] and *pratiṣṭhate* '. . . moves'. Which shows that Patañjali distinguishes among three cases:

---

[31] *adhyeti*: *adhi-s (su)* + ***ik*** + *laṭ*; *adhīte*: *adhi-s (su)* + *i* ***ṅ*** + *laṭ*. dhātupāṭha II. 37: *iṅ adhyayane*. dhātupāṭha II. 38: ***ik*** *smaraṇe*. The verb *i* (*iṅ*) which is used to signify the act of studying the Veda takes ātmanepada endings by *A*1.3.12. Note that, strictly speaking, *adhi* does not actually form a compound directly with the verb in the Pāṇinian derivation. *adhi* is a nipāta (*A*1.4.58) and an upasarga (*A*1.4.59), belonging to the nipāta class (*A*1.1.37). Therefore, the ending *su* is introduced after *adhi* (*A*2.3.46) and then dropped (*A*2.4.82).

1) The case where a certain verb deviates from a certain preverb (*yatra dhātur upasargaṃ vyabhicarati*).
2) The case where a certain verb does not deviate from a certain preverb (*yatra na khalu taṃ vyabhicarati*).
3) The case where a meaning totally separate from the one understood when a certain verb is used without a preverb is distinctly understood when the verb is used with the preverb (*vyaktam arthāntaraṃ gamyate*).

Interestingly, Patañjali's contribution to the point at issue was to show the limits of the *anvaya-vyatireka* method in specific cases and to introduce another way of establishing the relation of a linguistic item to its meaning.

4.5.1. *prapacati*

The instance *prapacati* illustrates case 1). The verb *pac* deviates from the preverb *pra* and hence can be used with other preverbs including a zero preverb. According to Patañjali, the preverb-verb complex of the *prapacati* type best serves as evidence of what is stated in the seventh vārttika. When the verb *pac* is used without the preverb *pra*, in other words, with the zero preverb, a bare act of cooking is understood; when it is used with *pra*, an excellent act of cooking, the act of cooking qualified by excellence is understood.[32]

Now we may say, following the sixth vārttika, that meanings of verbs do not differ when there are different preverbs with different meanings. Therefore, it is certain that the meaning

[32] *MBh* ad *A*1.3.1 (I.256.4): *pacatīti kriyā gamyate, tāṃ pro viśinaṣṭi* /
Nāgeśa explains that the meaning with which the preverb *pra* in *prapacati* has something to do is 'excellence' (*utkarṣa*). *Uddyota* on *MBh* ad *A*1.3.1 (II.184): *pro vīti / pacer utkṛṣṭakriyāparatvaṃ dyotayatīty arthaḥ* / On the basis of the seventh vārttika here, Bhartṛhari states as follows. *VP*2.187: *kvacit saṃbhavino bhedāḥ kevalair anidarśitāḥ / upasargeṇa saṃbandhe vyajyante praṇirādinā* // Puṇyarāja comments: *kvacit pacatyādau prakarṣādīnāṃ sambhavāt kevalais teṣām apratīter upasargasambandhāt tadavagama iti teṣūpasargāṇāṃ viśeṣadyotakatvam ucyate / ata eva coktam tam eva viśinaṣṭy anyaḥ iti.* A preverb manifests (*vyajyante, dyotaka*) factors differentiating an action. See the present section [4.5.4].

difference is not attributed to the complex *pra* + *pac* but to its components and that the meaning assignment by the *anvaya-vyatireka* method works properly: the *pra* is eligible for conveying the qualifier 'excellence' and the *pac* for the act of cooking.

4.5.2. *adhyeti/adhīte*

The instances *adhyeti* and *adhīte* meet case 2). Neither of the verbs used here (***ik*** in the former and ***iṅ*** in the latter) is used without the preverb *adhi*. Therefore, it is not so easy to justify Kātyāyana's statement that a preverb conveys a qualifier of an action. The following does not hold here: When the verb *i* (***ik/iṅ***) is used with the zero preverb, a certain action is understood; when it is used with the preverb *adhi*, the action qualified by a certain element is understood. Obviously, thus, it is not established that meanings of verbs do not differ when there are different preverbs with different meanings.[33] As a consequence of it, it will follow that in the instances *adhyeti* and *adhīte* the meaning difference is attributed to the complex *adhi* + *i* (***ik***, ***iṅ***) and therefore such a complex is undesiredly called *dhātu*.

In order to get over this difficulty, Patañjali notes the fact that in the above-mentioned instances, to be sure, the verb *i* does not deviate from the preverb *adhi*, but the latter deviates from the former.[34] And, on the basis of this observable fact, he states:

> *MBh* ad *A*1.3.1 (I.256.7–8): *te manyāmahe—ya evāsyādher anyatrārthaḥ sa ihāpīti / kaḥ punar anyatrādher arthaḥ / adhir uparibhāve vartate /*
>
> "We consider as follows: In the present instances also the preverb *adhi* has the same meaning as it does in other instances in which it is used with other verbs.
>
> [Question] But what is the meaning the preverb *adhi* has in other instances?

---

[33] See Section 3 [3.2.3].

[34] *MBh* ad *A*1.3.1 (I.256.5–6): *yatra na khalu taṃ vyabhicarati tatra katham adhyeti adhīta iti / yady apy atra dhātur upasargaṃ na vyabhicarati, upasargas tu dhātuṃ vyabhicarati /*

[Answer] [In other instances] the preverb *adhi* denotes 'being higher' (*uparibhāva*).[35]"

We have to notice that Patañjali here assumes that the verbal forms *adhyeti* and *adhīte* respectively convey the act of remembering qualified by *uparibhāva* and the act of studying the Veda, qualified by the same property; the former might mean 'he remembers excellently' and the latter 'he studies excellently the Veda'. Therefore, the point made by him is that for the reason mentioned above we cannot assign the meaning of *uparibhāva* to the preverb *adhi* in these instances.

What Patañjali means to say here is, accordingly, that the relation of the preverb *adhi* to the meaning *uparibhāva* which qualifies the acts of remembering and studying the Veda in the present instances is not established by the *anvaya-vyatireka* method but otherwise. If we take into consideration the argument Patañjali develops in connection with *pratiṣṭhate*, which will be taken up next, the relation at issue is established on the basis of the following inference:

[Thesis] The preverb *adhi* in *adhyeti* or *adhīte* manifests *uparibhāva.*
[Reason] Because of its property of being the item *adhi*.
[Example] Just like the preverb *adhi* which has been used with other verbs at a time in the past.[36]

Once the relation of the preverb *adhi* to the meaning *uparibhāva*

---

[35] See the *Kāśikāvṛtti* on *A*8.3.51: *adhyartha uparibhāvaḥ*. Nāgeśa comments that the term *uparibhāva* here means *utkarṣa* 'excellence'. *Uddyota* on *MBh* ad *A*1.3.1 (II.184): *utkarṣalakṣaṇa uparibhāvo 'dher arthaḥ* /

[36] The establishment of the relation of the preverb *adhi* in *adhyeti* / *adhīte* to the meaning *uparibhāva* through inference is suggested by Nāgeśa, who says as follows. *Uddyota* on *MBh* ad *A*1.3.1 (II.184): *dhātor upasargāvyabhicāre 'pi upasargasya dhātuvyabhicārād anyatra dyotyatvena niścito 'rtha evehāpy adheḥ* / According to him, even if the verb *i* does not deviate from the preverb *adhi*, the preverb deviates from the verb, so that the meaning as manifested by the preverb can be determined in other instances where the preverb is used with other verbs and hence the determined meaning is assumed to be ascribed to the present *adhi* in *adhyeti*/*adhīte* also.

is established through this inference, the condition is met that meanings of preverbs do not differ when there are different verbs with different meanings.[37] Consequently the meaning difference is not attributed to the complex *adhi* + *i*. It is thus established that the verb *i* has something to do with a meaning, the act of remembering or studying the Veda, and therefore that the item *i* is properly called *dhātu*.

4.5.3. *pratiṣṭhate*

The instance *pratiṣṭhate* covers case 3). What is observed with respect to this instance is: When the verb *sthā* (*ṣṭhā*) is used without the preverb *pra*, the absence (*nivṛtti*) of the act of going (*vrajikriyā*), that is, the act of staying, is understood; on the other hand, when it is used with the preverb *pra*, the act of going is understood. We cannot say that the act of going is one of the class of acts of staying nor that it is the act of staying which is qualified by a certain element. The two meanings in question are totally different from each other (*arthāntara*).[38]

In this case, obviously it does not hold that meanings of verbs do not differ when there are different preverbs with different meanings. But the fact that the condition which denies that the meaning difference is attributed to the complex *pra* + *sthā* is not met necessarily entails the difficulty that the *anvaya-vyatireka* method does not apply here and hence such a complex is undesiredly called *dhātu*.

In order to avoid such an undesired result Patañjali works out two solutions: he proposes that, instead of the *anvaya-vyatireka* method, we should resort to the familiarity (*prasiddha*, *prasiddhi*) of a particular meaning and to inference.

---

[37] This is why two conditions are stated for the meaning assignment to components of a complex in *vt*. 6. See Section 3 [3.2.3]. As said, here in the instances *adhyeti* and *adhīte* the reverse does not hold.

[38] *MBh* ad A1.3.1 (I.256.8–9): *iha tarhi vyaktam arthāntaraṃ gamyate —tiṣṭhati pratiṣṭhata iti / tiṣṭhatīti vrajikriyāyā nivṛttiḥ, pratiṣṭhata iti vrajikriyā gamyate /* dhātupāṭha I. 975: *ṣṭhā gatinivṛttau*. By A1.3.22 the verb *sthā* takes ātmanepada endings when it is preceded by the preverb *pra*.

4.5.3.1. Familiarity

On the point that when the verb *sthā* is used with the preverb *pra*, a meaning contrary to the one understood when it is used without that preverb is understood, Patañjali first states as follows:

> *MBh* ad *A*1.3.1 (I.9–10): *te manyāmahe—upasargakṛtam etad yenātra vrajikriyā gamyata iti* /
> "We consider: This is based upon the preverb *pra*. By virtue of it the act of going is understood [from *pratiṣṭhate*]."

According to Puṇyarāja, what Patañjali means to say by this Bhāṣya is explainable in the following manner: Of the verb *sthā*, its meaning, the absence of the act of going or the act of staying, is more familiar, so that we would not think of the same verb conveying the meaning of the act of going. Therefore we might well attribute that unfamiliar meaning to the preverb *pra*.[39] However, this is merely a tentative solution. Finally Patañjali resorts to inference.

4.5.3.2. Inference

Concerning the instances *adhyeti/adhīte* Patañjali has established the relation of the preverb *adhi* to the meaning *uparibhāva* on the basis of the observation that the preverb *adhi* has that meaning in other instances. Here also he finds the same sort of solution.

Patañjali forms two hypotheses:

1) From *pratiṣṭhate*, one understands the act of going which is qualified by *ādikarman* 'the initial moment of an action' or the property of having been just started, in other words, one understands that someone starts to go.
2) The verb *sthā* has more than one meaning so that it can convey the act of going as well as the absence of the act of going.

---

[39] Puṇyarāja on *VP*2.189: *gatinivṛttau tu prasiddhatvāt tiṣṭhateḥ praśabdasya gativācakatvam ucyate* . . . / Bhartṛhari is of the opinion that the familiarity of a meaning is a cause of the determination of a meaning with respect to a linguistic item. *Vṛtti* on *VP*1.106: *sarvatra hi prasiddhir evārthavyavasthākaraṇam* /

The second point is very important. For, in order to establish the relation of the preverb *pra* to the meaning *ādikarman* on the assumption that from *pratiṣṭhate* the act of going qualified by *ādikarman* is understood, it is necessary to justify that the verb *sthā* conveys the act of going also in addition to a more familiar meaning, the absence of the act of going. Note that from a viewpoint of Patañjali's semantics of verbs we cannot ask the question: Why does the verb *sthā* mean the act of going?[40] It is by its intrinsic denotative nature that the verb in question means that act. Therefore the point is how to justify that one and the same verb *sthā* conveys more than one meaning. If this is justified, there will be no harm in assuming that in the present instance *pratiṣṭhate*, the act of going is attributed to the verb *sthā*.

Now, with reference to the establishment of the relation of the preverb *pra* to the meaning *ādikarman* in *pratiṣṭhate*, Patañjali states:

> *MBh* ad *A*1.3.1 (I.256.10): *pro 'yaṃ dṛṣṭāpacāra ādikarmaṇi vartate* /
>
> "The preverb *pra* in the present instance, whose deviation from [the verb *sthā*] is observed (*dṛṣṭāpacāra*), denotes *ādikarman*."

The preverb *pra* may be used with verbs other than the verb *sthā*. If the preverb *pra* is used to convey *ādikarman* in other instances, why not in this instance? This is the underlying idea. Puṇyarāja formulates this argument as follows:

> [Thesis] The preverb *pra* at issue [in the instance *pratiṣṭhate*] manifests the meaning *ādikarman*.
> [Reason] Because of the property of being the item *pra*.
> [Example] Just like the preverb *pra* which has been observed in the past to be used with verbs such as *pac*.[41]

---

[40] See Section 5 [5.2.3.2].

[41] Puṇyarāja on *VP*2.189: *tatrāviśeṣeṇopasargāṇāṃ dyotakatvam / tathā ca praśabdo dharmī ādikarmadyotaka iti sādhyo dharmaḥ praśabdatvāt pūrvoditapacādidṛṣṭapraśabdavat iti viśeṣato dṛṣṭenānumānena / tad-dharmapraśabdasya samānadharmā sarvo 'pi prādir upasargo dyotaka-tvadharmayukta ucyata iti* /

This might remind us of the inference through which it is established that the preverb *adhi* in *adhyeti/adhīte* manifests *uparibhāva*. What is common to the preverbs under consideration is that they deviate from the verbs *i* and *sthā* respectively.

Concerning the establishment of the thesis that the verb *sthā* has more than one meaning, Patañjali states:

> *MBh* ad *A*1.3.1 (I.256.11–16): *na cedaṃ nāsti—bahvarthā api dhātavo bhavantīti / tad yathā—vapiḥ prakiraṇe dṛṣṭaś chedane cāpi vartate—keśaśmaśru vapatīti / . . . / evam ihāpi tiṣṭhatir eva vrajikriyām āha tiṣṭhatir eva vrajikriyāyā nivṛttim /*
> "It is not denied that there are also verbs which have many meanings (*bahvarthā api dhātavo bhavanti*). For example, the verb *vap* is observed to be used in the sense 'strew', and in the sense 'cut' as well, as in *keśaśmaśru vapati* 'He crops someone's hair and beard'. . . . In the same manner, in this case also, one and the same verb *sthā* denotes the act of going and the absence of the act of going as well."[42]

This argument of Patañjali's is formulated by Puṇyarāja as follows:

> [Thesis] The verb *sthā* has more than one meaning.
> [Reason] Because of the property of being a verb.
> [Example] Just like the verb *yaj* which both a proponent and an opponent agree has more than one meaning.[43]

---

[42] In addition to the verb *vap*, Patañjali mentions the verbs *īḍ*, *kṛ* as examples. Observation tells us that the verb *īḍ* has the meanings *stuti* 'praise', *codanā* 'directing', *yācñā* 'request', and *preraṇa* 'urging'; the verb *kṛ* the meanings *abhūtaprādurbhāva* 'the act of calling into existence something that has not yet come into existence', *nirmalīkaraṇa* 'polishing', *nikṣepaṇa* 'placing down'. It is to be noted in this connection that Patañjali mentions *abhūtaprādurbhāva* as the usual meaning of the verb *kṛ*. This is an important point especially when we consider the meaning of the term *kriyā* which is a derivate of the verb *kṛ*.

[43] Puṇyarāja on *VP*2.189: *dhātuś ca sāmānyato dṛṣṭenānumānenānekārthaḥ / yathā tiṣṭhatir dharmī anekārtha iti sādhyo dharmo dhātutvāt, ubhayavādisammatānekārthayajatyādidhātuvad iti / evaṃ sāmānyato dṛṣṭānumānāt taddharmānyo dhātur apy anekārtha ucyate . . . /*

Patañjali remarks that the verb *yaj* means various actions and hence denotes not only the act of making an oblation but also the act of bestowing. *MBh* ad *A*3.1.26 (II.34.4–6): *nānākriyā yajer arthaḥ /*

From the above, it has become clear that in the instance *pratiṣṭhate* Patañjali, assuming that from the item *pratiṣṭhate* one understands the act of going qualified by *ādikarman*, has established through inference the relation of the *pra* at issue to the property of *ādikarman* and the polysemy of the verb *sthā* which makes possible the assignment of the specific meaning, the act of going, to the verb *sthā*. And, now that the assignment of the meanings to the preverb and the verb has been established in this way, what is eligible for being called *dhātu* can be said to be neither the complex *pra* + *sthā* nor the preverb *pra* but the very verb *sthā*.

4.5.4. *dyotaka*

We have examined the question how we can avoid the over-application of the term *dhātu* to a preverb-verb complex under the *kriyā*-based definition. Patañjali does not say anything about the denotative function of *upasargas*. He only follows Kātyāyana's view.[44] As is well known, Pāṇinīyas like Bhartṛhari regard preverbs as *dyotakas* 'manifester, cosignifier'. Here it will suffice to adduce the kārikā stated by Bhartṛhari on the preverb.

*VP*2.187: *kvacit sambhavino bhedāḥ kevalair anidarśitāḥ / upasargeṇa sambandhe vyajyante pranirādinā //*

"Latent differentiating elements in certain [actions] are not pre-

---

nāvaśyaṃ yajir haviḥprakṣepaṇa eva vartate / kiṃ tarhi tyāge 'pi vartate / (For the punctuation *kiṃ tarhi tyāge 'pi*, see Section 2, fn. 8.)

Puṇyarāja presents the two forms of inference given here in commenting on *VP*2.189: *sthādibhiḥ kevalair yac ca gamanādi na gamyate / tatrānumānād dvividhāt taddharmā prādir ucyate //* This kārikā is stated by Bhartṛhari in view of the present Bhāṣya. In his *Vṛtti* he calls the inference for the preverb *pra*, *dṛṣṭānumāna* and that for the verb *sthā*, *sāmānyatodṛṣṭānumāna*. The inference called *dṛṣṭānumāna* or *viśeṣatodṛṣṭānumāna* (according to Puṇyarāja) is the inference from a specific property (*viśeṣa*) such as the property of being the item *pra* (*praśabdatva*) which is unique to the item *pra* and the inference called *sāmānyatodṛṣṭānumāna* is the inference from a generic property (*sāmānya*) such as the property of being a verb (*dhātutva*) which is common to all verbs. This is not the place to discuss these points in detail.

[44] *MBh* on *vt*. 4 ad *A*2.1.1 (I.365.17–18): *upasargāś ca punar evamātmakā yatra kaścit kriyāvācī śabdaḥ prayujyate tatra kriyāviśeṣam āha /*

> sented by verbs alone. They are manifested by preverbs such as *pra* and *nis* when the verbs are connected with the preverbs."[45]

Rather, what is important to note in the present Bhāṣya is, as said, that Patañjali has pointed out that there may be the limits of the *anvaya-vyatireka* method to be found in some of preverb-verb complexes and has shown the possibility of establishing the relation of a preverb to its meaning through inference.

---

[45] On the notion of *dyotaka*, see Cardona [1997: par. 688]. Cardona gives 'cosignifier' as a translation for the Sanskrit term *dyotaka*, in accordance with Nāgeśa's definition of the term: (*VSLM*584) *dyotakatvaṃ samabhivyāhṛtagatavṛttyudbodhakatvam* (according to Cardona, "[what constitutes an element's being a dyotaka] is the property of bringing to mind (*udbodhakatvam*) a word-meaning relation between a linguistic element and a meaning that properly pertains to another item, with which the former is used (*samabhivyāhṛta*).") If we attach weight to the fact that Nāgeśa characterizes a dyotaka as *udbodhaka*, we may also propose 'manifester' as a translation for '*dyotaka*', because a function of a dyotaka is said to manifest something that has not manifested itself, as shown in the kārikā cited here. See *Vṛtti* on *VP*2.164 also, where it is stated that the function of *dyotana* (lit. 'illuminating') is viewed in two ways: manifesting something that has not manifested itself, or restricting the possible things that can be assumed to obtain (*dyotanam api dvividham / anāvirbhūtāvirbhāvanam, avyudāsaprasaṅge vā prakārāntaravyudāsena kasya cid avadhāraṇam . . . /*). Suppose that the verb *pac* can signify the mere act of cooking and the act of cooking qualified by excellence: If the latter meaning is understood when the preverb *pra* is used with the verb *pac* as in *prapacati*, the denotation of meanings by this verb is said to be restricted by *pra* to that meaning. On the restrictive function of a dyotaka, see *Vṛtti* on *VP*2.187.

Section 4

Part 3: Bhāṣya on vārttikas 8–11 (*bhāva*-based definition)

4.6. On *vt.* 8

4.6.1. Preliminaries

In the eighth vārttika, Kātyāyana proposed an alternative semantic definition, a *bhāva*-based definition, with the aim of removing the difficulty which he had pointed out in his fifth vārttika that a semantic definition does not apply to items such as *as* 'be' if it is characterized as a *kriyā*-based definition. Regarding the *bhāva*-based definition also, before attempting to go forward in his discussion, Patañjali had certain tasks to fulfill. They are:

1) Inquiry into the meaning of the term *bhāva*
2) Looking into the evidence that items such as *pac* denote *bhāva*
3) Pursuit of the possibility of *A*1.3.1 being a semantic definition.

All of these shall be discussed in detail in the following sections. It is worth while examining them more closely in that they embody the essence of Patañjali's semantics of verbs. Therefore, in this section they shall be outlined only briefly.

Patañjali did not attempt any etymological or grammatical analysis of the term *kriyā* in the *kriyā*-based definition. With respect to the term *bhāva*, however, he had to be concerned specifically with its etymological or grammatical interpretations. As said, the *bhāva*-based definition was proposed by Kātyāyana as a definition which covers all items properly to be called *dhātu*, as compared to the *kriyā*-based definition as a narrower one. As is suggested by the introductory Bhāṣya to the eighth vārttika itself, the term *bhāva* involves ambiguity, so that he had to ask the question: When you say that a verb meaning is characterized as *bhāva*, what do you mean by the term *bhāva*?[1] In this regard, we

---

[1] *MBh* ad *A*1.3.1 (I.256.18–20): *yadi punar bhāvavacano dhātur ity etal lakṣaṇaṃ kriyeta / kathaṃ punar jñāyate—bhāvavacanāḥ pacādaya*

have to say, the intention with which Patañjali puts the question as to an action (*kā punaḥ kriyā*) is different from the one with which he poses the question about *bhāva* (*kaḥ punar bhāvaḥ*). He phrased the former question in order to establish an epistemological and ontological status of an action.[2]

There is still another reason for him to stick to the interpretation of the term *bhāva*. He attempted to read *A*1.3.1 as a semantic definition of the *bhāva*-based type. In such an attempt it was necessary to interpret the sūtra as that in which the term *bhū* equivalent to the term *bhāva* is used.

4.6.2. Three varieties of *bhāva*

4.6.2.1. The meaning of the verb *bhū*: *sattā* (existence) and *janman* (birth)

Patañjali has given three different interpretations of the term *bhāva*.

1) *bhāva* as existence (*bhavanam bhāvaḥ*)
2) *bhāva* as something that comes into being (*bhavatīti bhāvaḥ*)
3) *bhāva* as something that is brought into being (*bhāvyate yaḥ sa bhāva iti*)[3]

A few points have to be noted. First, of these three kinds of *bhāva* Patañjali describes the first kind of *bhāva*, or *bhāva* as existence, as *bhavateḥ svapadārthaḥ* 'the original, literal (*sva*)

---

iti / yad eteṣāṃ bhavatinā sāmānādhikaraṇyam—bhavati pacati, bhavati pakṣyati, bhavaty apākṣīd iti / kaḥ punar bhāvaḥ /

[2] See Section 4 [4.3.1].

[3] *bhāva*1: *bhū* + ***ghañ***; *A*3.3.24. *bhāva*2: *bhū* + *ṇa*; *vt. bhavateś ceti vaktavyam* (vārttika as quoted by the *Kāśikāvṛtti* ad *A*3.1.143). *bhāva*3: *bhū* + ***ṇic*** + *ac*; *A*3.1.32, 3.3.56. In connection with the third interpretation of the term *bhāva* it will be useful to quote from the *Tantravārttika* in which Kumārila glosses the term *bhāva* in *JS*2.1.1 (*bhāvārthāḥ karmaśabdās tebhyaḥ kriyā pratīyetaiṣa hy artho vidhīyate*) with the word *bhāvanā* 'the activity to cause something to come into being'. *TV* on *JS*2.1.1: *siddhāntavādī tu bhavater ṇijantāt er ac ity acpratyaye kṛte bhāvanāvācinaṃ bhāvaśabdaṃ vyutpādya . . . /* Patañjali's *bhāva*3 and Kumārila's *bhāva* differ in that the kṛt affix *ac* in the former denotes an object (*karman*), while the same affix in the latter denotes an act in the abstract (*bhāva*).

meaning (*artha*) understood from the word (*pada*) *bhū* itself'. According to Kaiyaṭa, by using such expression, Patañjali means to exclude the secondary, figurative meaning of the word *bhū* which is understood in dependence upon external factors such as context.[4] Therefore, it follows that what is understood from the verb *bhū* itself when *bhavati* is uttered, that is, the primary meaning of the verb *bhū*, is suggested by Patañjali to be spoken of as *bhāva*.

Interestingly, this suggestion implies that Patañjali admits that the verb *bhū* may also convey meanings other than its primary meaning. For, needless to say, the expression *svapadārtha* is used to exclude what is not a *svapadārtha* of the verb *bhū*. We find the following remarks in the commentaries by Kaiyaṭa and Nāgeśa:

With regard to the first interpretation of the term *bhāva*, Kaiyaṭa states: *ātmabharaṇavacano bhavatiḥ* 'here the verb *bhū* means self-maintenance (*ātmabharaṇa*)', whereon Nāgeśa comments: *ātmabharaṇaṃ cāṣaṣṭhād bhāvavikārād anusyūtaṃ sad iti pratyayavedyaṃ rūpam* 'and the self-maintenance, fastened to six modes of *bhāva* (*bhāvavikāra*) up to [but excluding] the sixth [i.e., perishing (*vinaśyati*)], is an aspect of things which is to be known on the basis of the understanding that they are existent (*sat*)'.[5] And besides, Nāgeśa explicitly remarks: *bhavanalakṣaṇa-*

---

[4] *Pradīpa* on *MBh* ad *A*1.3.1 (II.186): *svapadārtha iti / svagrahaṇam upacaritārthanivṛttyarthaṃ gauṇo 'pi padārtho bhavati, na tu svo, vyabhicārāt / padagrahaṇaṃ prakaraṇādyanapekṣatvapratipādanārtham /* For Pāṇinīyas like Bhartṛhari, the distinction between primary (*mukhya*) and secondary (*gauṇa*) meanings of a word is merely a matter of familiarity (*prasiddhi*). *VP*2.263: *anekārthatvam ekasya yaiḥ śabdasyānugamyate / siddhyasiddhikṛtā teṣāṃ gauṇamukhyaprakalpanā //* In *VP*2.264–65 Bhartṛhari states what are *gauṇārtha* and *mukhyārtha* or *svārtha*: *arthaprakaraṇāpekṣo yo vā śabdāntaraiḥ saha / yuktaḥ pratyāyayaty arthaṃ taṃ gauṇam apare viduḥ // śuddhasyoccāraṇe svārthaḥ prasiddho yasya gamyate / sa mukhya iti vijñeyo rūpamātranibandhanaḥ //*

[5] It is obvious that Kaiyaṭa and Nāgeśa here rest on the view Bhartṛhari set forth in his *VP*3.3.47ab: *ātmānam ātmanā bibhrad astīti vyapadiśyate /* See Section 6 [6.2]. For six modes of *bhāva*, see Section 4, Part 4 [4.8.3] and Section 6 [6.1].

bhāvasya sattārūpatvāt 'because the *bhāva* characterized as *bhavana* is in essence *sattā*'.

With reference to Kaiyaṭa's comment on the second interpretation of the term *bhāva*: *bhedādayo 'pi bhavantīti* 'acts denoted by items like *bhid* "break" are also spoken of by the word *bhavati*', Nāgeśa says: *janmavācī bhavatiḥ* 'here the verb *bhū* denotes *janman*'.

Moreover, in connection with the interpretation of *A*1.3.1 as a semantic definition of the *bhāva*-based definition type, Kaiyaṭa explicitly states: *bhavatir atra janmavācī gṛhyate na tu sattāvācī* 'the present verb *bhū* from which the derivate *bhū* is formed is taken as denoting *janman* and not as denoting *sattā*'.[6]

From these remarks it is clear that the commentators distinguish the meanings of the verb *bhū*: *sattā* and *janman* and that the meaning *sattā* is assigned to the verb *bhū* of the term *bhāva* in its first interpretation and the meaning *janman* to the same verb of that term in its remaining interpretations.

It is not unusual that a distinction is made between the two meanings of the verb *bhū*. For example, the *Kāśikāvṛtti* on *A*4.3.53 *tatra bhavaḥ*, distinguishing between those two meanings, states that the verb *bhū* from which the term *bhava* in this sūtra is derived is taken to mean *sattā* and not *janman* (*sattā bhavatyartho gṛhyate, na janma* . . .), so as to distinguish the sūtra in question from *A*4.3.25 *tatra jātaḥ*. *A*4.3.53 and *A*4.3.25 respectively account for a usage like *sraughna* 'located (*bhava*) in Srughna' and one such as *sraughna* 'born (*jāta*) in Srughna'.

Of these two meanings of the verb *bhū*, which is more familiar to us? To put it another way, of them, which is its primary meaning (*svapadārtha*)? As has already been suggested, it is the meaning *sattā*. The dhātupāṭha as handed down to us has the first entry *bhū sattāyām*. It has been said that later Pāṇinīyas like Kaiyaṭa are of the opinion that meaning entries such as *sattā* are given in the dhātupāṭha for illustration (*upalakṣaṇārtha*).[7] A

---

[6] See Section 7 [7.2.2].

[7] See Section 4 [4.2.5.1].

more familiar illustration is to be given. That is why Bhaṭṭoji Dīkṣita could say:

> *SK*2232: *sattādyarthanirdeśas copalakṣaṇam / yāgāt svargo bhavatītyādāv utpadyata ityādyarthāt /*
> "And meaning entries such as *sattā* are illustrative, for in utterances such as *yāgāt svargo bhavati* 'Through performing the sacrifice the heaven is produced' meanings such as *utpadyate* '. . . is born' are understood."

In sum: In his arguments on the *bhāva*-based definition, Patañjali assumes that the term *bhāva* is employed in the definition to refer to the meaning *sattā* (existence) of the verb *bhū*, to an agent with respect to the meaning *janman* (birth) of the verb *bhū*, and to an object with respect to the meaning of the derived verb *bhāvi* which is formed from the verb *bhū* with the meaning *janman*.[8]

4.6.2.2. *bhāva* vs. *svabhāvasiddha*

In discussing the third interpretation of the term *bhāva*, Patañjali makes the following statement:

---

[8] As we shall see later in Section 7 [7.2], Kaiyaṭa translates the third *bhāva* into the second *bhāva* (*yo hi bhavati sa eva bhāvyate nānyaḥ*). In this respect also, the verb *bhū* in the second interpretation and the one in the third interpretation should have the same meaning.

With reference to the second and third *bhāva*, the key to the question as to which of the two meanings, *sattā* and *janman*, is meant by the verb *bhū* from which the term *bhāva* is derived is found in the derivation of the third *bhāva* with the causative affix ***ṇic*** and in the fact that the second *bhāva* is taken as equivalent to the third *bhāva*. See *VP*3.7.126: *dravyamātrasya tu praiṣe pṛcchyāder loḍ vidhīyate / sakriyasya prayogas tu yadā sa viṣayo ṇicaḥ //* This kārikā states: The imperative affix (***loṭ***) is used after verb roots like *pracch* 'ask' as in *pracchatu mā bhavān* 'You ask me' (see *MBh* ad *A*3.1.26 [II.33.9]) when the bare substance is prompted; when the already active object is prompted, it comes within the scope of the use of the causative affix ***ṇic***. According to Bhartṛhari, the causative affix ***ṇic*** is introduced to a primitive verb to convey the situation in which one causes another who is already involved in the act signified by the verb not to stop the act. When the verb *bhū* signifies *sattā*, the derivate *bhāvi* should mean the activity to cause something to exist or the one to cause it not to stop existing, which activity is nothing but the act of maintaining. I cannot go further into details here.

> *MBh* ad *A* 1.3.1 (I.257.8–9): *kriyā caiva hi bhāvyate svabhāvasiddhaṃ tu dravyam* /
> "Indeed, an action (*kriyā*) alone is [that which is] brought into being. On the other hand, a substance (*dravya*) is something that has been established by 'own nature' (*svabhāvasiddha*)."

According to Patañjali, an action is viewed as being brought about, while a substance is viewed as something that is of its own nature already established, set, although given terms in contexts, relative terms (*sambandhiśabda*) such as *mātṛ* 'mother', serve to show that a given substance may be being produced. This statement is supremely important in terms of Patañjali's semantics of verbs. We have to note here the following points:

1) In the context of the *bhāva*-based definition the term *kriyā* occurs.
2) What is meant by the term *kriyā* is characterized as *bhāvyate* '[that which is] brought into being' whose substantial equivalent is *bhāva*.
3) What is meant by the term *kriyā* is placed in juxtaposition with *dravya* (substance), in accordance with which *bhāvyate* or *bhāva* is contrasted with *svabhāvasiddha*.
4) The notion of *svabhāva* 'own nature' is introduced.

These points also shall be dealt with later.[9] There is no need to add at the moment than that it is no exaggeration to say that Patañjali's introduction of the notion of *svabhāva* 'own nature' here forms his substantial contribution to the semantics of verbs.

4.6.3. Evidence for the denotation of *bhāva* by *pac*

As evidence that *pac* and the like denote actions (*kriyā*), Patañjali pointed out the collocation of the verb *kṛ* with the verb *pac* in the question-and-answer *kiṃ karoti—pacati*. Here in the context of the *bhāva*-based definition, the following triplet of utterances is introduced as evidence to show that items such as *pac* denote *bhāva*.[10]

---

[9] See Section 5 [5.2.3].

[10] See fn. 10 in the present section.

bhavati pacati; bhavati pakṣyati; bhavaty apākṣīt.

In this triplet of utterances we have three different forms of the verb *pac* with the same form *bhavati* (3rd sg. pres.): *pacati* (3rd sg. pres.), *pakṣyati* (3rd sg. fut.), *apākṣīt* (3rd sg. aor.). An appreciable difference between derivates of the verb *kṛ* used in expressions of the type *kiṃ karoti—pacati* and those of the verb *bhū* used in expressions of the type *bhavati pacati* is as follows: While according to cases the verb *kṛ* may take a verb ending for any tense, person, and number, the verb *bhū* remains taking the same verb ending *-ti*, 3rd sg. pres. Thus, for example, we have *kiṃ karoti—pacati, kim akārṣīt— apākṣīt, kiṃ kariṣyati—pakṣyati; bhavati pacati, bhavati pakṣyati, bhavaty apākṣīt.*[11] Needless to say, how the term *bhāva* is to be interpreted depends upon what meaning is to be ascribed to such an utterance as *bhavati pacati.*

Now, given utterances like *bhavati pacati*, what relation does there obtain between the meanings of the verbs *bhū* and *pac* and on what relation between them is it grounded to establish that the item *pac* denotes *bhāva*? Patañjali indicates that there can obtain two types of relations between them: the relation of concurrence (*sāmānādhikaraṇya*) and that of what is to be accomplished and what does the accomplishing (*sādhyasādhanabhāva*).

4.6.3.1. The relation of concurrence (*sāmānādhikaraṇya*)

Between the meanings of the verbs *kṛ* and *pac* in the question-and-answer *kiṃ karoti—pacati*, Patañjali has found the relation of concurrence (*sāmānādhikaraṇya*). He first tries to apply the same relation to the case at issue.[12]

If we find the relation of concurrence between the meanings of the verbs *bhū* and *pac* in the utterance *bhavati pacati*, the utterance will mean 'one who is currently cooking exists'. For, the relation

---

[11] *MBh* ad *A*1.3.1 (I.256.25–27): *karotiḥ pacādīnāṃ sarvān kālān sarvān puruṣān sarvāṇi vacanāny anuvartate, bhavatiḥ punar vartamānakālam caikatvaṃ ca* / We do not have utterances such as *bhaviṣyati pakṣyati* (3rd sg. fut.) and *bhavataḥ pacataḥ* (3rd du. pres.).

[12] *MBh* ad *A*1.3.1 (I.256.18–20): *kathaṃ punar jñāyate—bhāvavacanāḥ pacādaya iti / yad eteṣāṃ bhavatinā sāmānādhikaraṇyaṃ—bhavati pacati, bhavati pakṣyati, bhavaty apākṣīd iti* /

of concurrence which obtains here is such that the meaning of *bhū* and that of *pac* have the same locus, in other words, they have the same agent for their loci. Therefore it has to be understood that one who exists is the same as one who is currently cooking. As is evident, *bhū* means *sattā* 'be, exist' in this case. The acts of cooking and coming into being (*janman*) cannot take place concurrently.

The attempt in question to find the relation of concurrence between the meanings of the verbs *bhū* and *pac* in the given utterances, it is to be noted, is merely to offer a tentative solution. For, granted that there obtains the relation of concurrence between the meanings of the verbs *bhū* and *pac*, the relation cannot prove that the verb *pac* denotes a specific *bhāva* (**bhāvaviśeṣa*) as the relation between the meanings of the verbs *kṛ* and *pac* proves that the verb *pac* denotes a specific action (*kriyāviśeṣa*).[13]

4.6.3.2. The relation of what is to be accomplished and what does the accomplishing (*sādhyasādhanabhāva*)

In addition to the relation of concurrence, Patañjali finds another relation between the meanings of the verbs *bhū* and *pac*. He states as follows:

> *MBh* ad *A*1.3.1 (I.256.28): *pacādayaḥ kriyā bhavatikriyāyāḥ kartryo bhavanti* /
> "Actions that are denoted by items such as *pac* are agents (*kartṛ*) of the act denoted by the verb *bhū*."

The analysis given here of the meaning of the utterance *bhavati pacati* shows that the meaning of the verb *pac* serves as agent with respect to the accomplishment of the act denoted by the verb *bhū*.[14]

---

[13] See Section 4, Part 2 [4.3.3].

[14] This analysis of a sentence meaning assumed to be understood from an utterance such as *bhavati pacati* provides later Pāṇinīyas like Kauṇḍabhaṭṭa with grounds for their view of *dhātvarthamukhyaviśeṣyakabodha*, according to which a verb in a sentence contributes its meaning, an action, as the chief qualificand around which other meanings conveyed by other items gather as qualifier. See *VBhS* on *VSK*2: *bhūvādisūtrādisthakriyāprādhānyabodhakabhāṣyāc ca dhātvarthabhāvanāprādhā-*

As Kaiyaṭa explicates,[15] this amounts to saying that the relation obtaining between the meanings of the verbs *bhū* and *pac* is a relation of what is to be accomplished and what does the accomplishing (*sādhyasādhanabhāva*) and not a relation of concurrence in terms of the relation of universal and particular (*sāmānyaviśeṣabhāva*) on which the relation of concurrence between the meanings of the verbs *kṛ* and *pac* in *kiṃ karoti—pacati* is founded.[16]

Under this analysis, to be sure, the verb *bhū* may convey any of its two meanings, *sattā* and *janman*, but Patañjali, assuming that the verb *bhū* in question means *janman*, intends to demonstrate that items like *pac* denote *bhāva* as taken to be what comes into being. Therefore, one may understand from the utterance *bhavati pacati* that the act of cooking someone is currently performing is coming into being.

In effect, it is the relation thus described in the semantic structure of the utterance *bhavati pacati* that opens the door to the interpretation of the term *bhāva* as *bhavatīti bhāvaḥ* 'what comes into being is spoken of as *bhāva*' (the second interpretation of *bhāva*).

4.6.4. *A*1.3.1 as a *bhāva*-based definition

As I have mentioned in the beginning of this section, *A*1.3.1 *bhūvādayo dhātavaḥ* admits of an interpretation that the sūtra itself is a kind of *bhāva*-based definition of the term *dhātu*. According to Patañjali, we may take *A*1.3.1 as intending to say that a signifier (*vādi*) of what comes into being (*bhū*) is called *dhātu*. The key to this interpretation is to read into the present sūtra the term *bhū* which is derived from the verb *bhū* by adding the kṛt affix ***kvip*** to convey an agent. Under this interpretation the term *bhū* in the sūtra means 'that which comes into being'. It has to

---

nyam adhyavasīyate / *Darpaṇa* thereon: *itthaṃ hi tatra bhāṣyam—kā tarhīyaṃ vācoyuktiḥ pacati bhavati tvaṃ pacasi bhavasi pakṣyati bhavatīti / saiṣā vācoyuktiḥ, pacādikriyā bhavatikriyāyāḥ kartryo bhavanti iti / tena cāhatyaiva pacādyarthakriyākartṛkabhavanakriyāyāḥ prādhānyaṃ pratipādyate /*

[15] *Pradīpa* on *MBh* ad *A*1.3.1 (II.188): *pacādaya iti / sādhyasādhanabhāvaḥ sambandho na tu sāmānyaviśeṣabhāva ity arthaḥ /*

[16] See Section 4, Part 2 [4.3.3].

be noted in this connection that the present interpretation is proposed on the assumption that the dhātupāṭha is assigned new roles proposed by Kātyāyana in his twelfth and thirteenth vārttikas, the proposal being finally rejected by Patañjali.[17]

The interpretation of *A*1.3.1 made in this way shall be a target of an independent investigation.[18]

4.7. On *vt.* 11

4.7.1. Revision of the *bhāva*-based definition

The eleventh vārttika forms a solution for the problem brought up by the eighth vārttika. According to Kātyāyana, the *bhāva*-based definition involves an undesirable consequence that the verb ending is called *dhātu* which occurs after a verb when *bhāva*, the meaning of the verb, is to be signified, in order to avert which consequence a modification to the *bhāva*-based definition has to be proposed. The proposed definition with a modification is:

prathamabhāvavacano dhātuḥ.

With reference to this revised *bhāva*-based definition, Patañjali naturally imposed on himself a task of making clear how the compound *prathamabhāvavacana* is to be analyzed. What is to be noted in this context is that in carrying out the task, he discussed problems that would arise if only a semantic definition of the term *dhātu* were provided in Pāṇini's grammar.

4.7.2. *A*1.3.1 and *A*3.1.32

As has already been said, Pāṇini has two sūtras to assign the class name *dhātu* to items: A1.3.1 *bhūvādayo dhātavaḥ* and A3.1.32 *sanādyantā dhātavaḥ.* The distinction between these sūtras reflects the one between two groups of items which signify actions: items unanalyzable into their constituents and items analyzable into

---

[17] *MBh* ad A1.3.1 (I.257.11–14): *paṭhiṣyati hy ācāryo bhūvādipāṭhaḥ prātipadikāṇapayatyādinivṛttyartha iti / yāvatā paṭhiṣyati pacādayaś ca kriyā bhavatikriyāyāḥ kartryo bhavantīti astv ayaṃ kartṛsādhanaḥ. bhavatīti bhāva iti / kiṃ vaktavyam etat / na hi /* See Sections 7 [7.2] and 8.

[18] See Section 7.

their constituents.[19] It is natural to assume that these two sūtras have their respective domains of application. For example, the primitive verb *pac* (***ḍupacàṣ***) in *pacati* and the derived verb *putrīya* (*putra-am* + ***k****yac*; *A*3.1.8) in *putrīyati* '. . . desires a son for himself' are to have the name *dhātu* by *A*1.3.1 and *A*3.1.32, respectively, though the heading *A*3.1.91 *dhātoḥ* does not anticipate this distinction. However, such assumption is acceptable only if *A*1.3.1 is interpreted as the dhātupāṭha-based definition of the term *dhātu*. Consider what Patañjali says in his Bhāṣya on *A*3.1.32.

> *MBh* ad *A*3.1.32 (II.42.1–2): *kimarthaṃ punar idam ucyate / na bhūvādayo dhātava ity eva siddham / na siddhyati / pāṭhena dhātusaṃjñā kriyate na ceme tatra paṭhyante /*
> "[Objection] But for what purpose is this sūtra [*A*3.1.32] stated? Is it not established only by *A*1.3.1 that items ending in the affixes *sa**n*** etc. are called *dhātu*?
> [Answer] No, it is not established. [Pāṇini means by *A*1.3.1 that] the class name *dhātu* is assigned to items by virtue of their being listed in the dhātupāṭha. And these items [which end in the affixes *sa**n*** etc.] are not recited there in the dhātupāṭha."

From this statement, we clearly see that Patañjali here admits that *A*1.3.1 can be interpreted in two ways. First of all, Patañjali, who says *pāṭhena dhātusaṃjñā kriyate*, takes *A*1.3.1 as intended to be the dhātupāṭha-based definition of the term *dhātu* as Kātyāyana did in his first vārttika. As a matter of course, if *A*1.3.1 is interpreted in this way, *A*3.1.32 will have an independent domain of application, since, while the former applies to items listed in the dhātupāṭha, the latter applies to items which are not recited there. Patañjali points out, on the other hand, that *A*1.3.1 as otherwise interpreted includes the domain of application of *A*3.1.32. Then what interpretation of *A*1.3.1 could allow derived verbs such as *putrīya* to be called *dhātu*? Obviously, such an interpretation of *A*1.3.1 should be its interpretation as a semantic definition which is an alternative to its interpretation as the dhātupāṭha-based definition. As said, by *A*1.3.1 as a semantic def-

---

[19] See Introduction [0.2].

inition of the name *dhātu* it is intended that signifiers (*vādi*) of what comes into being (*bhū*) be called *dhātu*. According to Patañjali, if *A*1.3.1 is interpreted in this manner, items that end in affixes such as ***san*** may be called *dhātu* by the present sūtra itself in that they denote what comes into being.[20]

Here in his Bhāṣya on *A*1.3.1 also, Patañjali considers the same question of whether a semantic definition of the term *dhātu* can apply in the domain of application of *A*3.1.32, though here he speaks of a modified *bhāva*-based definition of the term *dhātu*: *prathamabhāvavacano dhātuḥ* (*vt.* 11) instead of *A*1.3.1 as semantically interpreted.[21]

---

[20] As Kaiyaṭa notes, we cannot take the dhātupāṭha-based definition Patañjali has in mind here simply as the same as that which has been proposed by Kātyāyana in his first vārttika. The dhātupāṭha-based definition here should be the one which is freed of the difficulties pointed out in *vts.* 2–3. Following Patañjali, Kaiyaṭa explains *A* 1.3.1 in two different ways. *Pradīpa* on *MBh* ad *A*3.1.32 (III.107–8): *bhuvo vādayo bhūvādaya ity arthāśrayaṇād iti bhāvaḥ / tataś ca kriyāvācitvāt sanādyantānāṃ dhātusaṃjñā sidhyatīty arthaḥ / pāṭheneti / ādiśabdasya pratyekaṃ sambandhād arthapāṭhābhyāṃ dhātusaṃjñā vihitā, tenāṇavayatyādayaḥ samānaśabdāś ca sarvanāmādayo nivartitā bhavanti . . . /* It is to be noted that Kaiyaṭa understands Patañjali to mean by *pāṭhena dhātusaṃjñā kriyate* that *A*1.3.1 be interpreted by taking into account both semantic (*artha*) and formal (*pāṭha*) aspects of items that are to have the name *dhātu*. According to Kaiyaṭa, if one takes the form *bhūvādayaḥ* in *A*1.3.1 as a ṣaṣṭhī tatpuruṣa paraphrased as *bhuvo vādayaḥ* (see the present section [4.6.4]) 'signifiers of what comes into being', the sūtra becomes a semantic definition of the term *dhātu*, so that it may cover the domain of application of *A*3.1.32. When he puts the question in the above-cited Bhāṣya, Patañjali has such an interpretation of the sūtra in mind. However, in answering the question, he has another interpretation of the sūtra. The interpretation is the one given by reading two *ādis*. See Section 7 [7.3].

[21] *MBh* ad *A*1.3.1 (I.258.2–6): *prathamabhāvagrahaṇaṃ ca kartavyam / prathamaṃ yo bhāvam āheti / kutaḥ punaḥ prāthamyam / kiṃ śabdata āhosvid arthataḥ / kiṃ cātaḥ / yadi śabdataḥ, sanādīnāṃ dhātusaṃjñā na prāpnoti—putrīyati vastrīyatīti / athārthataḥ, siddhā sanādīnāṃ dhātusaṃjñā, sa eva tu doṣo bhāvavacane tadarthapratyayapratiṣedha iti / evaṃ tarhi *nāpi śabdato nāpy arthataḥ / kiṃ tarhy abhidhānataḥ / sumadhyame 'bhidhāne yaḥ prathamaṃ bhāvam āha /* * I have adopted the reading in the Nirṇayasāgara Press and Rohatak editions. Kielhorn's edition reads: *naivārthato nāpi śabdataḥ*. In addition, I have corrected the punctuation for *kiṃ tarhi* in editions of the text for the reason stated

The modified *bhāva*-based definition admits of three different interpretations.

1) An item which denotes *bhāva* is called *dhātu* if it is the first one uttered. (*śabdataḥ* 'with respect to utterance')
2) An item which denotes the first *bhāva* is called *dhātu*. (*arthataḥ* 'with respect to meaning')
3) An item which first denotes *bhāva* is called *dhātu*. (*sumadhyame 'bhidhāne* 'with respect to denotation, faultless middle')[22]

According to the first interpretation, neither the affix *-e* in *śiśye* nor *putrīya* in *putrīyati* can be called *dhātu*. The affix *-e* is the second item which denotes *bhāva* so that it cannot be called *dhātu*. In the case of *putrīya*, the first item *putra* does not denote *bhāva* and it is the second item *-ya* (***kyac***) that denotes *bhāva* in the form of the act of desiring (*icchā*). Consequently, *putrīya* is not regarded as an item that ends in an item which denotes *bhāva* and which is the first one uttered.[23] Therefore it cannot be called *dhātu*.

The second interpretation allows both the affix *-e* and the item *putrīya* to have the name *dhātu*, since the former denotes the first *bhāva* in that it is a *svārthika* affix and the latter is an item ending in *-ya* which denotes the first *bhāva* in that the item *putra*, being a nominal base, does not denote *bhāva*.

The desired result is obtained under the third interpretation. In the case of *śiśye*, an item which first denotes *bhāva* is the base *śī* and not the affix *-e*, so that the affix *-e* cannot have the name *dhātu*. In the case of *putrīya*, the affix *-ya* first denotes *bhāva*, so that the item *putrīya* is properly deemed to be an item that

in Section 2, fn. 8.

[22] The denotative function (*abhidhāna*) is called *madhyama* 'middle' in that it is neither a linguistic unit nor a meaning conveyed by it.

[23] Note that in the domain of application of *A*3.1.32 *tadantavidhi* (*A*1.1.72) is taken into consideration so that *prathamabhāvavacano dhātuḥ* may be interpreted as *prathamabhāvavacanānto dhātuḥ*. *Uddyota* on *MBh* ad *A*1.3.1 (II.193): *lakṣaṇe bhāvavacanas tadantaś ca gṛhyate iti tadantasya dhātutvasiddhiḥ . . . |*

ends in an item which first denotes *bhāva* and hence is called *dhātu*. Thus it is plain that the third interpretation serves to block the over-application of the term *dhātu* to affixes which denote *bhāva* and makes it possible for the name *dhātu* to apply to items that end in the affix ***kyac***.

As is pointed out by Kaiyaṭa,[24] however, the modified *bhāva*-based definition as interpreted in 3), it is evident, cannot apply to items which terminate in affixes that are considered to be *svārthikas*. Take *gopāyati* '. . . guards' for example. The affix *āya*, being a *svārthika*, is introduced after the verb *gup* 'guard' to convey the meaning of that verb (*A*3.1.28). Now the item *gopāya* is not an item which ends in an item that first denotes *bhāva*, since in the sequence *gopāya* what first denotes *bhāva* is the primitive verb *gup*. Therefore, it follows that the revised *bhāva*-based definition of the term *dhātu* does not apply to all items which ends in affixes specified in *A*3.1.5–31 and hence *A*3.1.32 has for its domain of application items which end in *svārthika* affixes such as *āya*. With the result that, even if a semantic definition of the term *dhātu* alone were given, *A*3.1.32 would claim its own independent domain of application.

---

[24] *Pradīpa* on *MBh* ad *A* 1.3.1 (II.193): *atra pakṣe yathā śiśya iti pratyayasya dhātusaṃjñā na bhavati tathā svārthikānām āyādīnām api na prāpnoti—gopāyati kāmayate iti / tadarthaṃ sanādyantā dhātava iti paṭhitavyam eva / kāmayate* '. . . loves': *kāmi* (*kam* + ***ṇiṅ***; *A*3.1.30).

Section 4

Part 4: Bhāṣya on vārttikas 12–13 (roles of the dhātupāṭha)

4.8. On *vts.* 12–13

Arguments brought forward by Patañjali with reference to the twelfth and thirteenth vārttikas also deserve independent studies. I shall outline them only briefly here.

4.8.1. Preliminaries

As a semantic definition of the term *dhātu*, Kātyāyana finally accepted the revised *bhāva*-based definition: *prathamabhāvavacano dhātuḥ*, which Patañjali suggested reading as 'an item which first denotes *bhāva* is called *dhātu*'. Now the dhātupāṭha-based definition was such that items listed in the dhātupāṭha are called *dhātu*. Given that the term *dhātu* can be semantically defined in the above-mentioned way, what is the use of still having the dhātupāṭha in addition to the semantic definition? It was in order to answer this question that Kātyāyana stated the twelfth and thirteenth vārttikas.

As an indispensable preliminary to the discussion on the roles Kātyāyana assumed the dhātupāṭha to play, what Patañjali had to do were the following two things:

1) To make the *kriyā*-based definition equivalent to the *bhāva*-based definition so that one can have full definition of the term *dhātu* in either form.[1]

2) To give an interpretation of *A*1.3.1 in conformity with the framework created by Kātyāyana.

4.8.1.1. As has been seen in the preceding section, for Patañjali, a couple of rules, the rule for the revised *bhāva*-based definition and *A*3.1.32, taken together, cover all items to be called *dhātu* in

---

[1] As one can revise the *bhāva*-based definition, so also can one revise the *kriyā*-based definition to have *prathamakriyāvacano dhātuḥ*. *Pradīpa* on *MBh* ad *A*1.3.1 (II.193): *kevalaṃ prathamabhāvagrahaṇam apanīya prathamakriyāgrahaṇaṃ ceti kriyāgrahaṇaṃ kartavyam* / See Section 3 [3.2.4].

Pāṇini's grammar. In the course of arriving at this conclusion, he also makes clear the following point by arguing that *A*3.1.32 which does not presuppose the presence of the dhātupāṭha has an independent domain of application: That is, given a semantic definition in the form of the revised *bhāva*-based definition, there is no chance at all of the dhātupāṭha coming in, in such a way as to supply items to be called *dhātu*.

But if we were given a narrower semantic definition, we would not get rid of the need of the dhātupāṭha for defining the term. In this case, what else could allow one to assign the name *dhātu* to items which are not covered by the semantic definition in question? As said, the *kriyā*-based definition is said to be narrower in the sense that it does not apply to items such as *as*. Therefore, the upholders of the *kriyā*-based definition might claim that the dhātupāṭha is necessary to assign the name *dhātu* at least to items that are not covered by their definition.

In order to discuss the roles of the dhātupāṭha whose role of furnishing items to be called *dhātu* has been given up as the denial of the validity of the dhātupāṭha-based definition demands, thus, Patañjali had to take up again the *kriyā*-based definition and to try to make it exhaustive. He made such a trial in the way that he proved the meaning of the verb *as* to be an action (*kriyā*) exactly in the same sense as meanings of items such as *pac*.

Patañjali demonstrates that meanings of items like *as* are actions in two manners: by means of logical reasoning and *āgama* (traditional authorization). That is, he proves that items such as *as* and the like denote actions (*kriyā*), by means of finding in what are denoted by them those properties of an action (*kriyādharma*)[2] which are found in what are denoted by items of the *kṛ* type such as *pac*, and by virtue of resorting to the tradition which declares that a meaning of such an item as *as* comes under actions. Interestingly, in addition to these, he also examines in this context the claims for the non-occurrence of the question-and-answer *kiṃ karoti—asti* adduced as evidence in disproof of the view that the item *as* denotes an action.

---

[2]The term *kriyādharma* is used by Helārāja. See Section 6.

4.8.1.2. It is natural that once meanings of items like *as* are proved to be actions (*kriyā*), the *kriyā*-based definition of the term *dhātu* becomes exhaustive so that we do not have to expect the dhātupāṭha to play a part in defining the term. Before entering the discussion on the proof in question, Patañjali has stated that a *kriyā*-based definition has the same status as a *bhāva*-based definition except for the fact that the former does not apply to items such as *as*. Now that such a defect is eliminated from it, the *kriyā*-based definition is on a par with the *bhāva*-based definition.[3] At this point Patañjali can ask about a *raison d'être* of the dhātupāṭha.

But we must note the following point. The *bhāva*-based definition (with a modification) and the dhātupāṭha are in Kātyāyana's frame of reference, *A*1.3.1 being left aside. Patañjali, on the other hand, created a new frame of reference in which one could argue about the above, by proposing to read the sūtra in question from a different perspective, namely as involving the indication of the dhātupāṭha with new roles, the roles other than the one as a supplier of items to be called *dhātu*, as well as defining the term *dhātu* semantically.

4.8.2. Demonstration that the meaning of the verb *as* is an action: logical reasoning

As suggested above, Patañjali tries to prove that meanings of items such as *as* are actions by means of finding *kriyādharma* in those meanings. The *kriyādharma* is twofold: the property of excluding other actions and the property of being associated with time.

---

[3] *MBh* ad *A*1.3.1 (I.258.7–8): *iha ya eva bhāvavacane dhātau doṣās ta eva kriyāvacane 'pi* / *tatra ta eva parihārāḥ* / *tatredam aparihṛtam—astibhavatividyatīnāṃ dhātutvam iti* / *tasya parihāraḥ* / Needless to say, Patañjali can propose a revised *kriyā*-based definition such as *prathamakriyāvacano dhātuḥ* 'an item which first denotes an action is called *dhātu*'. See fn.1 in this section.

4.8.2.1. Exclusion of other actions

An action consists in exclusion of other actions (*kriyāyāḥ kriyā nivartikā bhavati*). This is grounded on the fact that the action may be regarded as what is defined as follows:

> *MBh* ad *A*1.3.1 (I.258.11): *kārakāṇāṃ pravṛttiviśeṣaḥ kriyā* /
> "An action consists in kārakas' different ways of performing activities."

This definition specifies that an action is a kāraka's activity which is differentiated from activities of other kārakas. When the utterance *devadatto dvidhā bhuṅkte* 'Devadatta is eating in two manners' is used, one understands that the activity of eating is differentiated in terms of the way in which it is performed.[5] What is more, when the item *bhuṅkte* '. . . is eating' is uttered, one understands that a certain agent is currently not cooking and, as a consequence, grasps the exclusion of the act of cooking which is understood from the item *pacati* '. . . is cooking'. In this way, according to Patañjali, an action consists in being excluded from other actions belonging to the same class (*sajātīya*) and to a different class (*vijātīya*).[6] If one can find this property of an action in what the item *as* denotes, then one may say that the meaning of the item *as* is also an action.

---

[4] Rocher [1969: 79]: "an action is a specific manifestation of the factors involved." Filliozat [1986: 51]: "La *kriyā* est lá mise en œuvre particulière des facteurs de réalisation." Joshi/Roodbergen [1994: 3]: "a *kriyā* is a particular way of *kārakas* becoming operative."

[5] Even with reference to one and the same agent Devadatta, we may speak of him as different kārakas according to different actions in which he is involved. That is why *A*2.3.7 *saptamīpañcamyau kārakamadhye* allows one to use the utterance *adya bhuktvā devadatto dvyahe bhoktā* 'After eating today, Devadatta will eat in two days'. The two actions of eating are differentiated from each other in time. One and the same agent Devadatta meets the condition *kārakamadhye* 'between two kārakas'.

[6] I just follow Helārāja who clearly states that the differentiation in activity holds with respect both to members of the same class and to those of a different class. *Prakāśa* on *VP*3.8.1: *viśeṣaś ca sajātīyād vijātīyāc ca* /

The context in which the definition of an action under consideration is proposed is as follows:

MBh ad *A*1.3.1 (I.258.8–11): *kāṃ punaḥ kriyāṃ bhavān matvāha—astibhavatividyatīnāṃ dhātusaṃjñā na prāpnotīti / kiṃ yat tad devadattaḥ kaṃsapātryāṃ pāṇinaudanaṃ bhuṅkta iti / na brūmaḥ kārakāṇi kriyeti / kiṃ tarhi / kārakāṇāṃ pravṛttiviśeṣaḥ kriyā /*

"[Question] But what do you have in mind as an action when you say that the name *dhātu* does not obtain for *as, bhū, vid*? Do you mean that a variety of kārakas as involved in the accomplishment of an act conveyed by the utterance *devadattaḥ kaṃsapātryāṃ pāṇinaudanaṃ bhuṅkte* 'Devadatta is eating rice-gruel in a bell-metal dish with his hand' are spoken of as an action?
[Answer] No, we do not mean that kārakas themselves are spoken of as an action (*kārakāṇi kriyā*).
[Question] Then what?
[Answer] We mean: *kārakāṇāṃ pravṛttiviśeṣaḥ kriyā*."

From this it is clear that Patañjali does not consider at first that the proposed definition of an action: *kārakāṇāṃ pravṛttiviśeṣaḥ kriyā* leads to a desired result that meanings of items such as *as* are actions. As he argues, it is because an action is defined in this way that items like *as* are not called *dhātu*. An idea underlying Patañjali's statement here is explained by Kaiyaṭa and Helārāja as follows:

Pradīpa on *MBh* ad *A*1.3.1 (II.114): *yathā ca bhojanakriyāṇāṃ parasparavailakṣaṇyāt pravṛttiviśeṣatvaṃ naivam astyādīnām /*

"It is not the case that just as acts like eating are differentiated activities (*pravṛttiviśeṣa*) because of their being different from one another, so also are meanings of items like *as*."

Prakāśa on *VP*3.8.1: *sattāyāś ca nirviśeṣatvād bhedābhāvaḥ /*

"In addition, *sattā* 'existence' is undifferentiated because of its being without distinction."

One thing is certain: If one takes the meaning of an item like *as* to be mere existence (*sattā*), one cannot apply the proposed definition of an action under consideration to it. In the case of the utterances *devadatto grāme 'sti* 'Devadatta is in the village' and *devadatto nagare 'sti* 'Devadatta is in the town', the existence itself of Devadatta is not differentiated. Patañjali was fully aware that one might argue from this perspective that the definition does not apply to meanings of items such as *as*, so that he introduced a special situation in which the verb *as* is used excluding other verbs and hence its meaning is regarded as a sort of activity in contrast with activities denoted by the latter. He placed the verb *as* in juxtaposition with the verb *mṛ* 'die'.

We also have to note the following point: The term *kāraka* in the statement *kārakāṇāṃ pravṛttiviseṣaḥ kriyā* may refer to any kāraka that gets involved in an action. Consider the following statement made by Bhartṛhari in the Sādhanasamuddesa of the *Vākyapadīya*:

> *VP*3.7.18: *niṣpattimātre kartṛtvaṃ sarvatraivāsti kārake / vyāpārabhedāpekṣāyāṃ karaṇatvādisambhavaḥ //*
> "Any kāraka has the property of being an agent (*kartṛtva*) with respect to the act in general of bringing about something (*niṣpattimātra*). However, when one expects a specific activity (*vyāpārabheda*) as what a kāraka brings about, the kāraka can be called *karaṇa* and so on."

As Bhartṛhari explicitly states, any kāraka involved in bringing an act to accomplishment is characterized as *niṣpādaka* or what brings about something; it brings about the main act through its own activity, that is, it functions toward the completion of the main action. Thus all the kārakas have their own activities, with respect to which they are regarded as agents. Now suppose that we have the utterance *x* (nom. sg.) *pravartate* with the variable *x*. Precisely for this reason we may put anything as functioning as kāraka into *x*.[7] For example, with respect to the situation conveyed

In addition, according to Patañjali, an agent is described as a *pravartayitṛ* 'one who causes another to perform an activity' of other kārakas by the utterance *devadatto 'sinā chinatti* 'Devadatta is cutting with an axe' where Devadatta and the axe serve respectively as agent and instrument, just as we can have *devadattaḥ pravartate* 'Devadatta is carrying out an activity', so can we have *asiḥ pravartate* 'The axe is carrying out an activity'. A full discussion shall be devoted to the problem relating to the interpretation of the present statement in Section 5.

4.8.2.2. Association with time

Patañjali observes that three time divisions, present, past, and future, are not manifested without an action (*nāntareṇa kriyāṃ bhūtabhaviṣyadvartamānāḥ kālā vyajyante*) and then applies this principle to the case in which the verb *as* is used: When the verb forms *asti* '. . . is', *abhūt* '. . . has been', and *bhaviṣyati* '. . . will be' are used, present, past, and future time are respectively manifested (*astyādibhiś cāpi bhūtabhaviṣyadvartamānakālā vyajyante*). According to Patañjali, this fact bears evidence that the item *as* denotes an action, since whatever is associated with time is nothing but an action. And, catching this aspect of an action, Bhartṛhari expressed it in the word *kālābhivyaktihetutva* 'the property of being a cause for time to manifest itself'.[8] Fuller discussion of how the association with time allows one to conceive that the meaning of the verb *as* is an action will be presented in Section 6.

(*MBh* ad *A*1.4.23 [I.326.10]: *yat sarveṣu sādhaneṣu saṃnihiteṣu kartā pravartayitā bhavati* /). When something is characterized as a *pravartayitṛ*, it is what causes others to perform an activity. From this also it is clear that all kārakas have their own *pravṛttis*. See also Section 4, Part 2, fn. 13.

[8] See Section 6, fn. 5. In his Bhāṣya on *A*3.1.67 Patañjali states that *tiṅabhihitabhāva* manifests time. What is called *tiṅabhihitabhāva* is nothing but a verb meaning. See Section 3, fn. 25.

4.8.3. Demonstration that the meaning of the verb *as* is an action: *āgama*

As regards the thesis that the meaning of the verb *as* is an action, Patañjali adds, we have the confirmatory testimony of the *Nirukta*. A relevant passage quoted therefrom is:

> *MBh* ad *A*1.3.1 (I.258.13–14): *ṣaḍ bhāvavikārā iti ha smāha bhagavān vārṣyāyaṇiḥ / jāyate 'sti vipariṇamate vardhate 'pakṣīyate vinaśyatīti /*[9]
>
> "Indeed, the Venerable Vārṣyāyaṇi said that there are six modes of *bhāva*. [The six modes of *bhāva* are:] *jāyate* '. . . is born', *asti* . . . is', *vipariṇamate* '. . . is changing', *vardhate* '. . . is growing', *apakṣīyate* '. . . is decaying', and *vinaśyati* '. . . is perishing'."

What Patañjali means to say is that *asti* is enumerated in the list of six modes of *bhāva* so that what is denoted by the verb *as* also claims to be an action. Of course, this is made possible by Patañjali's taking the term *bhāva* in the word *bhāvavikāra* as synonymous with the term *kriyā*.[10]

Interestingly Patañjali argues in this connection: If one says on the authority of the *Nirukta* that the meaning of the verb *as* enumerated in the list of six modes of *bhāva* is an action, then one can say in the same vein, on the authority of the *Nirukta*, that the meaning of the verb *sthā* 'remain, stand', which is not enumerated therein, is not an action.[11] However he continues to make clear that the meaning of the verb *sthā* is proved to be an action through inference from one of the *kriyādharmas*, the exclusion of other actions. By doing so, Patañjali has succeeded in showing that we can establish that a meaning of any verb is an

---

[9] *Nirukta*1.2. The word *bhagavān* is found neither in the original nor in the Nirnayasāgara Press edition.

[10] We know that Patañjali repeats the definition that a verb form (*ākhyāta*) is that whose principal meaning is *bhāva* (*bhāvapradhānam ākhyātam*), but says *kriyāpradhānam ākhyātam*. See *MBh* on *vt*. 2 ad *A*5.3.66 (II.418.15–16).

[11] *MBh* ad *A*1.3.1 (I.258.14–16): *sarvathā sthita ity atra dhātusaṃjñā na prāpnoti / bāhyo hy etebhyas tiṣṭhatiḥ /*

action if we accept the newly proposed definition of an action: *kārakāṇāṃ pravṛttiviśeṣaḥ kriyā.*

4.8.4. The rule of a question-and-answer

So far Patañjali has taken the following ground: While the answer *pacati* to the question *kiṃ karoti* proves that the verb *pac* denotes a particular action, the absence of the answer *asti* to the same question disproves the thesis that the verb *as* denotes a particular action. Now Patañjali argues that the non-occurrence of the question-and-answer *kiṃ karoti—asti* cannot be a negative evidence in disproof of the verb *as* denoting a particular action. According to him, the non-use of such a question-and-answer is not due to the fact that the verb *as* does not denote a particular action but to the fact that if one gives the answer *asti* to the question *kiṃ karoti*, this results in violating a certain rule as to the question-and-answer. Patañjali states:

> *MBh* ad *A* 1.3.1 (I.258.20): *nānyat pṛṣṭenānyad ākhyeyam* /
> "When one is asked a question about one thing, one should not say another thing in answer to the question."

What Patañjali means to say in this context is that in answer to the question *kiṃ karoti* which is put on the assumption that an agent with respect to the action denoted by the verb *kṛ* is existent, one cannot redundantly say *asti* 'he is existent'. The question is about a specific action which an existent agent is currently performing; and the answer refers to the existence itself of the agent. Obviously, one who makes an answer to the question *kiṃ karoti* by saying *asti* goes against the rule stated above. This implies that there may be a case in which the answer *asti* is used to the question *kiṃ karoti* on condition that the presence of an agent with respect to the meaning of the verb *kṛ* has not been ascertained.[12]

---

[12] See Section 6 [6.2].

4.8.5. Interpretations of *A* 1.3.1 both as indicating the dhātupāṭha with new roles and as defining the term *dhātu* semantically

As said, on the assumption that without the dhātupāṭha we can define the term *dhātu* solely from a semantic point of view, Patañjali provided a new frame of reference in which one could take *A*1.3.1 itself as indicating the dhātupāṭha and defining the term *dhātu* semantically, anticipating that the dhātupāṭha will embrace new roles replacing the role of supplying items to be called *dhātu*. This was done in a surprisingly skillful way.

Let us take the item *bhūvā* in the compound *bhūvādayaḥ* in *A*1.3.1 as a dvandva compound formed from the items *bhū* and *vā*. If we take the *bhū* as a mere form (*rūpa*) and the item *vā* as a meaningful unit (*arthavat*), or if we take the former as a meaningful unit and the latter as a mere form, then we can arrive at the indication of the dhātupāṭha as well as the semantic definition, with the help of the item *ādi*. On the assumption that the semantic definition available to us is satisfactory, new roles other than that of supplying items to be called *dhātu* are naturally to be allotted to the dhātupāṭha. But what is it that differentiates between the approaches to the item *bhūvā*—one takes the item *bhū* as a meaningful unit and the other takes the item *vā* as a meaningful unit? Now we have two kinds of semantic definitions: *kriyā*-based definition and *bhāva*-based definition. According to Patañjali, the upholders of the *kriyā*-based definition take notice of the item *vā* 'go, strike' as a meaningful unit, while the upholders of the *bhāva*-based definition take notice of the item *bhū* 'be, be born' as a meaningful unit. This is possible only if we assume that these two semantic definitions have different connotations, though they have something in common.[13]

[13]That is why Patañjali begins the argument under consideration by saying: *atha yady eva kriyāvacano dhātur ity eṣa pakṣo 'thāpi bhāvavacano dhātur iti kiṃ gatam etad iyatā sūtreṇa, āhosvid anyatarasmin pakṣe bhūyaḥ sūtraṃ kartavyam / gatam ity āha* (I.258.22–23) and goes on to take up the question concerning the role of the dhātupāṭha by stating: *yadi tarhi lakṣaṇaṃ kriyate, nedānīṃ pāṭhaḥ kartavyaḥ / kartavyaś ca / kiṃ prayojanam* (I.259.3). See Section 7 [7.3.2] and Section

As we shall see later in the next section, early teachers distinguish between *kriyā*-based and *bhāva*-based definitions in terms of whether verb meanings are viewed dynamically or statically.[14] Of course, if we stick to this kind of difference between *kriyā* and *bhāva*, it naturally follows that the *kriyā*-based definition which is applicable to the item *vā* does not apply to the item *bhū* and that the *bhāva*-based definition which is applicable to the item *bhū* does not apply to the item *vā*. That is why Patañjali suggests reading into the sūtra the word *ādi* used in the sense of *prakāra* 'similarity' (*sādṛsya*), whereby the different approaches to the item *bhūvā* may be made possible and the difference in connotation between the two semantic definitions may be ironed out. In this connection it cannot be emphasized too strongly that the semantic definitions in question as input are different from the ones as output on account of the introduction of the notion of similarity.

Not only is the word *ādi* used in the sense of *prakāra* read there, but also the word *ādi* used with reference to *vyavasthā* is read there. For, as said, the dhātupāṭha is indicated by using a bahuvrīhi compound with -*ādi* used in that sense.[15]

Thus, we see that Patañjali recognizes the following combinations as obtainable here:

1. *bhū* (form) + *ādi* (*vyavasthā*) *vā* (meaningful unit) + *ādi* (*prakāra*)
2. *bhū* (meaningful unit) + *ādi* (*prakāra*) *vā* (form) + *ādi* (*vyavasthā*)

According to Patañjali, one who adopts the *kriyā*-based definition will read A1.3.1 in conformity with combination 1 as follows:

Items which belong to the set beginning with *bhū* and which are like *vā* 'go, strike' are called *dhātu* (*bhū ityevamādayo vā ityevaṃprakārāḥ*).

---

8 [8.2.2.1].

[14] See Section 5 [5.1].

[15] See Section 4, Part 1 [4.1.1.2].

On the other hand, one who accepts the *bhāva*-based definition will interpret the sūtra in question in conformity with combination 2 in the following manner:

> Items which belong to the set beginning with *vā* and which are like *bhū* 'be, be born' are called *dhātu* (*vā ityevamādayo bhū ityevamprakārāḥ*).

These interpretations of *A*1.3.1 shall be treated again in Section 7.

4.8.6. Denial of the dhātupāṭha's functions

Kātyāyana, having ended the discussion on semantic definitions in the eleventh vārttika, went on to propose functions to be carried out by the dhātupāṭha in the twelfth and thirteenth vārttikas. An underlying idea was: When the purpose of defining the term *dhātu* has been established as satisfactorily accomplished by a semantic definition and therefore the way of defining it from a formal point of view has to be abandoned, what else than supply items to be called *dhātu* could the dhātupāṭha do?

The functions of the dhātupāṭha newly proposed by Kātyāyana in place of its function of supplying items to be called *dhātu* for the dhātupāṭha-based definition were: 1) to prevent the name *dhātu* from applying to nominal bases (*prātipadikanivṛttyartha*), 2) to prevent the name *dhātu* from applying to corruptions like *āṇapi*- (*āṇapayatyādinivṛttyartha*). In addition to these, Kātyāyana pointed out the following functions as those which Pāṇini's grammar itself presupposed: 3) to make known accentuations of base vowels (*svarajñāpanāya*), and 4) to make known markers (*anubandhajñāpanāya*). Functions 1) and 2) are looked for in order for the dhātupāṭha to supplement a semantic definition of the term *dhātu* and functions 3) and 4) for it to be ancillary to the sūtrapāṭha, the *Aṣṭādhyāyī*.

Interestingly and importantly enough, we find in the Bhāṣya on the vārttikas under consideration that Patañjali is severely critical of Kātyāyana who advances such an opinion.

With reference to the dhātupāṭha's functions of making known accentuations of base vowels and markers stated in *vt.* 13, Patañjali points out the difficulty that if we admitted that the dhātupāṭha has such functions, the necessity of being recited in the dhātupāṭha would be restricted to those verbs which are specified in operational rules. And besides, in relation to the function preventive of the over-application of the term *dhātu* to corruptions stated in *vt.* 12, he denies that the dhātupāṭha serves to perform such a function, based upon the fact that one may mistakenly use a corrupted form instead of using a correct form which is recited in the dhātupāṭha. According to Patañjali, such a prevention against the use of corruptions is possible only if we closely observe the usage of the śiṣṭas (*śiṣṭaprayoga*).

Notably, with regard to the remaining function of the dhātupāṭha, the function of avoiding the over-application of the term *dhātu* to nominal bases, he cites no example of nominal bases that are subject to having the name *dhātu*.

The argument developed by Patañjali under these vārttikas is very important from the point of view of his theory of semantics and grammar. He means to say that if the role of providing a definition of the term *dhātu* is assigned to a semantic definition, his semantic framework, as such, will not allow us to assume that the dhātupāṭha has the above-mentioned roles as Kātyāyana does. The key to an understanding of his attitude toward the dhātupāṭha here is his introduction of the notion of *svabhāva* 'own nature' or a linguistic item's intrinsic denotative nature.

Patañjali's approach to the dhātupāṭha also deserves an independent investigation.[16]

4.8.7. Survey of the *Mahābhāṣya* on A1.3.1

At this point, let us put the whole argument by Patañjali on *A*1.3.1 briefly from the point of view of how the sūtra in question is to be interpreted. He has offered its different interpretations by reading into the sūtra

1) the sound *-v-* meant for auspiciousness, whereby the dhātupāṭha-based definition of the term *dhātu* is accounted for;
2) the item *bhū* as an item ending in the kṛt affix ***kvip***, which

[16] See Section 8.

results in *A*1.3.1 being a purely semantic definition of the term *dhātu*;

3) two types of *ādi*, which leads to two kinds of definitions in both of which the indication of the dhātupāṭha with a role other than that of supplying items to be called *dhātu* and semantic definitions are merged.

What does this history of interpretations of *A*1.3.1 demonstrate? In connection with the first interpretation Patañjali showed its limits, with reference to the second he proposed it on the assumption that the dhātupāṭha has a complementary role, and concerning the third he denied the roles of the dhātupāṭha proposed by Kātyāyana. We clearly see that in his Bhāṣya on the sūtra in question Patañjali tries to show what would follow if we carried a formal definition based upon the dhātupāṭha or a semantic definition to its full extreme. According to him, the formal definition ends up requiring the segmentation of a sequence of sounds such as *bhvedha*, and the semantic definition results in denying the roles of the dhātupāṭha. In this connection it is important to keep in mind that in his formal definition no semantic considerations should be invoked at all, as he presupposes. In addition, it is certain that he considers a purely semantic interpretation of the sūtra, involving less prolixity, to be preferable from a theoretical point of view.

Apart from the question on the interpretation of *A*1.3.1, of the two kinds of semantic definitions Kātyāyana alternatively proposed, *kriyā*-based and *bhāva*-based definitions, with reference to the former, Patañjali tried to overcome the fault that it would not apply in items which convey the meaning 'be', whereas, with reference to the latter, Patañjali attempted a detailed analysis of the term *bhāva*. The reasons that Patañjali made an effort to clarify the notion of *bhāva* in the *bhāva*-based definition were as follows: First, the definition in question was proposed by Kātyāyana as that which has no fault of non-inclusion and in this regard it seemed to Patañjali that a verb meaning was something that could be understood as *bhāva*. Secondly, the *bhāva*-based definition had a great deal of relevance to a semantic interpretation of *A*1.3.1 according to which the form *bhū* that is derived from the verb *bhū* in the same way as the form *bhāva* is read into the sūtra.

What forms the core of the arguments Patañjali brings forward in his Bhāṣya on *A* 1.3.1 lies in his denial of the functions Kātyāyana claims the dhātupāṭha carries out in combination with a semantic definition of the term *dhātu*. Patañjali conceived a device which replaced the dhātupāṭha, a device which made it necessary to respect the usage of the śiṣṭas. The device is *svabhāva* or an intrinsic denotative nature of a linguistic item.

Section 5

kriyā and *bhāva*

5.0. *kriyā* and *bhāva*

Now what is a verb meaning (*dhātvartha*)? In order to answer this question, we have to consider what on earth are the action (*kriyā*) and *bhāva* which are respectively referred to in the *kriyā*-based definition and the *bhāva*-based definition.

Regarding the *kriyā*-based and *bhāva*-based definitions, the following has been made clear so far: For Kātyāyana, while the *kriyā*-based definition does not apply to verbs of the *as* 'be/become' class, the *bhāva*-based definition applies to verbs of the *kṛ* 'do/make' class as well as those of the *as* class. For Patañjali also, the same holds. However, for Patañjali, on the assumption that meanings of verbs of the *as* class and those of verbs of the *kṛ* class have common properties, it is also possible to treat the meanings of verbs of the *as* class as actions (*kriyā*) and therefore to let the *kriyā*-based definition apply to verbs of the *as* class. All this, of course, shows that a verb meaning can be viewed from various angles. But, when in this way Kātyāyana and Patañjali treat a verb meaning as *kriyā* or *bhāva*, what do they mean by the terms *kriyā* and *bhāva* at all?

As said, while Patañjali undertakes the task of clarifying the notions of *kriyā* and *bhāva,* Kātyāyana does not expressly tell us anything about the question of what he means by those terms. However, if we look into what later Pāṇinīyas say in connection with a classification of verbs, we may expect a clarification about how Kātyāyana conceives of *kriyā* and *bhāva*. But it is also to be noticed that the meanings of verbs of the *as* class which Kātyāyana cannot call *kriyā* can be termed *kriyā* by Patañjali. What is suggested by this fact is, undoubtedly, that we have to shun imposing Patañjali's way of viewing a verb meaning on Kātyāyana's. It will be proper to treat Kātyāyana's and Patañjali's notions of *kriyā* and *bhāva* separately. Thus this section shall be devoted to making clear what Kātyāyana means by the terms *kriyā* and *bhāva* in his semantic definitions and then what Patañjali intends by the very same terms.

5.1. *kriyā*-based and *bhāva*-based definitions by early teachers

According to Helārāja, the *kriyā*-based definition of the term *dhātu* which Kātyāyana proposed as an alternative to the dhātupāṭha-based definition is nothing but that which had already been framed by early teachers (*pūrvācāryalakṣaṇa*). That is, the definition is pre-Paṇinian.[1] Interestingly, in his commentary on the Kriyāsamuddeśa of the *Vākyapadīya* Helārāja does not refer to the *bhāva*-based definition whatsoever. Of course, this is simply due to the given context in which Bhartṛhari in the Kriyāsamuddeśa does not talk about a verb meaning but a *kriyā* as the verb meaning, and moreover because of the fact that, following Patañjali, Bhartṛhari regards *bhāva* in the *bhāva*-based definition as characterizing the *kriyā* as the verb meaning, which shall be discussed later. However, it is inconceivable that when Helārāja mentioned the *kriyā*-based definition as early teachers', he should have been ignorant of the *bhāva*-based definition as contrasted with it. And again, it is certainly unlikely that he considered Kātyāyana to have invented the *bhāva*-based definition as replacing the *kriyā*-based definition. Thus, viewed in this light, Helārāja's description of the *kriyā*-based definition implies not only that as the *Kāśikāvṛtti* does, he also understands the term *dhātu* for a verb to be a borrowing from early teachers' terminology, but also that the *bhāva*-based definition as an alternative to the *kriyā*-based definition is also pre-Pāṇinian. It is reasonable, first of all, to assume that Kātyāyana's treatment of semantic definitions of the term *dhātu* represents early teachers'

---

[1] *Prakāśa* on *VP*3.8.1: *iha kriyāvacano dhātur iti purvācāryalakṣaṇe astibhavatividyatīnāṃ dhātutvaṃ vaktavyam iti coditam / . . . / kiṃ ca parispandasvabhāvā loke kriyā prasiddhā / astibhavatividyatīnāṃ ca na parispandasvabhāvo 'rthaḥ . . . /* Here Helārāja mentions the *kriyā*-based definition as early teachers' and points out that in everyday life people speak of motion (*parispanda*) as *kriyā*, whereby he means to say that the definition of *kriyā* given by Bhartṛhari is different from the one given by early teachers and the *kriyā* is also far from being viewed as motion. See Introduction [0.3].

and that his task was to investigate the validity of Pāṇini's formulating *A*1.3.1 instead of semantic definitions which have been framed by early teachers. On this assumption, thus, we may safely suppose that Kātyāyana had before his eyes *A*1.3.1 interpreted as the dhātupāṭha-based definition and the two semantic definitions provided by early teachers.

5.1.1. As is indicated by *vt.* 5: *astibhavatividyatīnāṃ ca dhātutvam*, the contrast between *kriyā*-based and *bhāva*-based definitions of the term *dhātu* reflects the one between the meanings of the verbs *kṛ* and *as*. When early teachers defined the term *dhātu* as that which denotes an action (*kriyā*) or as that which denotes *bhāva*, what did they mean by the terms *kriyā* and *bhāva*?

Pāṇinīyas classify verbs under two categories: *sakarmaka* and *akarmaka*. Into the former category fall verbs that take objects (*karman*), i.e., transitive, into the latter verbs that do not take objects, i.e., intransitive. Not only do they have such a classification of verbs, but also they arrange another classification of verbs: *karmasthakriyaka* 'a verb, *kriyā* signified by which rests on an object' / *kartṛsthakriyaka* 'a verb, *kriyā* signified by which rests on an agent'—*karmasthabhāvaka* 'a verb, *bhāva* signified by which rests on an object' / *kartṛsthabhāvaka* 'a verb, *bhāva* signified by which rests on an agent'. First of all, verb meanings are divided into two categories: *kriyā* and *bhāva* and in accordance with it verbs are divided into two groups: a group of verbs which denote *kriyā* and a group of verbs which denote *bhāva*. Then again each group of verbs is classified into two types according to whether a certain specific feature is observable in an agent or an object: *kartṛstha* and *karmastha*.

Consider the following utterances.

A. *pacyate ghaṭaḥ svayam eva* /
'The clay pot is baking of itself.'
B. *bhidyate kusūlaḥ svayam eva* /
'The grain pot is breaking of itself.'
C. *māsam āste* /
'He is sitting for a month.'

D. *grāmaṃ gacchati* /
'He is going to the village.'

In A and C, the meanings conveyed by the verbs *pac* 'bake' and *ās* 'sit' are characterized as *bhāva*; in B and D, the ones conveyed by the verbs *bhid* 'break' and *gam* 'go' as *kriyā*. And further, the meanings of the verbs *pac* and *ās* in A and C are respectively regarded as *karmastha* and *kartṛstha*; those of the verbs *bhid* and *gam* in B and D are respectively regarded as *karmastha* and *kartṛstha*. Thus the verbs *pac*, *bhid*, *ās*, and *gam* are respectively spoken of as *karmasthabhāvaka*, *karmasthakriyaka*, *kartṛsthabhāvaka*, and *kartṛsthakriyaka*.[2]

Kaiyaṭa explains what are meant by the terms *kriyā* and *bhāva* in this classification of verbs as follows:

> *Pradīpa* on *MBh* ad *A*3.1.87 (IV.166): *aparispandanasādhanasādhyo dhātvartho bhāvaḥ* / *saparispandanasādhanasādhyas tu kriyā* /
> "A verb meaning which is to be brought to accomplishment by sādhanas without motion (*parispanda*) is spoken of as *bhāva*. On the other hand, a verb meaning which is to be brought to accomplishment by sādhanas with motion is spoken of as *kriyā*."[3]

---

[2] In the *Kāśikāvṛtti* on *A*3.1.87 the following verse is given: *karmasthaḥ pacater bhāvaḥ karmasthā ca bhideḥ kriyā* / *māsāsibhāvaḥ kartṛsthaḥ kartṛsthā ca gameḥ kriyā* // Note that *pacyate* of A and *bhidyate* of B are intransitive forms, which differ from those in the passive; the ātmanepada ending *te* here replaces the L-affix *laṭ* introduced to signify an agent-object (*karmakartṛ*). The ending *te* of *pacyate* in the passive replaces the affix *laṭ* introduced to signify an object (*karman*).

[3] On the distinction between *kartṛsthabhāvaka* and *karmasthabhāvaka*, Bhartṛhari states as follows. *VP*3.7.66ab: *viśeṣadarśanaṃ yatra kriyā tatra vyavasthitā* / Commenting on this line, Phullarāja gives the same description of *kriyā* and *bhāva* as Kaiyaṭa. And further, Phullarāja explains that Bhartṛhari uses the term *kriyā* instead of the term *bhāva* here because the former is treated as synonymous with the latter in Pāṇini's grammar. Phullarāja on *VP*3.7.66ab: *saparispandasādhanasādhyā kriyā, aparispandasādhanasādhyo bhāva iti viśeṣam anapekṣya sūtrakārābhiprāyeṇa kriyāpi bhāvo 'bhidhīyata iti ṭīkākārasyābhiprāyaḥ* / *tathā ca lakṣaṇahetvoḥ kriyāyāḥ, yasya ca bhāvena bhāvalakṣaṇam ityādāv abheda eva sūtrakārasya kriyābhāvayoś cetasi vartate* / In Helārāja's commentary on the Sādhanasamuddesa there are two

Clearly, the act of baking in A claims to be *bhāva* and the act of going in D *kriyā*, for example.

Kaiyaṭa's description of *kriyā* and *bhāva* here, it is reasonable to suppose, has something to do with the *kriyā*-based and *bhāva*-based definitions of the term *dhātu* established by early teachers. As a matter of fact, Kaiyaṭa is of such an opinion.

As has been said in Section 4 (Part 4 [4.8.5]), Patañjali proposes interpreting *A* 1.3.1 as containing the indication of the dhātupāṭha with new roles other than that of supplying items to be called *dhātu* and a semantic definition. In this interpretation, which of *bhū* and *vā* in the dvandva compound *bhūvau* is taken as a meaningful unit depends upon which of the *kriyā*-based and *bhāva*-based definitions is resorted to. One who accepts the *bhāva*-based definition takes *bhū* as a meaningful unit and one who accepts the *kriyā*-based definition takes *vā* as a meaningful unit. In this case these two semantic definitions are distinguished from each other by the fact that *kriyā* is different from *bhāva* in that the former has the form of motion and the latter does not (*parispandāparispandarūpatayā*), according to Kaiyaṭa.[4]

5.1.2. However, a question naturally arises: If *kriyā* and *bhāva* are distinguished from each other in this way, can one argue that the *bhāva*-based definition applies to items such as *pac* which may well be called *dhātu* by the *kriyā*-based definition? This question brings us to the next point.

On the Bhāṣya where Patañjali starts discussing the *bhāva*-based definition, Kaiyaṭa says as follows:

> *Pradīpa* on *MBh* ad *A*1.3.1 (II.185–86): *bhāvaśabdaḥ kriyāmātravācī / yathā yasya ca bhāveneti bhāve ghañ iti ca / tena pacādīnām api dhātusaṃjñā sidhyati, astibhavatividyatīnām api bhāvarūpārthābhidhāyitvāt /*
>
> "The term *bhāva* [in the *bhāva*-based definition] denotes an action in general (*kriyāmātra*). Just like the term *bhāva* in

---

gaps, which are said to have been filled up by Pullarāja. See Iyer [1963: INTRODUCTION, xiii].

[4] *Pradīpa* on *MBh* ad *A*1.3.1 (II.196): *parispandāparispandarūpatayā kriyābhāvayor bhedenopanyāsaḥ /*

A2.3.37 *yasya ca bhāvena bhāvalakṣaṇam* and A3.3.18 *bhāve*. Therefore, both items such as *pac* and the items *as*, *bhū*, and *vid* are equally established as being called *dhātu*, for they both denote the meaning in the form of *bhāva*."

It is obvious that when he states that the term *bhāva* in the *bhāva*-based definition denotes an action in general, Kaiyaṭa implies that the term *kriyā* in the *kriyā*-based definition denotes a specific action which cannot be conveyed by the verb *as*. What he means to say is as follows:

A2.3.37 accounts for both the utterance *goṣu duhyamānāsu gataḥ* 'He went off while the cows were being milked' in which a characterization of the meaning of the verb *gam* 'go off' by the meaning of the verb *duh* 'milk' is observed and the utterance *tasmin saty āgataḥ* 'When it occurred, he came' in which a characterization of the meaning of the verb *gam* preceded by the preverb *ā*- (*āṅ*) 'come' by the meaning of the verb *as* 'occur' is observed.[5] Similarly, A3.3.18 explains both the derivation of *pāka* 'cooking' from the verb *pac* and that of *bhāva* from the verb *bhū*, since Pāṇini, intending to let the sūtra apply to any verb, uses in the sūtra the term *bhāva* which is derived from the verb *bhū* that denotes an action in general (*kriyāsāmānya*).[6] Thus, taking into consideration Pāṇini's formulation of these sūtras, one may say that the term *bhāva* used in the *Aṣṭādhyāyī* covers both categories of verbs, verbs of the *kṛ* type and those of the *as* type.

---

[5]The utterances *goṣu duhyamānāsu gataḥ* and *tasmin saty āgataḥ* are respectively given as examples of A2.3.37 by the *Kāśikāvṛtti* on the same sūtra and the *Uddyota* on *MBh* ad A1.3.1 (II.185). We may recall that the latter is an example of what Patañjali calls the *satsaptamī*. See *MBh* ad A1.2.49 (I.225.20–22), which reads: *lukīty ucyate, na cātra lukaṃ paśyāmaḥ / lukīti naiṣā parasaptamī śakyā vijñātum, na hi lukā paurvāparyam asti / kā tarhi / satsaptamī / luki satīti /*

Note that A2.3.37 *yasya ca bhāvena bhāvalakṣaṇam*, in combination with A3.2.126 *lakṣaṇahetvoḥ kriyāyāḥ*, is adduced as evidence that Pāṇini does not distinguish between the terms *kriyā* and *bhāva* to refer to verb meanings. See Appendix 1 [1.3] and Appendix 1, fn. 15.

[6]*Kāśikāvṛtti* ad A3.3.18: *kriyāsāmānyavācī bhavatiḥ / tena arthanirdeśaḥ kriyamāṇaḥ sarvadhātuviṣayaḥ kṛto bhavati /*

But Kaiyaṭa should not have used here the expression *kriyāmātra* 'an action in general'. As Nāgeśa suggests, he should have used the expression *dhātvarthamātra* 'a verb meaning in general'.[7] For, Kaiyaṭa means simply to say that while the term *kriyā* is used to refer to a particular group of verb meanings, the term *bhāva* is used to refer to any verb meaning, and moreover, if we follow him, we will have to have two kinds of *kriyās* : *kriyā* as a verb meaning and *kriyā* characterizing a verb meaning, though this accords with Patañjali's treatment of the notion of *kriyā*.[8]

The point, in the given context, should be what are respectively meant by the terms *kriyā* and *bhāva* when the former is said to

---

[7] *Uddyota* on *MBh* ad *A*1.3.1 (II.185): *nanu bhāvavacana iti nyāse pacādiṣv avyāptir ata āha—kriyāmātreti / dhātvarthamātrety arthaḥ / mātrapadaṃ kārtsnye /* Probably Kaiyaṭa, in stating the present *Pradīpa*, bears in his mind the following Bhāṣya: *MBh* ad *A*3.3.18 (II.144.20–21): *kṛbhvastayaḥ kriyāsāmānyavācinaḥ, kriyāviśeṣavācinaḥ pacādayaḥ /* This Bhāṣya says that while the verbs *kṛ*, *bhū*, and *as* denote actions in general, verbs like *pac* denote specific actions (*kriyāviśeṣa*). Cardona [1999b: 231-33] treats Kātyāyana's vārttika and Patañjali's Bhāṣya on the sūtra.

[8] Here Kaiyaṭa follows Patañjali who describes a verb meaning as *kriyā*. See the present section [5.2.3.2]. Which implies, Kaiyaṭa knows that Pāṇini uses these terms, *kriyā* and *bhāva*, synonymously. But here the way to manage to distinguish between them has to be shown so that the distinction between the two semantic definitions under consideration may be made.

Kaiyaṭa points out, it is also to be noted, that although in certain contexts *kriyā* and *bhāva* are distinguished by Kātyāyana and Patañjali, in other contexts both of these are subsumed under *kriyā*. *Pradīpa* on *MBh* ad *A*8.3.87 (V.481): *karmasthabhāvakānāṃ karmasthakriyāṇām ity atra tu bhāvakriyayor bhedenopādānāt parispandalakṣaṇaviśiṣṭakriyāvṛttiḥ kriyāśabdaḥ, yatkriyāyuktā ityādau tu kriyāmātravṛttir ity avirodhaḥ /* (*MBh* ad *A*1.1.20 [I.75.2]: *yatkriyāyuktā prādayas taṃ prati gatyupasargasaṃjñe bhavataḥ /*) See Deshpande [1991: 470; fn. 21]. Of course, the *kriyā* under which *kriyā* and *bhāva* are subsumed is nothing but the one as characterizing a verb meaning, or what I call 'semantic *kriyā*'. See Section 5 [5.3.2]. Note that Kaiyaṭa states in his *Pradīpa* on *MBh* ad *A*1.3.1 (II.185): *bhāvaśabdaḥ kriyāmātravācī* 'the term *bhāva* deotes an action in general' and in his *Pradīpa* on *MBh* ad *A*8.3.87: *kriyāśabdaḥ . . . kriyāmātravṛttiḥ* 'the term *kriyā* occurs in the sense of an action in general'.

apply to meanings of a category of verbs of the *kṛ* type and the latter is said to apply to any verb meaning.

Recall that Kaiyaṭa knows in what respect *kriyā*-based and *bhāva*-based definitions are distinguished from each other. Thus his idea has to be reconsidered within the present context. On what grounds these semantic definitions are to be mutually distinguished, their domains of application considered?

It is Nāgeśa who considers the terms *kriyā* and *bhāva* in the definitions in this line. He clarifies the point:

> *Uddyota* on *MBh* ad *A*1.3.1 (II.185): *kriyāśabdaḥ saparispandasādhanasādhyārthe rūḍho bhāvaśabdaś ca saparispandāparispandānyatarasādhanasādhye* /
> "The word *kriyā* is conventionally used to refer to a verb meaning which is characterized as something to be brought to accomplishment by sādhanas with motion (*saparispandasādhanasādhya*); and the word *bhāva* is conventionally used to refer to a verb meaning which is characterized as something to be brought to accomplishment by sādhanas with or without motion (*saparispandāparispandānyatarasādhanasādhya*)."

According to Nāgeśa, the words *kriyā* and *bhāva* are conventionally used respectively to signify a verb meaning as that which is to be brought to accomplishment by a sādhana with motion and to signify it as that which is to be brought to accomplishment by a sādhana with or without motion. In other words, a verb meaning is generally referred to as *bhāva* and specifically, when it is viewed as something dynamic and not static, as *kriyā*.

It is, we may therefore reasonably conclude, the words *kriyā* and *bhāva* used in their conventional senses that are employed in the given semantic definitions of early teachers. So to speak, early teachers held *kriyā* to be a dynamic act and *bhāva* to be an act in general, dynamic and static. And such *bhāva* is precisely that which Yāska in his *Nirukta* deemed to be a meaning conveyed by a finite verb form (*ākhyāta*).[9]

---

[9] See Section 6 [6.1].

5.2. Patañjali's interpretation of the term *bhāva*

Patañjali devoted himself specifically to analyzing the term *bhāva* employed in the *bhāva*-based definition. As said, this was motivated by the fact that the *bhāva*-based definition, in which the term *bhāva* with ambiguity is employed, was supposed to cover any verb, and that *A*1.3.1 admitted of an interpretation that the sūtra itself formed a semantic definition equivalent to the *bhāva*-based definition.[10] As mentioned, Patañjali gives three interpretations of the term *bhāva*.[11] In the following let us examine each of these interpretations.

5.2.1. Being (*bhavana*): *bhāvasādhana*

5.2.1.1. The question-and-answer *kiṃ karoti—pacati* tells us, as Patañjali has observed with reference to the *kriyā*-based definition, that the verb *pac* denotes a specific action. This means: On the basis of the relation of concurrence (*sāmānādhikaraṇya*) between the meanings of the verbs *kṛ* and *pac*, one can establish that items such as *pac* denote actions (*kriyā*). With regard to the *bhāva*-based definition also, Patañjali sought the same semantic relation between the verbs *bhū* and *pac*. Under this semantic definition, he presented the following set of utterances as an instance to show that items such as *pac* denote *bhāva*:

bhavati pacati; *bhavati pakṣyati*; *bhavaty apākṣīt*.

In the first place, Patañjali assumed that there obtains the relation of concurrence between the meanings of the verbs *bhū* and *pac* in these utterances. This assumption presupposes the following: One understands from these utterances that one who is currently cooking exists (*bhavati pacati*), that one who will cook exists (*bhavati pakṣyati*), and that one who has cooked exists (*bhavaty apākṣīt*), respectively. Obviously, the relation of concurrence here is such that the meaning of the verb *bhū* abides in the same locus as that of the verb *pac*. In other words, the relation of concurrence obtains between the meanings of the verbs *bhū* and

---

[10] See Section 4, Part 3 [4.6.1].

[11] See Section 4, Part 3 [4.6.2].

pac only in the sense that the agent with respect to the meaning of the verb *bhū* is the same as the one with respect to the meaning of the verb *pac*.[12]

When one finds such a semantic relation between the meanings of the verbs *bhū* and *pac*, one can say that *pac* conveys the meaning of the verb *bhū*, namely *bhāva*. According to Kaiyaṭa, this is comparable to the case in which the utterance *śuklaṃ rūpam* 'white color' is used. He assumes that this utterance conveys that both the generic property of being white (*śuklatva*) and the generic property of being a color (*rūpatva*) abides in the quality white (*śuklaguṇa*). Given that the word *śukla* denotes the generic property of being white, it denotes the generic property of being a color which abides in the same locus as the generic property of being white; the locus being the quality white.[13]

As implied, the *bhāva* as the meaning of the verb *bhū* which stands in the relation of concurrence to that of the verb *pac* is

---

[12] *Uddyota* on *MBh* ad A1.3.1 (II.186): *evaṃ ca pacati bhavatītyāder yatkartṛkā pacikriyā tatkartṛkā satteti bodhaḥ / evaṃ ca bhavaty-arthapacatyarthayor ekādhikaraṇapravṛttitvam eva bhavatipacatyoḥ sāmānādhikaraṇyam iti bhāvaḥ /* According to Nāgeśa, the utterance *bhavati pacati* is considered to produce a verbal cognition conveyed by the paraphrase: *yatkartṛkā pacikriyā tatkartṛkā sattā* 'being (*sattā*), whose agent is the one that the action of cooking has for its agent'. As said in Section 4, Part 3 [4.6.2.1], Kaiyaṭa explains that the meaning of the verb *bhū* as forming the relation of concurrence to the meaning of the verb *pac* is *sattā* in the form of *ātmabharaṇa* 'self-maintenance', saying: *tac cātmabharaṇaṃ viruddhaikārthasamavāyaiḥ pācakatvādibhir aviruddhaikārthasamavāyam.* Devadatta can perform the acts of cooking, going, and so on. But they cannot occur concurrently. In this sense the properties of being a cook, of being a goer, and so forth are said to be contradictory to one another (*viruddha*). They are, however, not contradictory to *ātmabharaṇa* (*aviruddha*). They inhere in Devadatta concurrently with the latter (*ekārthasamavāya*).

Added to this, if we take the term *sāmānādhikaraṇya* as signifying coreferentiality, the utterance *bhavati pacati* can be explained as follows: With reference to Devadatta, he is spoken of as self-maintaining or existent and as being cooking. I do not dwell on this matter. See Section 4, Part 2, fn. 20.

[13] *Pradīpa* on *MBh* ad A1.3.1 (II.186): *yathā śuklaṃ rūpam iti śukle guṇe śuklatvaṃ rūpatvaṃ cāstīti śuklādayo rūpavacanāḥ, evaṃ pacādayo bhāvavacanāḥ /*

nothing but *sattā* 'existence, being'. Therefore, in reply to the question of what is meant by the word *bhāva*, Patañjali answers that the term *bhāva* in the definition means *bhavana* 'existence, being' (*bhavanaṃ bhāvaḥ*), which is what is primarily conveyed by the verb *bhū* itself, to put it another way, what comes readily to mind when it is heard (*bhavateḥ svapadārthaḥ*).

The gloss of the term *bhāva* with the word *bhavana* shows that the form *bhāva* is a *bhāvasādhana*. In this case, the term *bhāva* is a derivate formed from the verb *bhū* by adding the kṛt affix ***ghañ*** to be introduced to convey an action in the abstract (*A*3.3.18).[14]

5.2.1.2. According to Patañjali, the difficulties one has to face under this interpretation of the term *bhāva* are as follows:

The *bhāva*-based definition in which the term *bhāva* as described above is employed cannot be applied to items such as *bhid* 'break' and *chid* 'cut', since they denote non-existence (*abhāva*), contradictory (*vipratiṣiddha*) to , different from, existence (*bhāva*).[15]

And further, items such as *pac* result in not being called *dhātu*. Even if it may be said that there obtains the relation of concurrence between the meanings of the verbs *bhū* and *pac* in utterances such as *bhavati pacati*, this does not justify that the meaning of the verb *bhū* is connected with that of the verb *pac* in the same relation of universal and particular as the meaning of the verb *kṛ* is connected with that of the verb *pac* in the question-and-answer *kiṃ karoti—pacati*.[16] The concurrence relation in question between the meanings of the verbs *bhū* and *pac*, which is necessary for establishing that an item like *pac* denotes *bhāva*, has to be that which is established in terms of the universal-particular relation, in such a way that the meaning of the verb *pac* is a specific kind

---

[14] See Section 4, Part 3, fn. 1.

[15] *MBh* ad *A*1.3.1 (I.256.21–23): *yadi bhavateḥ svapadārtho bhavanaṃ bhāvo vipratiṣiddhānāṃ dhātusaṃjñā na prāpnoti bhedaḥ chedaḥ / anyo hi bhāvo 'nyo 'bhāvaḥ / ātaś cānyo bhāvo 'nyo 'bhāva iti yo hi yasya bhāvam icchati sa na tasyābhāvaṃ, yasya cābhāvaṃ na tasya bhāvam /*

[16] *MBh* ad *A*1.3.1 (I.256.23–25): *pacādīnāṃ ca dhātusaṃjñā na prāpnoti / yathā hi bhavatā kriyāvacane dhātau karotinā pacādīnāṃ sāmānādhikaraṇyaṃ nidarśitaṃ, na tathā bhāvavacane dhātau nidarśyate /*

of *bhāva* (**bhāvaviśeṣa*) as comparable to a specific action (*kriyāviśeṣa*) in the case of the question-and-answer *kiṃ karoti —pacati*. Patañjali explicitly states that one does not have utterances in which the items *bhū* and *pac*, whose meanings have the relation of concurrence in terms of the universal-particular relation, are used. Thus, he finally denies that the relation of concurrence between the meanings of the verbs *bhū* and *pac* in utterances like *bhavati pacati* can establish that the item *pac* denotes *bhāva*.[17]

5.2.2. What comes into being: *kartṛsādhana*

5.2.2.1. In utterances such as *bhavati pacati*, we can find out a different semantic structure which does not build up the relation of concurrence between the meanings of the verbs *bhū* and *pac*. As said, according to Patañjali, the relation of what is to be accomplished and what does the accomplishing (*sādhyasādhanabhāva*) can also be established between those two meanings.[18]

---

[17] *MBh* ad *A*1.3.1 (I.257.4–5): *yāvatātrāpy anyatvam asti, pacādayaś ca kriyā bhavatikriyāyāḥ katryo bhavantīti* / This Bhāṣya means the following: As long as the distinction is established between the meanings of the two same verbs in utterances such as *bhaved api bhavet* (see Section 5 [5.2.2.1]) and in utterances such as *pacati bhavati* the meanings of verbs like *pac* can be said to function as agents with respect to the meaning of the verb *bhū*, when a certain verb is uttered together with the verb *bhū*, we recognize that between the meanings of the two verbs in question there obtains the relation of *sādhyasādhanabhāva* and not that of *sāmānādhikaraṇya*. Therefore, it is not proper to define the term *dhātu* as *bhāvavacano dhātuḥ*. *Uddyota* on *MBh* ad *A*1.3.1 (II.189): *tad evam atra lakṣaṇe bhidādiṣv avyāptir bhavatisāmānādhikaraṇyābhāvāt pacādāv avyāptiś ceti dūṣaṇadvayaṃ sthitam / kartryo bhavantīty asyānupapannaṃ bhāvavacano dhātur iti lakṣaṇam iti śeṣaḥ / bhavatisāmānādhikaraṇyābhāvena bhāvavacanatvābhāvād iti bhāvaḥ* /

[18] See Section 4, Part 3 [4.6.3.2]. In this connection, Kaiyaṭa quotes a view some hold. According to them, an act conveyed by a finite verb form can be related to another act conveyed by another finite verb form in two ways: as agent and as object. A good example for the latter case is the utterance *paśya mṛgo dhāvati* 'Look, the deer runs', where the act of running conveyed by *dhāvati* functions as object with respect to the act of looking conveyed by *paśya*. In addition, in actual usage there is no utterance in which an act conveyed by a finite verb form is related as any of kārakas other than an agent and an object to another act conveyed by another finite verb form. *Pradīpa* on *MBh* ad *A*1.3.1 (II.188): *tatrāhuḥ—kartṛkarmabhāvena kriyā ākhyātavācyakriyayā sambadhyata*

With respect to that meaning of the verb *bhū* which is characterized as something to be brought to accomplishment (*sādhya*), the meaning of the verb *pac* serves as agent (*kartṛ*), one of sādhanas or kārakas. This means that the item *pac* denotes a meaning functioning as agent in relation to what the item *bhū* denotes. If you think of the verb *bhū* as signifying *sattā*, then the utterance *bhavati pacati* conveys that the act of cooking, referred to current time, whose agent is someone like Devadatta, exists.[19] By virtue of

---

eva bhavati pacati paśya mṛgo dhāvatīti / karaṇādibhāvena tu na sambadhyate, tathā prayogādarśanāt / See also *VP*2.449, which says: *tiṅantāntarayukteṣu yuktayukteṣu vā punaḥ / mṛgaḥ paśyata yātīti bhedābhedau na tiṣṭhataḥ //* According to Bhartṛhari, with respect to the utterance *mṛgaḥ paśyata yāti* 'You, look! The deer runs' two interpretations may be accepted. First, if we adopt the view of *tiṅantāntarayukta*, the nominal form *mṛgaḥ* is syntactically connected with the finite verb forms *yāti* and *paśya*, so that we have the sentence-split (*vākyabheda*) such as *mṛgo yāti, etaṃ mṛgaṃ paśya* 'The deer runs. You, look at this deer!'. Secondly, if we adopt the view of *yuktayukta*, the finite verb form *paśya* is syntactically connected with the finite verb form *yāti* which is syntactically connected with the nominal form *mṛgaḥ*, so that we do not have the sentence-split. The view relevant to the present context is the latter one, of course. It is to be noted that the difference between these two views comes from that of the views on *vākya* or sentence. One may hold the former view from the viewpoint of 'technical *vākya*' and the latter from the viewpoint of 'non-technical' *vākya*. See the present section, fn. 24.

[19]Similarly, on the assumption that the verb *bhū* denotes *sattā*, the utterances *bhavati pakṣyati* and *bhavaty apākṣīt* respectively convey that the act of cooking, referred to future time, whose agent is someone like Devadatta, currently exists and that the act of cooking, referred to past time, whose agent is someone like Devadatta, currently exists. As to the question of how it can be said that an action referred to past or future time currently exists, see the following remarks by Nāgeśa. *VSLM*796: *kiñca sarvatra prathamāntārthaṃ praty eva kriyāyā viśeṣaṇatvam iti pakṣe pākakriyā bhavatīty arthe pacati bhavatīty asya tavāsiddhiḥ / tad uktaṃ bhūvādisūtre bhāṣye kā tarhīyaṃ vācoyuktiḥ pacati bhavati, tvaṃ pacasi bhavati, pakṣyati bhavati iti praśne uttaraṃ pacādayaḥ kriyā bhavatikriyāyāḥ kartryo bhavanti iti / pakṣyati bhavatīty asya bhaviṣyantī pākakriyā satkāryavādāṅgīkārāt sūkṣmarūpeṇa bhavatīty arthān na doṣaḥ / Uddyota* on *MBh* ad A1.3.1 (II.187): *na caivaṃ pakṣyati bhavatīti kathaṃ prayogo, bhaviṣyatpāke vartamānasattāśrayatvāsambhavād iti vācyaṃ, bhūtabhaviṣyator api sūkṣmāvasthām ālambya sattāyā vartamānatvākṣater iti bhāvaḥ /* His justification of the use of the utterances under consideration is made on the basis of

resorting to this relation between the meanings of the verbs *bhū* and *pac*, as a matter of course, one fails to establish that the verb *pac* denotes *bhāva* in the form of *sattā*. However, if one takes the term *bhāva* as referring to an agent with respect to what the verb *bhū*, from which it is derived, denotes, one will succeed in establishing such a thesis on the basis of that very relation.

Now the question arises: On condition that the term *bhāva* in the *bhāva*-based definition is taken in the above-described way, granted that the *bhāva*-based definition justifies that items such as *pac* are called *dhātu*, how is it possible that the items *bhū*, *as*, and suchlike can be called *dhātu* by the same definition? What Patañjali has to do next is therefore to give examples to show that the meanings of items like *bhū* serve as agents with respect to themselves. He cites the following utterances to be considered:

bhaved api bhavet / (*bhū*1 + ***liṅ***1 *api bhū*2 + ***liṅ***2)
syād api syāt / (*as*1 + ***liṅ***1 *api as*2 + ***liṅ***2)
'May [Devadatta] be healthy, which is currently conjectured.'[20]

Patañjali's analysis of these utterances discloses the following: The meaning of *bhū*2 or *as*2 functions as agent in relation to the meaning of *bhū*1 or *as*1 and an agent with respect to the meaning of *bhū*2 or *as*2 is someone like Devadatta; ***liṅ***1 and ***liṅ***2 occurs respectively to signify wish (*prārthanā*)[21] and conjecture (*sambhāvanā*)[22]—***liṅ***1 is introduced with no specific time reference

the *satkāryavāda* or the doctrine of the pre-existing effect.

Needless to say, if the verb *bhū* signifies *janman*, the utterances *bhavati pakṣyati* and *bhavaty apākṣīt* may convey respectively that the act of cooking, referred to future time, whose agent is someone like Devadatta, currently comes into being and that the act of cooking, referred to past time, whose agent is someone like Devadatta, currently comes into being.

[20] *Uddyota* on *MBh* ad *A*1.3.1 (II.188): *sambhāvanāviṣayavartamānasattākartṛkā prārthyamānā satteti bodhaḥ* / ("Being wished (*prārthyamānā sattā*), whose agent is being (*sattā*) which is referred to current time (*vartamāna*) and which is an object on which conjectures are made (*sambhāvanāviṣaya*).") A verbal cognition produced by the utterance *bhaved api bhavet* or *syād api syāt* is conveyed by this paraphrase.

[21] *A*3.3.161.

[22] *Vt.* 1 ad *A*3.4.8: *upasaṃvādāśaṅkayor vacanānarthakyaṃ liṅartha-*

(*sarvakāla*) and the verb *bhū*2 or *as*2 to which *liṅ*2 is introduced signifies the meaning referred to current time (*vartamānakāla*).[23]

Now it is clear that Patañjali assumes a string such as *bhaved api bhavet* as well as a string such as *bhavati pacati* to be a single sentence (*vākya*),[24] on the same grounds that the relation

---

tvāt / The occurrence of *liṅ*2 in *api bhavet* / *api syāt* is accounted for by *A*3.3.152.

[23] Patañjali states that the meanings of *bhū*1 (*as*1) and *bhū*2 (*as*2) are distinguished from each other due to the difference in their agents and time reference. *MBh* ad *A*1.3.1 (I.257.2–4): *atrāpy anyatvam asti* / *kutaḥ* / *kālabhedāt sādhanabhedāc ca* / *ekasyātra bhavater bhavatiḥ sādhanaṃ sarvakālaś ca pratyayaḥ* / *aparasya bāhyaṃ sādhanaṃ vartamānakālaś ca pratyayaḥ* / The affix *liṅ* is said to be *sarvalakārāpavāda* or that which constitutes an exception to the affixes which are introduced under certain conditions of time reference (*kālaviśeṣavihitapratyaya*). See the *Kāśikāvṛtti* on *A*3.3.145, 3.3.157, 3.3.161. In the sense that the affix *liṅ* does not specify to which time the act signified by the verb after which it occurs is referred, it is called *sarvakāla* '[an affix introduced] with no specific time reference'. It goes without saying that such an act can be referred to any of past, future, and present time. On the other hand, it is justified that the meaning of *bhū*2 (*as*2) is referred to current time, for the particular reason that Devadatta's being healthy, which is wished as well as an object on which conjectures are made, should be referred to current time. *Pradīpa* on *MBh* ad *A*1.3.1 (II.188–89): *api bhaved ity atra yo bhavatis tasyārogyādiviśiṣṭadevadattādikartṛkā sattā vartamānārthaḥ* / *tathābhūtā hi sattā prārthyata iti vartamānakālaḥ* /

[24] As Bhartṛhari indicates in his *VP*2.3 (*nighātādivyavasthārthaṃ śāstre yat paribhāṣitam* / *sākāṅkṣāvayavaṃ tena na sarvam tulyalakṣaṇam* //), Pāṇinīyas distinguish between what one would technically call a *vākya* and what one would call a *vākya* in everyday speech. The 'technical' *vākya* is a speech unit which has a single finite verb form, as is defined by Kātyāyana in vārttikas 9–10 on *A*2.1.1. On the other hand, the 'non-technical' *vākya* is a stretch of speech which is composed of words that are semantically related so that their meanings are in a semantic expectancy for the meanings of other constituent words, as stated by Bhartṛhari in his *VP*2.4 following Mīmāṃsakas' view. *VP*2.4: *sākāṅkṣāvayavaṃ bhede parānākāṅkṣaśabdakam* / *karmapradnānaṃ guṇavad ekārthaṃ vākyam ucyate* // Bhartṛhari observes in *VP*2.6 that a *vākya* may contain more than one finite verb form if they are semantically related. In a string such as *bhavati pacati*, the fact that the meanings of the verbs *bhū* and *pac* form the relation of *sādhyasādhanabhāva* explains that the meanings are in a semantic expectancy for each other. *VP*2.6: *yathānekam api ktvāntaṃ tiṅantasya viśeṣakam* / *tathā tiṅantaṃ tatrāhus tiṅantasya viśeṣakam* // Any more words need not be wasted here. On

of *sādhyasādhanabhāva* is established between the meanings signified by the verbs of finite verb forms involved. It is noteworthy that he regards what is *sādhya* as the meaning of the verb *bhū* or its synonym *as* and, in the light of the verb *bhū* (*as*) being an intransitive (*akarmaka*), the sādhana with respect to it as agent. Obviously, all of this amounts to saying that whatever the verb may be, the meaning signified by it can function as agent with respect to the meaning of the verb *bhū*. Thus, as far as the term *bhāva* is taken as referring to an agent with respect to what the verb *bhū* signifies, the definition which employs the term ensues in applying to all verbs, including the verbs *as*, *bhū*, and *vid*.

5.2.2.2. The important point to note in connection with this interpretation of the term *bhāva* is that the term *bhāva* here does not refer to that which *exists* but to that which *comes into being*. As I have pointed out, Pāṇinīyas recognize that the verb *bhū* has two main meanings: *sattā* 'being, existence' and *janman* 'birth'.[25] We have to take it into consideration that Patañjali here also distinguishes between the two meanings of it.

Concerning the interpretation of the term *bhāva* as *bhavana* or *sattā*, Patañjali has pointed out that the *bhāva*-based definition does not apply to the verb *bhid*, because the verb, used to signify the sense 'break', is a word for non-existence (*abhāva*). If we accept the verb *bhid* as a word for non-existence, therefore, even if the utterance *bhavati pacati* may be understood to mean that the act of cooking exists, the utterance *bhavati bhinatti* cannot be taken to mean that the action of breaking exists. For, the utterance *bhavati bhinatti*, if so understood, would show self-contradiction in the sense that what is not existent is what is existent. Although Patañjali does not explicitly say so, judging from the fact that he considers existence (*bhāva*) and non-existence (*abhāva*) to be mutually contradictory in his first interpretation of the term *bhāva*,

---

Pāṇinīyas' notion of *vākya*, see Cardona [1983: 117–159].

It is to be noted in passing that the *Kāśikāvṛtti* on *A*8.1.28 cites *bhavati pacati* as a counter-example.

[25] See Section 4, Part 3 [4.6.2.1].

it is natural to assume that here he takes the verb *bhū*, from which the form *bhāva* is derived, to denote *janman*.

This is how the term *bhāva* in the definition is distinctly understood to mean what comes into being (*bhavatīti bhāvaḥ*). It is proper to say, therefore, that the form *bhāva* is a *kartṛsādhana*, considered to be derived from the verb *bhū* which signifies *janman* by introducing the kṛt affix ***ṇa*** to denote an agent.[26]

5.2.2.3. If we accept the term *bhāva* as referring to something that comes into being, the *bhāva*-based definition will apply to the item *bhid*, not to speak of the item *pac*. For, as Kaiyaṭa says, the former denotes the act of breaking as what comes into being (*bhedādayo 'pi bhavantīti*).[27]

The following is the difference between the *bhāva*-based definition which is formulated with the word *bhāva* for existence and that which uses the word *bhāva* for something that comes into being: While the former does not cover items for non-existence such as *bhid*, the latter undesiredly leads to the over-application of the term *dhātu* to nominal bases such as *vṛkṣa* 'tree', the referents of which are also considered to be what come into being (*etāny api hi bhavanti*).[28]

It is noteworthy that, with a view to interpreting *A*1.3.1 as a purely semantic definition, Patañjali returns to this second *bhāva*, what comes into being, through translating *bhāva* as what is brought into being. As shall be seen later, this translation is meant for the change of the level where the second *bhāva* is viewed, from ontological to semantic.[29]

---

[26] See Section 4, Part 3, fn. 3.

[27] See Section 4, Part 3 [4.6.2.1].

[28] *MBh* ad *A*1.3.1 (I.257.5–8): *astv ayaṃ kartṛsādhanaḥ—bhavatīti bhāva iti / kiṃ kṛtaṃ bhavati / vipratiṣiddhānāṃ dhātusaṃjñā siddhā bhavati / bhaved vipratiṣiddhānāṃ dhātusaṃjñā siddhā syāt, prātipadikānām api tu prāpnoti vṛkṣaḥ plakṣa iti / kiṃ kāraṇam / etāny api hi bhavanti /*

[29] See Section 7 [7.2].

5.2.3. What is brought into being: *karmasādhana*

5.2.3.1. In the interpretation of the term *bhāva* as what is brought into being, the form *bhāva* is a derivate formed from the derived verb *bhāvi*, in which the causative suffix ***ṇic*** occurs after the verb *bhū* that signifies *janman* (*A*3.1.26), by introducing to that derived base the kṛt affix ***ac*** which signifies an object (*bhāvyate yaḥ sa bhāva iti*). The form *bhāva*, therefore, is a *karmasādhana.*[30]

Now one might ask why the meaning of the verb *bhū* here is not *sattā* but *janman*. This question could be answered by taking into consideration the translation of *bhāva* as what is brought into being into *bhāva* as what comes into being, which is suggested by Kaiyaṭa.

As shall be discussed in detail later, Patañjali proposes reading in *A*1.3.1 the item *bhū* which is derived from the verb *bhū* by adding the kṛt affix ***kvip*** signifying an agent and not an object to that base. In this connection Kaiyaṭa explains why the affix to be introduced to the verb *bhū* is taken to signify an agent, saying as follows:

> *Pradīpa* on *MBh* ad *A*1.3.1 (II.190): *bhavatīti bhūr iti kartari kvib asti na tu karmaṇi / arthas tv abhinna eva / yo hi bhavati sa eva bhāvyate nānyaḥ /*
>
> "What comes into being is spoken of as *bhū* (*bhavatīti bhūḥ*). Therefore, after the verb *bhū* the affix ***kvip*** occurs here to signify an agent and not an object. But whichever the affix ***kvip*** here may signify, meanings of the derivate *bhū* do not differ at all. For what is spoken of as *bhāvyate* is nothing but what is spoken of as *bhavati.*"

Here Kaiyaṭa bears the following sūtra in mind:

> *A*1.4.52 *gatibuddhipratyavasānārthaśabdakarmākarmakāṇām aṇikartā sa ṇau //*

This sūtra provides that the agent of a noncausal action is object of causation if the former is movement (*gati*), thinking (*buddhi*), eating (*pratyavasāna*), an action whose object is a sound (*śabda-*

---

[30] See Section 4, Part 3, fn. 3.

karma), and intransitive (*akarmaka*). The verb *bhū* is an intransitive verb. Consider the following utterances:

A. *pāko bhavati* 'The act of cooking is coming into being'.
B. *devadattaḥ pākam bhāvayati* 'Devadatta has the act of cooking come into being'.

According to the present sūtra, utterance B, in which the act of cooking (*pāka*) is regarded as an object with respect to the meaning of the causative *bhāvi*, presupposes utterance A, in which the very same act of cooking is regarded as an agent with respect to the meaning of the verb *bhū* from which the causative is derived.

Now we have already established that the derivate *bhāva* as a *kartṛsādhana* refers to what comes into being because of the verb *bhū* signifying *janman*. Kaiyaṭa suggests that we return to the *bhāva* as referred to by the derivate by means of the translation of *bhāva* spoken of as *bhāvyate*. It follows therefore that what is nothing but something that comes into being is what is caused to come into being. Thus we can be fairly certain that in the case of the term *bhāva* as a *karmasādhana* also, the verb *bhū* from which it is formed signifies *janman* and not *sattā*.

5.2.3.2. We should notice that it is this interpretation of the term *bhāva* on which Bhartṛhari is based in formulating his definition of an action. And moreover, there is no doubt that, in so doing, he bases himself on the following statement which Patañjali has made so as to justify the present interpretation of the term *bhāva*.

MBh ad *A*1.3.1 (I.257.8–9): *kriyā caiva hi bhāvyate svabhāvasiddhaṃ tu dravyam* /
"Indeed, an action (*kriyā*) alone is [that which is] brought into being. On the other hand, a substance (*dravya*) is something that has been established by 'own nature' (*svabhāvasiddha*)."[31]

[31] The word *svabhāvasiddham* may be analyzed as *svabhāvataḥ siddham* 'something that has been established by 'own nature'. *MBh* on *vt*. 7 ad *A*1.1.50 (I.123.2–3): *svabhāvasiddhatvāt* / *svabhāvata etat siddham* /

5.2.3.2.1. In the preceding section, I have pointed out the following four points to be noted in this statement: 1) In the context of the *bhāva*-based definition the term *kriyā* occurs; 2) What is meant by the term *kriyā* is characterized as *bhāvyate* '[that which is] brought into being' whose substantial equivalent is *bhāva*; 3) What is meant by the term *kriyā* is placed in juxtaposition with *dravya* (substance), in accordance with which *bhāvyate* or *bhāva* is contrasted with *svabhāvasiddha*; 4) The notion of *svabhāva* 'own nature' is introduced.[32]

To begin with, we notice that, in the context where the question argued about is not what is meant by the term *kriyā* in the *kriyā*-based definition but what is meant by the term *bhāva* in the *bhāva*-based definition, Patañjali mentions the word *kriyā*. This is explainable in the following manner. In his *Mahābhāṣya* Patañjali reiterates: 'However what is the verb meaning? It is an action' (*kaḥ punar dhātvarthaḥ, kriyā*).[33] This shows that in some cases Patañjali means a verb meaning (*dhātvartha*) by the term *kriyā*. For him, saying that an action (*kriyā*) is that which is brought into being is equivalent to saying that a verb meaning (*dhātvartha*) is that which is brought into being. Thus we see that in the Bhāṣya under consideration Patañjali characterizes a verb meaning as what is brought into being and such a characterization of a verb meaning allows him to use the term *bhāva* as an equivalent of the term *kriyā* with reference to a verb meaning. As a consequence, therefore, it will follow that for Patañjali the action (*kriyā*) he himself regards as a verb meaning is identical with the *bhāva* which is interpreted as what is brought into being. This is the second point I have suggested noting.

5.2.3.2.2. The fourth point we notice here that Patañjali introduces the notion of 'own nature' (*svabhāva*) in this context is highly important from the point of view of his theory of semantics. For Patañjali, the 'own nature' has no ontological value; it is nothing less than an intrinsic denotative nature which a linguistic item

---

[32] See Section 4, Part 3 [4.6.2.2].

[33] See *MBh* ad *A*3.2.84, 3.2.115, 5.1.118. See Section 1, fn. 15.

has.[34] The intrinsic denotative nature of a linguistic item is precisely what Bhartṛhari refers to as *yogyatā* 'potential';[35] and moreover, its idea has already been advanced by Kātyāyana. Kātyāyana declares:

> *Vt.* 33 ad *A*1.2.64; *vt.* 15 ad *A*2.2.29: *abhidhānaṃ punaḥ svābhāvikam* /
> "However, [a linguistic item] denotes its meaning by its own nature."

In addition we find a parallel in the Bhāṣya also.

> *MBh* ad *A*2.1.1 (I.363.7): *svābhāvikaṃ śabdair arthābhidhānam* /
> "The denotation of meanings by linguistic items is determined by their own nature."

---

[34] Kaiyaṭa addresses this vital point by saying as follows. *Pradīpa* on *MBh* ad *A*1.3.1 (II.189): *svabhāvasiddham iti* / *śabdaśaktyanusāreṇaitad ucyate* / According to him, in his characterization of a substance as *svabhāvasiddha* Patañjali takes into account the denotative power of the word (*śabdaśakti*) which Pāṇinīyas consider to be eternal. See *VP*3.3.29: *indriyāṇāṃ svaviṣayeṣv anādir yogyatā yathā* / *anādir arthaiḥ śabdānāṃ saṃbandho yogyatā tathā* // and the next footnote. In this kārikā Bhartṛhari states: "Just as the sense-organs have a beginningless *yogyatā* with respect to their own objects, so also do words have a beginningless *yogyatā* with respect to their own meanings. The relation of words with their meanings is the *yogyatā*."

[35] In his *Vṛtti* on *VP*1.24–26 Bhartṛhari, saying: *yogyabhāvenāpi sambandha upavarṇitaḥ tatra tatra*, cites statements by Kātyāyana and Patañjali: [1] *abhidhānaṃ punaḥ svābhāvikam* / [2] *samāne varṇe śoṇakarkahemādīnām aśvaviṣayatvaṃ gavādiṣu cāpravṛttiḥ* / *tathedam uktam* / [3] *samānam īhamānānāṃ cādhīyānānāṃ ca kecid arthair yujyante, apare na ity evamādi*/ [4] *tathājātīyakāḥ khalv apy ācāryeṇa svaritañitaḥ paṭhitāḥ, ye ubhayavantaḥ, yeṣāṃ kartrabhiprāyaṃ cākartrabhiprāyaṃ ca kriyāphalam asti* / [1], [2] are taken up in this section and [4] in Section 8 [8.7.1.1]. The third statement asserts that even if they expend effort and study the Veda in like manner, some satisfactorily accomplish their purpose and others do not. According to Vṛṣabha, it is meant that even if linguistic items have equally the capacity to denote a certain thing and are equally uttered, not all of them convey the thing; some convey it and others do not; this distinction is due to their *yogyatās*. *Paddhati* on *Vṛtti* ad *VP*1.26: *samānam īhamānānām iti* / *yato 'rthābhidhānaśaktau satyām uccāraṇe ca niyatārthapratipādakatvaṃ yogyatāvaśena viviktam* /

This view that a linguistic item has an intrinsic denotative nature of its own is illustrated by Patañjali as follows:

> *MBh* ad *A*1.2.68–71 (I.251.5–7); *A*2.2.29 (I.433.12–14): *samāne rakte varṇe gaur lohita iti bhavaty aśvaḥ śoṇa iti / samāne ca kāle varṇe gauḥ kṛṣṇa iti bhavaty aśvo hema iti / samāne ca śukle varṇe gauḥ śveta iti bhavaty aśvaḥ karka iti /*
> "Although the brown color is the same, we say that an ox is *lohita*, while we say that a horse is *śoṇa*; although the black color is the same, we say that an ox is *kṛṣṇa*, while we say that a horse is *hema*; and, although the white color is the same, we say that an ox is *śveta*, while we say that a horse is *karka*."[36]

In actual usage, for example, the word *śoṇa* is not used with reference to a brown ox, nor is the word *lohita* used with reference to a brown horse. This restriction on the application of words is due to their intrinsic denotative nature. Furthermore, consider the following statement made by Patañjali:

> *MBh* ad *A*3.1.19 (II.27.17–19): *atha vā dhātava eva kyajādayo / na caiva hy arthā ādiśyante kriyāvacanatā ca gamyate / kaḥ khalv api pacādīnāṃ kriyāvacanatve yatnaṃ karoti / yenaiva khalv api hetunā pacādayaḥ kriyāvacanās tenaiva kyajādayo 'pi /*
> "Or rather, items ending in suffixes like ***kyac***[, denoting actions,] are nothing but what are called *dhātu*. Indeed, their meanings are never taught; but, it is understood [from their use] that they denote actions. Who on earth makes an effort at items such as *pac* denoting actions? Certainly, the items ending in the suffixes

---

[36]This is explained by Bhartṛhari as follows. *Vṛtti* on *VP*1.24–26: *samāne varṇe śoṇakarkahemādīnām aśvaviṣayatvaṃ gavādiṣu cāpravṛttiḥ* ("The words *śoṇa* 'brown', *karka* 'white', and *hema* 'black' have a horse for their domain of application and are not applied to objects such as an ox, even if they denote the same colors [as other words used for the latter].") See fn. 35 above.

It is, Patañjali explicitly stated, by its intrinsic denotative nature (*svabhāvataḥ*) that a certain linguistic item is applied to a certain thing in order to convey the thing (*MBh* ad *A*2.1.1 (I.363.11–12): *svabhāvata eteṣāṃ śabdānām eteṣv artheṣv abhiniviṣṭānāṃ* [*nimittatvenānvākhyānaṃ kriyate*]).

> *kyac* etc. also denote actions for the very same reason (*hetu*) as items such as *pac* do."

What Patañjali means is this. The item *putrīya* 'desire a son for oneself' in *putrīyati*, a derived verb by *A*3.1.8, and the item *pac* in *pacati*, a primitive verb, both denote actions. They both have the property of being signifiers of actions, which property is not created by human effort. The fact that they denote actions is owing to their intrinsic denotative nature, which is spoken of as *hetu*, a reason for items such as *putrīya* to denote actions, in the present Bhāṣya.[37] Of course, the exact reverse is the case from the point of view of Bhartṛhari's abstraction (*apoddhāra*) theory: theoretically speaking, an item such as *putrīya* which denotes an action is abstracted from a form such as *putrīyati* and from the item abstracted are further abstracted items such as *putra* and *ya* (***k**yac*).[38]

Now, as I have mentioned as the third point, Patañjali places *kriyā* in juxtaposition with *dravya* (substance), in conformity with which what is spoken of as *bhāvyate* or *bhāva* is contrasted with *svabhāvasiddha*. As he implies a verb meaning by the term *kriyā*, so he implies a meaning of a nominal base (*prātipadikārtha*) by the term *dravya*.[39] He characterizes a substance, a meaning

---

[37] It is important that Patañjali considers that items terminating in affixes such as ***k**yac* by nature denote actions so that they may be called *dhātu*. Recall that in his Bhāṣya on *A*3.1.32 he points out the possibility that *A*1.3.1 can apply to items ending in suffixes like ***san*** in the domain of *A*3.1.32 if *A*1.3.1 is semantically interpreted. This implies that *A*1.3.1 as interpreted semantically presupposes the intrinsic denotative nature of items to be called *dhātu*. See Section 4, Part 3 [4.7.2].

[38] See Introduction [0.2; fn. 5].

[39] The view that a substance is a meaning of a nominal base is stated by Patañjali as follows. *MBh* ad *A*5.3.55 (II.413.6–7): *kaḥ punar ṅyāp-prātipadikārthaḥ / dravyam /* ("[Question] However, what is the meaning of items with feminine affixes ***ṅī***, ***āp*** and nominal bases? It is a substance.") According to Kaiyaṭa, the substance referred to here is that which Bhartṛhari defines as follows. *VP*3.4.3: *vastūpalakṣaṇaṃ yatra sarvanāma prayujyate / dravyam ity ucyate so 'rtho bhedyatvena vivakṣitaḥ //* ("An object, with reference to which a demonstrative referring to a thing is used, is called *dravya* if it is intended to be conveyed as something to be differentiated [by a *guṇa*].") Bhartṛhari distinguishes

of a nominal base, as *svabhāvasiddha*. For this characterization of a substance we have a clarifying explanation by Helārāja.

> *Prakāśa* on *VP*3.8.1: *svabhāvasiddhaṃ tu dravyam ity uktam / vāstavena rūpeṇa sādhanādhīnasiddher anityasya dravyasya kathaṃ svābhāvikī siddhiḥ syāt / śābdena rūpeṇa vastu bhāvyamānātmakam api prātipadikaiḥ siddharūpam ucyate /*
> "Patañjali has stated: *svabhāvasiddhaṃ tu dravyam.* From the point of view of how things are (*vāstavena rūpeṇa*), a substance is impermanent (*anitya*) because it is brought to accomplishment in dependence on things that bring it to accomplishment (*sādhanādhīnasiddhi*); how could it be that such a substance is by nature something that is already brought to accomplishment (*svābhāvikī siddhiḥ*)? [Therefore] from the point of view of how things are spoken of (*śābdena rūpeṇa*), even if it is in essence something that is brought to accomplishment, an entity is denoted by nominal bases as something that has already been brought to accomplishment."[40]

First of all, according to Helārāja, one has to distinguish between how things are (*vāstavena rūpeṇa*) and how things are spoken of (*śābdena rūpeṇa*). A substance cannot be said to be *svabhāvasiddha* from the point of view of the former, for the reason that it is by its own nature something to be brought to accomplishment.

---

between two sorts of substances: according to Helārāja, a substance on the verbal level (*sāṃvyavahārikaṃ dravyam*) and the one on the level of the ultimate truth (*pāramārthikaṃ dravyam*). The substance as thus defined by Bhartṛhari is the former, whereas the latter is identified with the ultimate reality Brahman. *Prakāśa* on *VP*3.2.1: *dravyaṃ ca dvividham, pāramārthikaṃ sāṃvyavahārikaṃ ca / tatra dvitīyaṃ bhedyabhedakaprastāvena guṇasamuddeśe vakṣyate—vastūpalakṣaṇaṃ yatra ityādinā / anena ca dravyeṇa vyāḍidarśane sarve śabdā dravyābhidhāyino bhavanti / iha tu pāramārthikaṃ dravyaṃ nirūpyate /*

[40] Kaiyaṭa also states the same thing. *Pradīpa* on *MBh* ad *A*1.3.1 (II.189): *kṛtatākriyamāṇatākartavyatāyuktāny api dravyāṇi siddharūpāṇy eva prātipadikenābhidhīyante / śabdāntareṇa tu teṣām avasthāntaraṃ pratipādyate /* In the situation conveyed by the utterance *ghaṭaṃ karoti* 'He is making a pot', the substance pot has the property of being made (*kriyamāṇatā*), which occurs in it with respect to the act of making signified by the verb *kṛ* in *karoti*.

It is from the point of view of the latter that such a substance is considered to be *svabhāvasiddha*. The substance is what a nominal base denotes by its own nature as *siddha* irrespective of how it is. Clearly, thus, the term *svabhāva* refers to an intrinsic denotative nature of a linguistic item in Patañjali's semantics. This point is clearer when Kaiyaṭa remarks that Patañjali makes the statement *svabhāvasiddhaṃ tu dravyam* according to how denotative powers of linguistic items are (*śabdaśaktyanusāreṇaitad ucyate*) and when Nāgeśa elucidates the notion of *svabhāva* in question by saying that the *svabhāva* is of a denotative power of a linguistic item (*śabdaśaktisvabhāva*).[41]

Now, such being the case, considering that Patañjali admits verbs to denote actions by their own nature and contrasts *bhāvyate* with *svabhāvasiddha* here, what Patañjali means to say by the statement *kriyā caiva bhāvyate svabhāvasiddhaṃ tu dravyam* under discussion is as follows: A verb denotes by its own nature an action as that which is brought into being (*bhāvyate*), while a nominal base denotes by its own nature a substance as that which has already been brought to accomplishment (*siddha*).[42]

When actions are said to be denoted by verbs as things to be brought into being, the very fact that actions are brought into being indicates that they are put in the process of self-realization, as will be taken up later. And it is substances denoted as established by nominal bases that bring actions into being. What brings an action into being should be what has already been established and hence is already present (*siddha*). Thus only a substance characterized as such can come to be related to an action as a

---

[41] *Uddyota* on *MBh* ad *A*1.3.1 (II.189): *svabhāvena śabdaśaktisvabhāvena* . . . / For Kaiyaṭa's remark, see the present section, fn. 34.

[42] This point becomes clear when we consider the following statement by Helārāja. *Prakāśa* on *VP*3.8.12: *iha sādhyatvenābhidhīyamāno 'rthaḥ siddho 'pi kriyeti kriyā caiva hi bhāvyate, svabhāvasiddhaṃ dravyam iti śābdena rūpeṇa kriyālakṣaṇākhyānāt sattāpi ākhyātāt sādhyatayā pratīyamānā kriyā* / Helārāja explicitly states that the Bhāṣya under discussion defines an action from the point of view of how things are spoken of (*śābdena rūpeṇa*).

factor to bring the latter to accomplishment. This is explicitly stated by Patañjali as follows:

> *MBh* ad *A*3.1.67 (II.57.8–9): *dravyaṃ kriyayā samavāyaṃ gacchati / kaṃ samavāyam / dravyaṃ kriyābhinirvṛttau sādhanatvam upaiti /*
> "A substance forms a relation to an action. [Question] What relation? [Answer] A substance becomes a sādhana of bringing an action to accomplishment."

Precisely from this viewpoint that a substance serves as means for bringing an action to accomplishment, Patañjali regards the substance and action as forming a pair, treating them as contrasting with each other. It is with a view to sharply contrasting an action with a substance as something established (*siddha*) that Bhartṛhari uses the expression *sādhyatvena* 'as that which is to be brought to accomplishment' in his definition of an action. In this connection it will be useful to cite *VP*3.8.1 here again and its parallel, *VP*3.7.79.

> *VP*3.8.1: *yāvat siddham asiddhaṃ vā sādhyatvenābhidhīyate / āśritakramarūpatvāt tat kriyeti pratīyate //*
> "Whether it has or has not been brought to accomplishment, whatever is denoted as something yet to be brought to accomplishment (*sādhyatvenābhidhīyate*) because it assumes sequence is what one understands by the word *kriyā* [in grammar]."[43]
>
> *VP*3.7.79: *nirvartyo vā vikāryo vā prāpyo vā sādhanāśrayaḥ / kriyāṇām eva sādhyatvāt siddharūpo 'bhidhīyate //*
> "Whether it is something to be made (*nirvartya*), modified (*vikārya*), or reached (*prāpya*), a locus of a [capacity-]sādhana[, which is a substance,] is denoted as something that has already been brought to accomplishment (*siddharūpo 'bhidhīyate*) because an action alone is denoted as something that is to be brought to accomplishment."[44]

---

[43] See Introduction [0.3.1].

[44] Helārāja explains that the word *sādhanāśraya* means a locus of capacity (*śaktyādhāra*) and that the capacity-locus is what is in essence something

In this way, when it comes to Bhartṛhari, an action is what is denoted as something yet to be brought to accomplishment (*sādhyatvenābhidhīyate*) and a substance is what is denoted as something that has already been brought to accomplishment (*siddharūpo 'bhidhīyate*). It goes without saying that for Bhartṛhari also linguistic items have their denotation (*abhidhāna*) of meanings determined by their own nature, as Kātyāyaya and Patañjali hold.[45]

---

that has been realized (*niṣpannarūpa*) and is denoted by a nominal (*nāmapadair ucyate*) and further that such a locus is nothing but a substance (*dravya*). See *Prakāśa* on *VP*3.7.79.

According to Pāṇinīyas, an object by *A*1.4.49 has three subtypes: a thing which is made (*nirvartya*), modified (*vikārya*), and reached (*prāpya*). In *ghaṭaṃ karoti* 'He is making a pot' a substance referred to by the word *ghaṭa* serves as object of the *nirvartya* type, in *kāṣṭhaṃ bhasma karoti* 'He is turning the wood to ashes' a substance referred to by the word *kāṣṭha* serves as object of the *vikārya* type, and in *ādityaṃ paśyati* 'He is looking at the sun' a substance referred to by the word *āditya* serves as object of the *prāpya* type.

[45] In his *Vaiyākaraṇabhūṣaṇasāra* Kauṇḍabhaṭṭa explains what is meant by the word *sādhyatva* in *VP*3.8.1. *VBhS* on *VSK*2: *kriyāntarākāṅkṣānutthāpakatāvacchedakarūpaṃ sādhyatvam* / According to him, the property of being something to be brought to accomplishment (*sādhyatva*) is the property which delimits the property of not awakening expectations of an action different from what has the former property. For Nāgeśa, on the other hand, it is simply the property of being something to be brought to completion. *VSLM*551: *vastutaḥ sādhyatvaṃ niṣpādyatvam eva* / Nāgeśa describes in detail Kauṇḍabhaṭṭa's notion of *sādhyatva*. According to Nāgeśa, what is spoken of as *sādhya* is a thing which is a complex of component actions that occur in a sequence and which is fit to be connected with kārakas and further which does not awaken expectations of an action different from itself. *VSLM*550: *sādhyatvaṃ ca pūrvāparībhūtāvayavatvasamānādhikaraṇaṃ kārakānvayayogyatāvacchedakaṃ kriyāntarākāṅkṣānutthāpakatāvacchedakaṃ ca yad vaijātyaṃ tad rūpam* / As properties of an action Bhartṛhari has already pointed out the property of having an expectancy for sādhanas (*sādhanākāṅkṣatā*) as well as the property of being something to be brought to accomplishment. See Section 6, fn. 5.

It is to be noted in passing that in correlation with *sādhyatva* as held by Kauṇḍabhaṭṭa the property of being something that has already been brought to accomplishment (*siddhatva*) is defined as what delimits the property of awakening expectations of an action different from what has the former property. *VSLM*549-550: *siddhatvaṃ kriyāntarākāṅkṣotthāpakatāvacchedakaṃ yad vaijātyaṃ tad rūpam* /

5.2.3.3. If the term *bhāva* is interpreted as signifying that which is brought into being, Patañjali points out, the *bhāva*-based definition leads to an undesired result that relative terms (*sambandhiśabda*) such as *mātṛ* 'mother' are called *dhātu.*[46] The argument he has made is ingenious. He argues as follows: It is not the case that a certain woman is a mother by nature; she becomes a mother through her son being born. And the fact that she becomes a mother means that motherhood is brought about in her. In this case, thus, one may not say that a certain woman is endowed by her own nature with motherhood (*svabhāvasiddha*) but that her motherhood is something produced (*bhāvyate*). When this is what Patañjali means, the 'own nature' (*svabhāva*) is far from an intrinsic denotative nature of a linguistic item, having an ontological value. Thus it is clear that Patañjali points out that the *bhāva*-based definition under consideration leads to the undesired consequence that such a relative term as *mātṛ* is called *dhātu*, by consciously confusing a denotative 'own nature' with an ontological 'own nature'. Accordingly we have to note here that the relevant passage of the Bhāṣya might be paraphrased in two ways.

I. An action is that which is by nature something that is brought into being, while a substance is that which is by nature something that has already been brought into being.
II. An action is that which a linguistic item by its intrinsic denotative nature denotes as something that is brought into being, while a substance is that which a linguistic item by its intrinsic denotative nature denotes as something that has already been brought into being.

Needless to say, Patañjali adopts the first interpretation for the sake of argumentation and what he really means to say is that which is given by the second paraphrase, as we shall see later in Section 7 [7.2.2].

---

[46] *MBh* ad *A*1.3.1 (I.257.9–10): *evam api bhavet keṣāṃcin na syād yāni na bhāvyante / ye tv ete sambandhiśabdās teṣāṃ prāpnoti—mātā pitā bhrāteti /*

5.2.4. Verb meanings as in process

Now that we have seen that Patañjali characterizes a verb meaning as what comes into being (referred to by the term *bhāva* as a *kartṛsādhana*) and what is brought into being (referred to by the term *bhāva* as a *karmasādhana*), let us look at the question how the verb meaning is to be viewed given such a characterization of its own.

As said in Section 4 (Part 2 [4.3.2.2.1]), Patañjali finds a reason for an action being beyond perception in the fact that an action assumes the form of a mass (*piṇḍībhūtā*). Now consider the situation expressed by the utterance *devadattaḥ pacati* 'Devadatta is cooking'. What we conceive to be the action of cooking is a complex (*samūha*) of component actions (*avayavakriyā*) such as the act of putting a pot on the stove (*adhiśrayaṇa*). Patañjali states as follows:

> *MBh* ad *A*3.1.22 (II.28.15–16): *yady apy ekā sāmānyakriyā, avayavakriyās tu bahvyaḥ / adhiśrayaṇodakāsecanataṇḍulāvapanaidhopakarṣaṇakriyāḥ /*
>
> "Although an action which is common [to its component actions] is one, yet the component actions are many. [For example, the act of cooking is the composite of component actions such as] putting a pot on the stove (*adhiśrayaṇa*), pouring water and food grains in it (*udakāsecana*, *taṇḍulāvapana*), setting fire wood under it (*edhopakarṣaṇa*)."

The acts of putting a pot on the stove, pouring water in it, and so on constitute parts of cooking. Such component actions can never occur together. This is the reason why the composite action said to be denoted by a verb like *pac* is indeed not directly perceptible. The component actions of the act of cooking occur in a sequence to produce the result of the softening of rice grains, from the beginning of the composite act to its termination. And these component actions, coming into play with one single result as an intended goal, are made mentally unified; these unified component actions are spoken of as an action.[47]

[47] See *VP*3.8.4: *guṇabhūtair avayavaiḥ samūhaḥ kramajanmanām / bu-*

Now the situation conveyed by the utterance *devadattaḥ pacati* is the one expressed by the utterance *pāko jāyate* 'the act of cooking is coming into being' also. The paraphrase *pāko jāyate* of *devadattaḥ pacati* clearly shows that the act of cooking denoted by the verb *pac* is what is coming into being. Until the result of cooking has been achieved and, to convey such a stage, the utterance *pāko jātaḥ* 'the act of cooking has come into being' is used, the action of cooking is in the process of being brought to accomplishment, in which its component actions are brought about in a sequence by its sādhanas or participants in it such as Devadatta. In this sense the act of cooking is said to be what is brought into being in time. This amounts thus to saying: That an action is denoted as something that is brought into being means that it is denoted as something in the process of being brought to accomplishment. Patañjali's characterization of a verb meaning as what comes into being and as what is brought into being accordingly shows his view of the verb meaning as in process.

5.3. Patañjali's notions of *kriyā*

As said, Patañjali does not give any etymological explanation to the term *kriyā* as he does to the term *bhāva*. Nonetheless, we see that in his Bhāṣya on *A*1.3.1 Patañjali accepts three kinds of notions of *kriyā*.

1) Causal *kriyā*—activity to lead to a result (*abhūtaprādurbhāva*)
2) Semantic *kriyā*—*bhāva* as what is brought into being (*bhāvyate*)
3) Behavioral *kriyā*—differentiated activity (*pravṛttiviśeṣa*)

Now let us look closely at each of these sorts of notions of *kriyā*.

---

ddhyā prakalpitābhedaḥ kriyety vyapadiśyate // Kātyāyana observes that it is until the rice becomes soft that the fire-wood will burn. *Vt.* 10 ad *A*1.4.23: *edhāḥ pakṣyanty ā viklitter jvaliṣyanti /* Thus one may consider the result of the act of cooking to be the softening of food (*viklitti*). Note that, according to Bhartṛhari, the property of taking on the form a sequence (*kramarūpopagraha*) is one of the properties of an action. See Section 6, fn. 5.

5.3.1. Causal *kriyā*

What I call causal *kriyā* is precisely a meaning of the verb *kṛ*, an action denoted by that verb. The action of this kind, the causal *kriyā*, is mentioned by Patañjali in the following statement:

> *MBh* ad *A*1.3.1 (I.254.20–21): *kathaṃ punar jñāyate kriyāvacanāḥ pacādaya iti / yad eteṣāṃ karotinā sāmānādhikaraṇyam / kiṃ karoti, pacati / kiṃ kariṣyati, pakṣyati / kim akārṣīt, apākṣīd iti /*
> "[Question] How is it known that items such as *pac* denote actions?
> [Answer] [It is known from the fact] that [the meanings of] these items have the relationship of concurrence with [the meaning of] the verb *kṛ*, as shown in the question-and-answers *kiṃ karoti—pacati* 'What is he doing? He is cooking', *kiṃ kariṣyati—pakṣyati* 'What will he do? He will cook', *kim akārṣīt—apākṣīt* 'What has he done? He has cooked'."

This statement is made in connection with the *kriyā*-based definition Kātyāyana has proposed as an alternative to the dhātupāṭha-based definition. From the statement, we can recognize that Patañjali first of all takes the term *kriyā* in the *kriyā*-based definition as signifying the meaning of the verb *kṛ*. In his Bhāṣya on *vt.* 7 ad *A*1.3.1, in order to exemplify the polysemy of a single verb, Patañjali, taking up the verb *kṛ*, refers to *abhūtaprādurbhāva* as its general meaning, which in a sense can be regarded as a *svapadārtha* (primary meaning) of the verb *kṛ*.[48] The term *abhūtaprādurbhāva* means 'the act of calling into existence something that has not yet come into existence', which leads later Pāṇinīyas like Bhaṭṭoji Dīkṣita to treat the word *kriyā* as synonymous with the words *vyāpāra*, *bhāvanā*, *utpādanā*, *bhāva*.[49] The explanation

---

[48] *MBh* ad *A*1.3.1 (I.256.13–14): *karotir abhūtaprādurbhāve dṛṣṭo nirmalīkaraṇe cāpi vartate /* See Section 4, Part 2, fn. 42.

[49] See *VSK*5ab: *vyāpāro bhāvanā saivotpādanā saiva ca kriyā* and *SK*2756: *bhāvo bhāvanā utpādanā kriyā*. See also *BM* on *SK*3883: *abhūtaprādurbhāvo niṣpādanam.* Interestingly we find the *Kāśikāvṛtti* on *A*6.2.149 stating: *kṛtam iti kriyāsāmānye karotir vartate nābhūtaprādurbhāva eva*, according to which the verb *kṛ* in the derivate *kṛta* in the

of the word *kriyā* with these synonymous words indicates that the verb *kṛ* is an equivalent for the derived verb *bhāvi* which is formed from the verb *bhū* that signifies *utpatti* 'birth' with the causative affix ***ṇic***, as a consequence of which *karoti* means *bhāvayati* '. . . brings something into existence', in short that the word *kriyā* means 'the activity which leads to a result' (*phalotpattyanukūlo vyāpāraḥ*).[50] Recall that in explaining the term *kāraka* etymogically Patañjali states: *karoti nirvartayati*; *nirvartayati* in this gloss means 'brings something to accomplishment'.[51] This implies that he takes the verb *kṛ* to mean the activity of bringing something to accomplishment. I have pointed out that the term *kriyā*, as a *karmasādhana*, refers to something bought to accomplishment in correlation to kārakas. Here the term *kriyā*, as a *bhāvasādhana*, signifies an act in the abstract, the activity of bringing something to accomplishment.[52]

As has already been stated, Patañjali tries to show what is meant by the term *kriyā* in the *kriyā*-based definition Kātyāyana had proposed, by enumerating its synonymous terms *īhā*, *ceṣṭā*, and *vyāpāra*.[53] What we see from this enumeration is that *kriyā* is regarded as an activity (*vyāpāra*) which is common to mental and physical actions. There is no doubt that when Patañjali glosses the term *kriyā* with the term *vyāpāra*, he means by the latter term such a causal activity.

---

sūtra refers to an action in general (*kriyāsāmānya*) and not merely to *abhūtaprādurbhāva.* If we accept the verb *kṛ* in question as referring to *abhūtaprādurbhāva* alone, we would have to have only items such as *suptakṛtám* 'made during sleep' and *suptabhāvitám* 'brought about during sleep' and not items such as *suptapralapitám* 'uttered during sleep', according to the *Bālamanoramā*. It is to be noted that the item *kṛta* is treated as synonymous with the item *bhāvita* (*bhū* + ***ṇic*** + ***kta***) 'produced'.

[50] This is clearly stated by Nāgeśa as follows. *BŚIŚ*1954: *bhāvo bhāvaneti / utpattyarthāt bhavater ṇyantāt er aci bhāvaḥ / yuci bhāvanā / tad dhvanayann āha—utpādaneti / anena bhavater utpattyarthatvam, ṇyantasya bhavateḥ śuddhena karotinā tulyārthatvaṃ ca darśitam / sa ca phalotpattyanukūlo vyāpāraḥ /* As said in Section 4, Part 2 [4.3.2.1], later Pāṇinīyas come to view a verb meaning from its causal aspect.

[51] See Section 1, fn. 3.

[52] See Section 1 [1.4].

[53] See Section 4 [4.3.2.1].

It is thus obvious that when he speaks of *kriyā* as a meaning of the verb *kṛ*, he grasps it from a causal point of view as such an activity which brings about a result. Moreover, he stated in the same context of the argumentation on the *kriyā*-based definition that an action has to be known through inference and that one infers the action from its result such as reaching another place. If actions had been considered not to give rise to certain results, the theory of action-inference (*kriyānumāna*) itself could not have been propounded at all.[54] Thus Patañjali's theory of action-inference faithfully reflects his view of an action as a causal *kriyā*.

5.3.2. Semantic *kriyā*

Semantic *kriyā* is mentioned in connection with the third interpretation of the term *bhāva* in the *bhāva*-based definition. It is what Patañjali posits as a verb meaning (*dhātvartha*) and that which he characterizes as something that is brought into being (*bhāvyate*) and hence identifies with the third *bhāva* referred to by the term *bhāva* as a *karmasādhana*.

According to Patañjali, an action can be defined as that which a verb by its 'own nature' or its intrinsic denotative nature denotes as something that is brought into being. No doubt, this is exactly the same as what Bhartṛhari intends to say in *VP*3.8.1, where he formulates the definition of *kriyā* as what is denoted as something to be brought to accomplishment (*sādhyatvenābhidhīyate*). As said, an action, when viewed in correlation with kārakas, is described as *kriyā* or what is brought to accomplishment by them.[55] Thus we arrive at the semantic *kriyā* when we grasp an action on a semantic level by setting it into correlation with those kārakas involved in the action which are substances characterized as denoted as already established (*siddha*).

5.3.3. Behavioral *kriyā*

5.3.3.1. In addition to the above-mentioned two sorts of notions of *kriyā*, causal *kriyā* and semantic *kriyā*, Patañjali introduces the

[54] See Section 4, Part 2 [4.3.3.2].

[55] See Section 1 [1.5].

third notion of *kriyā*, that I call 'behavioral *kriyā*'. The introduction of the notion of behavioral *kriyā* was called for in order to demonstrate that meanings signified by items such as *as* are actions. As stated, Patañjali defines the *kriyā* of this sort as follows:

> *MBh* ad *A*1.3.1 (I.258.11): *kārakāṇāṃ pravṛttiviśeṣaḥ kriyā* /
> "An action consists in kārakas' different ways of performing activities."[56]

5.3.3.2. For the purpose of understanding what Patañjali means by this definition, it will be useful to quote the Bhāṣya on *A*5.3.42 *saṅkhyāyā vidhārthe dhā* in which the same definition of an action appears.

*A*5.3.42 provides that the affix *dhā* follows a number word used in the sense of *vidhā* 'manner', accounting for the derivation of items such as *dvidhā* 'in two ways' in the utterance *dvidhā bhuṅkte* 'He eats in two ways'. In his vārttika on this sūtra Kātyāyana proposed the reformulation of the present sūtra: *dhāvidhānaṃ dhātvarthapṛthagbhāve*, according to which the sūtra in question should be formulated as *saṅkhyāyā dhātvarthapṛthagbhāve dhā* 'the affix *dhā* follows a number word used to signify *dhātvarthapṛthagbhāva* 'the difference of *dhātvartha* (verb meaning)'. Under this vārttika Patañjali develops the following argument:

> *MBh* ad *A*5.3.42 (II.410.10–14): *kaḥ punar dhātvarthapṛthagbhāvaḥ / kiṃ yat tad devadattaḥ kaṃsapātryāṃ pāṇinaudanaṃ bhuṅkta iti / nety āha / kārakapṛthaktvam etat / yat tarhi tat kalye bhuṅkte sāyaṃ bhuṅkta iti / nety āha / kālapṛthaktvam etat / yat tarhi śītaṃ bhuṅkta uṣṇaṃ bhuṅkta iti / nety āha / guṇapṛthaktvam etat / kas tarhi dhātvarthapṛthagbhāvaḥ / kārakāṇāṃ pravṛttiviśeṣaḥ kriyā / yady evaṃ kriyāprakāre'yaṃ bhavati /*
> "[Question] But what is meant by the term *dhātvarthapṛthagbhāva* in the reformulation of the sūtra? Is it what is understood from the utterance *devadattaḥ kaṃsapātryāṃ pāṇinaudanaṃ*

---

[56] See Section 4, Part4 [4.8.2.1].

> *bhuṅkte* 'Devadatta is eating rice-gruel in a bell-metal dish with his hand'?
> [Answer] 'No,' he says. What is found in such an utterance is the difference among kārakas (*kārakapṛthaktva*).
> [Question] Then, is it what is understood from the utterance *kalye bhuṅkte sāyaṃ bhuṅkte* 'He eats in the morning and he eats in the evening'?
> [Answer] 'No,' he says. What is found in such an utterance is the difference of time (*kālapṛthaktva*).
> [Question] Then, is it what is understood from the utterance *śītaṃ bhuṅkta uṣṇaṃ bhuṅkte* 'He eats something hot and he eats something cold'?
> [Answer] 'No,' he says. What is found in such an utterance is the difference of quality (*guṇapṛthaktva*).
> [Question] Then, what is meant by the term *dhātvarthapṛthagbhāva*?
> [Answer] [The difference in action is meant, for] an action consists in kārakas' different ways of performing activities (*kārakāṇāṃ pravṛttiviśeṣaḥ kriyā*).
> [Objection] If so, the proposed reformulation amounts to saying that the affix *dhā* occurs after a number word used to signify *kriyāprakāra* 'manner of acting'. [As a result of it, there is no need for reformulating the present sūtra, since the term *vidha* means *prakāra*.]"

Patañjali states that from the utterances *devadattaḥ kaṃsapātryāṃ pāṇinaudanaṃ bhuṅkte*, *kalye bhuṅkte sāyaṃ bhuṅkte*, and *śītaṃ bhuṅkta uṣṇaṃ bhuṅkte* one respectively understands the difference in kāraka, the difference of time, and the difference of quality. What he means by stating so is that from the finite verb form *bhuṅkte*, even where it recurs, one cannot understand that the specific act of eating referred to by the verb *bhuj* is something differentiated from others, which he speaks of as *dhātvarthapṛthagbhāva* or *kriyāprakāra*. This is neatly set forth by Bhartṛhari as follows:

*VP*2.454: *nivṛttabhedā sarvaiva kriyākhyāte 'bhidhīyate / śruter aśakyā bhedānāṃ pravibhāgaprakalpanā //*
"In a finite verb form (*ākhyāta*) any action is denoted by it as something whose difference from others has disappeared (*nivṛttabhedā*). From an uttered item [which denotes its object in a general way] one cannot conceive of particular objects distinguished from one another."

According to Bhartṛhari, from the point of view of how the act of eating signified by the verb *bhuj* is, it may be said that there are a variety of acts of eating and hence that a particular act of eating is differentiated from other acts of eating; on the other hand, from the point of view of how it is denoted by the verb *bhuj*, it may be said that the verb *bhuj* does not signify a particular act of eating but any act of eating, in general. Thus, in order to denote the difference from other actions that an action as a verb meaning is assumed to have, one has to use an item ending in the affix *dhā* that is introduced to signify *dhātvarthapṛthagbhāva* or *kriyāprakāra*, such as *dvidhā* 'in two manners' as in *dvidhā bhuṅkte* 'he eats in two ways'. But on what grounds can one say that a particular act of eating is differentiated from other acts of eating? The notion of behavioral *kriyā* comes herein. According to Patañjali, an action is susceptible of differentiation because it is what is considered to consist in a kāraka's activity which is differentiated from activities of other kārakas.

5.3.3.3. It is necessary, at this point, to make clear what is meant by the phrase *kārakāṇām pravṛttiviśeṣaḥ* in connection with Patañjali's definition of behavioral *kriyā*. Patañjali explains the phrase with the following words:

MBh ad *A*1.3.1 (I.258.11–12): *anyathā ca kārakāṇi śuṣkaudane pravartante 'nyathā ca māṃsaudane /*
"Kārakas perform activities in one manner with respect to dry rice-gruel and in another manner with respect to rice-gruel with meat."

Here, by using the word *anyathā* 'otherwise', which is derived from the sarvanāman *anyad* 'other' by introducing the affix *thāl* to denote *prakāra* by *A*5.3.23 *prakāravacane thāl*, Patañjali means to say that the term *pravṛttiviśeṣa* signifies the difference in the manner in which an activity is carried out by a kāraka, or, to put it another way, an activity differentiated in manner from other activities. Now let us notice that Patañjali in his Bhāṣya on *A*5.3.42 glosses the term *dhātvarthapṛthagbhāva* with the term *kriyāprakāra*. Evidently the words *dhātvartha* 'verb-meaning' and *pṛthagbhāva* 'difference' correspond to the words *kriyā* and *prakāra*, respectively. There is no problem about equating *dhātvartha* with *kriyā*. Then what about the equation of *pṛthagbhāva* with *prakāra*? According to Bhartṛhari, in Pāṇini's grammar the term *prakāra* is used in two senses: *sādṛśya* 'similarity' and *bheda* 'difference, differentiation'.[57] In view of this, thus, we may justify the equation in question to say that in the term *kriyāprakāra* the word *prakāra* is used in the sense of *bheda*.[58] In this connection it is to be noted in passing that the term *prakāra* in *A*5.3.23 which accounts for the derivate *yathā* is also interpreted as signifying *bheda*.[59]

It has been stated that the manner how kārakas perform activities with reference to dry rice-gruel is different from the manner how they perform activities with reference to rice-gruel with meat. Consider the following utterances:

---

[57] *VP*3.14.619: *sādṛśyam eva sarvatra prakāraḥ kaiścid iṣyate / bhede 'pi tu prakārākhyā kaiś cid abhyupagamyate //*

[58] The term *prakāra* in the sense of *bheda* is explained in the *Kāśikāvṛtti* as follows. *Kāśikāvṛtti* ad *A*5.3.69: *sāmānyasya bhedako viśeṣaḥ prakāraḥ*, according to which *prakāra* is a specific feature which differentiates something general.

[59] See the *Kāśikāvṛtti* on *A*5.3.23: *sāmānyasya bhedako viśeṣaḥ prakāraḥ*. See fn. 58 above. When one has the utterance *yathā devadattaḥ pacati tathā yajñadattaḥ* 'As Devadatta cooks, so does Yajñadatta', one understands that there are two different manners of performing the action of cooking and that the manners have similarity; namely one understands Devadatta's action of cooking to be differentiated from Yajñadatta's and the former to be similar to the latter. For further details concerning the significance of the term *prakāra*, see Kapil Deo Shastri [1963] and Chaturvedi [2001: 184–190].

A. *devadatta odanaṃ bhuṅkte* /
'Devadatta is eating rice-gruel.'
B. *caitra odanaṃ bhuṅkte* /
'Caitra is eating rice-gruel.'
C. *devadattaḥ śuṣkaudanaṃ bhuṅkte* /
'Devadatta is eating dry rice gruel.'
D. *devadatto māṃsaudanaṃ bhuṅkte* /
'Devadatta is eating rice gruel with meat.')
E. *devadattaḥ pacati* /
'Devadatta is cooking.'

As said, the finite verb form *bhuṅkte* used in the utterances from A to D denotes its meaning, the act of eating, in a general form and not in a specific form. However, it is unlikely that Devadatta carries out an activity for accomplishing the act of eating rice-gruel exactly in the same manner as Caitra does. Similarly, the manner in which Devadatta eats dry rice-gruel is different from that in which he eats rice-gruel with meat; according to Kaiyaṭa, in the former case Devadatta goes at the act of eating reluctantly or with hesitation (*mandaprayatnaḥ*) and in the latter case aggressively or with alacrity (*saṃvegena*).[60] In short, whoever may eat and whatever one may eat, the act of eating is certainly denoted by the same finite verb form *bhuṅkte* in the same form; but, the manner to eat differs from kāraka to kāraka, as a matter of fact.

This is how a certain activity is clearly differentiated from other activities of the same class (*sajātīya*). Difference is also found between a certain activity and other heterogeneous activities of a different class (*vijātīya*).[61] If an activity is differentiated from other activities of the same class, how much more will it be so from those of a dissimilar class?[62] It is highly absurd to

[60] *Pradīpa* on *MBh* ad *A*1.3.1 (II.194): *śuṣkaudane mandaprayatnaḥ pravartate, māṃsaudane tu saṃvegena* /

[61] *Prakāśa* on *VP*3.8.1: *tathā hi sarvā pravṛttiḥ pravṛttyantarād bhidyamānā viśeṣarūpatām āpadyata iti sakalakriyānuyāyīdaṃ lakṣaṇam* / *viśeṣaś ca sajātīyād vijātīyāc ca* /

[62] *Prakāśa* on *VP*3.8.1: *vijātīyād bhedas tu pacati paṭhatītyādau spaṣṭa eva* /

assume that Devadatta performs the activity of eating in the same manner as he does the activity of cooking. In this way, in the light of the manner to perform an activity, it has to be concluded that any activity is differentiated from other activities, on which Kaiyaṭa remarks:

> *Pradīpa* on *MBh* ad *A*1.3.1 (II.194): *sarvā pravṛttiḥ pravṛtty-antarād bhidyate* /
> "Any activity is differentiated from other activities."

It is thus evident that, on the assumption that all activities in which kārakas are involved are differentiated from one another in terms of the manner to perform them, Patañjali has defined an action in this way, namely as *kārakāṇāṃ pravṛttiviśeṣaḥ kriyā.*[63] That is the behavioral *kriyā*.

5.3.3.4. What is noteworthy in connection with this definition of behavioral *kriyā* is, moreover, that Patañjali goes on to state the following on the basis of the given definition:

> *MBh* ad *A*1.3.1 (I.258.15–16): *kriyāyāḥ kriyā nivartikā bhavati, dravyaṃ dravyasya nivartakam* /
> "It is an action that excludes another action; and, it is a substance which excludes another substance."

It is natural for Patañjali to say that an action excludes another action from the viewpoint that an action consists in an activity which is differentiated from other activities. The exclusion of other actions is what Helārāja calls a property of an action (*kriyā-dharma*).[64] As shall be seen later, Patañjali introduces the notion of such a property of an action as the exclusion of other actions

---

[63] As is shown by Patañjali's explanation of the given definition, kārakas are regarded as agents with respect to the act of performing an activity (*kārakāṇi pravartante*). Here the term *kāraka* refers to any kāraka that is regarded as agent with respect to its own subsidiary action. See Section 4, Part 4, fn. 7. See also Helārāja's interpretation of the present definition of behavioral *kriyā* ([5.3.3.6]).

[64] *Prakāśa* on *VP*3.8.1: *yady api ca bhāvavikāreṣu tiṣṭhatir nopasaṅkhyā-taḥ tathāpi asyāsty eva kriyādharmānvayaḥ / tathā hi—kriyā kriyāyā ni-vartikā bhavati dravyaṃ dravyasya ity uktam* /

in the context where he discusses the question of how to demonstrate that the verb *sthā*, which is not enumerated in the list of *bhāvavikāra* in the *Nirukta*, denotes an action.[65] However, for him, the property of the exclusion of other actions is to be found in any verb meaning and therefore serves to prove that meanings of all verbs, including a verb like *as*, are actions.

5.3.3.5. Behavioral *kriyā* and Bhartṛhari's action-definition

Incidentally, it should be noted that the behavioral *kriyā*, which is defined as consisting in kārakas' different ways of performing activities, is not reflected in Bhartṛhari's definition of an action. According to Helārāja, the definition of an action from such a behavioral viewpoint applies universally to any verb meaning (*sakaladhātuvyāpakaṃ kriyālakṣaṇam*).[66] If so, one might suspect that in defining an action Bhartṛhari could have adopted such a definition of behavioral *kriyā*.

As has been pointed out, the action which Bhartṛhari tries to define is a semantic *kriyā* which is characterized as *bhāva* in the sense of that which is brought into being. What is the reason for that?

As said, for Bhartṛhari, a verb meaning is a meaning abstracted from a complex meaning of a larger linguistic unit such as a sentence or a word (*apoddhārapadārtha*), so that how a verb meaning is conceived of depends upon how a verb denotes its meaning by its intrinsic denotative nature. In his *VP*2.454 quoted above Bhartṛhari has pointed out that a verb denotes its meaning in a general form, as that whose differentiating feature has disappeared. This implies that when a verb meaning is abstracted from a complex meaning of a finite verb form, an action as the verb meaning is posited as being deprived of its property of the exclusion of other actions of the same class (*nivṛttabhedā*). Thus,

---

[65] *Prakāśa* on *VP*3.8.1: *tathā tiṣṭhater api kriyāntaranivṛttivacanatvād etad eva kriyālakṣaṇam anugāmi / tathā hi tiṣṭhatīty ukte na vardhate 'pakṣīyate veti gamyate / tathā ca kriyāntarāpākaraṇena kārakapravṛttiviśeṣatvāt kriyātvam /* See Section 6 [6.2].

[66] *Prakāśa* on *VP*3.8.1. *sakaladhātuvyāpakaṃ kriyālakṣaṇaṃ bhāṣye praṇītaṃ—kārakāṇāṃ pravṛttiviśeṣaḥ kriyā iti /*

in consequence of having to accept a verb's intrinsic denotative nature as it is in his theory of abstraction, Bhartṛhari inevitably cannot introduce the notion of behavioral *kriyā* into his definition of an action. The ground we must find for it is precisely that a verb does not relate itself to an action's differentiating aspect at a denotative level. Presumably, it is natural that Bhartṛhari who tries to define an action from a semantic point of view should not adopt the definition of an action Patañjali formulated on the basis of analyzing how actions are viewed when they are performed in reality (*vastvartha*). For Bhartṛhari an action is strictly a meaning understood from a linguistic item (*śabdārtha*).[67]

5.3.3.6. Helārāja on *kārakāṇāṃ pravṛttiviśeṣaḥ kriyā*

In his *Prakāśa* on *VP*3.8.1 Helārāja offers diverse interpretations Patañjali's statement: *kārakāṇāṃ pravṛttiviśeṣaḥ kriyā* admits of. They are worth a mention in passing.[68]

1. A single specific activity common to all kārakas that participate in bringing an action to completion is an action (*sarveṣāṃ ekaḥ pravṛttiviśeṣaḥ*).
2. A separate activity for each of kārakas that participate in bringing an action to completion (*pratikārakaṃ bhinnā pravṛttiḥ*) or a separate activity of each kāraka is an action (*yasya kārakasya yā pravṛttiḥ sā kriyā*).
3. A specific thing (*viśeṣa*) connected with activities of kārakas (*pravṛttīnāṃ viśeṣaḥ*) is an action. What is regarded as a specific thing connected with activities of kārakas is a product (*bhūti*)

[67] Pāṇinīyas make a sharp distinction between *śabdārtha* and *vastvartha*, the basis for which is provided by Patañjali who says: *śabdapramāṇakā vayam / yac chabda āha tad asmākam pramāṇam.* Helārāja reiterates. *iha vyākaraṇe na vastvartho 'rthaḥ api tu śabdārtho 'rthaḥ.* See *Prakāśa* on *VP*3.4.3, 3.7.5, 3.7.103, 3.8.1–2, 3.14.251, 3.14.572. See also *VP*3.7.110: *buddhiśabdau pravartete yathā bhūteṣu vastuṣu / teṣām anyena tattvena vyavahāro na vidyate //* (According to Iyer's edition, I have split *yathābhūteṣu* given by Rau.) This kārikā means to say the following: With reference to things as they are (*bhūteṣu vastuṣu*) cognition and the word occur; what bear up verbal activities are nothing but things as they are cognized and as they are spoken of. On Patañjali's declaration of the basic standpoint of grammarians, see Section 7 [7.2.3].

[68] For details, see Honda [1993].

as a result in the form of softening or the like, which product is yielded by all kārakas that participate in bringing an act such as cooking to accomplishment (*sakalakārakajanyā viklittyādirūpā bhūtiḥ phalabhūtā kārakapravṛtteḥ kriyā*).

4. A differentiated activity of an agent is an action (*kartur yā viśiṣṭā pravṛttiḥ sā kriyā*). Under this interpretation, an activity is regarded as something differentiated (*pravṛttir eva viśeṣaḥ*). This interpretation does not exclude the possibility that a differentiated activity of an object is an action (*karmaṇo 'pi sūcitatvāt kārakaśabdena tadvyāpāro 'pi kriyā*).

5. A specific activity of leading to a result (*phalajananā*), common to all kārakas that participate in bringing an action to completion, is an action (*phalajananaiva sādhāraṇātmikā kriyā pravṛttiviśeṣa ity ucyate; sarveṣāṃ hi kārakāṇām ekā pravṛttiḥ phalajananālakṣaṇā*).

Of these five interpretations, Helārāja categorically denies the first for the reason that it is absurd of a kāraka such as an agent to have the same activity as other kārakas like an instrument (*karaṇa*). With respect to the third and fifth interpretations, it is probable that he proposes them as theoretical possibilities, since he does not try to amplify them. With respect to the second and fourth interpretations, on the contrary, he brings forward arguments for them. What is characteristic of the arguments is that they are constructed from the point of view of how the given interpretations are suited to the thesis that a verb denotes an activity of either an agent or an object which is denoted by an L-affix (*kartṛkarmavyāpāra eva sarvatra dhātvarthaḥ*), which he thinks is taught by A3.4.69 *laḥ karmaṇi ca bhāve cākarmakebhyaḥ*. Under the second interpretation, he justifies it by saying that the statement in question is meant for stating what an action is (*kriyāsvarūpakathana*) and not for defining what a verb meaning is (*dhātuvācyatva*). Under the fourth interpretation, on the other hand, he justifies it by stating that the term *kāraka* in the statement at hand refers primarily to an agent and obliquely to an object.

Of the second and fourth interpretations, it is the latter that Helārāja tries to establish by basing himself on the Bhāṣya pertaining to the present statement. Which implies that he considers the fourth interpretation to have been originally intended by the statement. Thus, according to Helārāja, by the statement Patañjali means that a differentiated activity of either an agent or an object is an action.

Regarding the fourth interpretation, there are two points to be pointed out. First, as Helāraja himself admits in connection with the second interpretation, by the statement Patañjali does not intend to characterize an action as conveyed by a verb. As said, a verb does not touch on a differentiating aspect of its meaning. Patañjali's present statement should not be interpreted from a point of view of the semantics of verbs. Helārāja himself is aware that the differentiating aspect forms one of the properties of an action conveyed by a verb (*kriyādharma*). Second, we accordingly need not restrict what is referred to by the term *kāraka* to an agent and an object. As pointed out, with respect to any kāraka we can have the structure conveyed by *x pravartate*. In this case, it may be reasonably said that a kāraka functions as agent with respect to its own activity. Viewed in this light alone, it is permissible to take the term *kāraka* as referring to an agent.[69]

It is plain that Helārāja's confusion between objective and semantic levels in the denotation of an action by a verb makes his interpretations of the statement difficult to understand.[70]

---

[69] See Section 4, Part 4 [4.8.2.1].

[70] We may add that in his *Prakāśa* on *VP*3.8.37 Helārāja invokes Patañjali's statement at issue to explain that an ideal and universal action (*kriyā*), which is present in precedence to a substance-sādhana, becomes the specific acts of cooking, cutting, and so on (*pravṛttiviśeṣa*) when the former inheres in the substance-sādhana. See Ogawa [2000b: fn. 10]. We may also present here the Jain Siṃhasūri's (to be more precise, Mallavādin's) interpretation of Patañjali's definition of *kriyā*. *Nyāyāgamānusāriṇī* on *Dvādaśāra-Nayacakra* 5th Ara (II.399): *bhavanam evāviśiṣṭaṃ sarvatra kriyā ity āpādite tad amṛṣyatā idaṃ vaiyākaraṇena kriyālakṣaṇam abhidhīyate—pravṛttiviśeṣaḥ kriyā ity etaj jyāyaḥ kriyālakṣaṇam, na satatasampravṛttimātram / tatra kārakāṇāṃ ity etasya vyākhyānam udbhūtaśabdaiḥ kārakasyaiva kriyātvaṃ mā vijñāyi bhavatā, kārakapṛthagbhūtā gṛhyatām iti bhedadarśanārthā ṣaṣṭhī / viśeṣagrahaṇaṃ punaḥ kimartham iti cet, tata āha—sarvatra pravṛttisambhava ityādi / kenacit phaloddeśeneti sāṃvyavahārikam odanā-*

diphalam uddiśyate, kārakavatyā iti svāśrayapṛthagbhūtakaraṇādisādhanavatyā ity arthaḥ, sarvā hi kriyā kartṛsamavāyinī karmasamavāyinī vā syāt pacatibhinattivat phalavatīti evaṃrūpāyāḥ pacipaṭhigamyādeḥ parigrahārthaṃ bhidyādeś ca viśeṣagrahaṇam iti / I will not discuss this statement as a whole, which is beyond the scope of the present work. The point is: According to Siṃhasūri, *kārakāṇāṃ pravṛttiviśeṣaḥ kriyā* is the statement to the effect that an action is a specific activity (*pravṛttiviśeṣa*) as opposed to a generic activity taking place constantly (*satatasampravṛttimātra*), which is performed with the aim of attaining a certain practical result and which is related not only to an agent and an object but also to other kārakas (*kārakāṇām*).

From all these things, thus, we can recognize that Patañjali's statement in question admits of most diverse interpretations.

Section 6

Proof of the meaning of the verb *as* being an action

6. An action being the meaning of the verb *as*

As shown, early teachers recognize a distinction between the meanings of the verbs *kṛ* and *as* such that the meaning of the former is viewed dynamically and that of the latter statically,[1] whereas Patañjali sees a difference between their meanings such that the meaning of the former is a causal action and that of the latter existence (*bhavana*).[2] Interestingly, Patañjali not only contrasts the meanings of the verbs *kṛ* and *as* but also attempts to break down the barriers of the semantic discrimination between them. I have already shown what led him to make such an attempt: Patañjali, as a preliminary to the arguments on the dhātupāṭha brought forward by Kātyāyana in his twelfth and thirteenth vārttikas, had to make the *kriyā*-based definition be on a par with the *bhāva*-based definition.[3] It was thus from the viewpoint of the *kriyā*-based definition that Patañjali attempted to leave out the distinction between the meaning of the verb *kṛ* and that of the verb *as*. In this connection let us remind ourselves of the following fact: Kātyāyana, after pointing out in his fifth vārttika that the *kriyā*-based definition does not apply to the items *as*, *bhū*, and *vid*, proposed the *bhāva*-based definition in his eighth vārttika.

There are a few points to note in the arguments on the *bhāva*-based definition in this line. Obviously, for Kātyāyana, it is not the case that as the *kriyā*-based definition does not apply to items such as *as*, so does the *bhāva*-based definition not apply to verbs of the *kṛ* class: the *bhāva*-based definition should cover verbs of

---

[1] See Section 5 [5.1].

[2] By 'causal action' I mean an activity to lead to a result, which activity is considered to be signified by the verb *kṛ* in the question-and-answer *kiṃ karoti—pacati*. See Section 5 [5.3.1]. In addition, according to Patañjali, existence (*bhavanaṃ bhāvaḥ*) is the meaning which comes readily to mind when the verb *bhū* is heard (*svapadārtha*). See Section 4, Part 3 [4.6.2.1].

[3] For details, see Section 4, Part 4 [4.8.1].

the *kṛ* class as well as of the *as* class. What Patañjali did in this connection was to leave out a distinction between the meanings of the verbs *kṛ* and *as* by means of interpreting *bhāva* as what comes into being or what is brought into being. For, as long as the term *bhāva* is taken as signifying existence, we have to make a discrimination between them. What is more, it is important that Patañjali introduced the notion of semantic *kriyā* in the context of the *bhāva*-based definition: an action as a verb meaning, characterized as *bhāva* or what is brought into being. It goes without saying that if this semantic *kriyā* were meant by the term *kriyā* in the *kriyā*-based definition, there would be no room for the contrast between the meanings of the verbs *kṛ* and *as*. For, if so, the *kriyā*-based definition and the *bhāva*-based definition would have the same value in that both equally apply to items which denote what is brought into being or what comes into being. Into his justification of the thesis that the meaning of the verb *as* is an action, however, Patañjali will also incorporate the semantic *kriyā*.

As said, he tried to prove that the meaning of the verb *as* is an action, by means of:

1) finding in what is denoted by the verb *as* the properties of an action (*kriyādharma*) which are found in what is denoted by a verb of the *kṛ* type such as *pac*;
2) resorting to *āgama* which says that a meaning of the verb *as* comes under actions;
3) showing that the non-occurrence of the question-and-answer *kiṃ karoti—asti* does not disprove that the verb *as* denotes an action.[4]

The property of the exclusion of other actions and that of being a cause for time to manifest itself (*kālābhivyaktihetutva*) are what Helārāja calls 'the properties of an action' (*kriyādharma*) and the *āgama* cited as an authority is the *Nirukta*.[5] In this section,

---

[4] See Section 4, Part 4 [4.8.4].

[5] The term *kālābhivyaktihetutva* is used by Bhartṛhari in his *Vṛtti* on *VP*1.13: *atha vā pravṛttir janmādikriyā ākhyātapadanibandhanā / tasyāḥ pravṛttir iti samākhyātāyās tattvaṃ sādhyatvaṃ sādhanākāṅkṣatā kramarūpopagrahaḥ kālābhivyaktihetutvam /* According to him, an action

focussing upon the first two points, the proof in question shall be investigated.

6.1. *bhāva* in the *Nirukta* and Patañjali's *kriyā*

According to Patañjali, we see in the *Nirukta* that the inclusion of the meaning of the verb *as* in the six modes of *bhāva* (*bhāva-vikāra*) of Vārṣyāyaṇi is made, which indicates that the meaning of the verb *as* is *bhāva*, namely *kriyā*.[6] Kaiyaṭa explains:

---

as a verb meaning has the following properties: 1) that of being something to be brought to accomplishment (*sādhyatva*), 2) that of having an expectancy for sādhanas or means to bring it to accomplishment (*sādhanākāṅkṣatā*), 3) taking on the form a sequence (*kramarūpopagraha*), and 4) the property of being a cause for time to manifest itself (*kālābhivyaktihetutva*).

Bhartṛhari uses the term *kriyādharma* in *VP*3.14.438 in connection with *avyayakṛt*. See Section 8, fn.16. Helārāja uses the same term in his *Prakāśa* on *VP*3.7.79 (*sādhyatva*), 3.8.1 (exclusion of other actions), 3.8.12 (*kālābhivyaṅgyatva*), 3.9.30 (*krama*), 3.14.344, 3.14.437, 3.14.445. The term *kriyādharma* is also used in contrast with the terms *dravyadharma* and *sattvadharma*. According to Helārāja, what has the *dravyadharma* or *sattvadharma* is: 1) something capable of being referred to by demonstratives such as *idam* 'this' and *tad* 'that' (*idaṃ tad iti pratyavamarśayogyatva*), see Section 5, fn. 39; 2) something that has already been brought to completion (*pariniṣpannatā*), see Section 5 [5.2.3.2.2] and Section 7 [7.2.3]; 3) something that is viewed as independent compared to a *guṇa* 'quality' (*svātantrya*) , Section 5, fn. 39 and *VP*3.5.1; 4) something that is connected with gender and number (*liṅgasaṅkhyāyoga*), see Section 3, fn. 25. *Prakāśa* on VP3.1.13: *dravyadharmā idaṃ tad iti pratyavamarśayogyatvam, pariniṣpannatā, svātantryam, liṅgasaṅkhyāyogaś cetyevamādayaḥ* / We may add that in *VP*3.11.5 Bhartṛhari mentions the property of being to be differentiated (*bhedyabhāva*) as a *dravyadharma*.

[6] In his commentary on the Bhāṣya citing the *Nirukta*, Kaiyaṭa tries to give a metaphysical interpretation of the term *bhāva* following Bhartṛhari, identifying *bhāva* with Being (*sattā*), the ultimate reality, that is, Brahman. *Pradīpa* on *MBh* ad A1.3.1 (195): *bhāvasya sattāyā ete prakārāḥ / sattaivānekakriyātmikā sādhanasambandhād avasīyamānasādhyarūpā janmādirūpatayāvabhāsate /* ("The statement by Vārṣyāyaṇi means that there are these modes of *bhāva* or Being. The very reality, Being, appears as 'being born' (*janman*) and so forth, for it is not distinct from a variety of actions and hence it is determined as something to be brought to accomplishment in consequence of its connection with sādhanas.") The point is that the ultimate reality, Being, appears as something corporeal (*mūrti*) and as an action. *Vṛtti* on *VP*1.1: *mūrtikriyāvivartāv avidyāśaktipravṛttimātram* / This is not the place to discuss Bhartṛhari's

> *Pradīpa* on *MBh* ad *A*1.3.1 (II.194): *atraivārthe āgamam āha—ṣaḍ bhāvavikārā iti / bhāvasya kriyāyāḥ ṣaṭ prakārā ity arthaḥ / teṣu cāstiḥ paṭhita iti tasyāpi kriyātvam ity arthaḥ /* "For this very thesis [that items such as *as* denote actions], Patañjali quotes the *āgama* saying: *ṣaḍ bhāvavikārāḥ* 'there are six modes of *bhāva*'. The statement quoted means that there are six modes of *bhāva,* namely *kriyā.* And what Patañjali means that since the meaning of the verb *as* is counted among the six modes of *bhāva*, it is also regarded as an action (*kriyā*)."

As is made clear by Kaiyaṭa, in authorizing the thesis in question, Patañjali identifies *bhāva* in the six modes of *bhāva* the *Nirukta* discusses, with *kriyā.*[7] In equating *bhāva* in the *Nirukta* with his *kriyā,* what does he understand by the term *bhāva* and what does he mean by the term *kriyā*?

We already know that in his semantics of verbs Patañjali has three kinds of *bhāva* and three kinds of *kriyā*: *bhāva* as existence (*bhavanaṃ bhāvaḥ*), *bhāva* as what comes into being (*bhavatīti bhāvaḥ*), *bhāva* as what is brought into being (*bhāvyate yaḥ sa bhāva iti*); causal *kriyā,* semantic *kriyā*, behavioral *kriyā.*[8] It is unlikely that in the given context he has in mind a *bhāva* of a

---

metaphysics of Being. It will suffice here to quote the following kārikās. *VP*1.3: *adhyāhitakalāṃ yasya kālaśaktim upāśritāḥ / janmādayo vikārāḥ ṣaḍ bhāvabhedasya yonayaḥ //* *VP*3.1.36: *saiva [= sattaiva] bhāvavikāreṣu ṣaḍavasthāḥ prapadyate / krameṇa śaktibhiḥ svābhir evaṃ pratyavabhāsate //* The former kārikā states that the six modifications, being born and so on, which are the sources of a variety of *bhāva*, have their basis in the timepower of Brahman, a power on which parts are imposed. According to Vṛṣabha, the term *bhāva* here refers to verb meanings, actions such as cooking, and a set of actions is included in the six modifications because all verbs denote *bhāva*. *Paddhati* on *VP*1.3: *bhāvabhedasya iti / bhāvaḥ sattvaṃ dhātvarthaḥ, tasya bhedaḥ pacādikriyāḥ tāsām / yonayaḥ iti / yato 'yaṃ kriyāgrāma āsv eva ṣaṭsv antarbhavati yato bhāvavacanāḥ sarve dhātava iti /* The latter kārikā states that in the modifications of *bhāva* or Being the very *sattā* or Being assumes six states; on account of its powers, it appears so in a sequence. On outlines of Bhartṛhari's metaphysics, see Ogawa [2000a].

[7] On the identification of *bhāva* in the *Nirukta* with *kriyā* by Patañjali, see also Section 4, Part 4, fn. 10.

[8] See Section 5.

different kind from these *bhāvas* and a *kriyā* of a different sort from these *kriyās*.

Now, for considering the question at issue it will be useful to quote the following passage from the *Nirukta*:

> *Nirukta*1.1: *ada iti sattvānām upadeśaḥ / gaur aśvaḥ puruṣo hastīti / bhavatīti bhāvasya / āste śete vrajati tiṣṭhatīti /*
> "Substances (*sattva*) are denoted by the demonstrative *adas* 'that' [in a general way] and by the words *go* 'cow', *aśva* 'horse', and *hastin* 'elephant' [in a specific way]. *Bhāva* is denoted by the finite verb form *bhavati* [in a general way] and by the finite verb forms *āste* '. . . is sitting', *śete* '. . . is sleeping', *vrajati* '. . . is going', and *tiṣṭhati* '. . . is standing' [in a specific way]."

To be sure, it is arguable whether the form *bhavati* in the phrase *bhavatīti bhāvasya* in the *Nirukta* signifies 'something exists' or 'something comes into being'. In the *Niruktavṛtti* the form *bhavati* is taken as referring to existence in general (*astitvamātra*) and in the *Niruktabhāṣyaṭīkā* it is taken as referring to what is coming into being (*jāyamāna*), as a matter of fact.[9] Nevertheless, from the point of view of Patañjali's semantics of verbs, the equation under consideration excludes, first of all, the possibility of the word *bhavati* in the *Nirukta* signifying 'something exists'. For, as shown, Patañjali contrasts *bhāva* as existence and a causal action. The notion of *bhāva* as existence works only within the framework of a metaphysics as systematized by Bhartṛhari.[10] Thus, on the assumption that we have the alternative of 'something exists' or 'something comes into being' concerning what the word *bhavati* here signifies, it follows that the word *bhavati* in question has to be taken to signify the latter, 'something comes into being'

---

[9] *Niruktavṛtti* on *Nirukta*1.1: *tasmād bhavatīti sarvakriyāprasavabījabhūtam astitvamātram eva nirupapadena bhavatiśabdenocyate . . . / Niruktabhāṣyaṭīkā* on *Nirukta*1.1: *sarvasya bhāvasya jāyamānatvāt, jāyamānasya ca bhavatīty anenopadeśāt /*

[10] See the present section, fn. 6.

At this point it will also be of use to cite a passage preceding the one quoted above.

> *Nirukta*1.1: *pūrvāparībhūtaṃ bhāvam ākhyātenācaṣṭe vrajati pacatīti / upakramaprabhṛty apavargaparyantam /*
> "What one means to convey by a finite verb form (*ākhyāta*) such as *vrajati* '. . . is going' or *pacati* '. . . is cooking' is *bhāva* which occurs in a sequence (*pūrvāparībhūta*) from its commencement to its termination."

We have to note that Yāska views *bhāva* in process and characterizes it as what comes into being in a temporal sequence. As said, Patañjali fully shares this view.[11] Insofar as *bhāva* is referred to by the word *bhavati* and susceptible of such characterization, consequently, he will have no difficulty in taking *bhāva* in the *Nirukta* as signifying what comes into being.

Then what *kriyā* is meant when equated with such *bhāva*? In order to answer this question, let us note, to begin with, the following point: Patañjali translates *bhāva* as what is brought into being into *bhāva* as what comes into being so as to associate the latter with an intrinsic denotative nature (*svabhāva*).[12] For him, those two kinds of *bhāva* finally become quite equivalent. In addition, let us recall that Patañjali characterized *kriyā* as a verb meaning as what is brought into being, which *kriyā* I have called 'semantic *kriyā*'.[13] If one regards *kriyā* as what is brought into being, one may reckon it as what comes into being on the same level. Thus, what follows from this is obviously that *kriyā* which is equated with *bhāva* in the *Nirukta* as Patañjali understands it is nothing but the semantic *kriyā*.

Additionally, we may say that such equation in this context makes clear the following: What Patañjali intends to imply on the basis of the *Nirukta* is that the verb *as* denotes its meaning

---

[11] See Section 5 [5.2.4].

[12] Patañjali's translation of *bhāva* (*karmasādhana*) into *bhāva* (*kartṛsādhana*) shall be discussed in Section 7 [7.2].

[13] See Section 5 [5.3.2].

exactly in the same manner as other verbs like *pac*, as what comes into being or as what is brought into being.

6.2. Exclusiveness: the property of excluding other actions

Patañjali stated that it is an action that excludes other actions; and, it is a substance which excludes other substances (*kriyāyāḥ kriyā nivartikā bhavati*; *dravyaṃ dravyasya nivartaktam*). By this statement he means that there holds the invariable concomitance between the property of excluding an action and the property of being an action: Whatever excludes an action is an action (positive concomitance); whatever is not an action does not exclude an action (negative concomitance).[14] It is for the sake of illustrating the negative concomitance that he makes mention of a substance: a substance which is not an action does not exclude an action but a substance. As shown, the reason that one may claim so, of course, lies in the fact that an action is considered to consist in an activity being differentiated from other activities (*pravṛttiviśeṣa*). To put it another way, if we take behavioral *kriyā* into consideration, we arrive at the understanding that an action has the property of excluding other actions.

In the given context Patañjali deals with two instances: the verbs *sthā* 'remain, stand' and *as*, the arguments on which are to be understood as mutually complementary. In the case of the argument on the verb *sthā* he does not give a statement of the form *anyathā kārakāṇi pravartante 'nyathā* which shows that the action in question consists in a specific activity differentiated from other activities, while in the case of the argument on the verb *as* he does not mention the understanding of the exclusion of other actions. However, clearly the purposes of both of the arguments are the same: to establish that each of the meanings of the verb *sthā* and *as* is an action.

---

[14]The invariable concomitance in question, guaranteed between x and y: $x \rightarrow y$ (*anvaya*, positive concomitance) and $\bar{y} \rightarrow \bar{x}$ (*vyatireka*, negative concomitance), leads to establsihing the relation between what makes known (x) and what is known from it (y). We should notice that the reasoning described here is that of *anvaya* and *vyatireka* of the logical reason (*hetu*) in inference (*anumāna*), not the reasoning used in establishing the relation between cause and effect. See Section 3 [3.2.3].

Now let us start with the argument on the verb *sthā*. As said, the instance of the verb *sthā* was presented in connection with the proof on the authority of the *Nirukta* that the meaning of the verb *as* is an action. The objection raised was that the verb *sthā* is not enumerated in the list of six modes of *bhāva* in the *Nirukta*; in this respect, therefore, its meaning cannot be regarded as an action.[15] In order to resolve the objection, Patañjali introduces the proof on the basis of the property in question of excluding other actions that the meaning of the verb *sthā* is an action. An idea underlying such proof is: If one understands the exclusion of actions when a certain item is used, then the meaning of that item is considered to be an action for the very reason that the meaning in question has the property of excluding other actions. He states as follows:

> *MBh* ad A1.3.1 (I.258.16–18): *evaṃ hi kaścit kaṃcit pṛcchati —kimavastho devadattasya vyādhir iti / sa āha—vardhata iti / apara āha—apakṣīyata iti / apara āha—sthita iti / sthita ity ukte vardhateś cāpakṣīyateś ca nivṛttir bhavati /*
> "Indeed, someone asks another, 'How is Devadatta now?' (*kimavastho devadattasya vyādhiḥ*; lit. 'In what state is Devadatta's sickness?') He who has been asked answers, 'He is getting worse' (*vardhate*; lit. 'His sickness is aggravated.') A third answers, 'He is getting better' (*apakṣīyate*; lit. 'His sickness is passing.') The other answers, 'His condition remains the same (*sthitaḥ*).' When the word *sthitaḥ* '. . . remains the same' is uttered, there comes about [the understanding of] the exclusion of the meanings of the verbs *vṛdh* 'increase, grow (strong, old)' and *kṣi* with *apa* 'diminish'."

With reference to *vyādhi* (sickness, condition), we may have three kinds of utterances: *vyādhir vardhate*, *vyādhir apakṣīyate*, *vyādhiḥ sthitaḥ*. When the derivate *sthita* 'stable' (*sthā* + *kta*) of the verb *sthā* is used with reference to *vyādhi*, as Patañjali observes, the exclusion of the heterogeneous acts of increasing (*vṛddhi*) and diminishing (*kṣaya*) which are denoted respectively by the

---

[15] See Section 5 [5.3.3.4].

verbs *vṛdh* and *kṣi* preceded by the preverb *apa* is understood. According to Patañjali, this allows one to infer on the basis of the above-stated universal concomitance that the meaning of the verb *sthā* is an action in the following way:

If the meaning of the verb *sthā* were not an action, one could not understand the exclusion of the meanings of the verbs *vṛdh* and *kṣi* preceded by *apa* when the derivate *sthitaḥ* is used. But this is not the case. Therefore the meaning of the verb *sthā* is an action.[16]

Of course, in order to make the exclusiveness of the meaning of the verb *sthā* well-founded, we have to assume that the manner in which *vyādhi* performs its activity in the situation conveyed by the utterance *vyādhiḥ sthitaḥ* is different from those in which it carries out its activity in the situations conveyed by the utterances *vyādhir vardhate* and *vyādhir apakṣīyate*. That is, in this case we have to take it for granted that the act of staying as signified by the verb *sthā* consists in *vyādhi*'s activity—the *vyādhi* functions as agent here—which is differentiated from other activities performed by it where it is being aggravated and passing.

In the case of the verb *as*, Patañjali contrasts it with the verb *mṛ* 'die'. He assumes a certain special situation where one may have both *devadatto 'sti* and *devadatto mriyate* 'Devadatta is dying'. His idea is this: In such a situation, when the finite verb form *asti* is used, the exclusion of the meaning of the verb *mṛ*, dying, is understood, so that one may reason from this, on the

---

[16]This is explicitly stated by Kaiyaṭa. *Pradīpa* on *MBh* ad *A*1.3.1 (II.195): *anumānena sthānasya kriyātvaṃ pratipādayati / anyathā sthita ity ukte vṛddhikṣayanivṛttir na pratīyeta /* Raghunāthaśāstrī in his footnote in the second edition of the *Mahābhāṣya* (Nirṇayasāgara Press edition, 124: fn. 5) formulates the inference in question in a positive way as follows: *sthānaṃ kriyā vṛddhyādikriyānivartakatvāt, sāmānya-vyāptim āśrityānvaye gatyādinivartakaśayanādivad vyatireke dravyavad vā ity anumānena /* The formulation is as follows:

[Thesis] The meaning of the verb *sthā* is an action.

[Reason] Because it excludes actions like increasing.

[Example] (Positive) Whatever excludes other actions is an action, like lying and others which exclude going and so on. (Negative) Whatever is not an action does not exclude an action, like a substance.

basis of the very same universal concomitance, that the meaning of the verb *as* is an action.

But the question arises: If you accept the meaning of the verb *as* as exclusive, in what activity does it consist?

As said, the thesis that any action excludes other actions is rooted in the fact that an action consists in a kāraka's activity being differentiated from other activities (*pravṛttiviśeṣa*). In view of this, it is necessary, first of all, that the meaning of the verb *as* should be regarded as an activity (*pravṛtti*). Patañjali states:

> *MBh* ad *A*1.3.1 (I.258.12–13): *anyathā hi kārakāṇy astau pravartante 'nyathā hi mriyatau* /
>
> "For, in the situations for which the verb *as* is used kārakas perform activities in one way and in the situations for which the verb *mṛ* is used they perform activities in another way."

We have a parallel statement to this one: *anyathā ca kārakāṇi śuṣkaudane pravartante, anyathā ca māṃsaudane*, which was stated with reference to the act of eating. According to Patañjali, the situation conveyed by the utterance *devadattaḥ pacati* 'Devadatta is cooking' is one where Devadatta is involved in the actions of putting a pot on the stove, pouring water and food grains in it, setting fire wood under it, and so forth; only when he is performing those actions, such an utterance is used and the verb *pac* is considered to denote them.[17] The same may be said, no doubt, of the situation conveyed by the utterance *devadatto bhuṅkte* 'Devadatta is eating'. Then what about the situation to convey which an utterance such as *devadatto 'sti* 'Devadatta is' is used? The above-cited Bhāṣya constitutes an answer for it. For the Bhāṣya clearly shows that, in the situation expressed by the utterance *devadatto 'sti*, Devadatta who serves as agent does have a particular activity and hence that the situation at issue is one where Devadatta performs an activity which is to be denoted by the verb *as*.

---

[17] *MBh* ad *A*1.4.23 (I.324.19–20): *adhiśrayaṇodakāsecanataṇḍulāvapanaidhopakarṣaṇakriyāḥ kurvann eva devadattaḥ pacatīty ucyate* / *tatra tadā pacir vartate* /

Then what is the activity Devadatta performs in such a situation? Patañjali does not say anything about it. But, according to Bhartṛhari, the activity an agent such as Devadatta is supposed to perform in the given situation is what is called *ātmabharaṇa* 'self-maintenance'. He states:

> *VP*3.3.47ab: *ātmānam ātmanā bibhrad astīti vyapadiśyate* /
> "When a certain thing is maintaining itself by itself, it is referred to by the finite verb form *asti*."

Kaiyaṭa follows Bhartṛhari to say that in the case of the verb *as* the activity of self-maintenance is assumed to be referred to by it and adds that in the case of the verb *mṛ* the activity of self-abandoning (*ātmatyāga*) is assumed to be referred to by it.[18]

Thus, if we think of the meaning of the verb *as* as consisting in the activity of self-maintenance, which evidently is differentiated from another heterogeneous activity of self-abandoning, referred to by the verb *mṛ*, we may make the exclusiveness of the meaning of the verb *as* well-grounded. Such being the case, as suggested above, one may reason: The meaning of the verb *as* is an action. Because it excludes other actions. Just like the meaning of the verb *pac*.

So far, we have seen how it is established from the point of view of behavioral *kriyā* that the meaning of the verb *as* is an action. In this connection I would like to lay special emphasis on the following point: As a matter of fact, we can prove from the viewpoint of behavioral *kriyā* that the meaning of the verb *as* is an action, only if we find the aspect of causal *kriyā* in the meaning of the verb *as*. For, with reference to the situation

---

[18] *Pradīpa* on *MBh* ad A1.3.1 (II.194): *astāv ātmabharaṇarūpā pravṛttir mriyatau tattyāgarūpā* / *VP*3.3.47ab quoted here refers to *Nirukta*1.2: *astīty utpannasya sattvasyāvadhāraṇam*, which is interpreted as meaning 'one speaks of *avadhāraṇa* of something that has come into being as *asti*'. Helārāja takes the word *avadhāraṇa* in the sense of restriction, saying that the utterance *asti* means that something is maintaining itself and not perishing (*ātmānaṃ bibharty eva na dhvaṃsate*). That is, according to him, when the word *asti* is uttered, one understands the exclusion of the act of perishing. He glosses the word *avadhāraṇa* with the word *niścaya* 'determination'. See *Prakāśa* on *VP*3.8.26.

conveyed by the utterance *devadatto 'sti*, to say that Devadatta is involved in the activity of self-maintenance amounts to saying that he is performing the activity which leads to his own existence. This is why Kaiyaṭa does not deny that the question-and-answer *kiṃ karoti—asti* obtains in a certain situation, say, in the situation where Devadatta's last hour is coming, arguing that, in answer to the question *kiṃ karoti*, one can say *asti tāvat* 'he is alive up to now'.[19]

6.3. The property of being a cause for time to manifest itself

Patañjali describes the relationship between action and time (*kāla*) as follows:

> *MBh* ad *A*1.3.1 (I.258.19–20): *nāntareṇa kriyāṃ bhūtabhaviṣyadvartamānāḥ kālā vyajyante / astyādibhiś cāpi bhūtabhaviṣyadvartamānakālā vyajyante /*
> "Without an action [being understood], [three] time divisions: past (*bhūta*), present (*vartamāna*), and future (*bhaviṣyat*) are not manifested. And by [the use of] items such as *as* also [three] time divisions: past, present, and future are manifested."

In his *Vṛtti* on *VP*1.13 Bhartṛhari represents by the word *kālābhivyaktihetutva*, which he uses to say that an action has the property of being a cause for time to manifest itself, what Patañjali says of

---

[19] *Pradīpa* on *MBh* ad *A*1.3.1 (II.196): *yadā tu pratyāsannavināśaśaṅkayā devadattaḥ kiṃ karotīti praśnaḥ tadāsti tāvad iti prativacanaṃ bhavaty eva /* Nāgeśa assumes the activity which leads to the maintenance of existence (*tad[= sattā]-dhāraṇānukūlavyāpāra*) in the case of the verb *as* and the one which leads to the abandonment of existence (*tattyāgānukūlavyāpāra*) in the case of the verb *mṛ*. See *VSLM*556–557: *astibhavatividyatīnām arthaḥ sattā / . . . / yad vā sattāviṣayavyāpārārthakatvena kriyāvācakatvanibandhanadhātutvasiddhiḥ / . . . tadviṣayavyāpāraś cātmabharaṇasvarūpadhāraṇapadābhyām ucyate / ātmasvarūpaṃ ca sattaiva / sā cātra sthūlarūpātmikā / mriyatau tattyāgānukūlavyāpārasyevātra tadvaiparītyena taddhāraṇānukūlavyāpārasya pratīteḥ / spaṣṭaṃ cedaṃ bhūvādisūtre bhāṣye /* Concerning the verb *sthā* also, we may say that its meaning consists in a particular causal *kriyā*. According to Helārāja, the verb *sthā* as in *parvatas tiṣṭhati* 'The mountain stands' refers to an activity characterized as not leaving a certain spot (*ekadeśāparityāga*). *Prakāśa* on *VP*3.8.12: *tasmāt parvatāder apy ekadeśāparityāgalakṣaṇas tiṣṭhatau vyāpāro 'sty eva /*

an action in the present Bhāṣya.[20] In accordance with Patañjali, Vṛṣabha explains the notion of *kālābhivyaktihetutva* as follows.

> *Paddhati* on *Vṛtti* ad *VP*1.13: *kālavācibhir eva śabdair bhavatyādibhiḥ kriyāyāṃ pratipādyamānāyāṃ kālo vyajyate* /
> "When an action is understood from items such as *bhavati* which invariably denotes time, time divisions are manifested."

This explanation shows that finite verb forms such as *bhavati*, the affixes of which denote time, convey actions and at the same time manifest time divisions also. In this connection we also have to note Nāgeśa's remark that, on the basis of the above-cited Bhāṣya, Bhartṛhari states in his *VP*3.9.2c that time leads to differentiating an action (*kriyābhedāya kālaḥ*).[21] If we accept Nāgeśa's comment on the present Bhāṣya as relevant, what Bhartṛhari means by the expression *kālābhivyaktihetutva* is as follows: On the assumption that an action should be referred to any of three time divisions, when an action is understood from the finite verb form *bhavati*, the action is understood as qualified by current time.[22] If the action were not understood from *bhavati*, current time, as a qualifier of the action, would not be understood, either. Therefore, in the sense that the following both—if an action is understood, time as its qualifier is understood and if the action is not understood, time as its qualifier is not understood—hold, the action may be said to be a cause for the understanding of time.

---

[20] See the present section, fn. 5.

[21] *Uddyota* on *MBh* ad *A*1.3.1 (II.195): *etanmūlikaiva kriyābhedāya kālas tv iti vākyapadīyoktiḥ* /

[22] According to Bhartṛhari, time is a locus (*adhikaraṇa, ādhāra*) of actions. Being a locus of actions, it differentiates between them. See *VP*3.7.153ab: *kālāt kriyā vibhajyanta ākāśāt sarvamūrtayaḥ* / In his commentary to this kārikā Helārāja states: *kālaḥ kriyāsv ādhārabhāvopagamena pravibhāgam avasthāpayati.* In his *Vaiyākaraṇasiddhāntakārikā* Bhaṭṭoji Dīkṣita declares that the meanings of a verbal ending (*tiṅ*), an agent, an object, a number, and time, are the qualifiers (*viśeṣaṇa*) of an activity (*vyāpāra*) denoted by a verb after which the verbal ending occurs. *VSK*2: *phalavyāpārayor dhātur āśraye tu tiṅaḥ smṛtāḥ* / *phale pradhānaṃ vyāpāras tiṅarthas tu viśeṣaṇam* // See Section 10, fn. 5.

Linguistic items with the structure such that when an action is understood the time divisions are manifested are items ending in affixes introduced on the condition of time reference: items in verb endings and ones in krt affixes. Now consider the following instances:

A.	*pacati*	
	'He is cooking.'	(3rd sg. pres.; *laṭ*)
	apākṣīt	
	'He has cooked.'	(3rd sg. aor.; *luṅ*)
	pakṣyati	
	'He will cook.'	(3rd sg. fut.; *lṛṭ*)
B.	*ghaṭaḥ*	
	'the pot.'	
C.	*asti*	
	'He is.'	(3rd sg. pres.)
	abhūt	
	'He has been.'	(3rd sg. aor.)
	bhaviṣyati	
	'He will be.'	(3rd sg. fut.)

In A in which the verb *pac* accompanied by verb endings is used, one understands that the act of cooking which is denoted by that verb is referred to any of three time divisions. In B in which the nominal base *ghaṭa* followed by a nominal ending is used, the meaning of that nominal base, a pot as a substance, is not understood to be referred to any of three time divisions. In C in which the verb *as* with verb endings is used, specific time reference is known to be involved.[23] From these observations one may build up the following argument:

[Thesis] The meaning of the verb *as* is an action.
[Reason] Because of its being referred to any of three time divisions.

---

[23] *laṭ*: present (*A*3.2.123). *luṅ*: the past in general (*A*3.2.110). *lṛṭ*: the future in general (*A*3.3.13). In *bhaviṣyati*, *bhū* occurs instead of *as* by *A*2.4.52.

[Example] Just like the meaning of the verb *pac*.[24]

As long as C is accepted, it is established that the meaning of the verb *as* is an action. For the following universal concomitance holds: Whatever is referred to any of three time divisions is an action, just like the meaning of the verb *pac*; whatever is not an action is not referred to any of them, just like the substance pot.

But for what reason can one say that it is an action and not a substance which is connected with time? We know that Patañjali has characterized respectively a substance and an action as *siddha* 'what has been brought to accomplishment' and as *bhāvyate* 'that which is brought into being' or *sādhya* 'what is to be brought to accomplishment'. As shown in Section 5 ([5.2.4]), such characterization shows Patañjali's view of the verb meaning in process. He conceives of verb meanings as brought to accomplishment in time. Under the distinction between substance and action, thus, one has to admit that an action alone is connected with time. To put it another way, of what has been brought to accomplishment and what is to be brought to accomplishment it is the latter that is connected with time. Taking these into consideration, Kaiyaṭa says:

> *Pradīpa* on *MBh* ad *A*1.3.1 (II.195): *kriyāntaradharmasamanvayenāstyādīnāṃ kriyātvaṃ pratipādyate / ghaṭa ity ukte kālaviśeṣāvagatir nāsti / asti abhūd bhaviṣyatīti kālaviśeṣāvagamāt sādhyamānasya cārthasya kālena yogāt kriyātvāvasāyaḥ /*
> "One understands that meanings of items like *as* are actions, on the basis of their connection with a certain property that other actions [signified by items such as *pac*] have (*kriyāntaradharmasamanvaya*). When the nominal form *ghaṭaḥ* is uttered, no specific time reference is understood; when the verbal forms *asti*, *abhūt*, and *bhaviṣyati* are uttered, specific time references are understood. In addition, it is a thing being brought to

---

[24] This formulation of the argument is given by Raghunāthaśāstrī in his foot-note in the second edition of the *Mahābhāṣya* (Nirṇayasāgara Press, 124. fn. 9): *atrāyaṃ prayogo vivakṣitaḥ / astyādayaḥ kriyā bhūtādikālasambandhitvāt pākādivad iti /*

accomplishment that is connected with time. For these reasons one determines that the meaning of the verb *as* is an action."

It is clear that the connection of a verb meaning with time entails the aspect of an action, being something that is to be brought to accomplishment, the latter demonstrating that the verb meaning is an action. In view of this point, Bhartṛhari states:

> *VP*3.8.12ab: *kālānupāti yad rūpaṃ tad astīti pratīyate* /
> "From the finite verb form *asti* one understands the aspect which conforms to time,"

In his commentary on this kārikā Helārāja explicitly states that whatever is regarded as an action has the aspect which conforms to time in consequence of the action being characterized as something to be brought to accomplishment (*sādhya*).[25]

Now recall that a verb meaning which is characterized as what is to be brought to accomplishment is a semantic *kriyā*. In the present Bhāṣya, therefore, Patañjali speaks precisely of the semantic *kriyā*. If we look at the Bhāṣya under consideration from a different angle, we clearly see that Patañjali, who recognizes that time-connection is characteristic of a verb meaning, should necessarily admit that any verb denotes something that is brought to accomplishment in time.

6.4. Significance of the discovery of the properties of an action (*kriyādharma*)

What we have to note in Patañjali's attempts to prove that the meaning of the verb *as* is an action is his success in finding out with respect to an action its properties of excluding other actions and of being a cause for time to manifest itself, common to meanings of verbs of the *kṛ* type and of the *as* type. For Patañjali, whatever excludes an action or whatever is connected with time has to be considered to be an action. The meaning of the verb *as* excludes the meaning of the verb *mṛ* and is connected with time, so that it is reasonable to say that the meaning of the verb *as* is

---

[25] *Prakāśa* on *VP*3.8.12: . . . *sādhyatayā pratīyamānā kriyā* / *tathā ca kālāt kriyā vibhajyata iti kālānupātitā yathāyatham upapadyate, abhūd asti bhaviṣyatīti* /

an action. This also implies that the *kriyā*-based definition is freed of the difficulty that the name *dhātu* cannot be assigned to items such as *as*.

However, Patañjali's way of proving the thesis in question by resorting to such properties of an action indicates that he establishes the *kriyā*-based definition applicable to an item such as *as* from an angle different from that from which he establishes the *bhāva*-based definition. In the argument on the *bhāva*-based definition, Patañjali, with an eye to a linguistic item's intrinsic denotative nature, has investigated how items to be called *dhātu* denote their meanings, ending up with saying that an item called *dhātu* denotes its meaning as what comes into being or what is brought into being. In the argument about the *kriyā*-based definition, in contrast with that, he has investigated what are meanings of items to be called *dhātu*, so that he has followed a road to finding out the properties of an action. It is thus clear that Patañjali gives weight to the meaning of the item to be called *dhātu* in his *kriyā*-based definition and to the linguistic item to be so called in his *bhāva*-based definition.

6.5. Kaiyaṭa on the proof of the meaning of the verb *as* being an action

In his *Pradīpa*, Kaiyaṭa, taking up the proof considered to be against the thesis that the meaning of the verb *as* is an action, tries to demonstrate the thesis. His trial is worth a mention in passing.

He lists three reasons for not accepting the thesis:

1) The absence of the use of the question-and-answer *kiṃ karoti—asti*.
2) The fact that the following does not hold: On condition that all sādhanas are present, sometimes one rightly says *asti* '. . . is', and sometimes one does not have this.
3) The absence of the use of the comparative form *astitarām*.[26]

---

[26] *Pradīpa* on *MBh* ad *A*1.3.1 (II.193-94): *kiṃ karotīti praśne 'styādibhiḥ prativacanābhāvād'akriyāvacanatvam eṣāṃ manyate / yac cāpy uktam iha sarveṣu sādhaneṣu sannihiteṣu kadācit pacatīty etad bhavati kadācin neti tad astyādiṣu nāsti / na hy astīti kadācid bhavati, api tu sarvadeti*

Of these reasons the first is proved to be essentially irrelevant to the issue at hand by Patañjali who resorts to the rule of a question-and-answer.[27] The remaining two reasons are not dealt with by Patañjali at all.

6.5.1. With reference to the inference of the distinction between action and substance, Patañjali stated as follows:

> *MBh* ad *A*1.3.1 (I.254.17–18): *iha sarveṣu sādhaneṣu saṃnihiteṣu kadācit pacatīty etad bhavati, kadācin na bhavati* /
> "On condition that all participants in an action (sādhanas) are present, sometimes one rightly says *pacati* 'He is cooking', and sometimes one does not have this."[28]

Now let us consider the situation to convey which the utterance *devadattaḥ sthālyām odanaṃ kāṣṭhaiḥ pacati* 'Devadatta is cooking rice with firewood in a pot' is used. Unless the person called *devadatta* who functions as agent with respect to the act of cooking sets other kārakas such as firewood into play, the act of cooking does not take place even if all kārakas necessary to bring the act in question to accomplishment are present, in consequence of which one does not have *pacati.* On the other hand, on condition that such kārakas are present, one can have *asti* with respect to each of those kārakas irrespective of the activation of other kārakas by Devadatta: *devadatto 'sti, sthāly asti*, in this way.[29] The

pākādibhir vaidharmyam / yathā ca pacatitarām iti prakarṣo bhavati naivam astitarām iti / On the same issue Helārāja also mentions the same three reasons. *Prakāśa* on *VP*3.8.1: *nanv evam apy astyādīnāṃ kriyātvaṃ na syāt / na hi sarveṣu sādhaneṣu sannihiteṣu kadācid asti bhavati vidyate veti bhavati. sarvadābhāvāt / pacatitarām ityādāv iva cāstitarām ityādau prakarṣābhāvāt. kiṃ karoti pacatītyādivac ca kiṃ karoti astītyādipraśnaprativacanābhāvāt, sattāyāś ca nirviśeṣatvād bhedābhāvaḥ /*

[27] See Section 4 [4.8.4].

[28] See Section 4 [4.3.3.2].

[29] Strictly speaking, the rice-gruel (*odana*) is a resulting food of the rice (*taṇḍulavikārya*), so that in the given situation one cannot say *odanam asti* 'The rice-gruel exists'. *MBh* ad *A*1.4.49 (I.332.17–19): *iha hi taṇḍulān odanaṃ pacatīti dvyarthaḥ paciḥ / taṇḍulān pacann odanaṃ nirvartayatīti / ihedānīṃ taṇḍulānām odanaṃ pacatīti dvyarthaś caiva pacir vikārayoge ṣaṣṭhī / taṇḍulavikāram odanaṃ nirvartayatīti /*

reason for this is beyond question. In the given situation, the meaning of the verb *as*, existence, is a given with respect to each kāraka supposed to be involved in the act in question. On this assumption, the meaning of the verb *pac* is distinguished from that of the verb *as* in that the use of the verb *pac* occurs sometimes (*kadācit*) to convey its meaning, while the use of the verb *as* always occurs to convey its meaning (*sarvadā*) under the specified condition.

Kaiyaṭa expounds his views on this matter in his comments on the Bhāṣya in which Patañjali proposes a new notion of *kriyā*, behavioral *kriyā*, to have the *kriyā*-based definition cover verbs such as *as*.[30]

> *Pradīpa* on *MBh* ad *A*1.3.1 (II.194): *utpattiprabhṛtyā vināśāc ca sattānuṣaṅgād astīti pratyayasya sannihiteṣu sādhaneṣūtpattir avaśyaṃbhāvinīti kādācitkatvābhāvaḥ* /
> "It is inevitable that the utterance *asti* takes place with respect to present sādhanas, since they are accompanied by existence from their birth to destruction. Therefore, on condition that sādhanas are present, it is not established that sometimes one says *asti* and sometimes one does not have this."

Kaiyaṭa admits that under the specified condition one cannot establish that sometimes one says *asti* and sometimes one does not have this. But we should notice that, in the situation conveyed by the above-stated utterance, when Devadatta is not present, one does not have the utterance *devadatto 'sti* 'Devadatta is there' with respect to him, and when the verb *as* signifies *janman* 'birth' and not *sattā* 'existence', one can easily establish the above under the same condition.[31] This implies the following: The fact that under the specified condition one cannot establish that sometimes one says *asti* and sometimes one does not have this is due to the fact that the condition itself presupposes the existence of sādhanas involved in the act in question and not to the fact that the meaning of the verb *as* is not an action. This is comparable to the case of

---

[30] See Section 4, Part 4 [4.8.2.1].

[31] On the two meanings of the verb *as*, see Section 4, Part 4 [4.6.2.1].

the absence of the use of the question-and-answer *kiṃ karoti—asti*. According to Patañjali, one does not have the question-and-answer *kiṃ karoti—asti* not because the meaning of the verb *as* is not an action but because the use of it goes against the question-and-answer rule.[32]

6.5.2. In order to consider whether one can have utterances such as *astitarām*, let us adduce the form *pacatitarām* '. . . cooks quite well' as a plain example of a finite verb form followed by the comparative affix *tarap*. When Devadatta cooks better than Caitra, one says *pacatitarām* with reference to Devadatta.[33] In this case excellence in respect of the act of cooking is conveyed in dependence upon excellence in respect of what differentiates both the act of cooking in question performed by Devadatta and the same act by Caitra from the ones performed by others; both cook well and are good cooks. When the act of cooking by Devadatta is to be distinguished from the one by Caitra in respect of goodness, the utterance *devadattaḥ pacatitarām* is used. It is important to note that the utterance *devadatta āḍhyataraḥ* 'Devadatta is richer' is used in order to differentiate Devadatta who is rich from someone, say, Caitra, who is also rich.

What about the utterance *astitarām*? If one cannot find excellence in respect of what differentiates the existence of Devadatta and Caitra from that of others, then one cannot distinguish between the existence of Devadatta and that of Caitra, as a result of which one cannot have the utterance *devadatto 'stitarām*.[34]

Concerning this matter, Kaiyaṭa advances the following view:

---

[32] See Section 4 [4.8.4].

[33] By *A*5.3.37 the affix *tarap* is introduced to the finite verb form *pacati* and the derivate *pacatitara* takes the affix *āmu* by *A*5.4.11. The resulting form *pacatitarām* is called *avyaya* by *A*1.1.38. On the utterance for denoting excellence (*atiśāyana*), see also Section 1 [1.1].

[34] Helārāja explains that one does not have a specific existence and hence cannot make a distinction between the existence of one thing and that of another. *Prakāśa* on *VP*3.8.1: *sattāyāś ca nirviśeṣatvād bhedābhāvaḥ* / See Section 4, Part 4 [4.8.2.1].

Pradīpa on *MBh* ad *A* 1.3.1 (II.194): *prakarṣapratyayo 'pi dṛśyate vidyatetarām iha dhānyam iti* /
"Affixes for excellence (*prakarṣapratyaya*) are also observed to be used after items such as *asti*, as in *vidyatetarām iha dhānyam* 'Grain exists here quite well'."

According to Helārāja, the utterance *vidyatetarām* is explained as follows. The utterance *vidyate* '. . . exists' takes place in accordance with the presence of something that serves as agent with respect to the meaning of the verb *vid*. The presence of the agent is differentiated according to whether the agent is ever present or not. Just as a piece of cloth is distinguished from another piece of cloth in whiteness, similarly the existence of the agent who is ever present (*nityasannihita*) is distinguished from that of the agent who is not so (*anityasannihita*). Thus, in view of how agents with respect to the meaning of the verb *vid* are present, one is allowed to have the utterance *vidyatetarām*. Even if the meaning of the verb *vid*, existence, itself is not subject to differentiation, the differentiation of agents with respect to it justifies the use of such an utterance.[35]

[35] *Prakāśa* on *VP* 3.8.1: *prakarṣapratyayaś cāpi dṛśyate / vidyatetarām ayam iha nityasannidhānāt / anityasannihitād dhi nityasannihitasya sattā viśiṣyate / tena sādhanānyatvād abhidyamānāpi prakarṣeṇa yujyate* / *Uddyota* on *MBh* ad *A* 1.3.1 (II.194): *vidyatetarām ity api kārakagataprakarṣāropeṇaiva bodhyam* / In *vidyatetarām* what differentiates existence signified by the verb *vid* is considered to be an agent with respect to it. In this connection it is useful to consider one interpretation of the term *siddha* in the very first vārttika *siddhe śabdārthasambandhe* . . . given by Patañjali. He proposes taking it as signifying *atyantasiddha* 'absolutely existent'. According to Kaiyaṭa, the term *siddha* in this sense conveys excellence in *siddha*. *Pradīpa* on *MBh* (Paspaśā) [I.29]: *ihāpi nityānityayor niṣpannatvāviśeṣāt siddhaśrutir upāttā prakarṣaṃ gamayati* / Nāgeśa explains that as compared to a human being or a tree, the sky has the property of *atyantaṃ siddhatvam*. That is, the sky is ever present. *Uddyota* on *MBh* (Paspaśā) [I.29]: *manuṣyavṛkṣādyapekṣayākāśādīnām apy atyantaṃ siddhatvam* /

Section 7

Patañjali on *A* 1.3.1 as a semantic definition

7. Patañjali on *A* 1.3.1

A close examination of Kātyāyana's arguments on *A* 1.3.1 has revealed that, in the matter of the definition of the term *dhātu*, he supposes that the dhātupāṭha is given the alternative of playing the role of supplying items to be called *dhātu* or playing roles complementary to a semantic definition of the term *dhātu*.[1] First, noting the former role of the dhātupāṭha, he suggests reading *A*1.3.1 as a dhātupāṭha-based definition, which is obvious if we follow Patañjali's explication of the first vārttika: *pāṭhena dhātusaṃjñā* 'items are called *dhātu* by virtue of being recited'.[2] Then, alternatively, he suggests adopting semantic definitions such as have been established by early teachers— *kriyā*-based and *bhāva*-based definitions—and ends up with proposing the revised *bhāva*-based definition *prathamabhāvavacano dhātuḥ*, in expectation of the second alternative of the dhātupāṭha playing complementary roles to the semantic definition. This is the framework for the discussion on *A* 1.3.1 provided by Kātyāyana.

As said, Patañjali shows a tendency to pursue, within the given framework, the possibility of letting *A* 1.3.1 admit of several interpretations in conformity with Kātyāyana's suggestions and proposals.[3] Not only does he interpret the present sūtra as a dhātupāṭha-based definition, he also tries to interpret it as a semantic definition and further as forming both the indication of the dhātupāṭha with the complementary roles and a semantic definition, as I have already pointed out.[4]

What I have to do in this section is to consider Patañjali's treatment of *A* 1.3.1 in the latter line.

---

[1] Section 3 [3.2.6] and Section 4, Part 4 [4.8.6].

[2] *MBh* on *vt.* 1 ad *A*1.3.1. See Section 1 [3.2.1] and Section 4, Part 1 [4.1.1].

[3] See Section 4, Part 4 [4.8.7].

[4] See Section 4, Part 4 [4.8.5].

7.1. A single semantic definition of the term *dhātu*

In his Bhāṣya Patañjali puts a fourfold interpretation on *A*1.3.1.

1) Items of the set beginning with *bhū*, recited in the dhātupāṭha, are called *dhātu*.

2) Signifiers (*vādi*) of what comes into being (*bhū*) are called *dhātu*.

3) Those items which belong to the set beginning with *bhū* and which are like *vā* 'go, strike' are called *dhātu*.

4) Those items which belong to the set beginning with *vā* and which are like *bhū* 'be, be born' are called *dhātu*.

The first interpretation is what Patañjali presumes to be accepted by Kātyāyana and what I call 'dhātupāṭha-based definition'. As shown, under this interpretation Patañjali is extremely strict about not taking any semantic aspect of an item to be called *dhātu* into consideration.[5] Under the rest of the interpretations, however, he intends *A*1.3.1 to be an undoubted semantic definition and to imply a certain semantic definition. We have to take it for granted that his own semantics of verbs is reflected in these last three interpretations, for he must have interpreted the sūtra in question in such a way as to accord with his own semantic definition. He could not have otherwise suggested such interpretations at all. Then what is his semantic definition underlying such interpretations?

In response to Kātyāyana's suggestions of *kriyā*-based and *bhāva*-based definitions, Patañjali has examined their validity. On the one hand, presupposing that a verb meaning is treated as an action (*kriyā*), he characterizes it as *bhāva* in the sense of what is brought into being ('*bhāva*' as a *karmasādhana*) and does so with the introduction of the notion of *svabhāva* or an intrinsic denotative nature.[6] On the other hand, he makes both the definitions equivalent to each other by means of establishing that the meaning of the verb *as* can be regarded as an action as well as meanings of other verbs of the *kṛ* type. In establishing

---

[5] See Section 4, Part 1 [4.2].

[6] See Section 4, Part 3 [4.6.2.2].

the thesis that the meaning of the verb *as* is an action, he adopts a way of finding the properties of an action (*kriyādharma*) in the meaning of the verb *as*. He observes that an action has two properties: the property of excluding other actions (*kriyāyāḥ kriyā nivartikā bhavati*) and that of being associated with time (*kālā-bhivyaktihetutva*).[7] Apart from the former property which is in effect determined from the point of view of causal *kriyā*, the latter property is not determined without assuming a verb meaning in general to be what is brought into being in time.[8] Therefore, in the case of the establishment of the thesis at issue on the basis of an action's property of being associated with time, he obviously presupposes that a verb meaning is characterized as *bhāva* or what is brought into being. And further, more importantly, when he talks about such a property of an action, he focuses his gaze on a semantic structure of a linguistic item such as *pacati* which denotes an action and at the same time a specific time division as its qualifier (*viśeṣaṇa*). Which undoubtedly indicates that he has discovered the property of being associated with time from the point of view of how actions are spoken of. Thus his fundamental semantic definition should be framed from such a point of view, with the introduction of the notion of the denotative *svabhāva*. The semantic definition is:

> An item which denotes by its intrinsic denotative nature something that is brought into being—such a thing is referred to by the term *bhāva* or *kriyā*—is called *dhātu*.

In the following, how Patañjali interprets *A* 1.3.1 against a background of his own semantic definition shall be dealt with. Needless to say, interpretations of *A* 1.3.1 to be taken up are the second, third, and fourth.

---

[7] See Section 4, Part 4 [4.8.2] and Section 6.

[8] See Section 6 [6.3].

7.2. What comes into being: translation of what is brought into being (second interpretation)

7.2.1. As said, if the term *bhāva* in the *bhāva*-based definition is interpreted as what comes into being, the *bhāva*-based definition is freed of the difficulty that it is not applicable to items such as *pac* but leads to its over-application to nominal bases like *vṛkṣa* 'tree'. On the assumption that the term *bhāva* signifies what comes into being, Patañjali, leaving the role of preventing the over-application of the *bhāva*-based definition to the dhātupāṭha on the authority of *vt.* 12, which says that it is necessary for items to be called *dhātu* to be recited in the dhātupāṭha in order for nominal bases and corruptions not to be called *dhātu*, tries to deduce a semantic definition like the *bhāva*-based definition from *A*1.3.1 itself. He states:

> *MBh* ad *A*1.3.1 (I.257.11–14): *paṭhiṣyati hy ācāryo bhūvādi-pāṭhaḥ prātipadikāṇapayatyādinivṛttyartha iti / yāvatā paṭhiṣyati pacādayaś ca kriyā bhavatikriyāyāḥ kartryo bhavantīti astv ayaṃ kartṛsādhanaḥ, bhavatīti bhāva iti / kiṃ vaktavyam etat / na hi / katham anucyamānaṃ gaṃsyate / etenaivābhihitaṃ sūtreṇa bhūvādayo dhātava iti /*
>
> "For, the teacher [Kātyāyana] will state: 'The text in which items of the set beginning with *bhū* are recited serves to prevent the name *dhātu* from applying to nominal bases and [corruptions] such as *āṇapi-* 'order, command'.' (*vt.* 12) Insofar as he will state so, and since, as said, actions that are denoted by items such as *pac* are agents (*kartṛ*) of the act denoted by the verb *bhū*, let the term *bhāva* be a *kartṛsādhana*, analyzed as 'what comes into being is spoken of as *bhāva*' (*bhavatīti bhāvaḥ*).
>
> [Question] Then is it necessary to formulate a rule such as provides that an item which denotes *bhāva* or what comes into being be called *dhātu*?
>
> [Answer] Indeed, it is not.
>
> [Objection] Then how can it be understood [that an item which denotes *bhāva* or what comes into being is called *dhātu*], if no such statement is made?

[Answer] By this very sūtra *bhūvādayo dhātavaḥ* it is stated that an item which denotes *bhāva* or what comes into being is called *dhātu*."

What enables Patañjali to deduce from *A*1.3.1 a semantic definition, equivalent to the *bhāva*-based definition in which the term *bhāva* is taken as a *kartṛsādhana*, is his reading into the sūtra the derivate *bhū* which is formed from the verb *bhū* by introducing after that base the kṛt affix ***kvip*** to denote an agent. He states:

> *MBh* ad *A*1.3.1 (I.257.15): *nedam ādigrahaṇam / vader ayam auṇādika iñ kartṛsādhanaḥ—bhuvaṃ vadantīti bhūvādaya iti /* "Here [in the sūtra: *bhūvādayo dhātavaḥ*] the word *ādi* 'the first' is not mentioned. In this form [*bhūvādi*] the uṇādi affix ***iñ*** is introduced after the verb *vad* 'speak, utter'. [Therefore the word *vādi* is] that which is formed by adding to the base the kṛt affix to denote an agent (*kartṛsādhana*). [Thus] the word *bhūvādi* means 'items which signify *bhū* or what comes into being'."

As Kaiyaṭa explains, the form *bhū* in *bhuvaṃ vadantīti bhūvādayaḥ* is the derivate which is formed from the verb *bhū* 'be, be born' with the kṛt affix ***kvip*** to signify an agent (*bhavatīti bhūr iti kartari kvib asti*) and which Patañjali assumes to be synonymous with the form *bhāva* signifying what comes into being (*bhavatīti bhāvaḥ*).[9]

According to this interpretation, *A*1.3.1 is taken as follows:

> Signifiers (*vādi*) of what comes into being (*bhū*) are called *dhātu*.

---

[9]The occurrence of the uṇādi affix ***iñ*** after the verb *vad* is accounted for by *US*4.124: *vasivapiyajirājivrajisadihanivāśivādivāribhya iñ*. The form *bhū* as a derivate in the kṛt affix ***kvip*** is explained by *A*3.2.76 *kvip ca*. *Pradīpa* on *MBh* ad *A*1.3.1 (II.190): *bhavatīti bhūr iti kartari kvib asti na tu karmaṇi /* According to *A*3.4.67, the affix ***kvip*** signifies an agent. The compound *bhū-vādi*, formed by *A*2.2.8, is a ṣaṣṭhī-tatpuruṣa. See Section 2 [2.3.2].

7.2.2. Now let us consider here the development of Patañjali's argument in which he has arrived at his interpretation of *A*1.3.1 presented above. As is suggested by the above-cited Bhāṣya, it is within the framework of the *bhāva*-based definition that Patañjali comes to suggest reading the sūtra in question as such a semantic definition.

Stage 1. A difficulty is pointed out: If the term *bhāva* is taken to signify what comes into being, the *bhāva*-based definition is undesiredly applied to such a nominal base as *vṛkṣa*.
Stage 2. Another difficulty is pointed out: Alternatively, if it is taken to signify what is brought into being, the definition in question is undesiredly applied to a nominal base like *mātṛ*, a relative term. At this stage, the notion of 'own nature' (*svabhāva*) is also introduced. An action as a verb meaning, characterized as *bhāvyate* '[that which] is brought into being', is contrasted with a substance as a meaning of a nominal base, characterized as *svabhāvasiddha* 'something established in terms of *svabhāva*'.
Stage 3. It is pointed out that the definition of the term *dhātu*, formal or semantic, is unavoidably applied to nominal bases. The dhātupāṭha-based definition and the *bhāva*-based definition in which the term *bhāva* is interpreted as signifying what comes into being or what is brought into being equally lead to the difficulty that certain nominal bases are undesiredly called *dhātu*.[10]
Stage 4. A commission to prevent such over-application of the *bhāva*-based definition has been given to the dhātupāṭha. Patañjali returns to Stage 1.[11]
Stage 5. An interpretation of *A*1.3.1 as shown here is introduced.[12]

---

[10] *MBh* ad *A*1.3.1 (I.257.10–11): *sarvathā vayaṃ prātipadikaparyudāsān na mucyāmahe* / In the case of the dhātupāṭha-based definition, it has been pointed out that the name *dhātu* is undesiredly assigned to nominal bases homophonous with items recited in the dhātupāṭha. See Section 3 [3.2.1].

[11] See the Bhāṣya cited in the present section [7.2.1].

[12] On the development of Patañjali's argument under consideration, see Section 5 [5.2].

I have already shown that Patañjali might mean two things at Stage 2: (i) An action is that which is by nature something that is brought into being, while a substance is that which is by nature something that has already been brought into being; (ii) An action is that which a linguistic item by its intrinsic denotative nature denotes as something that is brought into being, while a substance is that which a linguistic item by its intrinsic denotative nature denotes as something that has already been brought into being.[13] Needless to say, if he had meant the latter, he could not have attained Stage 4. To put it the other way round, *svabhāva* as an intrinsic denotative nature considered, the *bhāva*-based definition the term *bhāva* of which is taken as a *karmasādhana* does not ask for the dhātupāṭha for the purpose of preventing it from applying to nominal bases. This is true of *A*1.3.1 interpreted as a semantic definition.

At this point let us see what Kaiyaṭa states in connection with Stage 5. He considers, as a matter of fact, that *A*1.3.1 as a semantic definition does not result in applying to nominal bases. He states:

> *Pradīpa* on *MBh* ad *A*1.3.1 (II.190): *jāyamānam arthaṃ ye 'bhidadhati te dhātava ity arthaḥ / bhavatir atra janmavācī gṛhyate na tu sattāvācīti siddhārthābhidhāyināṃ saṃjñā na bhavati /*
> "[By the paraphrase *bhuvaṃ vadantīti bhūvādayaḥ*] is meant that those items which denote a thing that is coming into being (*jāyamānam artham*) are called *dhātu*. The verb *bhū* here [from which the derivate *bhū* is formed] is taken to signify birth (*janman*) and not existence (*sattā*). Therefore, the term *dhātu* is not applied to items denoting things that have been brought to accomplishment (*siddhārtha*)."

Note that Kaiyaṭa draws a distinction between *jāyamāno 'rthaḥ* 'a thing that is coming into being' and *siddhārthaḥ* 'a thing that has been brought to accomplishment'. This distinction is parallel to the one made by Patañjali between an action as *bhāvyate* and

[13] See Section 5 [5.2.3.3].

a substance as *siddha* in Stage 2. According to Kaiyaṭa, owing to such a distinction, *A*1.3.1 as a semantic definition does not lead to its over-application to nominal bases. Granted that the terms *bhāva* in Stage 1 and *bhū* in the present sūtra are synonymous (*bhavatīti bhāvaḥ*; *bhavatīti bhūḥ*), for him, the semantic definition of the term *dhātu* which is deduced from *A*1.3.1 can evidently no longer serve to provide, at the same level as the *bhāva*-based definition which has been proposed in Stage 1 and which pertains to *bhāva* as what comes into being, that an item which denotes what comes into being is called *dhātu*. This is explained as follows:

As shown above, the semantic interpretation of *A*1.3.1 is proposed in Stage 5 after the *bhāva*-based definition, where the term *bhāva* is interpreted as signifying what is brought into being (*karmasādhana*), is introduced with the introduction of the notion of *svabhāva* in Stage 2. Patañjali's return to Stage 1 in Stage 4 is grammatically justifiable, since, as Kaiyaṭa explains, what is brought into being is nothing but what comes into being (*yo hi bhavati sa eva bhāvyate*).[14] But Kaiyaṭa sees in Patañjali's return to Stage 1 the translation of *bhāva* as what is brought into being into *bhāva* as what comes into being, in other words, the retaining of the value which the former *bhāva* has. What is viewed on a certain level as something that is brought into being has to be what is viewed on the same level as something that comes into being. This is clearly shown by the distinction made by Kaiyaṭa between *jāyamāno 'rthaḥ* and *siddhārthaḥ*, in which he does not basically change the characterization of a substance in the distinction made by Patañjali between *bhāvyate* and *svabhāvasiddha*. Thus, on the assumption that the term *svabhāva* refers to a linguistic item's intrinsic denotative nature, if an item, which denotes by its intrinsic denotative nature its meaning as what is brought into being, is called *dhātu*, one has to say that an item, which denotes by its intrinsic denotative nature its meaning as what comes into being, is also called *dhātu*.

---

[14] See Section 5 [5.2.3.1].

7.2.3. From a nominal base which denotes by its intrinsic denotative nature its meaning as something established, its meaning is understood to be something existent and not as something that is brought into being nor as something that comes into being. Patañjali explicitly states:

> *MBh* on *vt.* 5 ad *A*2.1.1 (I.366.12–14): *śabdapramāṇakā vayam / yac chabda āha tad asmākaṃ pramāṇam / śabdaś ceha sattām āha / ayaṃ daṇḍaḥ / astīti gamyate /*
> "We [grammarians] hold words as our standard. What words denote is our standard. And in the following instance a word denotes existence (*sattā*): *ayaṃ daṇḍaḥ* 'this stick'. Here we understand from this that [it] exists (*asti*)."

According to Patañjali, a nominal base such as *daṇḍa* 'stick' denotes existence (*sattā*).[15] That is, it denotes its meaning as something established or something that has been brought into being. And this is due to its intrinsic denotative nature, for a linguistic item's denotation of its meaning is conditioned by its intrinsic denotative nature (*arthābhidhānaṃ svābhāvikam*). Grammarians are not concerned with things as they are but as they are spoken of.[16] They have to accept such a denotative nature as it is. Such being the case, one may certainly say from an ontological point of view that the stick is something that is brought into being; but, at the same time, one may say from a semantic point of view that the stick in question as denoted by the nominal base *daṇḍa* is something that has already been existent.

This brings us to the following understanding: On condition that the definition that an item which denotes what comes into being is called *dhātu* is given, if its intrinsic denotative nature is not taken into consideration or if the 'own nature' is otherwise taken, it will ensue that nominal bases are undesiredly called *dhātu*, so that the dhātupāṭha has to be asked for in order to

[15]The present Bhāṣya taken into consideration, it is declared in the *Kāśikāvṛtti* that a meaning of a nominal base is existence. *Kāśikāvṛtti* on *A*2.3.46: *prātipadikārthaḥ sattā /*

[16]*Paddhati* on *Vṛtti* ad *VP*1.172: *śabdapramāṇakā iti / śabda eva pramāṇaṃ na pratyakṣādīni /* See also Section 5, fn. 67.

prevent such over-application of the definition. Of course, if as a linguistic item's intrinsic denotative nature the 'own nature' is properly taken into consideration, however, there will be no fear that by that definition nominal bases may be called *dhātu*. Strictly speaking, therefore, the semantic interpretation of *A*1.3.1, considered independently of the dhātupāṭha, should be as follows:

> Items which are by nature signifiers (*vādi*) of what comes into being (*bhū*) are called *dhātu*.

7.2.4. This interpretation is supported by Patañjali himself. As has been shown, in his Bhāṣya on *A*3.1.32 Patañjali remarked that *A*3.1.32 would not have its own independent domain if *A*1.3.1 were semantically interpreted and moreover in his Bhāṣya on *A*3.1.19 he observed that items ending in affixes such as ***kyac*** which are to have the name *dhātu* by *A*3.1.32 denote by nature actions, just as items such as *pac* do, so that they may be properly called *dhātu*.[17] It will be clear that, with regard to an item to be called *dhātu*, Patañjali considers its denotation of a meaning to be determined by its intrinsic denotative nature. Thus, for Patañjali, the notion of the intrinsic denotative nature may well be brought in the definition of the term *dhātu*.

7.2.5. However, in the Bhāṣya quoted in the present section [7.2.1], Patañjali proposes the interpretation of *A*1.3.1 as a semantic definition, on the hypothesis that the dhātupāṭha is required as a complementary to a semantic definition of the term *dhātu*. What does this mean? What is clear is that he considers as follows: The function of preventing an undesired application of the name *dhātu* to nominal bases is to be carried out either by resorting to the dhātupāṭha or by introducing the notion of the intrinsic denotative nature. It should be emphasized again that *A*1.3.1 as a semantic definition admits of two interpretations.

> A. Signifiers (*vādi*) of what comes into being (*bhū*) are called *dhātu* only if they are recited in the dhātupāṭha.

---

[17] See Section 5 [5.2.3.2].

B. Items for what comes into being are called *dhātu* only if they are by nature signifiers of it.

In this way it is in association either with the dhātupāṭha or with the intrinsic denotative nature that the semantic definition deduced from *A*1.3.1 attains its desired grammatical purpose. As shall be seen in the next section, Patañjali ultimately denies the need for the dhātupāṭha Kātyāyana envisages. Therefore, when he argues that if one takes the dhātupāṭha into consideration, it will become possible to interpret *A*1.3.1 as a semantic definition by means of reading into it the form *bhū* signifying what comes into being, he intends to imply that when the need for the dhātupāṭha is denied, the alternative to it is to take the intrinsic denotative nature into consideration.

7.2.6. To sum up: For Patañjali a common, general, definition of the term *dhātu* is, as said, that an item which denotes by nature what is brought into being is called *dhātu*. He has translated what is brought into being into what comes into being. This translation serves to preserve the value of what is brought into being. It is on the same level that what is brought into being is regarded as identical with what comes into being. If a semantic definition that an item which denotes what is brought into being is called *dhātu* expects help from the dhātupāṭha, a semantic definition that an item which denotes what comes into being is called *dhātu* also does so in a similar manner; and if the former does not, the latter does not, either. He has the alternative of the dhātupāṭha or an intrinsic denotative nature to prevent the over-application of the term *dhātu* to nominal bases. Therefore, as long as he finally denies the need for the dhātupāṭha in this sense, interpretation B above stated has to be what he really means to propose since it reflects his common, general, definition of the term *dhātu*.

7.3. Two kinds of *ādis*: *vyavasthā* 'arrangement' and *prakāra* 'similarity' (third and fourth interpretations)

7.3.1. As pointed out in Section 3, in his vārttikas on A1.3.1 Kātyāyana creates the framework where one has the alternative of a formal definition, the dhātupāṭha-based definition, and a semantic definition linked with the dhātupāṭha supposed to discharge four functions.[18] Within this given framework, Patañjali tries to interpret A1.3.1 itself as providing the indication of the dhātupāṭha with the four functions as well as a semantic definition. The results of such an attempt are the third and fourth interpretations of A1.3.1 stated earlier.

7.3.2. Now let us cite here the Bhāṣya dealing with the present issue. I will divide it into four parts as a matter of convenience.

> *Bh.* 1 (I.258.22–23): *atha yady eva kriyāvacano dhātur ity eṣa pakṣo 'thāpi bhāvavacano dhātur iti kiṃ gatam etad iyatā sūtreṇa, āhosvid anyatarasmin pakṣe bhūyaḥ sūtraṃ kartavyam / gatam ity āha /*
> "[Question] Now, if one holds the view that an item which denotes an action is called *dhātu*, or if one holds the view that an item which denotes *bhāva* is called *dhātu*, is such a semantic definition as one intends understood from this much sūtra (*bhūvādayo dhātavaḥ*), then?; or, in either view, should the sūtra in question be augmented in order to make the intended semantic definition understood from it?
> [Answer] He [who is an upholder of a semantic definition] says: '[The intended semantic definition is] understood from [this much sūtra].'"

This Bhāṣya forms an introduction to the third and fourth interpretations of A1.3.1. Before setting forth the present Bhāṣya Patañjali has already made clear the following points:

1) The revised *bhāva*-based definition *prathamabhāvavacano dhātuḥ* and A3.1.32, taken together, cover items to be called *dhātu*.

---

[18] See Section 3 [3.2.6].

2) On condition that *svabhāva* or a linguistic item's intrinsic denotative nature is not taken into consideration, a semantic definition will lead to the over-application of the term *dhātu* to nominal bases, which the dhātupāṭha serves to block.
3) A *bhāva*-based definition and a *kriyā*-based definition have the same value in that they are both freed of the difficulty that the name *dhātu* cannot be assigned to certain items which are to be legitimately called *dhātu*.

From points 2) and 3) it is clear that whichever of the *bhāva*-based and *kriyā*-based definitions one may adopt, one cannot evade its over-application to nominal bases so that one has to resort to the dhātupāṭha. Now that such a difficulty insuperable without introducing the *svabhāva* stated above is realized, what is the use of proposing interpreting *A*1.3.1 merely as a *kriyā*-based definition or a *bhāva*-based definition? Recall that Patañjali proposed interpreting the sūtra as a semantic definition, wishing to imply that if the dhātupāṭha is replaced by *svabhāva* a semantic definition provided by *A*1.3.1 becomes satisfactory. Here also he has a conscious intention. He is fully aware that the interpreting of *A*1.3.1 as a *kriyā*-based definition or as a *bhāva*-based definition involves the providing of the indication of the dhātupāṭha. If *A*1.3.1 serves to provide the indication of the dhātupāṭha as well as a semantic definition, then it will become satisfactory as a definition of the term *dhātu*.

7.3.3. A grammatical and syntactical explanation of the compound *bhūvādi*, which allows one to interpret the sūtra in question as such, is given in the following Bhāṣya.

Bh. 2 (I.258.24–27): *katham / ayam ādisabdo 'sty eva vyavasthāyāṃ vartate tad yathā devadattādīn samupaviṣṭān āha devadattādaya ānīyantām iti / ta utthāpyānīyante / asti prakāre vartate tad yathā devadattādaya āḍhyā abhirūpā darśanīyāḥ pakṣavantaḥ / devadattaprakārā iti gamyate /*

pratyekaṃ cādiśabdaḥ parisamāpyate bhvādaya iti ca vādaya iti ca /

"[Question] How?

[Answer] Certainly, this word *ādi* sometimes occurs with reference to *vyavasthā* 'arrangement'. An example of the use of the word *ādi* in the sense of *vyavasthā* is: Speaking of Devadatta and others who are sitting together, someone says *devadattādaya ānīyantām* 'Devadatta and the rest should be brought'; in this case these people are made to get up and brought.

[But] sometimes this very word occurs to signify *prakāra* 'kind, sort'.[19] An example of the use of the word *ādi* in the sense of *prakāra* is: One uses *devadattādaya āḍhyā abhirūpā darśanīyāḥ pakṣavantaḥ* 'A group of men like Devadatta are rich, learned, handsome, and have many followers'; in this case a group of men spoken of are understood to be like Devadatta in richness and other specified respects.

Furthermore, [in the compound *bhūvādi*] the word *ādi* is connected with each of the components *bhū* and *vā* of the compound *bhūvau*, so that one may have both *bhvādi* (*bhvādayaḥ*) and *vādi* (*vādayaḥ*)."

The point is that the form *bhūvādi* is the bahuvrīhi compound whose components are the dvandva compound *bhūvau* formed from *bhū* and *vā* and the ekaśeṣa ('single remainder') form *ādī* in which one of two *ādis* occurs as a single remainder. Thus we have the following string:

((*bhū* + *vā*) + (*ādi*1 + *ādi*2)) + *jas*
bhūś ca vāś ca bhūvau; *ādiś ca ādiś ca ādī*; *bhūvau ādī yeṣāṃ te bhūvādayaḥ*[20]

Now Patañjali states that the word *ādi* is connected with each of

---

[19]The formula *ayam -śabdaḥ asty eva . . . vartate . . . asti . . . vartate* occurs fairly frequently, when Patañjali deals with a polysemous term and illustrates how it is used. See Joshi/Roodbergen [1969: fn. 501] and [1975: fn. 877].

[20]A grammatical analysis, on which the interpretation of *A*1.3.1 as containing two *ādis* with different senses is based, is neatly given by Kauṇḍabhaṭṭa. *VBhS* on *VSK*9: *dhātusaṃjñāvidhāyakam—bhūvādayo dhātavaḥ iti sūtram / tatra bhūś ca vāś ceti dvandvaḥ / ādiśabdayor vyavasthāprakāravācinor ekaśeṣaḥ / ādiś ca ādiś ca ādī, tato bhūvau ādī yeṣāṃ te bhūvādayaḥ / bhūvau*: A2.2.29. *ādī*: A1.2.64. *bhūvau ādī yeṣāṃ te*: A2.2.24.

the components *bhū* and *vā* of the dvandva compound *bhūvau*. Therefore we have the following:

((*bhū* + *ādi*1) + (*vā* + *ādi*2)) + *jas*
bhvādayaḥ; *vādayaḥ*[21]

Thus what are to be termed as *dhātu* are in effect to be referred to by both of the bahuvrīhi compounds *bhvādi* (*bhvādayaḥ*) and *vādi* (*vādayaḥ*).

What is important to note here is that Patañjali assumes that there are two *ādis*: one which is used with reference to *vyavasthā* and the other that is used to signify *prakāra*. As shown, Patañjali uses bahuvrīhi compounds with *-ādi* to refer to a group of items recited in the text external to the corpus of sūtras, the *Aṣṭādhyāyī*; the word *ādi* being used with reference to *vyavasthā* such that a given element is the first of an ordered group.[22] In addition, as said, in Pāṇini's grammar the term *prakāra* is used in two senses: *bheda* 'differentiation' and *sādṛśya* 'similarity'.[23] Here the word *ādi* said to be used to signify *prakāra* means the latter, *sādṛśya*. Therefore, if its component *ādi* is taken as used with reference to *vyavasthā*, the bahuvrīhi compound *bhvādi* refers to members of the set beginning with *bhū*, recited in the dhātupāṭha, and, if taken as used in the sense of *prakāra*, the compound in question refers to a group of items like *bhū*.[24] It is thus clear that the word *ādi* used with reference to *vyavasthā* and the one used in the sense of *prakāra*, being a constituent of the bahuvrīhi compound,

---

[21] The connection of *bhū* and *ādi*1 and that of *vā* and *ādi*2 may be accounted for by the *yathāsaṅkhya* principle. See *A*1.3.10 *yathāsaṅkhyam anudeśaḥ samānām*.

[22] See Section 4 [4.1.1]. In *A*1.1.34 the term *vyavasthā* is used. The *Kāśikāvṛtti* thereon glosses it as follows: *svābhidheyāpekṣāvadhiniyamo vyavasthā*, according to which in such notions as 'in front of *x*' or 'the first of the ordered group *y*', the points of reference *x* and *y* are respectively called *vyavasthā*.

*A*1.1.34 provides that *pūrva* 'prior, eastern' and so on have the class name *sarvanāman* on condition that they are used with reference to something in a spatial or temporal arrangement (*vyavasthā*).

[23] See Section 5 [5.3.3.3].

[24] See also Section 4, Part 4 [4.8.5].

either *bhvādi* or *vādi*, respectively serve to indicate the dhātupāṭha and to provide a semantic definition.

7.3.4. Granted that a bahuvrīhi compound with *-ādi* used in the sense of *prakāra* serves to provide a semantic definition, however, how can one obtain each of the semantic definitions, *kriyā*-based and *bhāva*-based, from *A*1.3.1? When it has been established that both semantic definitions have the same value, moreover, what leads to such different approaches to the very same sūtra such that one takes it as providing the *kriyā*-based definition and the other takes it as providing the *bhāva*-based definition?

To begin with, we must admit that Patañjali assumes here a certain distinction between these semantic definitions. On this assumption he shows how an upholder of the *kriyā*-based definition and that of the *bhāva*-based definition each interpret *A*1.3.1.

Bh. 3 (I.258.27–259.1): *tad yadā tāvat kriyāvacano dhātur ity eṣa pakṣas tadā bhū ity atra ya ādiśabdaḥ sa vyavasthāyāṃ vartate, vā ity atra ya ādiśabdaḥ sa prakāre, bhū ityevamādayo vā ityevaṃprakārā iti /*

"First of all, therefore, when one has the view that an item which denotes an action is called *dhātu*, one understands as follows:

The word *ādi* which is connected with the item *bhū* occurs with reference to *vyavasthā* and the word *ādi* which is connected with the item *vā* occurs to signify *prakāra*. Consequently what is meant by the sūtra is: Those items which belong to the set beginning with *bhū* and which are like *vā* 'go, strike' are called *dhātu* (*bhū ityevamādayo vā ityevaṃprakārāḥ*)."

Bh. 4 (I.259.1–3): *yadā tu bhāvavacano dhātur ity eṣa pakṣas tadā vā ity atra ya ādiśabdaḥ sa vyavasthāyām, bhū ity atra ya ādiśabdaḥ sa prakāre, vā ityevamādayo bhū ityevaṃprakārā iti /*

"On the other hand, when one has the view that an item which denotes *bhāva* is called *dhātu*, one understands as follows:

The word *ādi* which is connected with the item *vā* occurs with reference to *vyavasthā* and the word *ādi* which is connected with the item *bhū* occurs to signify *prakāra*. Consequently what is meant by the sūtra is: Those items which belong to the set beginning with *vā* and which are like *bhū* are called *dhātu* (*vā ityevamādayo bhū ityevaṃprakārāḥ*)."

Bh. 3 and *Bh.* 4 are stated from the viewpoint of the *kriyā*-based definition and from that of the *bhāva*-based definition, respectively. What we see from these is: An upholder of the *kriyā*-based definition obtains from the sūtra a semantic definition such that a group of items which are like *vā* in that they denote actions are called *dhātu*; an upholder of the *bhāva*-based definition, on the other hand, obtains from the same sūtra a semantic definition such that a group of items which are like *bhū* in that they denote *bhāva* are called *dhātu*. The point is that the dvandva compound *bhūvau* is assumed to be a component of the compound *bhūvādi* and further the constituents *bhū* and *vā* of that dvandva compound are assumed to be distinguished from each other in some respect.

I have already pointed out that in order to interpret *A*1.3.1 as providing the indication of the dhātupāṭha as well as a semantic definition one has to take the components *bhū* and *vā* of the dvandva compound *bhūvau* either as a mere form and a meaningful unit, respectively, or as a meaningful unit and a mere form, respectively.[25] Then on what grounds can one say that the item *bhū* as a meaningful unit is different from the item *vā* as a meaningful unit? At least, one may not say that they are different so long as the *kriyā*-based and *bhāva*-based definitions are considered to have the same value, for one can say in that case that the item *vā* denotes *bhāva* as well as an action and that the item *bhū* denotes an action as well as *bhāva*. This being the case, Kaiyaṭa had to comment upon *Bh.* 1 as follows:

> *Pradīpa* on *MBh* ad *A*1.3.1 (II.196): *parispandāparispandarūpatayā kriyābhāvayor bhedenopanyāsaḥ* /
> "[In the present Bhāṣya] an action and *bhāva* are represented as mutually distinct. The reason for this is that the former consists in motion and the latter does not."

---

[25] See Section 4, Part 4 [4.8.5].

This reminds us of the *kriyā*-based and *bhāva*-based definitions given by early teachers. As has already been shown, the *kriyā*-based and *bhāva*-based definitions as held by early teachers are respectively that an item which denotes something that is to be brought to accomplishment by sādhanas with physical motion is called *dhātu*, and that an item which denotes something that is to be brought to accomplishment by sādhanas without physical motion is called *dhātu*.[26]

Now we have the dvandva compound whose components are *bhū* and *vā*. Viewed as a meaningful unit, the item *bhū* may be understood to convey the meaning of existence or birth and the item *vā* to convey the meaning of the act of going or striking. Needless to say, the former meaning is consonant with their notion of *bhāva* and the latter meaning with their notion of *kriyā*. Furthermore, when either of the components is taken as a meaningful unit, the item *ādi* which is connected with it cannot be the one used with reference to *vyavasthā*. Suppose that the *vyavasthā-ādi* were connected with the item *bhū* as a meaningful unit and the *prakāra-ādi* with the item *vā* as a mere form. That would lead to the result that items similar in form with *vā* are called *dhātu*, which is highly absurd.

In the first place, thus, those who accept early teachers' *kriyā*-based definition, fixing their eyes upon the item *vā* which is supposed to be a meaningful unit, interpret A1.3.1 as follows:

> A. *MBh* ad A1.3.1 (I.258.29): *bhū ityevamādayo vā ityevaṃprakārāḥ* /
> "Those items which belong to the set beginning with *bhū* and which are like *vā* 'go, strike' are called *dhātu*."

As said, the item *vā* signifies the act of going or striking, which conforms with early teachers' notion of *kriyā*, a dynamic act. On the other hand, those who accept early teachers' *bhāva*-based definition, having an eye to the item *bhū* as a meaningful unit, interpret the sūtra at issue as follows:

---

[26] See Section 5 [5.1].

B. *MBh* ad *A*1.3.1 (I.259.2): *vā ityevamādayo bhū ityevaṃprakārāḥ* /
"Those items which belong to the set beginning with *vā* and which are like *bhū* 'be, be born' are called *dhātu*."

It goes without saying that early teachers regarded the meaning of the verb *bhū* as signifying something that is brought to accomplishment by sādhanas without physical motion, a static act, so to speak.

7.3.5. The important point to note in these interpretations of *A*1.3.1 is that Patañjali points out that a bahuvrīhi compound with *prakāra-ādi* provides a semantic definition. Let us take interpretation A for example. We have the following possibilities of interpretation with respect to the aspect of a semantic definition.

1. An item which, like the item *vā* 'go, strike', denotes such an action as is to be brought to accomplishment by sādhanas with physical motion is called *dhātu*.
2. An item which, like the item *vā* 'go, strike', denotes such an action as is to be brought to accomplishment is called *dhātu*.

If we adopt the former alternative, we will obviously face the undesired consequence that the item *bhū* is not called *dhātu*. We cannot say that the item *bhū* is similar to the item *vā* in that it signifies an action as something to be brought to accomplishment by sādhanas with physical motion. Then in what respect the items *bhū* and *vā* should be said to be alike?

Recall that Patañjali has the notion of semantic *kriyā*: he presupposes that a verb meaning is spoken of as *kriyā* and characterizes it as *bhāvyate* or *bhāva*, that which is brought into being. In this sense also we may consider that the *kriyā*-based and *bhāva*-based definitions have the same value. Thus Patañjali has to say that the items under consideration are alike in that they denote something that is brought into being, in other words, something to be brought to accomplishment.[27] Therefore, if we adopt the latter

[27] According to Nāgeśa, the similarity between the terms *bhū* and *vā* consists in their denoting things as they are in the state of being to be brought to accomplishment and which have not been denoted by other

alternative, we will not have the adverse consequence stated above.

In the case of interpretation B also, there is no doubt that we cannot have the semantic definition such that an item which, like the item *bhū* 'be, be born', denotes such *bhāva* as is to be brought to accomplishment by sādhanas without physical motion is called *dhātu*.

7.3.6. The third and fourth interpretations of *A*1.3.1 are: 3) Those items which belong to the set beginning with *bhū* and which are like *vā* 'go, strike' are called *dhātu*; 4) Those items which belong to the set beginning with *vā* and which are like *bhū* 'be, be born' are called *dhātu*. It is interesting that in the interpretations of *A*1.3.1 *kriyā*-based and *bhāva*-based definitions as input are different from those as output. The difference is due to the reading of *prakāra-ādi* into the sūtra. And, more importantly, the *kriyā*-based and *bhāva*-based definitions as output are no longer distinct from each other, having the same value.

Those who accept the *kriyā*-based and *bhāva*-based definitions of early teachers should respectively understand *A*1.3.1 to intend the following:

A. Those items which belong to the set beginning with *bhū* and which, like *vā* 'go, strike', denote something to be brought to accomplishment or something that is brought into being are called *dhātu*.

B. Those items which belong to the set beginning with *vā* and which, like *bhū* 'be, be born', denote something to be brought to accomplishment or something that is brought into being are called *dhātu*.

I have already stated that Patañjali has a single semantic definition of the term *dhātu*.

---

items. *Uddyota* on *MBh* ad *A*1.3.1 (II.196): *sādṛśyaṃ cānyānabhihitasādhyāvasthāpannārthavācitvena*. The qualification of the things denoted by 'which have not been denoted by other items' (*anyānabhihita*) is necessary to exclude *svārthika* verb endings such as *-e* in *śiṣye*. See Section 3 [3.2.4].

> An item which denotes by its intrinsic denotative nature something that is brought into being—such a thing is referred to by the term *bhāva* or *kriyā*—is called *dhātu*.[28]

In the third and fourth interpretations of *A*1.3.1, the dhātupāṭha simply replaces *svabhāva* or a linguistic item's intrinsic denotative nature. As said, Patañjali considers that the dhātupāṭha and *svabhāva* alternate in performing certain roles complementary to a semantic definition.[29] Thus we clearly see here that each of the intended semantic definitions as output is nothing but his single semantic definition of the term *dhātu* and hence that, as far as the aspects of the semantic definitions provided by *A*1.3.1 are concerned, they are not mutually distinct in these interpretations.

7.3.7. In connection with the fourth interpretation of *A*1.3.1 on the part of the upholders of the *bhāva*-based definition, Patañjali suggests having the indication of *vādigaṇa* or the set beginning with *vā* by means of connecting *vyavasthā-ādi* with the item *vā*. We should not overlook this.

As is well known, the verbs of Pāṇini's dhātupāṭha are arranged in ten major groups (*gaṇa*), the first items of which are as follows: I. *bhū́* 'be', II. *adá* 'eat', III. *hu* 'offer oblations', IV. *dívú* 'play, gamble', V. *ṣuñ* 'press juice out of something', VI. *tudà* 'shove, goad, wound', VII. *rudhìr* 'hold in, oppress, besiege', VIII. *tánù* 'stretch', IX. *ḍukrīñ* 'buy', X. *cura* 'steal'. While *bhvādayaḥ* 'members of the set beginning with *bhū*' refers to verbs of the dhātupāṭha, *adiprabhṛtibhyaḥ* 'members of the set beginning with *ad*' (*A*2.4.72) refers to a subgroup in the dhātupāṭha that begins with (*-prabhṛti*) *ad*. Now the item *vā* is a member of the set beginning with *ad*. We do not have the set beginning with *vā*. But, under the fourth interpretation of *A*1.3.1, we expect that, like *bhvādayaḥ*, *vādayaḥ* also refers to verbs of the dhātupāṭha. How is it possible for the bahuvrīhi compound *vādi* to refer to them? In this case, according to Kaiyaṭa, we have both to change the order in which items are arranged in the subgroup *adādigaṇa*

---

[28] See the present section [7.1].

[29] See the present section [7.2.5].

so as to have the item *vā* for its first entry and to change the order in which ten major groups are arranged in the dhātupāṭha to have the subgroup *vādigaṇa* for its first major group.[30]

It is to be noted, however, that in his fourth interpretation of A1.3.1 Patañjali does not in reality intend to propose the rearrangement of the dhātupāṭha but simply to show one theoretically conceivable interpretation of the sūtra. At the bottom of his heart he knows that the dhātupāṭha serves no longer any practical purpose in Pāṇini's grammar once a semantic definition of the term *dhātu* with the notion of *svabhāva* or a linguistic item's intrinsic denotative nature taken in is introduced.[31]

7.4. Patañjali on the ślokavārttika

As shown in Section 2, we have the ślokavārttika which aims at telling how A1.3.1 is interpreted differently. It goes:

bhūvādīnāṃ vakāro 'yaṃ maṅgalārthaḥ prayujyate /
bhuvo vārthaṃ vadantīti bhvarthā vā vādayaḥ smṛtāḥ //

As I pointed out in the very same section, Patañjali adduces only the first half of this verse, of which he makes use to account for the interpretation of A1.3.1 as the dhātupāṭha-based definition,

[30] *Pradīpa* on *MBh* ad A1.3.1 (II.196): *adādīnām ādau vā gatigandhanayor iti paṭhitavyam / adādigaṇo 'pi gaṇānām ādau / tena sarve dhātupāṭhasanniviṣṭā gṛhītā bhavanti /* Other interpretations of the bahuvrīhi compound *vādayaḥ* to refer to verbs of the dhātupāṭha are given by Haradatta in his *Padamañjarī* on the ślokavārttika taken up in Section 2 [2.3.2.2]. We have A2.4.72 *adiprabhṛtibhyaḥ śapaḥ*, which provides that after verbs of the set beginning with *ad* the vikaraṇa affix *śap* which has been introduced by A3.1.68 is replaced by zero (*luk*). Nāgeśa works out two solutions to the problem of how the sūtra is to be treated on the assumption that *vā* precedes *ad* in the given subgroup *adādigaṇa*: the first alternative to take is to have *vāprabhṛtibhyaḥ śapaḥ* instead of *adiprabhṛtibhyaḥ śapaḥ*; the second is to take the form *adiprabhṛti* as the single remainder (*ekaśeṣa*) of the tatpuruṣa compound *adiprabhṛti*, which means 'the item which precedes *ad*' to refer to the item *vā*, and the bahuvrīhi *adiprabhṛti*, which means 'items of the set beginning with *ad*' and which alone remains (See Section 2, fn. 21). *Uddyota* on *MBh* ad A1.3.1 (II.196): *adiprabhṛtibhya ity asya sthāne vāprabhṛtibhya ity eva paṭhanīyam / adiprabhṛtibhya ity atra bahuvrīhitatpuruṣayor ekaśeṣo vā bodhyaḥ /*

[31] See Section 8 [8.7] and Appendix 1 [2.2.2].

and does not refer to its second half. The ślokavārttika in question gives three different interpretations of *A*1.3.1. According to the *Nyāsa* we have the following:

1) Items of the set beginning with *bhū*, recited in the dhātupāṭha, are called *dhātu*.
2) Signifiers (*vādi*) of *bhū* or an action in general are called *dhātu*.
3) A set of *vā*-like items which signifies *bhū* or an action in general is called *dhātu*.

And according to the *Padamañjarī*:

1) Items of the set beginning with *bhū*, recited in the dhātupāṭha, are called *dhātu*.
2) Signifiers (*vādi*) of *bhū* or an action in general are called *dhātu*.
3) A set of items preceding *vā* and items of the set beginning with *vā* are called *dhātu* if they signify *bhū* or an action in general.

From the point of view of grammatical analysis, the first and second interpretations of the *Nyāsa* are the same as those of the *Padamañjarī*; and also, they correspond to Patañjali's interpretations of *A*1.3.1 as the dhātupāṭha-based definition and a purely semantic definition, respectively.[32] On the other hand, the third interpretation of the *Nyāsa* is different from that of the *Padamañjarī* and none of these corresponds to Patañjali's interpretation of *bhūvādayaḥ* as consisting of *bhvādayaḥ* and *vādayaḥ* (his third and fourth interpretations). Let us look more closely at the third interpretation by each of the *Nyāsa* and the *Padamañjarī*.

Nyāsa:
Items of the *vā*-type (*vādi*; *vā* 'go, strike' [II. 41]), which, being spoken of as *bhvartha* (*bhū-artha*) because of (*iti*) denoting

[32] Note that, in the interpretation of the sūtra as a purely semantic definition, while the *Nyāsa* and *Padamañjarī* take the form *bhū* as an action noun (*bhāvasādhana*), Patañjali takes it as an agent noun (*kartṛsādhana*). See the present section [7.2.1].

(*vadanti*) the meaning of the verb *bhū* (*bhuvo 'rtham*), denote *bhū* [i.e., an action in general (*kriyāsāmānya*)], are intended [to be understood as the named] (*smṛtāḥ*).

Padamañjarī:

Two sets of items that denote *bhū* [i.e., an action in general] are intended [to be understood as the named] (*bhvarthā vā vādayaḥ smṛtāḥ*): a set of items which precede, or are recited prior to, *vā* (*vādayaḥ*) and items of the set which begins with *vā* (*vādayaḥ*).

Note their interpretations of the compound *bhūvādayaḥ*. Both in the *Nyāsa* and in the *Padamañjarī* it is the ṣaṣṭhī tatpuruṣa formed of *bhū* and *vādi*; according to the *Nyāsa* it is analyzed as *bhuvo vādayaḥ* and according to the *Padamañjarī* as *bhuvo vādayaś ca vādayaś ca*. In either of them, two *ādis* with different values are not read into the sūtra as in the Bhāṣya, nor does the term *bhū* refer to the entry *bhū* in the dhātupāṭha.

Of course, we clearly see that the third interpretation by the *Padamañjarī* is similar to Patañjali's fourth interpretation. However, if Patañjali hesitated to adduce the second half of the ślokavārttika relevant to *A*1.3.1 granted that he was aware of the whole ślokavārttika, the reason for that should be that, as I have made clear, within the framework created by Kātyāyana, Patañjali had to attempt to interpret A1.3.1 itself as providing the indication of the dhātupāṭha with the four functions as well as a semantic definition. He wanted both the indication of the dhātupāṭha and the provision of a semantic definition out of *A*1.3.1, which were impossible without reading two *ādis*: *vyavasthā-ādi* and *prakāra-ādi* into the compound *bhūvādayaḥ*.

Section 8

Patañjali on the dhātupāṭha and its roles

8. Patañjali on the dhātupāṭha

As shown, in his vārttikas on *A* 1.3.1 Kātyāyana assumes that, with respect to the definition of the term *dhātu*, the dhātupāṭha has the alternative of carrying out the role of supplying items to be called *dhātu* or filling roles complementary to a given possible semantic definition of the term *dhātu*.[1] Patañjali is severely critical of Kātyāyana who considers the latter alternative in his twelfth vārttika. Patañjali disputes and finally denies the need for the dhātupāṭha Kātyāyana has seen with respect to its complementary roles to a semantic definition. Moreover, with reference to the roles of the dhātupāṭha which Kātyāyana in his thirteenth vārttika asserts as necessary for Pāṇini's grammatical system also, posing such a problem that we can consider the preventive role of the dhātupāṭha regarding corruptions, he denies such a role for the dhātupāṭha. It is a matter of serious concern to Patañjali whether the dhātupāṭha can preclude one from committing misuse (*viparyāsa*) at all.[2]

The aim of this section is to clarify what makes him take a negative attitude toward the roles Kātyāyana finds for the dhātupāṭha. We will see that the question is deeply involved with Patañjali's own theory of semantics.

8.1. Kātyāyana on roles of the dhātupāṭha

Let us now confirm what Kātyāyana says in his twelfth and thirteenth vārttikas.

> *Vt.* 12: *bhūvādipāṭhaḥ prātipadikāṇapayatyādinivṛttyarthaḥ* //
> "The text in which items of the set beginning with *bhū* are recited serves to prevent the name *dhātu* from applying to nominal bases and [corruptions] such as *āṇapi-* 'order, command'."

---

[1] See Section 3 [3.2.6] and Section 4, Part 4 [4.8.6].

[2] See Section 4, Part 4 [4.8.6].

Vt. 13: *svarānubandhajñāpanāya ca* //
"And also, items of the set beginning with *bhū* should be recited in order to make known the distinctive accentuations of base vowels and markers."

As said, these vārttikas are stated from the point of view of what functions the dhātupāṭha fulfills on condition that the revised *bhāva*-based definition *prathamabhāvavacano dhātuḥ*, which, according to Patañjali, is to be taken as intending that an item which first denotes *bhāva* is called *dhātu*, is provided. For Kātyāyana, even if one were given a semantic definition of such a form, it would still be necessary to list verbs in the dhātupāṭha for the following reasons:

1) To prevent the name *dhātu* from applying to nominal bases (*prātipadikanivṛttyartha*). [*Vt.* 12]
2) To prevent the name *dhātu* from applying to corruptions like *āṇapi-* (*āṇapayatyādinivṛttyartha*). [*Vt.* 12]
3) To make known accentuations of base vowels (*svarajñāpanāya*). [*Vt.* 13]
4) To make known markers (*anubandhajñāpanāya*). [*Vt.* 13][3]

According to Kātyāyana, the revised *bhāva*-based definition certainly does not allow the name *dhātu* to apply to affixes such as *-e* in *śiśye* which denotes *bhāva* as has already been denoted by bases.[4] However, there are other items that denote *bhāva* as denoted by verbs. They are certain nominal bases and certain corruptions like *āṇapi-*. In spite of its applying successfully in the domain of syntactic units ending in verbal affixes, one might claim, the revised semantic definition does not apply appropriately in the domain of the above-mentioned items. Thus Kātyāyana suggests allotting the dhātupāṭha the role of excluding from the *dhātu* class the nominal bases and corruptions which denote *bhāva.*

In addition, he points out that in Pāṇini's system of grammar the dhātupātha bears a decisive part. First, the dhātupāṭha makes

---

[3] See Section 3 [3.2.6].
[4] See Section 3 [3.2.4].

known accentuations of base vowels (*svarajñāpanāya*). For example, we know from the dhātupāṭha that *bhū́*, *édha*, *dhvánsu*, *lúncá*, *údjhá*, *nṛ́tī́* have high-pitched base vowels (*udātta*). Secondly, it also makes known markers (*anubandhajñāpanāya*). For instance, we are told that ***ñibhī*** and *ṣu**ñ*** are marked with *ñi* and *ñ*. In this way, not only from the point of view of how the dhātupāṭha serves a semantic definition but also from the point of view of Pāṇini's system of grammar, that is, of how the dhātupāṭha is linked with the *Aṣṭādhyāyī*, he argues that one cannot dispense with the dhātupāṭha.

In this connection it has to be noted that, after all, Kātyāyana recognizes that the dhātupāṭha has a fivefold role. What is to be added to the above-mentioned roles is the role of supplying items to be assigned the class name *dhātu*, needless to say.

8.2. Patañjali on vārttikas 12–13

8.2.1. A premise of the argument

Unlike Kātyāyana, Patañjali sets himself the task of interpreting *A*1.3.1. Not only does he justify the interpretation of the rule as the dhātupāṭha-based definition in connection with the condition imposed by Kātyāyana in his first vārttika for assigning the class name *dhātu*: *pāṭhena dhātusaṃjñāyām* and its interpretation as a purely semantic definition in connection with a *bhāva*-based definition Kātyāyana proposed as an alternative to the dhātupāṭha-based definition. He also justifies the interpretation of the sūtra in question as intending both the indication of the dhātupāṭha with a complementary role to a semantic definition and the semantic definition. All this has been made clear so far.[5] For Patañjali, therefore, Kātyāyana's vārttikas 12–13 are taken into the context of the last interpretation of *A*1.3.1.

The interpretation was made in a twofold way:

A. Those items which belong to the set beginning with *bhū* and which, like *vā* 'go, strike', denote something to be brought to accomplishment or something that is brought into being are called *dhātu*.

---

[5] See Section 7.

B. Those items which belong to the set beginning with *vā* and which, like *bhū* 'be, be born', denote something to be brought to accomplishment or something that is brought into being are called *dhātu*.

Here the indication of the dhātupāṭha is provided by the bahuvrīhi compound *bhvādayaḥ* or *vādayaḥ* with *vyavasthā-ādi* and the semantic definition by the bahuvrīhi *vādayaḥ* or *bhvādayaḥ* with *prakāra-ādi*. We have here a common semantic definition to which the dhātupāṭha plays a complementary role. That is:

An item which denotes something to be brought to accomplishment or something that is brought into being is called *dhātu*.

And if regarded as independent of the dhātupāṭha, the intended semantic definition is:

An item which denotes by its intrinsic denotative nature (*svabhāva*) something that is brought into being—such a thing is referred to by the term *bhāva* or *kriyā*—is called *dhātu*.

It will be useful to keep these points in mind as we examine Patañjali's argument on vārttikas 12–13.[6]

8.2.2. *Mahābhāṣya* on vārttikas 12-13

We have taken a brief look at Patañjali's interpretations of *A*1.3.1. Now we see what led Patañjali to take up the question of the need for the dhātupāṭha. For Patañjali, the question is whether it is in reality necessary to accept help from the dhātupāṭha at all when we have a semantic definition of the term *dhātu*, granted that *A*1.3.1 admits of interpretations A and B shown above. Therefore, in the context of interpretations A and B, this question assumes the form of the question whether it is necessary to read *vyavasthā-ādi* as well as *prakāra-ādi* in the sūtra.[7] On the

[6]On the interpretations of *A*1.3.1, see Section 7.

[7]This point is clearly stated by Nāgeśa in connection with *Bh.* 1 cited below. Kaiyaṭa explains the intention of *Bh.* 1 (see the present section [8.2.2.1]) as follows. *Pradīpa* on *MBh* ad *A*1.3.1 (II.196): *kriyāvacano dhātur iti vā bhāvavacano dhātur iti vā lakṣaṇaṃ kriyatāṃ nārthaḥ pāṭhenety arthaḥ* / ("What *Bh.* 1 means is: Let the definition of the term *dhātu* be made as *kriyāvacano dhātuḥ* or *bhāvavacano dhātuḥ*,

assumption that the bahuvrīhi compound *bhūvādayaḥ* is formed from the dvandva compound *bhūvau* and *prakāra-ādi*, we can interpret the sūtra as intending a semantic definition without indicating the dhātupāṭha in the following manner:

> Items which are like *bhū* 'be, be born' and which are like *vā* 'go, strike' are called *dhātu*;[8] or, items which are like *bhū* 'be, be born' and *vā* 'go, strike' are called *dhātu*.

Of course, if the dhātupāṭha has to be linked here also with the sūtra in question as interpreted in this way, then it will have only to be taken to serve as a kind of ākṛtigaṇa 'type-listing'.[9]

Thus our next step is to consider, in view of these, what Patañjali says in connection with the *raisons d'être* of the dhātupāṭha Kātyāyana has pointed out. Let us first have an overview of the Bhāṣya at issue.

---

there is no purpose to be served by the dhātupāṭha.") To elucidate this passage of the *Pradīpa*, Nāgeśa states as follows. *Uddyota* on *MBh* ad *A*1.3.1 (II.196): *nanu vyavasthāvācyādiśabdāntarbhāveṇa pāṭhasyāpi lakṣaṇenāpekṣaṇīyatvān nedānīm ity ayuktam ata āha—kriyāvacana iti / vyavasthāvācyādiśabdasya prayojanapraśna ity arthaḥ /* According to Nāgeśa, interpretations A and B of *A*1.3.1 given here both assume that the sūtra in question contains the *vyavasthā-ādi* and hence expect the dhātupāṭha to contribute to defining the term *dhātu*. In *Bh*. 1 Patañjali argues that even though any semantic definition of the term *dhātu* is given, we should have the dhātupāṭha and then asks the question as to what purpose the dhātupāṭha serves under the given condition. Thus, according to Nāgeśa, for Patañjali asking the above-stated question amounts to raising the question of the purpose of reading the *vyavasthā-ādi* in the sūtra (*vyavasthāvācyādiśabdasya prayojanapraśnaḥ*).

[8] In a statement in which an item whose referent forms a certain group is used, a syntactic relation is built up by taking its members either singly (*pratyekavākyaparisamāpti*) or collectively (*samudāyavākyaparisamāpti*). See *MBh* on *vt*. 12 ad *A*1.1.1, *VP*2.375–76; 391, and *PIS*107–108. In this case, by the rule of *pratyekavākyaparisamāpti*, the single item *ādi* is connected with each of the components *bhū* and *vā* of the dvandva compound *bhūvau*. The second interpretation presented here follows the rule of *samudāyavākyaparisamāpti*. See also the Bhāṣya (*Bh*. 2) cited in Section 7 [7.3.3].

[9] On ākṛtigaṇa, see the present section [8.6.1.2].

8.2.2.1. Introduction to vārttikas 12-13

To begin with, Patañjali makes an introductory remark to vārttikas 12–13 as follows:

Bh. 1 (I.259.3): *yadi tarhi lakṣaṇaṃ kriyate, nedānīṃ pāṭhaḥ kartavyaḥ / kartavyaś ca / kiṃ prayojanam /*
"[Objection] Then if the [semantic] definition of the term *dhātu* is given, it is not now necessary to recite items [in the dhātupāṭha].
[Answer] But reciting items in the dhātupāṭha is necessary.
[Question] For what purpose?"

Let us confirm here again that this Bhāṣya is stated after establishing that either of the *kriyā*-based and *bhāva*-based definitions, which are in effect equivalent to each other, is obtained through reading the *prakāra-ādi* in *A*1.3.1. In the light of the context, it is evident that Patañjali here brings up the question about the use of reading in the sūtra the *vyavasthā-ādi* which serves to indicate the dhātupāṭha, as is pointed out by Nāgeśa.[10]

8.2.2.2. Patañjali's interpretation of vārttika 12

With reference to vārttika 12, what he states is this:

Bh. 2 (I.259.5–7): *bhūvādipāṭhaḥ kartavyaḥ / kiṃ prayojanam / prātipadikāṇapayatyādinivṛttyarthaḥ / prātipadikanivṛttyartha āṇapayatyādinivṛttyarthaś ca / ke punar āṇapayatyādayaḥ / āṇapayati vaṭṭati vaḍḍhatīti /*
"Items of the set beginning with *bhū* should be recited.
[Question] For what purpose?
[Answer] For the purpose of preventing the name *dhātu* from applying to nominal bases and [corruptions] such as *āṇapi*-.
Items of the set beginning with *bhū* should be recited both for the purpose of preventing the name *dhātu* from applying to nominal bases and for the purpose of preventing the name from applying to [corruptions] such as *āṇapi*-.
[Question] But what are meant by *āṇapayatyādayaḥ* '[corruptions] such as *āṇapi*-'?

---

[10] See the present section, fn. 7.

[Answer] *āṇapayati*, *vaṭṭati* 'occur', and *vaḍḍhati* 'grow'—these items are meant."

This Bhāṣya intends merely to gloss on vārttika 12. Importantly, while Kātyāyana considers the dhātupāṭha to serve to prevent the term *dhātu* from applying to certain nominal bases (*prātipadikanivṛttyartha*), Patañjali gives no instance of the over-application of the term *dhātu* to them.

8.2.2.3. Patañjali's interpretation of vārttika 13

In the Bhāṣya on vārttika 13, the arguments on the roles of the dhātupāṭha are brought forward.

Bh. 3 (I.259.9–10): *svarānubandhajñāpanāya ca pāṭhaḥ kartavyaḥ / svarānubandhāṃś ca jñāsyāmīti / na hy antareṇa pāṭhaṃ svarā anubandhā vā śakyā vijñātum /*

"And also, items of the set beginning with *bhū* should be recited in order to make known the distinctive accentuations of base vowels and markers.

With the intention, 'I will know accentuations of base vowels and markers,' one resorts to the dhātupāṭha. Indeed, one can know neither accentuations of base vowels nor markers without the dhātupāṭha."

Bh. 4 (I.259.10–11): *ye tv ete nyāyyavikaraṇā udāttā ananubandhakāḥ paṭhyanta eteṣāṃ pāṭhaḥ śakyo 'kartum /*

"[Objection] However, items after which the vikaraṇa *śap*, a vikaraṇa provided for by the general rule (*nyāyya*) *A* 3.1.68,[11] those the base vowels of which are high-pitched (*udātta*), and

[11]Kaiyaṭa explains the word *nyāyya* of the compound *nyāyyotpatti* in the Bhāṣya on *A*2.3.1 as referring to *utsarga* ('general rule'), saying that early teachers (*pūrvācārya*) commonly understood *utsarga* by the word *nyāyya*. *Pradīpa* on *MBh* ad *A*2.3.1 (II.752): *utsargaḥ pūrvācāryaprasiddhyā nyāyya ucyate /* It is also appropriate to mention here *Ṛgvedaprātiśākhya* 1.53: *nyāyair miśrān apavādān pratīyāt*, in his commentary on which Uvaṭa glosses: *nyāyāḥ utsargāḥ mahāviṣayā vidhayaḥ / apavādāḥ alpaviṣayā vidhayaḥ / tān utsargaiḥ miśrān ekīkṛtān jānīyāt.* The word *nyāyya* is a derivate formed from *nyāya* with the taddhita affix *yat* (*A*4.4.92).

those which are unmarked (*ananubandhaka*) are recited here in the dhātupāṭha. These items can be left unlisted."

Bh. 5 (I.259.11–12): *eteṣām apy avaśyam āṇapayatyādinivṛttya-rthaḥ pāṭhaḥ kartavyaḥ* /
"[Answer] These items mentioned above also should be recited so that one may prevent the name *dhātu* from applying to [corruptions] such as *āṇapi-*."[12]

Bh. 6 (I.259.1213): *na kartavyaḥ* / *śiṣṭaprayogād āṇapaya-tyādīnāṃ nivṛttir bhaviṣyati* /
"[Answer] They do not have to be recited. On the authority of the usage of the śiṣṭas (*śiṣṭaprayoga*), an élite of model speakers, [corruptions] such as *āṇapi-* will be prevented from being called *dhātu*."

---

[12] Kaiyaṭa explains this Bhāṣya as follows. *Pradīpa* on *MBh* ad *A*1.3.1 (II.197): *teṣām apāṭhe nivṛttir āṇavayatyādivat syāt tasmād āṇavayatyā-diṣv eṣāṃ nivṛttir yathā syāt tanmadhye mā pravikṣann ityevamarthas teṣām api pāṭhaḥ kartavya ity arthaḥ* / ("What the present Bhāṣya means is this: If those items were not recited in the dhātupāṭha, they would be excluded from the category of items listed therein, just as items like *āṇavi-* (= *āṇapi-*). Therefore, they have to be recited in the dhātupāṭha so that they may be excluded from the category of [corrup-tions] such as *āṇavi-*, in other words, so that they should not fall under the category of such [corruptions].") Nāgeśa comments thereon. *Uddyota* on *MBh* ad *A*1.3.1 (II.197): *pāṭhābhāve hi te 'pi āṇavayatyādivad bahir bhaveyur iti āṇavayatyādibhyo nivṛttyartho bhedārtha iti bhāṣyārtha iti bhāvaḥ* / ("An idea underlying Kaiyaṭa's statement is as follows. What Patañjali means by the present Bhāṣya is: Indeed, if the items in question were not listed in the dhātupāṭha, they would be outside the dhātupāṭha, as items like *āṇavi-*; therefore, the dhātupāṭha serves to differentiate them from such items as *āṇavi-*, namely to distinguish the former from the latter.") Clearly Kaiyaṭa takes the phrase *āṇapayatyādinivṛttyartha* in the present Bhāṣya as meaning 'for the purpose of distinguishing the items in question from [corruptions] such as *āṇapi-*'. According to him, if verbs which are not specified in the operational rules were not listed in the dhātupāṭha, they would not be differentiated from corruptions in that they are not found in the dhātupāṭha. Thus one has to make a distinction between such verbs and corruptions corresponding to them in such a way that the former are listed therein and the latter not. I take the present Bhāṣya as intending to say that verbs unspecified in the operational rules need also to be recited in the dhātupāṭha in order that corruptions corresponding to them may not be called *dhātu*.

Bh. 7 (I.259.13–14): *sa cāvaśyaṃ śiṣṭaprayoga upāsyo ye 'pi paṭhyante teṣām api viparyāsanivṛttyarthaḥ / loke hi kṛṣyarthe kasiṃ prayuñjate, dṛśyarthe ca disim /*
"Moreover, the usage of the śiṣṭas [which is resorted to for the exclusion of corruptions] is necessarily respected in order to prevent the misuse (*viparyāsa*) of those items also which deserve to be recited. For in the world of everyday usage (*loke*) one uses *kas* in the sense of *kṛṣ* 'plow' and *dis*[13] in the sense of *dṛś* 'see'."

What is especially noteworthy in the Bhāṣya on vārttika 13 is Patañjali's making much of the dhātupāṭha's role of preventing the term *dhātu* from applying to corruptions and his denial of it through introducing the notion of the respect for the usage of the śiṣṭas (*śiṣṭaprayoga upāsyaḥ*).

8.3. *prātipadikanivṛttyartha*

Of the four functions Kātyāyana in his twelfth and thirteenth vārttikas assumes the dhātupāṭha to have, let us first take up its function to exclude nominal bases from the domain of application of the name *dhātu*. Strangely enough, however, in his Bhāṣya on vārttika 12, Patañjali does not present any examples to illustrate the point made with regard to nominal bases (*Bh.* 2). How should we understand this?

On this question Nāgeśa expounds his views as follows:

Uddyota on *MBh* ad *A*1.3.1 (II.197): *vārttike prātipadikagrahaṇaṃ tu prauḍhyaiva / ata eva tadudāharaṇānuktir bhāṣye /*
"But it is precisely owing to his perfectionism (*prauḍhi*, lit. 'boldness') that Kātyāyana makes mention of the word *prātipadika* in his twelfth vārttika. For this very reason Patañjali does not adduce a single example of the over-application of the term *dhātu* to nominal bases in his Bhāṣya."

What does Nāgesa see here in the Bhāṣya? In giving this statement, what does he wish to imply?

---

[13] Kielhorn's edition gives *diśim*. I follow the Rohatak edition and the Nirnayasāgara Press edition.

8.3.1. We have two sūtras which provide that certain items have the class name *prātipadika* 'nominal base'.

> A1.2.45 *arthavad adhātur apratyayaḥ prātipadikam* /
> A1.2.46 *kṛttaddhitasamāsāś ca* /

Nominal bases are either primitive or derived. A primitive nominal base such as *go* 'cow' has the class name *prātipadika* by A1.2.45. A1.2.46 provides that certain derivates also have the class name *prātipadika*: those that end in kṛt and taddhita affixes and compounds.

In the present context we need not take into consideration nominal bases such as *vā* 'or' which would be called *dhātu* if the dhātupāṭha-based definition were given. Nominal bases we have to consider are the ones which would be undesiredly called *dhātu* if a semantic definition alone were given.

8.3.2. So far we have seen that, in connection with the *bhāva*-based definition, nominal bases such as *vṛkṣa* 'tree' and *mātṛ* 'mother' are mentioned by Patañjali. These nominal bases are primitive. As shown, these nominal bases denote by their intrinsic denotative nature their meanings, substances, as things that have already been brought to accomplishment (*svabhāvasiddha*). As a matter of course, if the following semantic definition is given, the intrinsic denotative nature of a nominal base prevents the term *dhātu* from applying to the nominal base.

> An item which denotes by its intrinsic denotative nature (*svabhāva*) something that is brought into being—such a thing is referred to by the term *bhāva* or *kriyā*—is called *dhātu*.

I have said that this semantic definition is totally independent of the dhātupāṭha.[14] In this respect, therefore, we cannot assume that the dhātupāṭha has the role of blocking the over-application of the term *dhātu* to nominal bases such as *vṛkṣa* and *mātṛ*.

However, what would happen if we had certain nominal bases which denote by its intrinsic denotative nature something that is brought into being?

---

[14] See Section 7 [7.1-2].

8.3.3. In place of Patañjali, Kaiyaṭa enumerates examples of nominal bases at issue. They are:

1. The derivate *pāka* which ends in the kṛt affix ***ghañ*** (*A*3.3.18) as in *bhoktum pākaḥ* 'cooking to eat'.
2. The derivate *śayitavya* which ends in the kṛtya affix *tavya* (*A*3.1.96) as in *devadattena śayitavyam* 'Devadatta should sleep'.[15]
3. Certain nominals called *avyaya* and characterized as *kriyā-pradhāna*, such as *hiruk* 'without' and *pṛthak* 'except'.[16]

The derivates *pāka* and *śayitavya* are derived nominal bases, having the class name *prātipadika* by *A*1.2.46. Items such as *hiruk* and *pṛthak* are primitive nominal bases, being called *prāti-padika* by *A*1.2.45.

8.3.3.1. *bhoktuṃ pākaḥ*

The occurrence of the affix ***tumun*** after the verb *bhuj* 'eat' in the utterance *bhoktuṃ pākaḥ* is accounted for by the following sūtra:

A3.3.10 *tumunṇvulau kriyāyāṃ kriyārthāyām* /

This sūtra provides that ***tumun*** or ***ṇvul*** follows a verb (V1) whose meaning is referred to the future, if this is used with another verb

---

[15] The kṛt affix *tavya* has the name *kṛtya* also by *A*3.1.95.

[16] *Pradīpa* on *MBh* ad *A* 1.3.1 (II.197): *yathā bhoktuṃ pāka iti kriyāśrayāṇi tumunādīni bhavanti tathā dhātusaṃjñāpi syād iti pākādīnāṃ śayi-tavyādīnāṃ ca prātipadikānāṃ pāṭhenāsau nivartyate / tathā hiruk pṛthag ityādīnāṃ ca kriyāpradhānānām avyayānām /* To these examples Nāgeśa adds derivates that end in affixes called *avyayakṛt* such as *bhoktum* in *bhoktuṃ vrajati* 'He goes to eat' and *bhuktvā* in *bhuktvā vrajati* 'He goes after eating'. Pāṇinīyas call affixes such as ***tumun*** and ***ktvā*** *avya-yakṛt*. Patañjali states that kṛt affixes called *avyayakṛt* occur to signify *bhāva* (*MBh* ad *A*3.4.9 [II.171.16]: *avyayakṛto bhāve bhavanti*). Since they are *svārthika* affixes, the *bhāva* as denoted by them is nothing but a verb meaning, *ābhyantarabhāva* 'internal *bhāva*'. See the present section, fn. 18. Bhartṛhari describes such kṛt affixes as connected with properties of an action denoted by a verb (*kriyādharmasamanvita*), point-ing out that items ending in such kṛt affixes are not distinguished from finite verb forms in their denotation of an action. *VP*3.14.438: *ye cāvyayakṛtaḥ kecit kriyādharmasamanvitāḥ / teṣām asattvavācitvaṃ tiṅantair na viśiṣyate //*

(V2) the action denoted by which has as its purpose the act which the first verb (V1) signifies. What has to be noticed is that the sūtra presupposes that a derivate of the second verb (V2) denotes an action in process, as in *bhoktuṃ pacati* 'He cooks to eat'; V1 being *bhuj* and V2 *pac*.[17] Now the item *pāka* is derived from the verb *pac* by adding the kṛt affix ***ghañ***, which is introduced to signify *bhāva* or an act in the abstract, to that verb. According to Patañjali, the following is commonly accepted:

> *MBh* ad *A*3.1.67 (II.57.8): *kṛdabhihito bhāvo dravyavad bhavati* /
> "*Bhāva* which is denoted by a kṛt affix behaves like a substance."

Just as a substance as the meaning of the nominal base *vṛkṣa* is connected with a certain gender (*liṅga*), a certain number (*saṅkhyā*) and serves as kāraka, so *bhāva* as denoted by a kṛt affix such as ***ghañ*** also is connected with them and serves as kāraka. As one says *vṛkṣo vartate* 'A tree is there', *vṛkṣā vartante* 'The trees are there', similarly one says *pāko vartate* 'The act of cooking is taking place', *pākā vartante* 'The acts of cooking are taking place'.[18]

Obviously, however, if we accept the present item *pāka* as denoting such *bhāva*, we cannot derive the utterance *bhoktuṃ pākaḥ*, nor does the intended semantic definition have the chance of over-application to the item *pāka* in question. Therefore we have to get a new angle on this matter.

In his Bhāṣya on *A*6.2.139, Patañjali, taking up the derivate *bhavana* which ends in the kṛt affix ***lyuṭ*** that is introduced, like the affix ***ghañ***, to signify *bhāva* or an act in the abstract (*A*3.3.115), describes its character as follows:

---

[17] See the present section, fn. 19.

[18] Patañjali distinguishes *bhāva* as in *A*3.3.18 and *bhāva* as in *A*3.4.69, calling the former *bāhyabhāva* 'external *bhāva*' and the latter *ābhyantarabhāva* 'internal *bhāva*'. The internal *bhāva* is nothing but a verb meaning. See Section 3 [3.2.4] with fn. 25.

> *MBh* ad *A*6.2.139 (III.136.4–6): *nanu cāyaṃ tasyaivārthasya vācakaḥ prabhavanam iti / eṣo 'pi dravyaviśiṣṭasya / katham / kṛdabhihito bhāvo dravyavad bhavati kriyāvad apīti /*
> "[Objection] And the word *prabhavana* 'production' here denotes only that meaning [of an action].
> [Answer] This word also denotes something qualified by [the properties of] a substance.
> [Question] How?
> [Answer] *Bhāva* which is denoted by a kṛt affix behaves like a substance and like an action as well (*kṛdabhihito bhāvo dravyavad bhavati kriyāvad api*)."

Patañjali describes *bhāva* denoted by a kṛt affix as behaving like an action as well as a substance, on the basis of which Kaiyaṭa in his *Pradīpa* on this Bhāṣya explicitly states the introduction of the affix *tu**mun*** to the verb *bhuj* in *bhoktuṃ pākaḥ* is justified.[19] Thus we see that the key to the over-application of a semantic definition to the item *pāka* lies in its behaving like an action (*kriyāvat*) according to cases.

Then what does it mean that *bhāva* denoted by a kṛt affix behaves like an action? Kaiyaṭa explains:

> *Pradīpa* on *MBh* ad *A*5.4.19 (IV.255): *avipratipattiviṣayākhyātavācyakriyāpekṣaś ca kriyāvad ity atideśaḥ /*
> "And, it is indisputable that a finite verb form denotes an action; by saying *kriyāvat* 'like an action', Patañjali, in view of such an action as denoted by a finite verb form, means that properties of the action are extended [to *bhāva* denoted by a kṛt affix]."

It is clear from this that by extension (*atideśa*) properties of an action denoted by a verb are extended to *bhāva* denoted by a kṛt affix to which the properties would otherwise not pertain and thereby the latter is treated as behaving like an action.

All this makes it clear that, in Kaiyaṭa's view, in *bhoktuṃ pākaḥ* the affix *tu**mun*** is introduced to the verb *bhuj* by virtue of *bhāva* denoted by the kṛt affix ***ghañ*** in *pāka*, that is, the act of

---

[19] *Pradīpa* on *MBh* ad *A*6.2.139 (IV.570): *tena bhoktuṃ pāka ityādau kriyopapadāśrayaḥ pratyayaḥ /*

cooking in the abstract, being treated as behaving like an action denoted by the verb *pac*, that is, the act of cooking in process, and, precisely for this reason the item *pāka* has the chance of being assigned the name *dhātu* by the intended semantic definition.[20]

8.3.3.2. *śayitavya*

Concerning the derivate *śayitavya* that ends in the kṛtya affix *tavya*, we have to consider the following sūtra:

A3.4.70 *tayor eva kṛtyaktakhalarthāḥ* /

According to this sūtra, kṛtya affixes occur only in two meanings given in the preceding sūtra A3.1.69: an object and *bhāva*. The affix *tavya* in *śayitavya* denotes the same *bhāva* as the verb ending *-te* in *śayyate devadattena* 'Devadatta is sleeping'. The *bhāva* as denoted by verb endings is called *tiṅabhihitabhāva* '*bhāva* denoted by a verb ending', characterized as internal *bhāva* (*ābhyantarabhāva*) which is nothing but a verb meaning.[21] What results from this is that the *bhāva* as denoted by kṛt affixes is also nothing but a verb meaning, an action in process. Thus, apart from its modal meanings, the derivate *śayitavya* can be regarded as the same as the verb *śī*, so that it is subject to the application of the intended semantic definition.[22]

8.3.3.3. *hiruk, pṛthak*

According to Patañjali, of the items called *avyaya* some are characterized as *vibhaktyarthapradhāna* and others as *kriyāpradhāna*.[23] For example, *uccasis* 'high, loud', coming under

---

[20] Nāgeśa, on the other hand, does not accept sentences such as *bhoktuṃ pākaḥ* as correct usage. *Uddyota* on *MBh* ad A1.3.1 (II.197): *pākapadena siddhāvasthasya bhānād bhoktuṃ pāka iti prayogo 'pi cintyaḥ . . .* / See also *Uddyota* on *MBh* ad A2.2.19 (II.692). I do not think that there is a need to go into details about this matter.

[21] See the present section, fn. 18.

[22] On modal meanings of derivates ending in kṛtya affixes, see A3.3.163–172.

[23] *MBh* ad A1.1.38 (I.95.19–20): *kiṃcid avyayaṃ vibhaktyarthapradhānaṃ, kiṃcit kriyāpradhānam / uccair nīcair iti vibhaktyarthapradhānam, hiruk pṛthag iti kriyāpradhānam /*

the former category, has a meaning of a nominal ending of the seventh triplet (*saptamīvibhakti*) for its principal meaning, paraphrased as *uccadeśe* 'in [on, at] a high place'.[24] What we are concerned with are items such as *hiruk* 'without' which fall under the latter category. The item *hiruk* is said to convey the meaning of the act of excluding (*varjana*).[25]

Now, if the expression *kriyāpradhāna* is taken to mean 'what has an action for its principal meaning', then the item *hiruk*, being understood to convey the act of excluding as its principal meaning, certainly has the name *dhātu* by the intended semantic definition. This is the idea Kaiyaṭa holds here.

However, as Nāgeśa points out,[26] this interpretation of the expression *kriyāpradhāna* goes against his own interpretation found in his *Pradīpa* on *MBh* ad *A*1.1.38, where he suggests that we should take that expression as meaning 'what qualifies an action' (*kriyāviśeṣaṇa*) or what has an action for its chief qualificand.[27] Following this interpretation, we naturally cannot claim that the item *hiruk* denotes an action. Thus we need not take into account here items such as *hiruk* which are characterized as *kriyāpradhāna*.

8.3.4. From the above we are now certain that the item *pāka* in *bhoktuṃ pākaḥ* has the chance of the intended semantic definition being applied to itself through the extension of properties of an action to it and the item *śayitavya* is susceptible to the application of the intended semantic definition by virtue of being an equivalent to the verb *śī*. Interestingly, however, from the viewpoint of Pāṇini's derivational system, even if these items are given the name *dhātu*, no undesirable consequence ensues.

---

[24] *Uddyota* on *MBh* ad *A*1.2.29–30 (II.43): *uccaiḥ uccadeśe* /

[25] *VBhS* on *VSK*9: *atra kriyāvācitvamātroktau varjanādirūpakriyāvācake hiruk nānā ityādāv ativyāptir iti bhvādigaṇapaṭhitatvam uktam* /

[26] *Uddyota* on *MBh* ad *A*1.3.1 (II.197): *hirug iti / kriyāntarākāṅkṣādarśanenaiṣāṃ kriyāvācitvaṃ cintyam / ata eva taddhitaś cāsarvavibhaktir iti sūtre kriyāmātraviśeṣaṇatvāt kriyāpradhānatvam eṣāṃ svayam uktam* /

[27] *Pradīpa* on *MBh* ad *A*1.1.38 (I.304): *kriyāviśeṣaṇatvād eṣāṃ kriyāprādhānyam / kriyāpadaprayogam antareṇāpi pṛthag devadatta ityādiprayogaḥ kriyākṣepād upapadyate* /

Take the item *pāka* for example. Let us suppose that the item *pāka* is called *dhātu* by the intended semantic definition. It is also called *prātipadika* by *A*1.2.46. Therefore, with reference to it, we have simultaneous application of operations provided for by sūtras headed by *A*3.1.91 *dhātoḥ* and *A*4.1.1 *ṅyāprātipadikāt*. But we have *A*1.4.2 *vipratiṣedhe paraṃ kāryam* which provides that, if two operations conflict, the subsequently stated one takes preference. By this sūtra, consequently, operations provided for by sūtras headed by *A*3.1.91 do not apply to the item *pāka*. For example, we have the sequence *pāka* + ***sup*** and not *pāka* + ***tiṅ***.[28]

It must be recalled here that, with reference to primitive nominal bases such as *vṛkṣa*, their intrinsic denotative nature precludes the intended semantic definition from applying to them, so that there is no room for the dhātupāṭha to come in. In the case of the primitive nominal bases, the intrinsic denotative nature blocks the over-application of the term *dhātu* to them instead of the dhātupāṭha, and, in the case of derived nominal bases such as *pāka* in *bhoktuṃ pākaḥ* and *śayitavya* in *śayitavyaṃ devadattena*, which are regarded as denoting by nature actions, *A*1.4.2 blocks the undesired application of operational rules to them which results from the application of the intended semantic definition of the term *dhātu* to them. The latter proves clearly that there is no need for the dhātupāṭha to prevent the intended semantic definition from applying to the derived nominal bases.

What all these things make clear is: Even if the intended semantic definition alone is given, we need not expect that the dhātupāṭha will serve to block its over-application to nominal bases. We may thus safely say that for this reason Patañjali does not adduce any example of nominal bases to which the name *dhātu* is assigned in this context.

---

[28] *Uddyota* on *MBh* ad *A*1.3.1 (II.197): *vastuta eṣāṃ dhātutve phalābhāvaḥ / na ca prātipadikatvābhāvaḥ phalam / kṛdantatvena tadabhāvasya vaktum aśakyatvāt / ubhayoḥ sattve 'pi liḍ ityādāv iva paratvāt supām evotpattisiddheḥ /*

8.4. *āṇapayatyādinivṛttyartha*

The second reason Kātyāyana brings forward in favor of the view that the dhātupāṭha is still required even if the intended semantic definition is given is that the dhātupāṭha is necessary to prevent the class name *dhātu* from applying to corruptions like *āṇapi-* (*āṇapayati*). Patañjali adds two other examples: *vaṭṭati, vaḍḍhati.* Obviously, these are Middle Indic forms corresponding to Old Indo-Aryan *ājñāpayati* 'commands', *vartate* 'occurs, is', *vardhate* 'grows' (*Bh.* 2). As Cardona points out, there is no doubt that Kātyāyana envisages the possibility of a grammar like Pāṇini's having to exclude Middle Indic forms because they were in use at the same time as the language described in the *Aṣṭādhyāyī.*[29]

As shall be seen later, Patañjali has to be keenly interested in the present function of the dhātupāṭha from the point of view of his theory of semantics and grammar.

8.5. *svarānubandhajñāpanāya*

8.5.1. In his thirteenth vārttika, in view of Pāṇini's system of grammar Kātyāyana gives two more reasons for the necessity of the dhātupāṭha: to make known an accentuation of a base vowel and to inform us of a marker attached to a verb.

As shown in *Bh.* 4, Patañjali considers the bearing of the dhātupāṭha upon grammatical operations with reference to these three points: 1) the introduction of affixes called *vikaraṇa* to verbs, 2)

---

[29] See Cardona [1992] and [2002: 17-18]. Regarding the exclusion of corruptions from a class of correct speech forms, Haradatta states in his *Padamañjarī* on A1.3.1 as follows: *yadi tv anādṛtya pāṭham, kriyāvacano dhātur ity ucyeta / kuto nu khalv etad āṇavedv ityādayo 'pabhraṃśā iti / yāvato ye śāstreṇānugamyante te sādhavaḥ /* ("However, if, without taking the dhātupāṭha into consideration, the rule were formulated as *kriyāvacano dhātuḥ,* then how could it ever be that items such as *āṇavedu* (Śaurasenī, = *ājñāpayatu*) are corruptions, as far as items with which grammar conforms are considered to be correct speech forms?") According to Haradatta, the grammatical rule *kriyāvacano dhātuḥ* results in authorizing corruptions to be correct (*sādhu*). He considers so from the viewpoint of *prāpti* or a resultant from grammar. See the present section [8.6.2.1].

accentuations of base vowels (*svara*), and 3) markers (*anubandha*).[30] Now let us consider the following rules pertaining to those points:

A3.1.69 *divādibhyaḥ śyan* // [*vikaraṇa*]
A7.2.10 *ekāca upadeśe 'nudāttāt* // [*svara*]
A1.3.12 *anudāttaṅita ātmanepadam* // [*anubandha*]

A3.1.69 states that the vikaraṇa ***śyan*** occurs after verbs of the subset beginning with *div*, on condition that the verbs occur with sārvadhātuka affixes signifying an agent. By this rule, the introduction of the affix ***śyan***, as in *dīvyati* '. . . is gambling', is accounted for. A7.2.10 provides that *iṭ* does not occur in an ārdhadhātuka affix that begins with a consonant other than *y* (*val*) if this follows a verb which, when it is taught (*upadeśe*), is monosyllabic (*ekācaḥ*) and has a low-pitched base vowel (*anudāttāt*). For example, the affix ***tumun*** is not augmented with *iṭ* as in *attum* (*ad-tum*; *ad* 'eat'). By A1.3.12 ātmanepada affixes are allowed to follow a verb that has a low-pitched vowel or *ṅ* for a marker (*anudāttaṅitaḥ*). The item *é**dha*** is marked with a low-pitched vowel *a* so that one has *edhate*.

As is clear, A3.1.69 specifies that a verb to which the vikaraṇa ***śyan*** is introduced is the one which is a member of the subset in the dhātupāṭha that begins with *div*. In the same manner, A7.2.10 and A1.3.12 respectively specify that a verb after which a certain ārdhadhātuka affix (A3.4.114–116) does not take *iṭ* is the one which has a low-pitched base vowel, and that a verb which an ātmanepada affix follows has a low-pitched vowel or *ṅ* for a marker.

Then where can one know the verbs specified in these rules? From the dhātupāṭha, of course. Without the dhātupāṭha, one could not know these specified verbs. This is what is said by Patañjali in *Bh.* 3. However, this being so, one might say that items which have to be listed in the dhātupāṭha should be the

---

[30] Additional affixes whose introduction to verbs is determined by verbal affixes are called *vikaraṇa* by Pāṇinīyas.

items specified in operational rules. With the intention of implying this, Patañjali states *Bh.* 4.[31]

8.5.2. A theoretical assumption underlying *Bh.* 4 is that the necessity of being recited in the dhātupāṭha is restricted to those verbs which are specified in operational rules. Consider the following rules:

A3.1.68 *kartari śap* //
A7.2.35 *ārdhadhātukasyeḍ valādeḥ* //
A1.3.74 *ṇicaś ca* //
A1.3.78 *śeṣāt kartari parasmaipadam* //
A3.1.25 *satyāpapāśarūpavīṇātūlaślokasenālomatvacavarma-varṇacūrṇacurādibhyo ṇic* //

A3.1.68 is a general rule to which A3.1.69 *divādibhyaḥ śyan* is an exception, providing that if a verb occurs with a sārvadhātuka affix (A3.4.113) signifying an agent (*kartari*), the suffix ***śap*** follows that verb, as in *bhavati* (*bhū-a-ti*). Unlike A3.1.69 this rule does not specify verbs. A7.2.35 is the rule according to which the augment *iṭ* occurs as part of an ārdhadhātuka affix that begins with a consonant other than *y*, so that one has *bhavitum* (*bhū-tum*). A7.2.10 *ekāca upadeśe 'nudāttāt* is a negative rule that disallows the addition of *iṭ*. In A7.2.35 Pāṇini does not specify the verbs after which specified ārdhadhātuka affixes take *iṭ*. Items of the subgroup beginning with *cur* (*curādigaṇa*) have final vowels like *a* of *cur**a*** (A3.1.25). But they are not markers accented in a manner to show that a verb takes an ātmanepada affix, a parasmaipada affix, or both. For the use of ātmanepada and parasmaipada affixes with derived verbs containing ***ṇic*** is covered in general by A1.3.74, 78; in the case of *cur**a***, one has *corayati*. Just like *hu* 'offer oblations', they have zero markers.

[31] From a different angle Haradatta stresses the need for the dhātupāṭha. *Padamañjarī* on *Kāśikāvṛtti* ad A1.3.1: *avaśyaṃ cānubandhādiviśiṣṭaṃ rūpaṃ pāṭhenaiva darśanīyam, na hi tadrūpaṃ prayoge sambhavati* / The point is that forms of verbs qualified by elements such as markers are not found in actual usage, so that the dhātupāṭha is necessary to show such forms.

Thus verbs that are not specified in operational rules are as follows:

1) Verbs after which the vikaraṇa ***śap*** occurs.
2) Verbs whose base vowels are low-pitched and the ārdhadhātuka affixes following which take the initial augment *iṭ*.
3) Verbs with no markers attached to them.[32]

Given such a restriction on verbs to be listed in the dhātupāṭha, what would follow? Theoretically, if only the verbs which are specified in operational rules had to be recited in the dhātupāṭha, verbs of the above-mentioned sort could not be recited in the dhātupāṭha for the reason that they have no connection with operational rules whatever. As Patañjali argues, the restriction on verbs to be recited in the dhātupāṭha thus leads to the consequence that it is not necessary to list in the dhātupāṭha the verbs which are not specified in operational rules.

8.5.3. Let us summarize here the main points that have been made with reference to the dhātupāṭha's function of feeding information on accentuations of base vowels and markers.

A student of the *Aṣṭādhyāyī*, when encountering the rules in which verbs are specified in terms of their base vowels and markers, will seek for a text which give information about such verbs. The text is the dhātupāṭha. However, if this argument were accepted, one could not avoid the consequence that there is a fear that the need for the dhātupāṭha might be restricted to those verbs which have a connection with operational rules. This is the point Patañjali makes in connection with the dhātupāṭha's

[32]In addition to these, there are verbs which do not undergo operations connected with subgroups (*antargaṇa*) included in ten major groups of verbs. For example, in *A*3.1.55 *puṣādidyutādyḷditaḥ parasmaipadeṣu* the subgroups *puṣādigaṇa* (the set beginning with *puṣ**á*** 'nourish, feed') and *dyutādigaṇa* (the set beginning with *dyú**ta*** 'shine') are referred to by *puṣādi* and *dyutādi*, respectively. The *puṣādigaṇa* is included in *divādigaṇa* and the *dyutādigaṇa* in *bhvādigaṇa*. This sūtra specifies that verbs of such subgroups are subject to the replacement of ***aṅ***. See *Padamañjarī* on *Kāsikāvṛtti* ad *A*1.3.1: *asmin pakṣe gaṇapāṭhasāmarthyāt so 'py aṅgīkriyate, anyathā śabvikaraṇā ye seṭo niranubandhakā antargaṇakāryavarjitā bhūprabhṛtayas teṣāṃ pāṭho 'narthakaḥ syāt* /

function of conveying information about accentuations of base vowels and markers, pertaining to verbs.

8.6. Patañjali on *āṇapayatyādinivṛttyartha*

Kātyāyana enumerated four functions of the dhātupāṭha: on the assumption that the dhātupāṭha carries out roles complementary to the intended semantic definition, he mentioned the role of preventing the semantic definition from applying to nominal bases and that of preventing it from applying to corruptions; on the assumption that the dhātupāṭha is a requisite for Pāṇini's derivational system, he specified the role of informing us of accentuations of base vowels and that of making known markers of verbs. As said, of the four functions of the dhātupāṭha what involves Patañjali in a detailed discussion is the second one, that is, the function of preventing the intended semantic definition from applying to corruptions. The keys to his discussion on that function are the notions of *viparyāsa* 'misuse' and *śiṣṭaprayoga* 'the usage of the śiṣṭas', and further his theory of semantics and grammar. In my view, the argument he brings forward in this context forms a core of the Bhāṣya on *A*1.3.1.

8.6.1. *viparyāsa* 'misuse'

With Patañjali, the use of corruptions is a matter of misuse (*viparyāsa*), a mistake in usage; the misuse consists in using a certain corrupted form instead of using a corresponding correct form.[33] It is in this frame of reference that Patañjali argues against assuming that the application of the name *dhātu* to corruptions by the intended semantic definition is prevented by virtue of the dhātupāṭha.

As has been said, Patañjali does not accept the view that the dhātupāṭha serves to make known accentuations of base vowels

[33]That Patañjali means misuse by the term *viparyāsa* is clear from his comments on *vt*.8 ad *A*3.3.133: *asiddhaviparyāsāc ca. MBh* on *vt*. 8 ad *A*3.3.133 (II.160.22–23): *asiddhaś ca viparyāsaḥ / na hīha kaścid kūpo 'stīti prayoktavye kūpo 'bhūd iti prayuṅkte /* ("And, misuse is not established. Indeed, in this everyday world, no one uses the utterance *kūpo 'bhūt* 'there was a well' when the utterance *kūpo 'sti* 'There is a well' is to be used.")

and markers attached to verbs, on the grounds that such an assumption would entail the undesirable consequence that only the verbs specified in operational rules have to be listed in the dhātupāṭha. To his denial of such functions of the dhātupāṭha, an objection is raised: Unspecified verbs should also be listed in the dhātupāṭha so as to prevent the over-application of the name *dhātu* to the corruptions corresponding to them (*Bh*. 5). As argued, however, if it is necessary to list unspecified verbs in the dhātupāṭha to prevent such an undesirable application, then the same will be true of the verbs having a connection with the operational rules. Thus Patañjali states *Bh*. 7.

8.6.1.1. When he says in his twelfth vārttika that the dhātupāṭha serves to deny the name *dhātu* to corruptions, Kātyāyana means the following:

The name *dhātu* applies to an item which denotes *bhāva* if and only if the item is listed in the dhātupāṭha. A corruption like *āṇapi-* denotes *bhāva* but is not listed in the dhātupāṭha. Consequently such a corruption does not have the name *dhātu*. Without being assigned the name *dhātu*, corruptions could not be subject to any grammatical operations linked with items termed *dhātu*, as a consequence of which one would not have a derivative like *āṇapayati*.

This is precisely the way Kātyāyana considers how the dhātupāṭha could prevent one from using such a corrupted form which is observed to be in actual use.

But Patañjali wonders:

Suppose that a certain item is listed in the dhātupāṭha. Can one be prevented from using a corresponding corrupted form which conveys the same meaning as that item, simply by virtue of the item being recited in the dhātupāṭha? In the dhātupāṭha, while *dṛś* is recited, its corrupted form *dis* is not. But in the everyday world it is observed that one misuses *dis* when *dṛś* is to be used. Thus, if we take what is found in actual usage into consideration, we have to admit that what is meant by Kātyāyana is theoretically conceivable, but not likely. According to Patañjali, it is the usage of the śiṣṭas (*śiṣṭaprayoga*) and not the dhātupāṭha that one should resort to in order to prevent the name *dhātu* from applying to corruptions (*Bh.* 6: *śiṣṭaprayogād āṇapayatyādīnāṃ nivṛttir bhaviṣyati*).[34]

8.6.1.2. ākṛtigaṇa-*prayogadarśana*

Now what we see from an argument Patañjali has built up in *Bhs.* 4–6 is the following.

Patañjali proposes:

1. Verbs which are specified in operational rules should be recited in the dhātupāṭha for the purpose of serving the operational rules.
2. Verbs which are not specified in operational rules should be recited in the dhātupāṭha for the purpose of preventing the name *dhātu* from applying to their corresponding corruptions.

As said above, the second point is denied in *Bh.* 6 for the reason that instead of the dhātupāṭha the usage of the śiṣṭas serves to prevent the name from applying to corruptions.

If, as Patañjali argues in *Bh.* 4, verbs which are not specified in operational rules did not have to be recited in the dhātupāṭha, the dhātupāṭha would not be that in which a group of verbs are exhaustively listed. And if the application of the name *dhātu* by the intended semantic definition to verbs which are not listed in the dhātupāṭha and the avoidance of its over-application to their corresponding corruptions were established on the authority of the usage of the śiṣṭas, the same is the case with type listings (*ākṛtigaṇa*) in the gaṇapāṭha. That is to say, we may regard the dhātupāṭha as functioning as a kind of ākṛtigaṇa when we take into consideration corrupted forms corresponding to verbs listed in the dhātupāṭha.

It is well known that Pāṇinīyas distinguish two kinds of groups (*gaṇa*) in the gaṇapāṭha. First, there are groups whose members

---

[34] According to Patañjali, a correct speech form (*śabda*) and an incorrect speech form (*apaśabda*) corresponding it serve to produce the same understanding of a meaning. *MBh* (Paspaśā) [I.8.20–21]: *evam ihāpi samānāyām arthagatau śabdena cāpaśabdena ca dharmaniyamaḥ kriyate* / See the present section, fn. 39.

are exhaustively listed in a given order. In addition, there are type listings such that only illustrative instances of a class are recited in the gaṇapāṭha. According to the *Padamañjarī*, the type listing is defined as follows:

> *Padamañjarī* on *Kāśikāvṛtti* ad *A*2.1.59: *prayogadarśanenā-kṛtigrāhyo gaṇaḥ ākṛtigaṇaḥ* /
> "ākṛtigaṇa is a gaṇa whose [unlisted] members are to be understood, on the basis of the observation of their actual use (*prayoga-darśanena*), following items cited as examples (*ākṛti*)."

In the ākṛtigaṇa, in this manner, items which are not actually listed in a gaṇa are posited, through the observation of their actual use, as the members of the gaṇa because of the similarity between those unlisted items and listed items. Let us apply this structure of ākṛtigaṇa to that of the dhātupāṭha as assumed by Patañjali in this context.[35]

Suppose that there are both a certain item x listed in the dhātupāṭha and a certain item y unlisted there. According to Patañjali, the item y has a relation to the item x such that the use of the item y instead of the item x is called misuse; the item x being a

[35] What Pāṇinīyas call *ākṛtigaṇa* is referred to by a bahuvrīhi compound containing *prakāra-ādi*. One of the meanings of the word *prakāra* is *sādṛśya* 'similarity', as said before. Thus such a bahuvrīhi compound refers to a group of items like listed items, so that instances similar to cited items are to be posited as coming under the group in question through observing usage. See *MBh* ad *A*2.1.59 and also Section 5 [5.3.3.3]. *A*2.1.59 *śreṇyādayaḥ kṛtādibhiḥ* provides for the compounding of syntactic units (*pada*) formed from bases of the set that begins with *śreṇi* 'row, group' (*śreṇyādi*) and coreferential syntactic units formed from terms of the type *kṛta* 'made' (*kṛtādi*). Patañjali considers *śreṇyādi* and *kṛtādi* as exhaustive listing and type listing, respectively (*śreṇyādayaḥ paṭhyante, kṛtādir ākṛtigaṇaḥ*). Kaiyaṭa comments on the Bhāṣya as follows. *Pradīpa* on *MBh* ad *A*2.1.59 (II.635): *ata evātrādiśabdo vyavasthāvācī, kṛtādir ity atrādiśabdaḥ prakāravācī / prayogadarśanāc codāharaṇasthānīyāḥ katipaye vṛttikāraiḥ pradarśitā /* ("From this statement of Patañjali's we understand that the item *ādi* here in *śreṇyādi* signifies *vyavasthā* and the item *ādi* in *kṛtādi* signifies *prakāra*. [In the case of the latter] some items that are similar to an illustration are presented by commentators on the sūtras on the basis of the observation of the usage.")

correct speech form, *dṛś*, the item *y* a corrupted speech form *dis*. The items *x* and *y* are alike in that both of them denote the act of seeing. As a result, on the basis of the observation of its actual use, the item *y* is posited as a verb. However, if a restriction on the users of the item *y* is made, the item will not be accepted as correct for the reason that the item *y* is not actually used by the śiṣṭas.

This is, according to Patañjali, how the usage of the śiṣṭas serves to prevent the misuse of corruptions (*Bh*. 6).

8.6.2. dhātupāṭha and *śiṣṭaprayoga*

So far we have seen that Patañjali holds that what serves to prevent the misuse of corruptions is not the dhātupāṭha but *śiṣṭaprayoga* or the usage of the śiṣṭas instead. Now we can move on to the next issue: How is the *śiṣṭaprayoga* linked with the denial of the dhātupāṭha's preventive function aimed at corruptions?

8.6.2.1. The śiṣṭas are the authority with respect to correct usage (*MBh* ad *A* 6.3.109 [III.174.10]: *śiṣṭāḥ śabdeṣu pramāṇam*). As Patañjali characterizes them,[36] the śiṣṭas are brāhmaṇas who dwell in Āryāvarta, following established rules of correct behavior without having to be given any immediate cause for this, and who by their favor of fate or their nature, in other words, thanks to their innate linguistic capacity, use correct speech forms without receiving instruction in grammar. They are said to be inferred from the *Aṣṭādhyāyī* (*śiṣṭajñānārthāṣṭādhyāyī*).[37]

---

[36] *MBh* ad A6.3.109 (III.174.6–10): *evaṃ tarhi nivāsata ācāratas ca / sa cācāra āryāvarta eva / kaḥ punar āryāvartaḥ / prāg adarśanāt pratyak kālakavanād dakṣiṇena himavantam uttareṇa pāriyātram / etasminn āryanivāse ye brāhmaṇāḥ kumbhīdhānyā alolupā agṛhyamāṇakāraṇāḥ kiṃcid antareṇa kasyāścid vidyāyāḥ pāragās tatrabhavantaḥ śiṣṭāḥ /* See Cardona [1997: par. 834]. As said in Introduction [0.3.3.2], for later Pāṇinīyas such as Bhartṛhari, the śiṣṭas are grammarians also who are representatives for the śiṣṭas as users of correct speech forms.

[37] *MBh* ad A6.3.109 (III.174.10–15): *yadi tarhi śiṣṭāḥ śabdeṣu pramāṇaṃ kim aṣṭādhyāyyā kriyate / śiṣṭajñānārthāṣṭādhyāyī / kathaṃ punar aṣṭādhyāyyā śiṣṭāḥ śakyā vijñātum / aṣṭādhyāyīm adhīyāno 'nyaṃ paśyaty anadhīyānaṃ ye 'tra vihitāḥ śabdās tān prayuñjānam / sa paśyati—nūnam asya daivānugrahaḥ svabhāvo vā yo 'yaṃ na cāṣṭādhyāyīm adhīte ye*

The relation of the śiṣṭas to grammar is such that, as in the case of derivates such as **ādityadarśa* ('one who sees the sun'), what is grammatically well formed is not necessarily what is actually used by the śiṣṭas; and, as in the case of *pṛṣodara* ('spotted-belly'), what is actually used by the śiṣṭas is not necessarily what is grammatically accounted for. The derivate **ādityadarśa* as corresponding to the phrase *ādityaṃ paśyati* is what results (*prāpti*) from an operation provided for in A3.2.1 *karmaṇy aṇ* but not what is desired (*iṣṭi*).[38] The item *pṛṣodara*, on the other hand, is treated as a compound equivalent to *pṛṣad udaraṃ yasya* ('[someone] whose belly is spotted'). No rule of the *Aṣṭādhyāyī* explicitly provides for deleting *-t* of *pṛṣat*. Instead, Pāṇini gives *pṛṣodara* as a ready-made form (*nipātana*) in A6.3.109 *pṛṣodarādīni yathopadiṣṭam.* Derivates such as *pṛṣodara* are accepted as taught.

8.6.2.2. In view of the above-described relation of the śiṣṭas to grammar, the thesis put forward by Kātyāyana that the dhātupāṭha plays a critical role in preventing the name *dhātu* from applying to corruptions turns out to be subject to two ways of refutation.

There is a principle that the rules of grammar should conform with usage; on the contrary, usage does not have to conform with the rules of grammar.[39] However, if priority were given to usage,

---

cāsyāṃ vihitāḥ śabdās tāṃś ca prayuṅkte / nūnam ayam anyān api jānāti / evaṃ eṣā śiṣṭajñānārthāṣṭādhyāyī / The structure of the inference of the śiṣṭas from the *Aṣṭādhyāyī* (*śiṣṭānumāna*) is as follows: A certain person who studies the *Aṣṭādhyāyī* observes that a certain speaker who has not studied the *Aṣṭādhyāyī* uses correct speech forms explained by the *Aṣṭādhyāyī*. On the basis of this observation the person reasons that it is by his favor of fate or his nature that the speaker uses those correct forms without depending on the *Aṣṭādhyāyī* and therefrom that the speaker knows correct forms which are not enjoined by the *Aṣṭādhyāyī*. See Cardona [1997: par. 834].

[38]This principle is called *anabhidhāna* 'forms resulting from the application of rules are not used to convey the intended meanings'. See *vt.* 5 ad A3.2.1: *anabhidhānāt*.

[39]The principle as formulated is stated by Bhartṛhari in his *Vṛtti* on VP2.59: *ataḥ śāstreṇa nityasya lakṣyasyānuvidhānaṃ kartavyaṃ na tu nityena lakṣyeṇa śāstram anuvidheyam /* Obviously, this principle is based upon what Kātyāyana says in his very first vārtttika: *siddhe śabdārthasambandhe lokato 'rthaprayukte śabdaprayoge śāstreṇa dha-*

it would follow that whatever is observed in usage is considered to be correct. On the other hand, if priority were given to grammar, whatever is deduced from grammar would be held to be correct. Therefore restrictions have to be placed on usage and on grammar.

As said, it is the śiṣṭas who are the authority with respect to correct usage. It is hardly possible that a corrupted form is posited as a verb from the observation of the usage of the śiṣṭas, since it is not used by them. A grammar does not explain speech forms which are not observed to be in actual use, from which it follows that such a grammatical rule as semantically defines the term *dhātu* has no possibility of applying to corruptions. In consequence, the purpose of the dhātupāṭha will not be found in preventing the over-application of the name *dhātu* to corruptions. Where there is no possibility of the application of the rule, there is no possibility of the prevention of its application at all. This is how one can deny such a purpose of the dhātupāṭha from a theoretical point of view. On this point Kaiyaṭa states as follows.

Pradīpa on *MBh* ad *A*1.3.1 (II.197–98): *prayuktānām idam anvākhyānaṃ na cāṇavayatyādayaḥ śiṣṭaiḥ prayujyante iti nāsti teṣāṃ śāstreṇānuvidhānam iti bhāvaḥ* /

"What Patañjali means to say is this: This [science of grammar]

---

rmaniyamaḥ yathā laukikavaidikeṣu. The points Kātyāyana addresses here are as follows: 1) Linguistic items (*śabda*), their meanings (*artha*), and the relation (*sambandha*) between them are fixed (*siddha*) and permanent, perennial (*nitya*); 2) the use of a word is prompted by a meaning in that one uses words to convey meanings; 3) there is the same comprehension of a meaning through a correct form and an incorrect form; 4) the grammar serves to establish a restriction intended for merit such that the meaning in question should be expressed by means of a correct form, not an incorrect one; 5) for grammar unbroken tradition of usage is a given. It is to be noted in passing that what is to be characterized by rules of the grammar (*lakṣya*) is the speech (*śabda*), which is *nitya* 'perennial'; and the corpus of rules is *lakṣaṇa* 'what characterizes the speech'. See *vt*. 14 (Paspaśā): *lakṣyalakṣaṇe vyākaraṇam* //

Following Haradatta (see the present section, fn. 29), on the assumption that grammar should follow usage, one cannot but grant the same status as correct speech to corruptions because they are in use. Any semantic definition of the term *dhātu* allows an item, which denotes a certain meaning specified in itself, to be called *dhātu*, irrespective of whether it is correct or not.

> is a means of explaining items in actual use. But [corruptions] such as *āṇavayati* are not used by the siṣṭas. Therefore the rules of grammar do not conform with those [corruptions]."[40]

In addition, applying the same principle to the case where the item *pāka* in *bhoktuṃ pākaḥ* might have the name *dhātu* by the intended semantic definition by virtue of its referent being treated as behaving like an action (*kriyāvat*), Kaiyaṭa states as follows.

> *Pradīpa* on *MBh* ad *A*1.3.1 (II.198): *etenaiva nyāyena prātipadikanivṛttyartho 'pi pāṭho nopayujyate / na hi pākādayaḥ śabdā dhātuvihitapratyayaparā loke prayujyante /*
> "By this very same principle, the dhātupāṭha is not useful for preventing the over-application of the name *dhātu* to nominal bases. For items such as *pāka* [in *bhoktuṃ pākaḥ*] are not used accompanied by affixes to be introduced by rules headed by *A*3.1.91 in everyday speech."

According to him, in everyday communication the item *pāka* is not used accompanied by affixes whose occurrence is provided for by rules headed by *A*3.1.91 *dhātoḥ*, so that the item *pāka* does not come under the domain of application of the intended semantic definition in grammar.[41]

On the other hand, if one looked only to strict abidance by the rule providing for a semantic definition of the term *dhātu*, one would thereby be led to accept the undesired consequence that a corrupted speech form might be called *dhātu*, as one would be led to form a derivate such as **ādityadarśa* by *A* 3.2.1. But such an undesired result would be avoided on the authority of the usage of the siṣṭas. This is an indirect denial of the dhātupāṭha's preventive function aimed at corruptions, which seems to be in effect assumed by Kātyāyana and Patañjali.

---

[40] Kaiyaṭa gives the reading *āṇavayatyādayaḥ* instead of *āṇapayatyādayaḥ*. The corruption *āṇavayati* also corresponds to *ājñāpayati*. See *Uddyota* on *MBh* ad *A*1.3.1 (II.175): *ājñāpayatīty arthe āṇavayatīti prākṛtam /*

[41] Nāgeśa adds that operations linked with accentuations of base vowels of verbs and markers attached to them are also established on the basis of the observation of the usage of the siṣṭas. *Uddyota* on *MBh* ad

8.6.3. As shown, with reference to the prevention of the over-application of the term *dhātu* to corruptions, Patañjali views the dhātupāṭha in contrast with the usage of the śiṣṭas. From the above his idea on this matter has become clear. According to him:

When a restriction is made on users of speech forms to be accounted for by grammar and it is taken for granted that what should obtain by rules are to be attested in the usage of the śiṣṭas, it can no longer be said that the dhātupāṭha serves to prevent the name *dhātu* from applying to corruptions.

In everyday speech one is exposed to the danger of mistakenly using incorrect speech forms instead of using correct ones. In this sense one may be said to be expected to have the correctness of one's speech guaranteed by the usage of the śiṣṭas. What we have to respect is the usage of the śiṣṭas and not the dhātupāṭha, symbolic of grammar. At this point a conclusion can be thus drawn:

> Insofar as the śiṣṭas are the authority with reference to correct speech, it is sufficient to have a given semantic definition in order to assign the name *dhātu* to items proper to be called *dhātu*; there is no room for the dhātupāṭha to take part in.

8.7. dhātupātha and Patañjali's theory of semantics and grammar

As suggested, strictly speaking, Kātyāyana found five roles in the dhātupāṭha:

1. to supply items to be called *dhātu*;
2. to prevent the intended semantic definition from applying to nominal bases;
3. to prevent the intended semantic definition from applying to corruptions;
4. to make known accentuations of base vowels of verbs;

A1.3.1 (II.198): *idaṃ upalakṣaṇam / svarānubandhakāryam api śiṣṭaprayogād eveti bodhyam /* The point is that what Nāgeśa asserts here becomes possible if one is assumed to be a *vṛttajña* or one who is familiar with usage. See the present section [8.7.1].

5. to make known markers attached to verbs.

With reference to the first role, Kātyāyana himself and Patañjali pointed out that a formal definition of the term *dhātu* dependent upon this role of the dhātupāṭha leads to grammatical difficulties. Kātyāyana considered that its remaining four roles form the reasons for the dhātupāṭha being still required even if a semantic definition is given. With respect to the second role of the dhātupāṭha, Patañjali denied it on the grounds that a semantic definition with an intrinsic denotative nature taken in does not apply to primitive nominal bases and, even if it may apply to certain derived nominal bases, nominal bases that end in certain kṛt affixes, Pāṇini's derivational system does not allow them to have operations linked with verbs. Concerning its fourth and fifth roles, we cannot say that Patañjali intends to deny the dhātupāṭha those roles, since, if he did so, he would have to change drastically Pāṇini's derivational system itself. Therefore, he set up only a paradox as a theoretical possibility that items to be listed in the dhātupāṭha are restricted to those which are linked with operational rules. Lastly, regarding the third role of the dhātupāṭha, he demanded respect for the usage of the śiṣṭas in the use of correct speech forms and thereby denied the dhātupāṭha that role.

We are now in a good position to consider what provides Patañjali with such a negative attitude towards the dhātupāṭha meant for preventing the misuse of corruptions and with the respect for the usage of the śiṣṭas.

8.7.1. Patañjali's treatment in this line of the dhātupāṭha in his Bhāṣya on *A*1.3.1 is comparable to his treatment of markers attached to verbs.

8.7.1.1. Let us take up the following sūtra:

*A*1.3.72 *svaritañitaḥ kartrabhiprāye kriyāphale* //

This sūtra provides that ātmanepada affixes follow a verb marked with a svarita vowel or *ñ* if an agent is to be signified and the result of the act in question is intended for that agent. In his Bhāṣya on this sūtra, Patañjali, considering the need to include *svaritañitaḥ* in the rule and claiming *svaritañitaḥ* can be omitted, states as follows:

MBh ad A 1.3.72 (I.292.18-23): *svaritañita iti kimartham / yāti vāti drāti psāti / svaritañita iti śakyam akartum / kasmān na bhavati yāti vāti drāti psātīti / kartrabhiprāye kriyāphala ity ucyate, sarveṣāṃ ca kartrabhiprāyaṃ kriyāphalam asti / ta evaṃ vijñāsyāmaḥ / yeṣāṃ kartrabhiprāyam akartrabhiprāyaṃ ca kriyāphalam asti tebhya ātmanepadaṃ bhavatīti / na caiteṣāṃ kartrabhiprāyam akartrabhiprāyaṃ ca kriyāphalam asti / tathājātīyakāḥ khalv ācāryeṇa svaritañitaḥ paṭhitā ya ubhayavanto yeṣām kartrabhiprāyaṃ cākartrabhiprāyaṃ ca kriyāphalam asti /*

"[Question] For what purpose is the word *svaritañitaḥ* included in the rule?

[Answer] For the purpose of disallowing the introduction of ātmanepada affixes after bases such as *yā* 'go' (*yāti*), *vā* 'blow' (*vāti*), *drā* 'run', *psā* 'eat' (*psāti*).

[Objection] The word *svaritañitaḥ* can be left unsaid.

[Question] Then how comes it that there do not occur ātmanepada affixes after bases such as *yā, vā, drā, psā*?

[Answer] The rule formulated as *kartrabhiprāye kriyāphale* provides that ātmanepada affixes occur with a verb if the result of an action denoted by the verb is intended for its agent. Moreover, acts denoted by all verbs can have results intended for their agents.

[From the rule as formulated] we will understand in the following way: An ātmanepada affix occurs after verbs denoting actions whose results can be both intended and not intended for their agents.

The bases *yā* and so forth are such that the acts they signify are not spoken of as having results intended for their agents and also not so intended.

Indeed, the teacher [Pānini] listed in the dhātupāṭha verbs such as take both parasmaipada and ātmanepada affixes and denote actions whose results can be both intended and not intended for their agents, marking them with svarita vowels or *ñ*."

Actions denoted by all verbs can have results intended for their agents (*sarveṣāṃ ca kartrabhiprāyaṃ kriyāphalam asti*).[42] Then on this assumption the condition stated by *kartrabhiprāye kriyāphale* would be meaningless. The condition given presupposes that there is an action which is to be excluded by saying *kartrabhiprāye kriyāphale*, namely, the action whose result is not intended for its agent (*akartrabhiprāyaṃ kriyāphalam*).[43]

In the case of the verb *yā* (*yā*), the act denoted by it is not spoken of as having a result both intended for its agent and not so intended, so that one has *yāti*. On the other hand, in the case

---

[42]Kaiyaṭa states in his *Pradīpa* on this Bhāṣya that the expression *kartrabhiprāye kriyāphale* in the sūtra may be interpreted in two ways. *Pradīpa* on *MBh* ad A1.3.72 (II.286–87): *kartrabhiprāye kriyāphala ity anena saṃvidhānalakṣaṇa eva kriyāviśeṣa upalakṣyate / . . . anye tv āhuḥ—svārthaṃ yaḥ kriyām ārabhate tatrātmanepadaṃ, parārthārambhe tu parasmaipadam /* That is, some hold that the expression in question implies a specific action characterized as the act of making provision for an act to be carried out (*saṃvidhāna*), and others consider that the expression refers to an aspect of act such that one takes action for one's own benefit so as for its main fruit to go to its agent (*svārthatā*). This is how the present Bhāṣya: *sarveṣāṃ ca kartrabhiprāyaṃ kriyāphalam* comes to mean that all verbs may convey the idea of *saṃvidhāna* or that actions denoted by all verbs may be performed for their agents' own benefit. *Pradīpa* on *MBh* ad A1.3.72 (II.287): *sarveṣāṃ ceti / sarvatra saṃvidhānasya sambhavāt sarvatra ca svārthānuṣṭhānasambhavād iti bhāvaḥ /*

It is to be noted that Kaiyaṭa here simply follows Bhartṛhari who introduces the view of *svārthatā* in his *VP*3.12.5 and that of *saṃvidhāna* in his *VP*3.12.8–9. For the latter view, see fn. 45 in the present section. In connection with the former view Bhartṛhari states as follows. *VP* 3.12.5: *kriyāpravṛttāv ākhyātā kaiścit svārthaparārthatā / asatī vā satī vāpi vivakṣitanibandhanā //* ("Some declare that one takes action for one's own benefit or for another's benefit. Whether such a distinction (*svārthaparārthatā*) is real or not, it depends upon a speaker's intention.") According to the *Bālamanoramā*, what is meant by the term *kriyāphala* is that with the aim of which one takes action. *BM* on *SK*2159: *lokato vedato vā yaduddeśena kriyāpravṛttiḥ tayaivātra kriyāphalaśabdena vivakṣitatvāt /*

[43]*Uddyota* on *MBh* ad A1.3.72 (II.288): *yatra dhātau kartrabhiprāya ity asya vyāvarttyasambhavas tatraivāsya pravṛttiḥ /*

of *nī* (*ṇīñ*) 'lead, take somewhere', the act which it denotes is spoken of in both ways, and one says both *nayate* and *nayati*. It is, what is important, verbs such as *nī* that Pāṇini is said to have marked with svarita vowels or *ñ*.

8.7.1.2. Naturally, the question arises: What makes a distinction between *yā* and *nī* if it is assumed that acts denoted by all verbs can have results intended for their agents? Here the notion of an intrinsic denotative nature (*svabhāva*) comes in. Let us consider the following kārikās in the *Vākyapadīya*, which concern the discussion given above.[44]

> *VP*3.12.11: *kriyāviśeṣavacane sāmarthyam uparudhyate / keṣāṃ cid anye tu kṛtāḥ svariteto ñitas tathā //*
> "For some verbs the capacity (*sāmarthya*) to signify a particular sort of action [that is, the action of *saṃvidhāna*] is suppressed, while there are others for which this does not hold: these are marked with svarita vowels and *ñ* as they are recited in the dhātupāṭha."
> *VP*3.12.12: *anubandhaś ca siddhe 'rthe smṛtyartham anuṣajyate / tulyārtheṣv api cāvaśyaṃ na sarveṣv ekadharmatā //*
> "When a particular meaning has been established [as signified by particular verbs] (*siddhe 'rthe*), markers are appended to those verbs for the sake of calling to mind that the verbs in question signify the particular meaning.
> And, although all verbs have in common that they signify acts, it does not necessarily mean that all verbs have the same property [of conveying such a particular meaning]."

In *VP*3.12.8–9[45] Bhartṛhari states that a particular feature of an

---

[44] The very same discussion is also dealt with in the *Vṛtti* on *VP*1.26 in connection with *yogyatā* as a relation between words and meanings. See Section 5, fn. 35 and also Cardona [1999b: 142–144].

[45] *VP*3.12.8–9: *saṃvidhānaṃ pacādīnāṃ kva cid arthaḥ pratīyate / tannimittā yathānyāpi kriyādhiśrayaṇādikā // kartrabhiprāyatā sūtre kriyābhedopalakṣaṇam / tathābhūtā kriyā yā hi tatkartā phalabhāg yataḥ //* ("Sometimes, from verbs such as *pac* one understands the meaning of *saṃvidhāna*, just as one also understands from them other actions like putting the pot on the fire which are caused by the *saṃvidhāna*. The

action, that its result is intended for the agent (*kartabhiprāya-kriyāphala*), implies a particular action of *saṃvidhāna* or the act of making provision for an act to be carried out; thus, for example, as is stated by Helārāja, while the utterance *pacati devadattaḥ* has its equivalents such as *adhiśrayati* '[Devadatta] puts a pot on the stove' and *udakam āsecayati* '[Devadatta] pours in water', the utterance *pacate devadattaḥ* is paraphrased as *saṃbhāraṃ ḍhaukayati* '[Devadatta] is getting a complete set of requisites for the act of cooking'.[46] Since Bhartṛhari takes in this manner the term *kartrabhiprāye kriyāphale* as implying *saṃvidhāna*, therefore for him the present Bhāṣya means to say that although all verbs can denote *saṃvidhāna*, still in reality some denote it and others do not; Pāṇini attached the markers to the former.

Bhartṛhari says that verbs such as *yā* have the capacity to signify *saṃvidhāna* suppressed; verbs to which markers are attached are those which have such a denotative capacity unsuppressed. Recall Patañjali's remark of the application of the words *śoṇa* and *lohita*, namely that both words signify the color brown but the former is used with reference to a horse and the latter to an ox.[47] Obviously the difference in intrinsic denotative nature makes this difference; and, the intrinsic denotative nature in question, it is to be noted in passing, is nothing but *yogyatā* in Bhartṛhari's terminology, as said before.[48]

Moreover, we have to note the phrase *siddhe 'rthe* in *VP* 3.12.12, which indicates that language is prior to grammar. It goes without saying that in saying *siddhe 'rthe* Bhartṛhari is quite conscious of the premise on which grammar starts off, stated in Kātyāyana's

---

expression *kartrabhiprāye kriyāphale* in the sūtra implies a particular action. Indeed, an agent of such an action enjoys the fruit [aimed at through performing an action like cooking] in consequence of that action.") According to Bharṛhari, it is only when the action of cooking is accompanied by the act of *saṃvidhāna* by its agent that the agent enjoys the fruit of the action.

[46] Nāgeśa glosses *saṃvidhāna* as *sāmagrīsaṅghaṭana*. See *Uddyota* on *MBh* ad *A* 1.3.72 (II.286). In the form of **ḍupacàṣ** with a svarita vowel *à*, the verb *pac* 'cook' is recited in the dhātupāṭha.

[47] See Section 5 [5.2.3.2].

[48] See Section 5 [5.2.3.2].

very first vārttika beginning with *siddhe śabdārthasambandhe*.[49] Therefore Bhartrhari, it is obvious, understands that as a given, Pāṇini accepts the use of the verbs *nī* and so on to signify *saṃvidhāna*. Then this brings up the following question: For what purpose did Pāṇini append markers to such verbs? Bhartṛhari says that Pāṇini did so merely for the purpose of calling such usage to mind (*smṛtyartha*).

8.7.1.3. Bhartṛhari here in *VP*3.12.11–12 clearly stands on the *Mahābhāṣya.* In his Bhāṣya on *A*1.3.9, Patañjali discusses the issue pertaining to markers. There he first puts forward the view that after observing what has resulted from applying a rule one should determine what marker is appended to a certain given affix.

> *MBh* ad *A*1.3.9 (I.266.18–19): *vṛttād vā punaḥ siddham etat / vṛddhimantam ādyudāttaṃ dṛṣṭvā ñid iti vyavaseyam / antodāttaṃ dṛṣṭvā kid iti /*
> "Alternatively, however, this is established on the basis of usage (*vṛtta*). After observing an item [such as *gā́rgyaḥ*] whose first vowel is replaced by a vṛddhi vowel and is high-pitched, one should determine that the affix in question is marked with *ñ*. [In addition,] after observing an item [such as *nāḍāyanáḥ*] whose final vowel is high-pitched, one should determine that the affix in question is marked with *k*."[50]

No doubt this view is presented from the viewpoint that speech is produced (*kārya*) and not eternal (*nitya*).[51] Thus, from the

---

[49] See fn. 39 in this section.

[50] *A*7.2.117 provides that the first vowel of a presuffixal base called *aṅga* is replaced by a vṛddhi vowel before a taddhita affix that is marked with *ñ* or *ṇ*. This accounts for *gārgya* 'gotra descendant of Garga' (*garga-yañ*: *A*4.1.92, 105). Since it is derived with the taddhita suffix ***yañ***, by *A*6.1.197 its first vowel is high-pitched (*ādyudāttam*), so that one has *gā́rgyaḥ*. The derivate *nāḍāyanáḥ* 'gotra descendant of Naḍa', formed with the taddhita suffix *pha**k*** which is marked with *k* (*A*4.1.99), has its final vowel high-pitched by *A*6.1.165.

[51] Pāṇinīyas distinguish two kinds of eternity: *vyavahāranityatā* and *paramārthanityatā.* The former consists in an uninterrupted succession of verbal activities and the latter in a sort of ontological and metaphysical

opposed viewpoint that speech is eternal or perennial, he next sets forth the following view:

> *MBh* ad *A*1.3.9 (I.266.19–21): *yuktaṃ punar yad vṛttanimittako nāmānubandhaḥ syān nānubandhanimittakena nāma vṛttena bhavitavyam / vṛttanimittaka evānubandhaḥ / vṛttajño hy ācāryo 'nubandhān āsajati /*
>
> "However, it is proper to say that one should append markers to [linguistic elements] based upon usage but one should indeed not have usage based upon markers. Appending markers to linguistic elements is based exclusively upon usage. For the teacher [Pāṇini] who is familiar with usage appends markers to [linguistic elements]."[52]

The point is that one who appends markers to linguistic elements is characterized as *vṛttajña* 'one who is familiar with usage'. This characterization of a marker-giver indicates that appending markers to linguistic elements is meant for those who are not familiar with usage, as already suggested by Bhartṛhari saying *smṛtyartham* in *VP*3.12.12. The following statement made by Helārāja is relevant to this.

---

eternity. Grammar has to do with the former eternity. *MBhD* I.8.1: *nityatā cāpi dvividhā / vyavahārāśrayā paramārthāśrayā ca / . . . / evam ihāpi pāṇininānyena vā śabdāḥ [smṛtā] eva svato 'rthapratyāyakā iti vyavahāranityataivehopakāriṇī /* See Section 3 [3.2.5] and also *VP*1.28: *nityatve kṛtakatve vā teṣām ādir na vidyate / prāṇinām iva sā caiṣā vyavasthānityatocyate //* In this kārikā Bhartṛhari uses the term *vyavasthānityatā* 'eternity of a settled state' instead of *vyavahāranityatā*. Patañjali observes that the word *nitya* is not used necessarily with reference to permanent immutable objects (*kūṭastheṣv avicāliṣu bhāveṣu*); it also occurs in the sense of repetition (*ābhīkṣṇya*). An idea represented by the word *nitya* used in the sense of repetition is of course linked with what the term *vyavahāranityatā* means. *MBh* (Paspaśā) (I.7.3-4): *ayaṃ khalv api nityaśabdo nāvaśyaṃ kūṭastheṣv avicāliṣu bhāveṣu vartate / kiṃ tarhy ābhīkṣṇye 'pi vartate /* (For the punctuation concerning *kiṃ tarhi*, see Section 2, fn. 8.)

[52] According to Helārāja's *Prakāśa* on *VP*3.12.12, the term *vṛtta* means either the usage of the word (*prayoga*) or the denotative function of the word (*vartana*). Here Kaiyaṭa takes it as meaning the former.

> *Prakāśa* on *VP*3.12.12: *yo hi prayogād eva svabhāvaviśeṣam avadhārayitum aśaktas taṃ prati smṛtyartho 'nubandhāsaṅgaḥ, prayogajñaṃ tu prati nārthas tena / tathā ca prayogadarśinaṃ ca prati svaritañidgrahaṇaṃ śakyam akartum iti pratyākhyātaṃ etad bhāṣye / vacanānusāriṇaṃ tu prati kriyata evaitat /*
> "Indeed, markers are appended to linguistic elements, for the sake of those who are unable to determine the particular denotative nature of the elements (*svabhāvaviśeṣa*) merely from usage, so that the markers can bring the usage to mind. For those who are familiar with the usage, on the other hand, there is no purpose to be served by the markers.
> Such being the case, for the sake of those who observe usage (*prayogadarśin*), the word *svaritañitaḥ* can be left unsaid [in *A* 1.3.72]. Accordingly this inclusion of the word *svaritañitaḥ* in the rule is rejected in the Bhāṣya. For the sake of those who go by the statements made in the grammar (*vacanānusārin*), on the other hand, it is imperative that the inclusion in question is made (*kriyata eva*)."

Following Bhartṛhari, Helārāja here obviously regards *vṛttajña* as *svabhāvajña* 'one who is familiar with an intrinsic denotative nature'.[53] It is thus clear from this remark of Helārāja's that the distinction is made between *prayogadarśin* and *vacanānusārin*; the former, being familiar with usage, is able to determine a linguistic item's denotative nature from usage and the latter is not so, and that grammatical devices such as a marker are meant for the latter. After citing the Bhāṣya's statement with a slight modification as *vṛttajño hy ācāryaḥ tatsamarthān anubandhān āsajati* and explaining the term *vṛtta*, Helārāja goes on to spell out Patañjali's statement quoted above.

> *Prakāśa* on *VP*3.12.12: *tajjñaḥ sūtrakāro vacanānusāriṇam avṛttajñaṃ prati ñakāram āsajatīty arthaḥ /*
> "What is meant by the Bhāṣya is this: the author of sūtras who

[53] See *VP*1.135cd: *svabhāvajñaiś ca bhāvānāṃ dṛśyante śabdaśaktayaḥ / Paddhati* on *VP*1.135cd: *ye tu śiṣṭāḥ padārthaśaktim pratyakṣeṇa te pṛṣodarādivat sarvān sādhūn vidantīti tān praty anarthakaṃ vyākaraṇam / tacchiṣṭaparijñānārthan tu vyākaraṇam iti /*

is familiar with that [i.e., *vṛtta* 'usage'] appends the sound *ñ* as a marker for the sake of those who are not familiar with usage and hence [have to] follow the statements made in the grammar."

Helārāja here bears in mind the following view held by Bhartṛhari:

VP3.14.79: *prakṛtipratyayāv ūhyau padāt tābhyāṃ padaṃ tathā / anubandhasvarādibhyaḥ śiṣṭaiḥ śāstraṃ na tān prati //*
VP3.14.80: *śāstradṛṣṭis tu śāstrasya prāptimātre 'py aniścite / yujyate pratyavāyena śāstraṃ cakṣur apaśyatām //*
"A base and an affix are elements to be posited, through reasoning, by means of their abstraction from a word. The śiṣṭas account for a word by means of those posited elements with devices such as markers and accentuations. Grammar is not for the sake of such śiṣṭas (*śāstraṃ na tān prati*)."
"On the other hand, one who sees rules of grammar (*śāstradṛṣṭi*) assumes a sin (*pratyavāya*) if using what should obtain by a rule without attesting it in usage even if there is a mere applicability of the rule. For those who cannot see usage, grammar is their eyes to see it (*śāstraṃ cakṣur apaśyatām*)."

Here are shown two standpoints, which concern persons respectively spoken of as *lakṣyaikacakṣuṣka* 'those whose eyes are solely fixed on the usage to be described' and *lakṣaṇaikacakṣuṣka* 'those whose eyes are solely fixed on the rules of grammar' in later grammarians' terminology.[54] Grammar is not for the sake of the śiṣṭas, characterized as *prayogadarśins* and as *lakṣyaikacakṣuṣkas*, but for the sake of those who do not observe usage, characterized as *vacanānusārins* and as *lakṣaṇaikacakṣuṣkas*; for the latter, grammar serves as their eyes to see usage.[55]

---

[54] See Joshi/Roodbergen [1969: vii, fn. 20] and Aklujkar [forthcoming]. It is important to note that, as Cardona points out (Aklujkar [forthcoming: fn. 48]), Patañjali's distinction between a *prāptijña* 'one who knows what results' and an *iṣṭijña* 'one who knows what is desired' can be considered to be a precursor of the distinction between a *lakṣaṇaikacakṣuṣka* and a *lakṣyaikacakṣuṣka*.

[55] For Bhartṛhari, ancient grammarians such as Pāṇini become the śiṣṭas, who have a direct mystical insight into the true nature of Sanskrit. See Deshpande [1993].

Grammar is not for the sake of the śiṣṭas. As a matter of course, the dhātupāṭha accompanying as an ancillary text the *Aṣṭādhyāyī*, the core of Pāṇini's grammar, is also not for the sake of the śiṣṭas, just as appending markers to verbs. For the sake of those who are comparable to them, namely who are able to determine the particular intrinsic denotative nature (*svabhāvaviśeṣa*) from usage, there is no use of listing verbs with specific features in the dhātupāṭha.

Suppose that items listed in the dhātupāṭha are posited as verbs, through the analysis of usage, by grammarians such as Pāṇini who have an insight into the denotative nature of given linguistic items. For what purpose is such a procedure taken? The answer for it will leave no room for dispute. Thus, we may consider that the reason for listing verbs in the dhātupāṭha is the same as that for using devices such as markers. The reciting of verbs in the dhātupāṭha is for the sake of those who have no access to the usage of the śiṣṭas and who have no insight into such a denotative nature even if they have this access, just as markers are appended to items for the purpose of calling it to mind.

8.7.2. Now it has been made clear that there are two situations with respect to the usage of the śiṣṭas. In one situation one can observe their usage and in the other situation one cannot. In addition, in the former situation some have an insight into the denotative nature of language and others do not. Moreover, even in the situation where the usage of the śiṣṭas is observed, not only a correct speech form but also an incorrect speech form is used to produce the same understanding of a meaning, as is said by Patañjali.[56] Needless to say, by definition linguistic units that are used by the śiṣṭas are regarded as correct.

Thus if we describe the situation which Patañjali assumes for

[56] *MBh* (Paspaśā) [I.8.20–22]: *evam ihāpi samānāyām arthagatau śabdena cāpaśabdena ca dharmaniyamaḥ kriyate / śabdenaivārtho 'bhidheyo nāpaśabdeneiti /* See *VP* 1.27 also: *śiṣṭebhya āgamāt siddhāḥ sādhavo dharmasādhanam / arthapratyāyanābhede viparītās tv asādhavaḥ.* For details of the problem concerning the status of *apaśabda* and *sādhuśabda*, see Cardona [1999a].

his argumentation in the context at issue, it is the one in which the use of both correct and incorrect speech forms is actually observed and its observers can be considered to have an insight into the intrinsic denotative nature of linguistic units.

In his *Bh.* 7 Patañjali has stated:

> *Bh.* 7: *sa cāvaśyaṃ śiṣṭaprayoga upāsyo ye 'pi paṭhyante teṣām api viparyāsanivṛttyarthaḥ / loke hi kṛṣyarthe kasiṃ prayuñjate, dṛśyarthe ca disim /*
>
> "Moreover, the usage of the śiṣṭas [which is resorted to for the exclusion of corruptions] is necessarily respected in order to prevent the misuse (*viparyāsa*) of those items also which deserve to be recited. For in the world of everyday usage (*loke*) one uses *kas* in the sense of *kṛṣ* 'plow' and *dis* in the sense of *dṛś* 'see'."

On this Bhāṣya Nāgeśa comments as follows:

> *Uddyota* on *MBh* ad *A*1.3.1 (II.198): *nanu śiṣṭaprayogālambanena pratyākhyāne śāstravaiphalyam ata āha bhāṣye—sa cāvayśyam iti / evaṃ cākṛtigaṇeṣv iva tadupāsanāvaśyakatve kiṃ pāṭheneti bhāvaḥ /*
>
> *nanu tadvad eva nidarśanārthaḥ katipayapāṭho 'py āvaśyaka iti cet / astu, atyantāvaśyakatā nety eva bhāṣyatātparyād iti dik /*
>
> "[Objection] If [the usefulness of the dhātupāṭha were] denied on the basis of [the respect for] the usage of the śiṣṭas, grammar itself would be fruitless.
>
> [Answer] In answer to this objection Patañjali in his Bhāṣya says: 'the usage of the śiṣṭas [which is resorted to for the exclusion of corruptions] is necessarily respected.'
>
> And, such being the case, his underlying idea is that if, as in the case of the ākṛtigaṇa, the usage of the śiṣṭas has to be necessarily respected, what is the use of listing verbs in the dhātupāṭha?
>
> [Objection] As in the case of the ākṛtigaṇa, some verbs are to be recited in the dhātupāṭha for illustration.
>
> [Answer] Be it so. But this is because Patañjali in this Bhāṣya

> intends to say precisely that it is not absolutely necessary to list verbs in the dhātupāṭha. This is a general line of the present argument."

Here again we have to note that the dhātupāṭha can be regarded as a kind of ākrtigaṇa. As shown, in the case of the ākṛtigaṇa, members of a certain set which are not listed in the set are posited as members of the set by resorting to the usage of the śiṣṭas. However, as Helārāja suggested, mere observation of the usage of the śiṣṭas does not lead to positing correct forms as the members of the set, so that one has to determine their intrinsic denotative nature from the usage of the śiṣṭas. Thus the respect for the usage of the śiṣṭas presupposes that one can determine the intrinsic denotative nature from their usage. Now Pāṇinīyas such as Patañjali and Bhartṛhari consider that appending markers to verbs, symbolic of grammar, is not for the sake of the śiṣṭas, or those who are able to determine the intrinsic denotative nature from the usage of the śiṣṭas. Thus if one were a *vṛttajña* or *svabhāvajña* like a śiṣṭa, there would be no use of listing verbs in the dhātupāṭha for the sake of them. As Nāgeśa argues, granted that the dhātupāṭha has the role of illustrating verbs to be used, the role is not essential for the dhātupāṭha, since what forms of verbs are to be used is determined by the usage of the śiṣṭas. Of course, it is an undeniable fact that the dhātupāṭha is useful for those who cannot but see the usage of the śiṣṭas through the eyes of grammar. This being the case, thus, one can safely state, following Nāgeśa, that it is not absolutely necessary to recite verbs in the dhātupāṭha (*atyantāvaśyakatā na*).

8.7.3. I have said that the respect for the usage of the śiṣṭas presupposes that one can determine an intrinsic denotative nature from their usage. At this point let us recall that Patañjali has the following semantic definition of the term *dhātu*:

> An item which denotes by its intrinsic denotative nature (*svabhāva*) something that is brought into being—such a thing is referred to by the term *bhāva* or *kriyā*—is called *dhātu*.[57]

[57] See Section 7 [7.1].

How things are in reality is not a matter of important concern to grammarians. Grammarians are *śabdapramāṇakas.* Then what does language tell us? They see that it is not nominal bases but verbs that by their intrinsic denotative nature denote their meanings as things which are brought into being; to echo Bhartṛhari in his *VP*3.12.11, nominal bases have their capacities to signify such meanings suppressed. Those who are familiar with usage will also distinguish between linguistic items which respectively denote something established and something yet to be established, and will correctly know which linguistic item is used to signify its meaning as something that is to be brought to accomplishment. And they can abstract through analysis such an item which denotes its meaning as such from a single whole unit (*saṅghāta*) in actual use. We must not forget that Kātyāyana in his fourth and sixth vārttikas claims that the application of a semantic definition of the term *dhātu* presupposes the analysis of the real unit of actual communication into component elements through the reasoning from *anvaya* and *vyatireka*.

However, even if certain linguistic items are known to be used to signify such meanings, not all of them can be correct speech forms. Correct forms such as *dṛś* and incorrect forms such as *dis* both signify the same meaning which is characterized as such. This is the reason why the usage in which one is expected to determine the intrinsic nature of linguistic items actually used has to be confined to that of the śiṣṭas.

The definition of the term *dhātu*, with the intrinsic denotative nature brought in, bases itself on actual usage. Therefore, when only the śiṣṭas are viewed as the authority with respect to correct usage, such a definition will not lead to the over-application of the term *dhātu* to corruptions. As a sort of device which can alternate with the dhātupāṭha, Patañjali introduced the notion of the intrinsic denotative nature into the definition of the term *dhātu*. This is likened, though the case is just reversed, to the fact that in order to account for the occurrence of ātmanepada affixes after certain verbs Pāṇini invented markers which might alternate with such intrinsic denotative nature. It is the introduction of such nature that demanded the usage of the śiṣṭas as that from which the intrinsic denotative nature is determined and accepted as it is. Thus, insofar as the usage of the śiṣṭas is respected, *A*1.3.1 *bhūvādayo dhātavaḥ*, which is interpreted as a purely semantic definition, cannot have its validity disputed.

8.7.4. Let us turn to the starting point of Patañjali's discussion on the roles of the dhātupāṭha. Within the framework created by Kātyāyana in which the question is discussed what roles are to be carried out by the dhātupāṭha on condition that a semantic definition of the term *dhātu* is provided, Patañjali sees the same framework in *A*1.3.1 by interpreting it as containing the indication of the dhātupāṭha as well as a semantic definition. As said, to ask what roles are to be played by the dhātupāṭha on a given condition is to ask whether the indication of the dhātupāṭha by using *vyavasthā-ādi* is necessary for defining the term *dhātu*.[58] Now the conclusion is drawn. It is not necessary to read *vyavasthā-ādi* in the sūtra. If one still wishes to read *prakāra-ādi* there, a resulting semantic definition will be ultimately the same as Patañjali's basic semantic definition as stated above.

In concluding this section, let me stress again that Patañjali's theory of semantics in which a linguistic item's intrinsic denotative nature has a special status leads him to introduce such a nature into his definition of the term *dhātu* and to suggest accepting the nature as it is determined from the usage of the śiṣṭas. What is clear in Patañjali's argument on the roles Kātyāyana claims the dhātupāṭha to play is his respect or predilection for *svabhāva* or the intrinsic denotative nature.

---

[58] See Section 7 [7.3].

Section 9

A roundup of Patañjali's interpretations of *A*1.3.1

9. Two extremes

In this section let us look back how Patañjali interpreted *A*1.3.1 and thereby make clear what his interpretations of it reveal.

9.1. We have the following interpretations of *A*1.3.1 Patañjali sets forth explicitly.

1) Items of the set beginning with *bhū*, recited in the dhātupāṭha, are called *dhātu.*[1]
2) Signifiers (*vādi*) of what comes into being (*bhū*) are called *dhātu.*[2]
3) Those items which belong to the set beginning with *bhū* and which are like *vā* 'go, strike' are called *dhātu.*
4) Those items which belong to the set beginning with *vā* and which are like *bhū* 'be, be born' are called *dhātu.*[3]

And further we also have its interpretations implicitly accepted by him.

A. Signifiers (*vādi*) of what comes into being (*bhū*) are called *dhātu* only if they are recited in the dhātupāṭha.
B. Items for what comes into being are called *dhātu* only if they are by nature signifiers of it.[4]
C. Those items which belong to the set beginning with *bhū* and which, like *vā* 'go, strike', denote something to be brought to accomplishment or something that is brought into being are called *dhātu.*
D. Those items which belong to the set beginning with *vā* and which, like *bhū* 'be, be born', denote something to be brought

---

[1] See Section 3 [3.2.1] and Section 4, Part 1 [4.1].
[2] See Section 4, Part 3 [4.6.4] and Section 7.
[3] See Section 4, Part 4 [4.8.5] and Section 7.
[4] See Section 7 [7.2.5].

> to accomplishment or something that is brought into being are called *dhātu*.
>
> E. Items which are like *bhū* 'be, be born' and which are like *vā* 'go, strike' are called *dhātu*; or, items which are like *bhū* 'be, be born' and *vā* 'go, strike' are called *dhātu*.[5]

Interpretation 1), what I call the 'dhātupāṭha-based definition', is what Patañjali assumes Kātyāyana to accept. According to this interpretation, in assigning the name *dhātu* to items listed in the dhātupāṭha one has to take note only of their formal aspects without invoking any semantic considerations whatever. What is characteristic of this interpretation is that items recited in the dhātupāṭha are merely taken as conveying their own forms and not as meaningful units.

Interpretation 2) is in effect given the alternatives of A or B. In view of the fact that Patañjali finally denies the dhātupāṭha roles complementary to a semantic definition, he obviously chooses alternative B. The semantic definition given by interpretation B reflects Patañjali's fundamental semantic definition, which is as follows:

> An item which denotes by its intrinsic denotative nature something that is brought into being—such a thing is referred to by the term *bhāva* or *kriyā*—is called *dhātu*.[6]

Interpretations 3) and 4) are to suggest taking *A*1.3.1 as intending both to indicate the dhātupāṭha and to provide a semantic definition. In these interpretations the dhātupāṭha is assumed to carry out functions complementary to the intended semantic definition. The difference between interpretation 3) and interpretation 4) arises according to which of the constituents *bhū* and *vā* of the dvandva compound *bhūvau* is taken as a meaningful unit. As a result of reading in the sūtra *prakāra-ādi*, the word *ādi* used in the sense of similarity, the semantic definitions obtained in 3) and 4) become the same. If in the sūtra one does not read two *ādis*, *vyavasthā-ādi* and *prakāra-ādi*, but only the latter *ādi*, for the reason that the

[5] See Section 8 [8.2.2].

[6] See Section 7 [7.1].

dhātupāṭha is denied its complementary roles to a semantic definition, then one may have interpretation E, which also Patañjali's basic semantic definition underlies. What is characteristic of his interpretations of the sūtra as semantic definitions is that he, accepting an intrinsic denotative nature of a verb as it is, tries to define the term *dhātu* from that point of view.

9.2. As has already been seen, Patañjali shows that the dhātupāṭha-based definition leads to a grammatically insuperable difficulty of its over-application to non-verbs homophonous with items listed in the dhātupāṭha (*samānaśabdātiprasaṅga*)[7] and that a semantic definition with an intrinsic denotative nature of a verb taken in leads to the denial of the status of the dhātupāṭha in Pāṇini's grammar.[8] These imply that if one follows up a formal definition standing solely on formal aspects of verbs listed in the dhātupāṭha, one reaches such an extreme that one has to face the grammatically insuperable difficulty; if, on the other hand, one follows up a semantic definition standing solely on a semantic aspect of verbs, one has to reach, in another respect, such an extreme that one has to introduce a radical change in Pāṇini's system of grammar.

9.3. As I have already suggested, the original dhātupāṭha as known to Kātyāyana and Patañjali, which does not contain meaning entries (*arthapāṭha*), goes like this:[9]

*bhū́ édh**a** spárdh**a*** . . .

The verbs shown here have high-pitched (*udātta*) base vowels; *bhū́* has a zero marker, while *édh**a*** and *spárdh**a*** have vocalic markers attached to them: low-pitched *a*. It is with the dhātupāṭha of this form that Patañjali brings forward his argument on *A* 1.3.1.

In the preceding section we have seen how Patañjali viewed Pāṇini's attaching markers to linguistic elements. Patañjali's

---

7 See Section 4, Part 1 [4.1.2].

8 See Section 8.

9 See Section 4, Part 1 [4.2].

root idea on that matter was fully expressed in the following statement:

> *MBh* ad *A*1.3.9 (I.266.20–21): *vṛttajño hy ācāryo 'nubandhān āsajati* /
> "For the teacher [Pāṇini] who is familiar with usage appends markers to [linguistic elements]."[10]

Bhartṛhari explained what Patañjali meant to say by the above-cited Bhāṣya.

> *VP*3.14.79: *prakṛtipratyayāv ūhyau padāt tābhyāṃ padaṃ tathā / anubandhasvarādibhyaḥ śiṣṭaiḥ śāstraṃ na tān prati //*
> "A base and an affix are elements to be posited, through reasoning, by means of their abstraction from a word. The śiṣṭas account for a word by means of those posited elements with devices such as markers and accentuations. Grammar is not for the sake of such śiṣṭas (*śāstraṃ na tān prati*)."[11]

Of course, theoretically speaking, the same is true of the accentuation of base vowels of verbs. That is, Pāṇini who is familiar with usage added accentual features to verbs. As said, the appending of markers to verbs and the specific accentuation of base vowels of verbs serve metalinguistic purposes.[12] They have their places as means for describing usage in a grammar. This is clearly stated by Bhartṛhari here. But the important point to note here is that verbs which, characterized by their metalinguistic accentual features and markers, are recited in the dhātupāṭha, are regarded as linguistic units abstracted from units of communication found in actual usage through analysis (*prakṛtipratyayāv ūhyau padāt*). In view of the analytic procedure which leads to abstracting bases and affixes from larger units through reasoning from *anvaya* and *vyatireka*, therefore, one has to recognize that items found in the dhātupāṭha are listed there as distinct meaningful units.[13]

---

[10] See Section 8 [8.7.1.3].
[11] See Section 8 [8.7.1.3].
[12] See Section 3 [3.2.6] and Section 8 [8.5].
[13] See Section 3 [3.2.3].

Thus if we accept Patañjali's view, amplified by Bhartṛhari, on devices Pāṇini contrived concerning verbs listed in the dhātupāṭha, there would be no doubt that in positing basic verb forms Pāṇini (on the assumption that he composed the dhātupātha) treated them as meaningful units, so that he could feature them with accentuations and markers so as to account for usage.

9.4. As shown, if one wishes to carry a formal definition to its full extreme on the basis of the dhātupāṭha, one has to disregard, with reference to verbs listed therein, their specific accentuations of base vowels and markers attached to them. For these distinctive features presuppose the meaningfulness of the verbs. As long as the purpose of such devices is to characterize items abstracted from units found in actual usage, one has to accept items listed in the dhātupātha as distinct meaningful units. And the disregard for the meaningfulness of items listed there brings us to such a treatment of them that we have to regard *édha*, for example, as a mere sequence of sounds without its base vowel accented: *edha* and in consequence to have a stretch of sounds *bhvedha* in which the pitch feature of the verb *bhū́* is also obscured.[14] Let me stress again that in the dhātupāṭha-based definition meant by *pāṭhena dhātusaṃjñā* no semantic considerations are invoked.

On the other hand, if one wishes to carry a semantic definition to its logical extreme, one has to trace the analytic procedure, which allowed Paṇini to posit his verbs, to its starting point. That is, in this case one is expected to become a *vṛttajña* 'one who is familiar with usage' or, according to Bhartṛhari, *svabhāva-jña* 'one who is able to determine a linguistic item's intrinsic denotative nature', for whom, as said, the dhātupāṭha serves no longer any purpose.[15] One has only to observe the usage of the śiṣṭas and to determine from it the intrinsic denotative nature of verbs. We might assume that Pāṇini who is a *vṛttajña*, grasping certain items as denoting things yet to be brought to accomplishment, posited them as verbs. If one were a Pāṇini, therefore, one

[14] See Section 4, Part 1 [4.2].

[15] See Section 8 [8.7].

could know what items found in actual usage denote things to be brought to accomplishment following the same analytic procedure as Pāṇini, so that, by Patañjali's fundamental semantic definition of the term *dhātu*, one could call *dhātu* the items which denote the things characterized as such.

9.5. However, grammar is a means of teaching correct speech forms (*śabdānuśāsana*).[16] It is true that grammar is not for the sake of those who have an insight into the intrinsic denotative nature of a linguistic item (*śāstraṃ na tān [śiṣṭān] prati*), but one cannot deny that grammar is for the sake of those who do not have it and who cannot observe the usage of the śiṣṭas (*śāstraṃ cakṣur apaśyatām*).[17] In view of this the dhātupāṭha must be granted recognized status in grammar.

Where do the two extremes of the definition of the term *dhātu*, described above, spring from? Needless to say, from the dhātupāṭha that Patañjali has. In his dhātupāṭha items are given as conveying their own forms (*svarūpa*) and their meanings (*artha*). Now let us consider Pāṇini's derivational procedure which leads to the form *edhate* 'thrives'.

*éd**ha***	
edh	
edh + ***laṭ***	(*A*3.2.123)
edh + ta	(*A*3.4.78)
edh + ***śap*** *+ ta*	(*A*3.1.68)
edh + a + te	(*A*3.4.79)
edhate	

We have to note the form *éd**ha*** at the very initial stage of the derivation in question, or at the stage of *upadeśa* 'teaching', at which it has been introduced but has not yet undergone grammatical operations.[18] The form *éd**ha*** is provided by the dhātupāṭha. The

[16] See Cardona [1997: par. 827].

[17] See Section 8 [8.7.1.3].

[18] On the notion of *upadeśa*, see Cardona [1980: III.1.3.5c; III.1.3.7; III.1.5.3c]. See also *A*1.3.2 given below.

vocalic marker is unconditionally dropped (*A*1.3.9) and the accentual feature of the base vowel achieves its purpose in specifying grammatical operation provided for by sūtras such as *A*7.2.35. The form *edh* at the second stage is nothing but what is intended to be understood as a verb in the dhātupāṭha and hence to have the name *dhātu* by *A*1.3.1. This means that as at the stage of *upadeśa*, so also in the dhātupāṭha *edh* presented as *édha* is already meaningful. As said, for Pāṇinīyas, *edh* with its accentual feature and marker has to be an item gotten through abstraction. Thus it is plain how Patañjali considered *A*1.3.1 was to be understood. He doubtless presupposed that, under the given dhātupāṭha which goes: *bhū́ édha spárdha* . . . , the sūtra would be interpreted as follows:

> Meaningful units (*arthavat*) such as *bhū*, *edh*, *spardh*, and so on, which are listed in the dhātupāṭha, are called *dhātu*.[19]

Clearly the sūtra as interpreted in this way provides two aspects of an item to be called *dhātu*: formal and semantic. And this is comparable to the case in which, by *A*1.4.57 *cādayo 'sattve*, meaningful units like *ca*, *vā*, *ha*, and so on, which are listed in the *cādigaṇa*, are called *nipāta*. It must be recalled that, when he suggests reading the *prakāra-ādi* in the form *bhūvādayaḥ* of *A*1.3.1 Patañjali asks one to take either *bhū* or *vā* of the dvandva compound *bhūvau* as a meaningful unit, which decidedly indicates that items listed in the dhātupāṭha can be taken as meaningful in themselves.[20]

What is more, one may notice that this interpretation of *A*1.3.1 is nothing but a revised dhātupāṭha-based definition. If semantic considerations are invoked in the original dhātupāṭha-based definition, one will get this definition. In this connection we have to note that the ślokavārttika Patañjali adduced in favor of the dhātupātha-based definition does not contradict the revised dhātupāṭha-based definition shown above.[21]

[19] On the point that the assignment of the name *dhātu* presupposes the meaningfulness of items eligible for it, see Section 4, Part 1 [4.2.2.1].

[20] See Section 7 [7.3].

[21] See Section 2 [2.3.2].

And further, it is also noteworthy that if the dhātupāṭha Patañjali knew had contained meaning entries, he could not have reached such an extreme that he had to introduce the notion of the intrinsic denotative nature of verbs into his semantic definition of the term *dhātu*. We should not overlook that the application of Patañjali's theory of semantics and grammar to his dhātupāṭha led him to carry his formal and semantic definitions of the term *dhātu* to the furthest extreme and that his dhātupāṭha was susceptible to such an application.

9.6. At this point let us recall the interpretation of *A*1.3.1 attempted in the *Kāśikāvṛtti*. There the following interpretation was offered:

> *Kāśikāvṛtti* ad *A*1.3.1: *bhū ityevamādayaḥ śabdāḥ kriyāvacanā dhātusaṃjñā bhavanti* /
> "Items of the set beginning with an item such as *bhū*, denoting actions (*kriyā*), are called *dhātu*."[22]

We have to consider why the semantic condition 'denoting actions' came to be introduced in the interpretation of the sūtra. The following sūtras help account for the point at issue.

> A1.3.2 *upadeśe 'j anunāsika it* //
> A1.3.11 *svaritenādhikāraḥ* //

*A*1.3.2 provides that a nasalized vowel at the stage of *upadeśa* is called *it*. For example, the low-pitched vowel *a* in *édha* and *spárdha* are called *it* by this sūtra. *A*1.3.11, on the other hand, provides that an element understood to be in force in sūtras after the one in which it first occurs (*adhikāra*) is recognized by a special feature of pronunciation, a svarita vowel. As the *Kāśikāvṛtti* notes, the distinctive nasalization and distinct accents in the tradition of Pāṇinian recitation including the svarita were given up and are recognized by Pāṇinīyas by convention in accordance with what authoritative teachers have established earlier (*pratijñānunāsikyāḥ pāṇinīyāḥ; pratijñāsvaritāḥ pāṇinīyāḥ*).[23]

---

[22] See Section 2 [2.3].

[23] Note that the distinctive accentuations of base vowels and markers are not retained in the dhātupāṭha as handed down by commentators

It is possible to set up a hypothesis that the introduction of the meaning condition into the interpretation of *A*1.3.1 is connected with the loss of the nasalization and the distinct accents stated above. As shown, verbs recited in the dhātupāṭha have their base vowels accented and vocalic markers attached to them, and these features, with which verbs are recited in the dhātupāṭha, form indicators pointing to verbs with them being meaningful units. Thus the loss of the nasalization and accentuation in the tradition of Pāṇinian recitation means the loss of the indicators of verbs listed in the dhātupāṭha being meaningful. It is not hard to imagine that such loss of the indicators results in making it obscure that items listed in the dhātupāṭha are verbs. Just as one has to accept that a given vowel was originally nasalized as a marker according to what authoritative teachers have said earlier, so also does one have to be taught that items listed there are verbs in that they denote actions. In this line meaning entries came to be introduced into the dhātupāṭha. Thus under these circumstances it became necessary to impose semantic conditions on assigning the name *dhātu* to items listed in the dhātupāṭha.

On the other hand, if we turn to the need for the dhātupāṭha, the following may be said. In his *VP*3.14.80 Bhartṛhari declared that for those who do not observe the usage of the śiṣṭas, grammar is their eyes to see it (*śāstraṃ cakṣur apaśyatām*).[24] It is beyond question that verbs listed in the dhātupāṭha were posited in consequence of the analysis of the usage of the śiṣṭas. As Bhartṛhari explicitly states, at his time one could no longer observe the usage of the śiṣṭas. Which implies that the dhātupāṭha became the eyes for those who no longer had access to the usage of the śiṣṭas to know the correctness of verbs. When the dhātupāṭha is reasonably regarded as an authority representative of the usage of the śiṣṭas, we are naturally led to consider that verbs to be used have to be restricted to those which are listed therein for their correctness.

---

like Kṣīrasvāmin, Maitreya, and Sāyaṇa.

[24] See Section 8 [8.7.1.3].

Thus, on account of the development in these directions, at some time after Patañjali, the restriction of items to be called *dhātu* to those which were listed in the dhātupāṭha and the semantic condition for assigning the name *dhātu* to those items became essential. Consequently we have to think that the interpretation of *A*1.3.1 offered in the *Kāśikāvṛtti* is an accurate reflection of such development.

9.7. Patañjali has shown the absolute extremes of formal and semantic definitions of the term *dhātu*, and that *A*1.3.1 itself admits of different interpretations in keeping with such extremes. The two extremes of interpretation concerning the sūtra grew out of two factors inherent in the original dhātupāṭha: formal and semantic. In the original dhātupāṭha items to be called *dhātu* were given as showing their own forms and as verbs, meaningful units. It turns out, therefore, that this is precisely what Patañjali tried to prove through some sort of *reductio ad absurdum.* In addition, it is to be noted that, in following up a semantic definition in particular, Patañjali has developed his theory of semantics and grammar founded on the notion of *svabhāva* or an intrinsic denotative nature of a linguistic item.

Section 10

Bhartrhari and his predecessors on the verb meaning (*dhātvartha*): Concluding remarks

10. *kāraka* and *svabhāva*

This section shall be devoted to a review of what Pāṇini and the Pāninīyas, Kātyāyana and Patañjali, say of verb meanings to conclude the present work whose chief aim is to trace Bhartrhari's semantics of verbs to its source.

10.1. Pāṇini: *kriyā-kāraka, sādhya-sādhaka*

The kāraka categories Pāṇini introduced as syntactico-semantic categories presuppose that a verb meaning is viewed as correlative to a kāraka. The term *kāraka*, which he uses without defining (*A*1.4.23 *kārake*), refers to what contributes to something being accomplished. In correlation to a kāraka what is signified by a verb is thus viewed as something brought to accomplishment by the kāraka. This correlation between kāraka and verb meaning properly allows one to consider a verb meaning as something to be called *kriyā* 'that which is brought to accomplishment'. Pāṇini's derivational system accounts for the derivation of the term *kriyā* used in this sense (*karmasādhana*). It is beyond discussion that in view of such correlation between kāraka and verb meaning, the reverse may also be true: what brings something to be signified by a verb to accomplishment is termed *kāraka* because what is considered to be denoted by a verb is called *kriyā*.

In addition, in *A*1.4.42 *sādhakatamaṃ karaṇam* Pāṇini characterizes a kāraka as *sādhaka* or that which accomplishes. This characterization of a kāraka reveals that Pāṇini doubtless considers what a verb signifies to be spoken of as *sādhya* in correlation with a sādhaka.

He could have adopted a *sādhaka* system instead of the *kāraka* system and could have characterized a *sādhaka* as *kāraka*. But he did not. This seems to imply that he supposes that a verb meaning is to be called *kriyā*.[1]

10.2. Kātyāyana: *saparispanda/aparispanda*

As shown, for Kātyāyana who had to define the term *dhātu*, the choices were restricted to the following: *A*1.3.1 formulated by Pāṇini, *kriyā*-based and *bhāva*-based definitions formulated by early teachers. The *kriyā*-based definition is that an item which denotes *kriyā* is called *dhātu* (*kriyāvacano dhātuḥ*) and the *bhāva*-based definition is that an item which denotes *bhāva* is called *dhātu* (*bhāvavacano dhātuḥ*). These two definitions have in common that they are formulated from a semantic point of view. *A*1.3.1 taken as an alternative to these semantic definitions, on the other hand, is a formal definition based solely on the dhātupāṭha such that items which are recited in the dhātupāṭha are called *dhātu*. Kātyāyana considered that, of the two semantic definitions, the *bhāva*-based definition was preferable to the *kriyā*-based definition in that while the latter had difficulty in applying to items such as *as* which mean existence, the former did not.

Now, as far as Kātyāyana accepts them as deserving to be proposed, it seems reasonable to suppose that the semantic definitions by early teachers represent Kātyāyana's view of the verb meaning. And, on this assumption, it is taken for granted that his proposal of the *bhāva*-based definition with the aim of getting around such a difficulty as involved in the *kriyā*-based definition clearly shows that he regarded *bhāva* as a meaning common to all verbs.

I have already pointed out that early teachers' distinction between *kriyā* and *bhāva* has something to do with the classification of verbs Kātyāyana knows: *karmasthakriyaka*, *karmasthabhāvaka*; *kartṛsthakriyaka*, *kartṛsthabhāvaka*.[2] According to him, whatever verb meaning is regarded as *kriyā* is called *bhāva* but whatever verb meaning is regarded as *bhāva* cannot be called *kriyā*. For example, the meaning of the verb *pac* is subject to being characterized as *bhāva* as well as *kriyā*, but the meaning of the verb *as*

---

[1] I have shown how Pāṇini viewed verb meanings in Section 1.

[2] See Section 5 [5.1].

is not subject to being characterized as *kriyā*. For Kātyāyana who draws such a distinction between *kriyā* and *bhāva*, thus, in accordance with the conventional use of the terms *bhāva* and *kriyā*, a verb meaning is generally spoken of as *bhāva*, and specifically as *kriyā* when a dynamic aspect of the verb meaning is taken into account. According to later Pāṇinīyas like Kaiyaṭa, the term *kriyā* is conventionally used to signify something that is to be brought to accomplishment by sādhanas with motion (*saparispandasādhanasādhya*) and the term *bhāva* is conventionally used to signify something that is to be brought to accomplishment by sādhanas without motion (*aparispandasādhanasādhya*). And, as a matter of course, like Nāgeśa we have to say that the term *bhāva* is used to signify both.[3]

There is an important thing to note in Kātyāyana's treatment of a semantic definition of the term *dhātu*. That is: He is fully conscious that the application of the semantic definition of the term *dhātu* presupposes the abstraction, through the reasoning from *anvaya* and *vyatireka*, of items to be called *dhātu* from the complex items which include such items and which are usable in actual communication.[4] This implies that he already knows that a semantic characterization of verb meanings has to be made in conformity with usage.

10.3. Patañjali: *svabhāva*

When he proposed the *kriyā*-based and *bhāva*-based definitions, Kātyāyana, treating *kriyā* and *bhāva* as if their notions had been established as a given, did not explicitly state what they were. Patañjali, on the other hand, went into the question in detail since he had to assess the validity of the two semantic definitions. As a result of the consideration of the question at issue, he made clear the following various features of a verb meaning.

---

[3] See Section 5 [5.1]. We see of course that later Pāṇinīyas' way of explaining *kriyā* and *bhāva* is completely in the frame of reference Patañjali and Bhartṛhari have already provided.

[4] See Section 3 [3.2.2].

A verb meaning is:

1) an activity which leads to its result (*abhūtaprādurbhāva*; *phalānukūlavyāpāra*; *phalotpattyanukūlavyāpāra*);[5]

2) what consists in the exclusion of other actions (*pravṛttiviśeṣa*);

3) what is connected with time (*kālābhivyaktihetu*);

4) what comes into being (*bhāva, bhū*);

5) what is brought into being by substances which serve as sādhanas (*bhāva*, *bhāvyate*).

Features 1), 2), and 3) are those which pertain to what a verb denotes, being made clear through examining the *kriyā*-based definition.[6] Features 4) and 5) are those which pertain to how a verb meaning is spoken of, being revealed through examining the *bhāva*-based definition.[7] It is remarkable that Patañjali's examination of the *bhāva*-based definition results in not characterizing a verb meaning as existence/being (*bhavana*) and what exists/is (*bhāva*).[8]

10.3.1. What is of crucial importance in Patañjali's treatment of verb meanings is that he applies his theory of semantics and grammar to a semantics of verbs. That is, he introduced the notion of 'own nature' (*svabhāva*) or a linguistic item's intrinsic denotative nature in describing feature 5) and restricted the usage from which one was supposed to determine such an intrinsic denotative nature to that of the śiṣṭas (*śiṣṭaprayoga*). The former, the introduction of the intrinsic denotative nature, is a necessary

---

[5] See Section 5 [5.3.1]. Neo-grammarians like Bhaṭṭoji Dīkṣita developed their theory of verb meanings based on this aspect of the verb meaning. Bhaṭṭoji Dīkṣita, for example, declares: *VSK*2: *phalavyāpārayor dhātur āśraye tu tiṅaḥ smṛtāḥ / phale pradhānaṃ vyāpāras tiṅarthas tu viśeṣaṇam //* ("The following has been traditionally handed down: A verb denotes both an activity and its result; verb endings denote their locus. The activity is the principal [significand] with respect to its result; on the other hand, the meaning of the verb ending is its qualifier.") See also Section 6, fn. 22.

[6] See Section 5 [5.3].

[7] See Section 5 [5.2].

[8] See Section 5 [5.2]. The terms *bhāva* for *bhavana* and *bhāva* for what exists/is are derived from the verb *bhū* which denotes *sattā* and not *janman*.

consequence of Pāṇinīyas' *svabhāva*-based semantics (*abhidhānaṃ punaḥ svābhāvikam*).[9] And the latter, implying the respect for the usage of the śiṣṭas, leads him even to deny the need of Pāṇini's grammar having the dhātupāṭha.[10] At this point let us recall Patañjali's characterizations of the meaning of the verb (*dhātvartha*), an action, and of the meaning of the nominal base (*prātipadikārtha*), a substance.

MBh ad *A*1.3.1 (I.257.8–9): *kriyā caiva hi bhāvyate svabhāvasiddhaṃ tu dravyam* /
"Indeed, an action (*kriyā*) alone is [that which is] brought into being. On the other hand, a substance (*dravya*) is something that has been established by 'own nature' (*svabhāvasiddha*)."[11]

Pāṇinīyas' *svabhāva*-based semantics reflects their basic outlook on the world, which in his *Mahābhāṣya* Patañjali repeatedly declares.

MBh on *vt*. 5 ad *A*2.1.1 (I.11.1–2; 366.12–13): *śabdapramāṇakā vayam / yac chabda āha tad asmākaṃ pramāṇam* /
"We [grammarians] hold words as our standard. What words denote is our standard."

Grammarians such as Pāṇinīyas are not concerned with things as they are (*vastvartha*) but as they are spoken of (*śabdārtha*).[12] Now let us consider how this outlook on the world leads to Patañjali's semantics of verbs.

Suppose that Pāṇini himself composed the dhātupāṭha. The usage of the śiṣṭas was given to him as the established. And, on the basis of its observation, he posited the item *pac* as a verb to present it as ***ḍupacàṣ*** with a low-pitched base vowel and the markers *ḍu*, *à*, *ṣ* in the dhātupāṭha. In doing so he took the following procedure: He first determined the intrinsic denotative nature of the complex unit *pacati* which was actually used by the

---

[9] See Section 5 [5.2.3.2].

[10] See Section 8.

[11] See Section 5 [5.2.3.2].

[12] Helārāja describes things opposed to those denoted by words as *vastvartha*. See Section 5 [5.3.5.3] and Section 7 [7.2.3].

śiṣṭas and then found in its meanings a certain meaning which has the aspect of being something that comes into being or something that is brought into being, on the basis of which he applied the method of analysis that allowed him to abstract the item *pac* from that complex unit *pacati*. It also has to be considered to be due to its intrinsic denotative nature that the abstracted item *pac*, to which the abstracted meaning is attributed, denotes that meaning as something that comes into being or something that is brought into being. This analytic procedure for positing verbs demands that grammarians be concerned primarily with what and how linguistic items in actual use convey in accordance with their intrinsic denotative nature. In view of grammarians' basic outlook on the world, therefore, presumably it was a necessity that Patañjali brought the notion of an intrinsic denotative nature into his semantics of verbs.

10.3.2. I have said that a verb meaning has the five features according to Patañjali. However, when he takes an intrinsic denotative nature of a verb into consideration, he speaks of a verb meaning only as characterized as what comes into being (*bhavatīti bhāvaḥ*) or as what is brought into being (*bhāvyate yaḥ sa bhāva iti*).[13] As said, this is because in doing so he wishes to describe a verb meaning from the point of view of how a verb conveys its meaning. In this connection it is to be noted in passing that feature 2) of a verb meaning, the exclusion of other actions, is not considered from a semantic point of view.[14]

For Patañjali, the term *dhātu* is to be defined as follows:

> An item which denotes by its intrinsic denotative nature something that is brought into being—such a thing is referred to by the term *bhāva* or *kriyā*—is called *dhātu*.[15]

Patañjali observes features 4) and 5) in a verb meaning, namely that a verb meaning is conveyed as what comes into being and that it is conveyed as what is brought into being. These two

---

[13] See Section 5 [5.2.3.2].

[14] See Section 5 [5.3.3.5].

[15] See Section 7 [7.1].

features hold true for a verb meaning on the same level. For, the characterization of a verb meaning as what comes into being presupposes its characterization as what is brought into being, since for Patañjali what comes into being is obtained through the translation of what is brought into being on the same level. That is, if a certain item denotes by its intrinsic denotative nature its meaning as what is brought into being, then the item denotes its meaning in like manner, by its intrinsic denotative nature, as what comes into being.[16] That is why the above-mentioned definition of the term *dhātu* can be deemed to be Patañjali's fundamental semantic definition of it.

10.3.3. In his Bhāṣya on *A*1.3.1 Patañjali deals with three kinds of *kriyās*: causal, semantic, and behavioral.[17] Of these the semantic *kriyā*, a *kriyā* which Patañjali accepts as a verb meaning without defining, is identical with the *bhāva* as what is brought into being, because he characterizes the *kriyā* as *bhāvyate* '[that which] is brought into being'.[18] This can be easily explained if we take the verb *kṛ* in *karoti* as synonymous with the derived verb *bhāvi* in *bhāvayati* which is derived from the verb *bhū* by adding the causative affix *ṇic* to that verb. The forms *kriyā* and *bhāva*, taken as *karmasādhanas*, respectively mean 'what is brought to accomplishment' and 'what is brought into being'.[19]

As said, Pāṇini viewed a verb meaning in correlation with a kāraka and characterized the kāraka as *sādhaka* 'that which accomplishes'. It is likely that within this frame of reference he regarded such a verb meaning as *kriyā* and considered it to be something to be brought to accomplishment (*sādhya*). And this is faithfully reflected in Patañjali's treatment of the verb meaning.

When Patañjali is asked the question: "What is a verb meaning?" (*kaḥ punar dhātvarthaḥ*), he answers, "It is an action" (*kriyā*). When he answers so, he bears in mind the verb meaning as correlative to kārakas, the notion of which is well grounded on

[16] See Section 7 [7.2].

[17] See Section 5 [5.3].

[18] See Section 4, Part 3 [4.6.2.2], and Section 5 [5.2.3.2].

[19] See Section 1 [1.4].

Pāṇini's derivational system. Furthermore, if he continues to be asked the question: "What is the action?" then he may answer, "It is *bhāva* or what is brought into being" (*kriyā caiva hi bhāvyate*).[20]

To put it the other way round, this clearly shows that Patañjali's description of a verb meaning is in conformity with Pāṇini's. Thus we may say that Pāṇini's kāraka categories allow Patañjali to characterize a verb meaning, the semantic *kriyā*, as *bhāva* or something brought into being and to provide that an item which denotes such a *bhāva* by its intrinsic denotative nature is called *dhātu*.

10.4. Bhartṛhari: *yathāgamam*

Bhartṛhari defined an action as follows:

> *VP*3.8.1: *yāvat siddham asiddhaṃ vā sādhyatvenābhidhīyate* /
> *āśritakramarūpatvāt tat kriyeti pratīyate* //
> "Whether it has or has not been brought to accomplishment, whatever is denoted as something yet to be brought to accomplishment because it assumes sequence is what one understands by the word *kriyā* [in grammar]."[21]

We find a parallel in his semantics of nominal bases.

> *VP*3.7.79: *nirvartyo vā vikāryo vā prāpyo vā sādhanāśrayaḥ* /
> *kriyāṇām eva sādhyatvāt siddharūpo 'bhidhīyate* //
> "Whether it is something to be made (*nirvartya*), modified (*vikārya*), or reached (*prāpya*), a locus of a [capacity-]sādhana[, which is a substance,] is denoted as something that has already been brought to accomplishment because an action alone is denoted as something that is to be brought to accomplishment."[22]

What has to be noticed in these kārikās is that he uses the word *abhidhīyate* '. . . is denoted'. What is called *kriyā* is something that *is denoted* as what is to be brought to accomplishment (*sādhyatvena*) and what is considered to be a locus of a capacity

---

[20] See Section 5 [5.2.3.2] and [5.3.2].

[21] See Introduction [0.3].

[22] See Section 5 [5.2.3.2].

to bring an act to accomplishment, that is, a substance (*dravya*), is something that *is denoted* as what has already been brought to accomplishment (*siddharūpa*). Bhartṛhari declared that he only followed a tradition (*yathāgamam*) in presenting word meanings.[23] Recall that Kātyāyana set forth the view that a linguistic item denotes its meaning by its own nature (*abhidhānaṃ punaḥ svābhāvikam*) and Patañjali expressed it as *svābhāvikaṃ śabdair arthābhidhānam*.[24] From this it is clear that when Bhartṛhari uses the word *abhidhīyate* he presupposes that the denotation of meanings by linguistic items is determined by their own nature, their intrinsic denotative nature.

And further, his characterization of a verb meaning as what is to be brought to accomplishment is doubtless based on Patañjali's and hence on Pāṇini's.

All this makes it clear that every aspect of the description of a verb meaning by Patañjali and Bhartṛhari had already been anticipated by Pāṇini in his grammar.

---

[23] See Introduction [0.3.3].

[24] See Section 5 [5.2.3.2].

Appendix 1

A survey of previous researches on the *Mahābhāṣya* ad *A*1.3.1

0. Previous researches on the *Mahābhāṣya* ad *A*1.3.1

A French translation of the *Mahābhāṣya* on *A*1.3.1 together with the *Pradīpa* and *Uddyota* was made by Pierre-Sylvain Filliozat [1986]. There is also an English translation by P. S. Subrahmanya Sastri [1951–62], which, being a literal translation without annotations, serves only as a survey of the arguments stated in the text.[1]

The Bhāṣya which comments on vārttikas 1–2 on *A*1.3.1 has been an object of study in connection with the question whether the original dhātupāṭha associated with the *Aṣṭādhyāyī* included meaning entries.[2] Surprisingly few studies have so far been made of the Bhāṣya on *A*1.3.1 in its entirety. To my knowledge, studies which take the entire text in their purview have been made only by Rosane Rocher [1969] and by S. D. Joshi and J. A. F. Roodbergen [1994]. In this Appendix 1, I will take up their studies on the Bhāṣya on *A*1.3.1 to consider the points developed by them.[3]

---

[1] In addition to these, there is the Marathi translation of the *Mahābhāṣya* in question by V. S. Abhyankar edited by his son [1938–54], of which I could not make use.

[2] See Cardona [1980: 161–163; 1999b: 140–144]. It seems to me that, in dealing with the problems the first and second vārttikas and the Bhāṣya thereupon bring up, few scholars have given due attention to the frame of reference within which Kātyāyana and Patañjali discussed the validity of the dhātupāṭha-based definition of the term *dhātu*. See Section 9.

[3] Subramania Iyer [1950–51] also dealt with the *Mahābhāṣya* on *A*1.3.1, but his study was basically meant for making clear the notion of an action (*kriyā*) on the basis of the Kriyāsamuddeśa of the *Vākyapadīya*.

1. The distinction between *kriyāvacana* and *bhāvavacana* verbs

Joshi, S. D. and Roodbergen, J. A. F.
The Aṣṭādhyāyī of Pāṇini, Volume III (1.3.1–1.3.93); with Translation and Explanatory Notes. New Delhi: Sahitya Akademi, 1994.

This work is one of the volumes in which S. D. Joshi and J. A. F. Roodbergen have undertaken a joint translation of the *Aṣṭādhyāyī.*

1.1. Interpretation of *A* 1.3.1

As has been seen in Section 9, in his Bhāṣya on *A* 1.3.1 Patañjali makes clear that the present sūtra admits of four different interpretations.

1) Items of the set beginning with *bhū*, recited in the dhātupāṭha, are called *dhātu*.
2) Signifiers (*vādi*) of what comes into being (*bhū*) are called *dhātu*.
3) Those items which belong to the set beginning with *bhū* and which are like *vā* 'go, strike' are called *dhātu*.
4) Those items which belong to the set beginning with *vā* and which are like *bhū* 'be, be born' are called *dhātu*.

Of these interpretations the third and fourth are offered in the following Bhāṣya.

> *Bh.* 1 (I.258.27–259.3): *tad yadā tāvat kriyāvacano dhātur ity eṣa pakṣas tadā bhū ity atra ya ādiśabdaḥ sa vyavasthāyāṃ vartate, vā ity atra ya ādiśabdaḥ sa prakāre, bhū ityevamādayo vā ityevaṃprakārā iti* /
>
> *yadā tu bhāvavacano dhātur ity eṣa pakṣas tadā vā ity atra ya ādiśabdaḥ sa vyavasthāyām, bhū ity atra ya ādiśabdaḥ sa prakāre, vā ityevamādayo bhū ityevaṃprakārā iti* /

This Bhāṣya can be rendered as follows:

> "First of all, therefore, when one has the view that an item which denotes an action is called *dhātu*, one understands as follows:

The word *ādi* which is connected with the item *bhū* occurs with reference to *vyavasthā* and the word *ādi* which is connected with the item *vā* occurs to signify *prakāra*. Consequently what is meant by the sūtra is: Those items which belong to the set beginning with *bhū* and which are like *vā* 'go, strike' are called *dhātu* (*bhū ityevamādayo vā ityevaṃprakārāḥ*).

On the other hand, when one has the view that an item which denotes *bhāva* is called *dhātu*, one understands as follows:

The word *ādi* which is connected with the item *vā* occurs with reference to *vyavasthā* and the word *ādi* which is connected with the item *bhū* occurs to signify *prakāra*. Consequently what is meant by the sūtra is: Those items which belong to the set beginning with *vā* and which are like *bhū* 'be, be born' are called *dhātu* (*vā ityevamādayo bhū ityevaṃprakārāḥ*)."

As shown, the third and fourth interpretations of A1.3.1 are proposed by Patañjali within the framework created by Kātyāyana such that even if a semantic definition of the term *dhātu* is given, the dhātupāṭha is still necessary for complementing it through playing the role of preventing its over-application to certain nominal bases and corruptions. Within this framework, according to Patañjali, one has to interpret the sūtra as both indicating the dhātupāṭha and providing a semantic definition.[4]

Now, concerning the present Bhāṣya, Joshi/Roodbergen [1994: 4] state:

"Now Patañjali's idea is that to have the sense of *kriyāvacana* from *bhūvādayaḥ* analysed as *bhū-ādayaḥ* + *vā-ādayaḥ* we will take *ādi* in connection with *bhū-* in the sense of *vyavasthā*, and *ādi* in connection with *vā-* in the sense of *prakāra*. Thus *bhūvādayaḥ* is taken to mean '*bhū-*, etc. (in the arrangement of the *Dhp.*) and *vā*-type forms'. . . . In order to have the sense of *bhāvavacana* from *bhūvādayaḥ* in the the [*sic.*] same analysis we will take *ādi* in connection with *bhū-* in the sense of *prakāra*, and *ādi* in connection with *vā* in the sense of *vyavasthā*. Thus

---

[4] See Section 7 [7.3].

bhūvādayaḥ is taken to mean '*bhū*-type forms and *vā*-, etc. (in the arrangement of the *Dhp.*)' . . ."

There are two points to be noted. First, Joshi/Roodbergen take what are meant by the compound *bhūvādayaḥ* as follows:

A. *bhū*-, etc. (in the arrangement of the *Dhp.*) and *vā*-type forms

B. *bhū*-type forms and *vā*-, etc. (in the arrangement of the *Dhp.*)

The upholders of the *kriyā*-based definition and those of the *bhāva*-based definition respectively adopt alternatives A and B. The interpretations A and B of the compound *bhūvādayaḥ* they give clearly show that they understand that, whichever of A and B may be adopted, items to be called *dhātu* are divided into two classes. In A one has the class the first member of which is *bhū* and the class the members of which are similar to *vā*. In B, on the other hand, one has the class the first member of which is *vā* and the class the members of which are similar to *bhū*.

However, interpretations A and B are both fundamentally unsound, from a grammatical point of view and from the point of view of the framework in which A1.3.1 is interpreted in these manners.

1.1.1. What in the given context Patañjali understands by the bahuvrīhi compound *bhūvādayaḥ* is explainable with the following equivalent string:

bhūvau ādī yeṣāṃ te [śabdāḥ].

According to Patañjali, the compound *bhūvādayaḥ* is a single bahuvrīhi compound formed from the dvandva compound *bhūvau* whose constituent elements are *bhū* and *vā* and the item *ādī* obtained as a result of the ekaśeṣa operation applied to two *ādis* with different senses.[5]

By contrast, Joshi/Roodbergen consider in all but name the

---

[5] See Section 7 [7.3.3].

compound *bhūvādayaḥ* to be an alternant of the following utterance:

bhūḥ ādir yeṣāṃ te ca vāḥ ādir yeṣāṃ te ca.

Patañjali gives the paraphrase *bhū ityevamādayo vā ityevamprakārāḥ* with regard to the *kriyā*-based definition and the paraphrase *vā ityevamādayo bhū ityevamprakārāḥ* with reference to the *bhāva*-based definition. It is obvious that Joshi/Roodbergen take the compound *bhūvādayaḥ* as formed from a double bahuvrīhi, so that they mean that, in the case of the former, *bhū ityevamādayaḥ* forms one bahuvrīhi and *vā ityevamprakārāḥ* forms another; in the case of the latter, *vā ityevamādayaḥ* and *bhū ityevamprakārāḥ* form different bahuvrīhis.

Grammatically speaking, when the compound *bhūvādayaḥ* is taken as a bahuvrīhi, it cannot be interpreted as Joshi/Roodbergen understand it should be. For in the light of *A*2.2.24 *anekam anyapadārthe* which provides for the derivation of a bahuvrīhi compound the meanings of the constituent *padas* should function as qualifiers of something distinct from what the constituent *padas* signify and hence the meaning of the conjunctive *ca* 'and' referred to by the item *ādī* (*ādiś ca ādiś ca*) obtained from the application of ekaśeṣa also should be regarded as one of the qualifiers.

But, there is no evidence to show that the compound *bhūvādayaḥ* in this context is formed from the two constituent bahuvrīhis. On the contrary, later Pāṇinīyas like Kauṇḍabhaṭṭa support my interpretation. What Patañjali means by the above-mentioned paraphrases of the compound in question is that items to be called *dhātu* are those which belong to the class beginning with *bhū*/*vā* and whose similarity is to *vā*/*bhū*, literally speaking.[6]

Probably, Joshi/Roodbergen misunderstood the following Bhāṣya which was stated to explain the combination of two *ādis*, *vyavasthā-ādi* and *prakāra-ādi*, and the constituents *bhū* and *vā* of the dvandva compound *bhūvau.*

Bh. 2 (I.258.27): *pratyekaṃ cādiśabdaḥ parisamāpyate bhvādaya iti ca vādaya iti ca* /

[6] See Section 7, fn. 20.

> "Furthermore, [in the compound *bhūvādi*] the word *ādi* is connected with each of the components *bhū* and *vā* of the compound *bhūvau*, so that one may have both *bhvādi* (*bhūvādayaḥ*) and *vādi* (*vādayaḥ*)."[7]

This Bhāṣya does not mean that there are two groups: one is that whose *ādi* is *bhū* and the other that whose *ādi* is *vā*, but that, with reference to a group of items, they are spoken of as *bhvādi* and as *vādi* as well. If the *bhvādi* contains *vyavasthā-ādi* and the *vādi prakāra-ādi*, then the group of items both refer to has items which belong to the set beginning with *bhū* and which are like *vā*.

1.1.2. What is more, if we accepted interpretations A and B, then we could not reasonably explain the original intention of Patañjali who proposes the third and fourth interpretations of A1.3.1. Within Kātyāyana's framework noted above, two conditions are to be specified in a desirable definition of the term *dhātu* as follows:

> Items are called *dhātu* if they denote *kriyā/bhāva*, and are listed in the dhātupāṭha.

The second condition that items to be called *dhātu* should be listed in the dhātupāṭha is necessary for the name *dhātu* not to apply to certain nominal bases and corruptions, as said. If we have a group of verbs listed in the dhātupāṭha on the one hand and another group of verbs similar to *bhū/vā* on the other, the difficulties pointed out with respect to the dhātupāṭha-based definition and a semantic definition would again arise since there is no interrelation to be found between those two groups of verbs. Joshi/Roodbergen, as we understand, propose only the combination of the dhātupāṭha-based definition and a semantic definition. This is never the case. Here Patañjali, following Kātyāyana, accepts a semantic definition of the term *dhātu* as its one and only definition.

---

[7] See Section 7 [7.3.3].

1.2. *kriyā*-based and *bhāva*-based definitions and interpretations of *A*1.3.1

By stating the following Bhāṣya, Patañjali introduces *Bh.* 1.

> *Bh.* 3 (I.258.22–23): *atha yady eva kriyāvacano dhātur ity eṣa pakṣo 'thāpi bhāvavacano dhātur iti kiṃ gatam etad iyatā sūtreṇa, āhosvid anyatarasmin pakṣe bhūyaḥ sūtraṃ kartavyam / gatam ity āha /*
>
> "[Question] Now, if one holds the view that an item which denotes an action is called *dhātu*, or if one holds the view that an item which denotes *bhāva* is called *dhātu*, is such a semantic definition as one intends understood from this much sūtra (*bhūvādayo dhātavaḥ*), then?; or, in either view, should the sūtra in question be augmented in order to make the intended semantic definition understood from it?
>
> [Answer] He [who is an upholder of a semantic definition] says: '[The intended semantic definition is] understood [from this much sūtra].'"[8]

Patañjali says that *kriyā*-based and *bhāva*-based definitions are obtained from the sūtra itself by means of interpreting it in the above stated manner (Interpretations of *A*1.3.1 3 and 4). On this point, Joshi/Roodbergen make the following remark:

> Joshi/Roodbergen [1994:4]: ". . . how exactly the meaning *kriyāvacana* is obtained from the analysis '*bhū*-, etc. and forms similar to *vā*', and the meaning *bhāvavacana* from the analysis 'forms similar to *bhū*-and *vā*-, etc', is not clear. Apparently, in the combinations indicated by 'and' the portion 'similar to' is the dominating portion, or so Patañjali thinks."

It is not unclear how the *kriyā*-based and *bhāva*-based definitions are obtained from *A*1.3.1. By reading the *prakāra-ādi* in the sūtra Patañjali intends it to provide them. The *kriyā*-based and *bhāva*-based definitions which we can get from the sūtra are as follows:

---

[8] See Section 7 [7.3.2].

kriyā-based definition:
A. Items which, like *vā* 'go, strike', denote actions (*kriyā*) are called *dhātu*.
bhāva-based definition:
B. Items which, like *bhū* 'be, be born', denote *bhāva* are called *dhātu*.

The point is that one who entertains the view of the *kriyā*-based definition takes the component *vā* of the dvandva compound *bhūvau* as a meaningful unit and one who maintains the view of the *bhāva*-based definition interprets the component *bhū* of the same compound as a meaningful unit. The difference between these two approaches to the dvandva compound in question stems from the difference between the meanings of the items *vā* and *bhū*. It goes without saying that Patañjali treats the meaning of the item *vā* as *kriyā* and that of the item *bhū* as *bhāva*.

We have to note that in his *Mahābhāṣya* on *A*1.3.1 Patañjali speaks of different notions of *kriyā*—causal, semantic, behavioral *kriyās*, and *kriyā* as conceived of by early teachers—and of different notions of *bhāva*—existence, what comes into being, what is brought into being, and *bhāva* as conceived of by early teachers.[9] Joshi/Roodbergen do not take this into consideration at all. The meanings of verbs, *kriyā* and *bhāva*, given by Patañjali here as being distinct from each other are of early teachers, according to whom they differ from each other depending on whether those which bring them to accomplishment have motion or not.

Moreover, we have to note that the term *prakāra-ādi* here refers to similarity (*sādṛśya*), the significance of which Joshi/Roodbergen miss. It is because he has the idea, following early teachers, that the meanings of the items *bhū* and *vā* have a difference in one way and a similarity in another between themselves that Patañjali can introduce the item *ādi* used in the sense of *prakāra*. One has to say that the item *bhū* is like the item *vā* in that the former denotes *kriyā* and that the item *vā* is like the item *bhū* in that the former denotes *bhāva*. First of all, the *kriyā*-based def-

[9]See Section 5.

inition A has to apply to the item *bhū* and the *bhāva*-based definition B has to apply to the item *vā*.

This brings us to the second question: What is the *kriyā* which covers meanings of all verbs and what is the *bhāva* which covers them?

The present Bhāṣya (*Bh.* 3) should not be considered apart from the context, which Joshi/Roodbergen do not take into consideration at all. What is important is that before he undertakes interpreting *A*1.3.1 in the above-stated manner, Patañjali has already established his basic semantic definition of the term *dhātu*, which is as follows:

> An item which denotes by its intrinsic denotative nature something that is brought into being—such a thing is referred to by the term *bhāva* or *kriyā*—is called *dhātu*.[10]

Thus, in the third and fourth interpretations of *A*1.3.1 the *kriyā*-based and *bhāva*-based definitions as input are different from the ones as output. In the *kriyā*-based and *bhāva*-based definitions as output, the terms *kriyā* and *bhāva* employed therein refer to the same thing, what is brought into being. Regrettably, Joshi/Roodbergen fail to depict accurately what Patañjali means by *Bh.* 3. The main reason for that lies in their overlooking the framework in which Patañjali proposes those interpretations of the sūtra.

1.3. *kriyāvacana* and *bhāvavacana* verbs

Pāṇini had predecessors in the field of grammar. And the pre-Pāṇinian grammarians had already established the *kriyā*-based and *bhāva*-based definitions of verbs using the term *dhātu*. In such a situation Pāṇini, following their terminology, formulated *A*1.3.1. One of the tasks imposed on Patañjali in his *Mahābhāṣya* on *A*1.3.1 was to go deeply into the semantics of verbs to show how verbs were to be defined semantically. Accordingly, it was essential for him to reexamine the notions of *kriyā* and *bhāva*. His reexamination of them is doubtless a rich source of information about the question of what aspects a verb meaning has.

---

[10] See Section 7 [7.1].

Nonetheless, Joshi/Roodbergen touch only on what I call 'behavioral *kriyā*' and the establishment of the meaning of the verb *as* as an action on the authority of the *Nirukta*, leaving aside the interpretations of the term *bhāva* which were given by Patañjali. As shown, Kātyāyana regarded the *bhāva*-based definition as preferable to the *kriyā*-based definition which does not apply to the verbs *as*, *bhū*, and *vid*.[11] In addition Patañjali treated *bhāva* as characterizing a verb meaning spoken of as *kriyā*.[12] It is beyond question that we must look carefully into what the terms *kriyā* and *bhāva* mean when used to describe verb meanings. As said, in the *Mahābhāṣya* on A1.3.1 we find various kinds of *kriyās* and different sorts of *bhāvas*.

kriyā :

1. early teachers' *kriyā*
2. causal *kriyā*
3. semantic *kriyā*
4. behavioral *kriyā*

bhāva :

1. early teachers' *bhāva*
2. existence
3. what comes into being
4. what is brought into being[13]

Leaving out of account the fact that these notions of *kriyā* and *bhāva* are dealt with therein, Joshi/Roodbergen observe that a distinction is drawn between *kriyāvacana* and *bhāvavacana* verbs in Pāṇini's grammar.

> Joshi/Roodbergen [1994: 5]: "In the A. the word *kriyāvacana* is not used, whereas the word *bhāvavacana* has been used just once (in P. 3.3.11) in the sense of an action noun.
>
> But, apart from terminology, does Pāṇini provide clues for the factual distinction between *kriyāvacana* and *bhāvavacana* verbs?

---

[11] See Section 3 [3.2.5].

[12] See Section 4, Part 3 [4.6.2.2].

[13] See Section 5.

> One case in point is P. 3.3.10. This rule prescribes the suffix *tumUN* in the sense of *kriyā* 'action' performed for another action. An example is *bhoktuṃ vrajati* 'he goes in order to eat'. But usages like *bhavituṃ vrajati* 'he goes in order to be' or *gantuṃ bhavati* 'he is in order to go', in which *bhū-* is a *bhāvavacana* verb, are not attested. Therefore we may take it that Pāṇini's expression *kriyāyāṃ kriyārthāyām* 'in the sense of action (performed) for the sake of another action' factually excludes the addition of *tumUN* in the case of a verbal base which is not *kriyāvacana* but *bhāvavacana*."

We will notice immediately that Joshi/Roodbergen do not follow the arguments advanced by Kātyāyana and Patañjali over *A*1.3.1. They take items such as *bhuj* 'eat' and items such as *bhū* as *kriyāvacana* and *bhāvavacana* verbs, respectively. For Kātyāyana who has brought in the *kriyā*-based and *bhāva*-based definitions as established by pre-Paṇinian grammarians, the verb *bhuj* is called *dhātu* by the *bhāva*-based definition as well as by the *kriyā*-based definition, but the verb *bhū* is so called only by the *bhāva*-based definition. For Patañjali who has established that the *kriyā*-based and *bhāva*-based definitions are equivalent to each other, on the other hand, both the verbs are properly called *dhātu* by any of the two definitions. If Pāṇini, as Joshi/Roodbergen argue, distinguishes between *kriyāvacana* and *bhāvavacana* verbs, Kātyāyana's *bhāva*-based definition and Patañjali's *kriyā*-based and *bhāva*-based definitions will lose support from Pāṇini.

To be sure, as shown, early teachers distinguish between *kriyā* and *bhāva* and the distinction between them is recognized by Kātyāyana and Patañjali when they classify verbs into *karma (kartṛ)sthakriyaka* and *karma(kartṛ)sthabhāvaka* verbs in a different way from that in which Pāṇini divides verbs into two categories: *akarmaka* and *sakarmaka* verbs. And further, Patañjali certainly notes that there is the difference between causal *kriyā* and existence, though he finally succeeds in placing the latter in the same category as the former. But, the question confronts us: Does Pāṇini's formulation of *A*3.3.10 *tumunṇvulau kriyāyāṃ* *kriyārthāyām* support that he himself draws a distinction between *kriyāvacana* and *bhāvavacana* verbs?

*A*3.3.10 provides that ***tumun*** and ***ṇvul*** alternately follow a verb whose meaning is referred to the future, if this is used with another verb the action denoted by which has as its purpose the act which the first verb signifies (*kriyāyāṃ kriyārthāyām*). For example, this sūtra accounts for the derivate *bhoktum* in the utterance *bhoktuṃ vrajati*. Joshi/Roodbergen consider the items *bhuj* 'eat' and *vraj* 'go' to be *kriyāvacana* verbs, that is, the verbs which denote *kriyā*. What they argue is: The fact that usages like *bhavituṃ vrajati* or *gantuṃ bhavati* are not attested indicates that *A*3.3.10 does not have *bhāvavacana* verbs such as *bhū* in its domain of application, in the light of which Pāṇini is proved to make a distinction between *kriyāvacana* and *bhāvavacana* verbs.

However, their argument seems not to be convincing. Consider the following sūtra:

*A*2.3.37 *yasya ca bhāvena bhāvalakṣaṇam* //

This sūtra provides that an ending of the seventh triplet follows a nominal if an act (*bhāva*) connected with what it signifies serves as a means of characterizing another act (*bhāvalakṣaṇam*). By the sūtra are accounted for the occurrence of the seventh triplet ending in *tasmin* of the utterance A *tasmin sati tad bhavati* 'If x occurs, y occurs' but also that of the seventh triplet ending in *goṣu* of the utterance B *goṣu duhyamānāsu gataḥ* 'He went off while the cows were being milked'.[14] According to Joshi/Roodbergen's classification of verbs, the verbs *as* and *bhū* in A are characterized as *bhāvavacana* and the verbs *duh* 'milk' and *gam* 'go off' in B as *kriyāvacana*. If their argument were valid, they would have to say that usage B is not attested.

According to Kaiyaṭa, *A*3.3.10, which Joshi/Roodbergen consider to provide a clue for the factual distinction between *kriyāva*-

[14]The introduction of the seventh triplet endings in *sati* and *duhyamānāsu* is accounted for by *A*3.2.124. For these examples, see Cardona [1970: 215] and also Section 5, fn. 5. In his *Uddyota* on *MBh* ad *A*2.3.37 (II.803) Nāgeśa gives the utterance *dhūme sati vahnir bhavati* 'If smoke is present, then fire is present'.

cana and *bhāvavacana* verbs, contrary to their assumption, indicates that Pāṇini uses the term *bhāva* to refer to a meaning of any verb.[15] The point made by Joshi/Roodbergen is in essence a matter of *anabhidhāna* principle, namely that grammatically correct items cannot always be attested, as in the case of **ādityadarśa* which is what should obtain by *A*3.2.1 but is not attested in actual usage.[16] It seems reasonable to suppose that Pāṇini uses the terms *kriyā* and *bhāva* with no distinction to refer to verb meanings.[17]

I will not examine all the occurrences of the terms *kriyā* and *bhāva* in the *Aṣṭādhyāyī*. However, one may say for certain the following with respect to Pāṇini's use of the term *bhāva* in sūtras headed by *A*3.1.91 *dhātoḥ*.

In the sūtras headed by *A*3.1.91 *dhātoḥ*, which provide for the introduction of the verb endings (*tiṅ*) and the kṛt affixes to items called *dhātu*, Pāṇini uses the term *bhāva* in order to refer to a verb meaning in two different ways: as undifferentiated from the verb meaning and as differentiated from it. For example, in the utterance *āsyate devadattena* 'Devadatta is sitting', the affix *-e* in *āsyate* denotes *bhāva* by *A*3.4.69 *laḥ karmaṇi ca bhāve cākarmakebhyaḥ*. The *bhāva* in question is nothing but the meaning of the verb *ās*. And besides, in the utterance *āsitavyaṃ bhavatā* 'You should sit down' the kṛt affix *-tavya* denotes *bhāva* by *A*3.4.70 *tayor eva kṛtyaktakhalarthāḥ*. This *bhāva* is also not distinct from the meaning of the verb *ās*. On the other hand, in

[15] See *Pradīpa* on *MBh* ad *A*1.3.1 (II.185): *bhāvaśabdaḥ kriyāmātravācī / yathā yasya ca bhāveneti bhāve ghañ iti ca / Uddyota* thereon: *kriyāmātreti / dhātvarthamātrety arthaḥ /* See also Section 5 [5.1.2]. For the equivalency of these terms, see Cardona [1970]. In *A*3.2.126 *lakṣaṇahetvoḥ kriyāyāḥ* which provides that the affixes *śatṛ* and *śānac* replace *laṭ* as in *śayānā bhuñjate yavanāḥ* 'The Yavanas eat reclining', Pāṇini uses the term *kriyā* to refer to a verb meaning in the relation of *lakṣyalakṣaṇabhāva* or the characteristic-characterized relation.

[16] See Section 8 [8.6.2.1].

[17] We may add that in *A*3.4.1 *dhātusambandhe pratyayāḥ* he uses the term *dhātu* so as to refer to its meaning (*dhātvartha*). In *A*5.1.118 *upasargāc chandasi dhātvarthe* the word *dhātvartha* is used. But Pāṇinīyas like Patañjali take it to refer to kārakas. See *MBh* thereon.

the case of the nominal base *pāka* which is derived from the verb *pac* by adding the kṛt affix ***ghañ*** to that verb by *A*3.3.18 *bhāve*, the affix ***ghañ*** nominalizes the verb *pac*. The term *bhāva* here refers to any verb meaning viewed in the abstract.[18]

However that may be, what has to be noticed in dealing with the notions of *kriyā* and *bhāva* found in the sūtras of the *Aṣṭādhyāyī* is that we should free ourselves from all preconceptions of them. As a matter of fact, as is shown by Patañjali in his *Mahābhāṣya* on *A*1.3.1, the terms *kriyā* and *bhāva* have so multiple meanings that we cannot easily determine what they signify in a given context. We have to be patient in dealing with the notions of *kriyā* and *bhāva* in Pāṇini's grammar. One thing is certain: the *kriyās* and *bhāvas* as described by Pāṇinīyas represent different aspects of the verb meaning.

2. Preferential solution and an explicit choice

Rocher, Rosane.
"The concept of verbal root in Indian grammar (a propos of Pāṇini 1.3.1)." *Foundation of Language* 5 (1969): 73–82.

As far as I know, this is the only paper that has so far been intended as a close investigation of the *Mahābhāṣya* on *A*1.3.1.

2.1. Return to the *kriyā*-based definition

From two angles, Patañjali establishes that the *kriyā*-based and *bhāva*-based definitions of the term *dhātu* are equivalent to each other.

1) The establishment of the meaning of a verb like *as* as action (*kriyā*).

This is made through the following: First, through finding the properties of an action in the meaning of the verb *as*; secondly, through resorting to the authority of the *Nirukta*; thirdly, through denying that having no question-and-answer *kiṃ karoti—asti* disproves that the meaning of the verb *as* is an action.

2) The synonymy of the terms *kriyā* and *bhāva*.

---

[18] For two kinds of *bhāva*: the *bhāva* which is denoted by verb endings (*tiṅabhihitabhāva*) and the *bhāva* which is denoted by kṛt affixes (*kṛdabhihitabhāva*), see Section 3 [3.2.4].

As said, they both denote what is brought into being.[19] With reference to a verb meaning (*dhātvartha*), Patañjali speaks of it as *kriyā* and describing it as *bhāva*. That is, for him, the semantic *kriyā* is nothing but *bhāva* (what is brought into being).

Rocher says as follows of Patañjali who, from the viewpoint of 1), tries to establish the equivalence between the *kriyā*-based and *bhāva*-based definitions:

> Rocher [1969: 79]: "It is clear at this point that, although he does not say so explicitly, Patañjali is conscious of the fact that the Aṣṭādhyāyī does not really authorize his statement that the root expresses *bhāva*. He therefore returns to the former alternative, according to which the verbal root expresses an action."

As shown in Section 4 (Part 4), it is after he first deals with the *kriyā*-based definition proposed by Kātyāyana in his third vārttika and then goes on to develop an argument about the *bhāva*-based definition in accordance with the context in which Kātyāyana discusses it in his vārttikas 8–11 that Patañjali returns to the *kriyā*-based definition. Rocher considers the reason for his return to the *kriyā*-based definition to be that the *bhāva*-based definition is not borne out by the *Aṣṭādhyāyī*. This is rather pointless. The case is as follows:

In Patañjali's argumentation on *A*1.3.1 we find two stages: the stage in which he discusses problems involved in a semantic definition of the term *dhātu* as opposed to its formal definition on the assumption that the *bhāva*-based definition has the domain of application which does not overlap that of the *kriyā*-based definition, and the stage in which he discusses the problem whether there is still the need for the dhātupāṭha granted that a semantic definition of any form is given. In order to make a transition from the former stage to the latter he should make the *kriyā*-based and *bhāva*-based definitions equivalent to each other so that he may have a single semantic definition.

Here again I have to stress that Patañjali develops an argument in accordance with the framework Kātyāyana has constructed.

---

[19] Section 5 [5.3.2].

Kātyāyana has succeeded in establishing a semantic definition of the term *dhātu* by making a revision of the *bhāva*-based definition. The revised *bhāva*-based definition *prathamabhāvavacano dhātuḥ* deprives the dhātupāṭha of its function of supplying items to be called *dhātu*, which function was essential for the dhātupāṭha-based definition, so that it may make the dhātupāṭha purposeless. On the assumption that verbs are defined semantically, the dhātupāṭha has to be made purposeful by allotting it new functions: to prevent the semantic definition from applying to certain nominal bases and corruptions (*vt.* 12).

Now, if the *kriyā*-based definition remained narrower with respect to its domain of application, the dhātupāṭha would still be necessary for items not covered by such a kriyā-based definition to be called *dhātu*. Obviously, one who holds the view of the *kriyā*-based definition cannot have his semantic definition fit into Kātyāyana's framework. In order to discuss the dhātupāṭha's functions replacing its function of supplying items to be called *dhātu*, a semantic definition has to be established as covering all verbs, whatever it may be. This is why Patañjali returns to the *kriyā*-based definition. And, through this return, he wishes to change the *kriyā*-based definition, proposed by Kātyāyana according to early teachers, into his own one. This is evident from the fact that after returning to the definition in question he goes on to present the third and fourth interpretations of *A*1.3.1 in which no distinction can be made between those two semantic definitions. The return to the *kriyā*-based definition has nothing to do with the question of whether the *Aṣṭādhyāyī* authorizes the *bhāva*-based definition or not. If, on the contrary, it seems that the *Aṣṭādhyāyī* authorizes the *kriyā*-based definition, it is simply because Pāṇini adopted the *kāraka* system instead of the *sādhaka* system.[20]

2.2. Patañjali's interpretations of *A*1.3.1

As is shown by the passage quoted above, Rocher consistently treats the *kriyā*-based definition and the *bhāva*-based definition

---

[20] See Section 1.

as placed in juxtaposition with each other. She considers that Patañjali who is selective in his choice of a semantic definition prefers the *kriyā*-based definition to the *bhāva*-based definition. The tendency to try to understand Patañjali to choose between the *kriyā*-based and *bhāva*-based definitions is noticeable when she reads the Bhāṣya (*Bh.* 1, quoted in subsection 1.1) which presents the third and fourth interpretations of *A*1.3.1.

2.2.1. She expounds the Bhāṣya at issue as follows:

> Rocher [1969: 80]: "If one adopts the definition that the verbal root expresses an action, the sūtra *bhūvādayo dhātavaḥ* can be interpreted as follows: "roots are *bhū* 'exist' and those following after it in the Dhātupāṭha, and *vā* 'blow' and similar ones (i.e., roots expressing an action)." If, on the contrary, one prefers the definition that the root expresses existence, one may interpret thus: "roots are *bhū* 'exist' and similar ones (i.e., roots expressing existence), and *vā* 'blow' and those following after it in the Dhātupāṭha."''

We may point out that in interpreting the bahuvrīhi compound *bhūvādayaḥ* Rocher makes the same mistake as Joshi/Roodbergen. She interprets the compound as follows:

> *bhū* 'exist' and those following after it in the Dhātupāṭha, and *vā* 'blow' and similar ones (i.e., roots expressing an action);
> *bhū* 'exist' and similar ones (i.e., roots expressing existence), and *vā* 'blow' and those following after it in the Dhātupāṭha.

I have already shown how the compound under consideration is to be interpreted when dealing with its interpretation by Joshi/Roodbergen. The point is that, as Joshi/Roodbergen do, so also does Rocher interpret the compound *bhūvādi* as, for both of the upholders of the *kriyā*-based definition and those of the *bhāva*-based definition, referring to two groups of items to be called *dhātu*. According to her, from the point of view of the former, the compound refers to members of the set beginning with *bhū* and a group of items like *vā*; from the point of view of the latter, members of the set beginning with *vā* and a group of items like *bhū*; the upholders of the *kriyā*-based definition bend their eyes on a group of items like *vā* and those of the *bhāva*-based definition on a group of items like *bhū*. However, as I have already pointed out in connection with Joshi/Roodbergen's interpretation of the present Bhāṣya, to interpret the bahuvrīhi compound *bhūvādayaḥ* in this manner is not justifiable in terms of its derivation and in view of the context where Patañjali proposes the third and fourth interpretations of *A* 1.3.1.

2.2.2. After presenting her own interpretation of the Bhāṣya in question, Rocher continues to say:

> Rocher [1969: 80–81]: "The striking fact is that, in his final analysis, Patañjali thus allows both semantic definitions to subsist alongside one another. He abandons the discussion here, as he does frequently, leaving open various possibilities. This does not mean that Patañjali was himself unable to choose one possibility over the others. As on many other occasions in the Mahābhāṣya, all elements indicative of a preferential solution are present in the text, but the author refrains from making an explicit choice, leaving it to the reader to draw his own conclusions."

According to Rocher, *A* 1.3.1, based upon its third interpretation, has the aspect of the semantic definition of the *kriyā*-based definition, and, based upon its fourth interpretation, has the aspect of that of the *bhāva*-based definition. In addition, Patañjali seems to accept that both of the semantic definitions hold side by side with each other but in reality he chooses between them, though the choice is not explicitly made. Such being the case, it is a reader's task to determine which semantic definition Patañjali prefers to the other. Thus Rocher goes on to try to clear up the question.

Rocher, for the reason that the fourth interpretation compels one to assume the group *vādigaṇa* or the class beginning with *vā* which is not found in the dhātupāṭha as preserved to us, makes a concluding remark.

> Rocher [1969: 81]: "Given the fact that all commentators, and Patañjali in particular, are extremely reluctant to change the traditional reading of texts such as the Dhātupāṭha, there can be little doubt that Patañjali prefers an alternative which obviates the need for such emendation."

It is true that, as Rocher states, the third and fourth interpretations respectively presuppose *bhvādigaṇa* or the set beginning with *bhū* and *vādigaṇa* or the set beginning with *vā*, which is made possible by reading in the sūtra the item *vyavasthā-ādi*. But, is it possible to reason from Patañjali's assuming the *vādigaṇa* that he intends to give a preference to the *kriyā*-based definition for the reason Rocher described? The answer to that is in the negative.

As said, preliminary to the discussion as to whether there is the need for the dhātupāṭha on condition that a semantic definition is given, Patañjali put the third and fourth interpretations on A1.3.1 which require that the terms *vyavasthā-ādi* and *prakāra-ādi* should be read in the sūtra. Now when certain members of an ordered set are referred to by a bahuvrīhi compound with the term *vyavasthā-ādi* used in a sūtra, it is indicated that they are recited in a text external to the corpus of sūtras, the *Aṣṭādhyāyī*. Therefore, as Kaiyaṭa notes, in order for the compound *vādayaḥ* to refer to all the items recited in the dhātupāṭha, the item *vā* should be made the first member of the set beginning with the item *ad* (*adādigaṇa*) and the set beginning with the item *vā* has to be the first set of the ten sets like the set beginning with the item *bhū* (*bhvādigaṇa*).[21] In this regard, as Rocher points out, the fourth interpretation entails the rearrangement of items and sets arranged in the dhātupāṭha.

However this implicit proposal of the rearrangement of items and sets arranged in the dhātupāṭha implies that Patañjali is not fettered by how the dhātupāṭha is in reality and hence that he proposes the fourth interpretation as a theoretical possibility. As said, the framework created by Kātyāyana in his vārttikas 12–13

---

[21] *Pradīpa* on *MBh* ad *A*1.3.1 (II.196): *adādīnām ādau vā gatigandhanayor iti paṭhitavyam / adādigaṇo 'pi gaṇānām ādau / tena sarve dhātupāṭhasanniviṣṭā gṛhītā bhavanti /* See Section 7 [7.3.7].

brings Patañjali to proposing the third and fourth interpretations of *A*1.3.1. According to what Patañjali argues under vārttikas 12–13, if one follows up a semantic definition of the term *dhātu*, the dhātupātha becomes of no practical use in Pāṇini's grammar.[22] It is precisely because at the bottom of his heart he knows there to be no role for the dhātupāṭha to play if a semantic definition is provided that he can propose the fourth interpretation which presupposes as a theoretical possibility the set *vādigaṇa* which is not found in the dhātupāṭha in reality. It does not matter to Patañjali whether or not such set is found in the given dhātupāṭha since for him the dhātupāṭha has no role to play at all in this context.

Here also we will see how important it is to understand the Bhāṣya in its proper context. In the given context Patañjali does not distinguish between the third and forth interpretations of *A*1.3.1 in any sense, in consequence of which he does not indicate preference for any of the *kriyā*-based and *bhāva*-based definitions, nor are we allowed to choose between them.

2.3. Action—what is it?

As said above, Rocher holds the view that Patañjali prefers the *kriyā*-based definition. An idea underlying her view was that even if the third and fourth interpretations of *A*1.3.1 are equally valid from a theoretical point of view, the former is preferable to the latter on the principle of brevity (*lāghava*). As evidence in support of her view, she goes on to adduce the statement by Patañjali: *kaḥ punar dhātvarthaḥ, kriyā* in the Bhāṣya on *A*5.1.118 (II.365.3); the *kriyā* mentioned in which is what I describe as semantic *kriyā*.

> Rocher [1969: 81]: "As a matter of fact, elsewhere in his commentary, Patañjali unequivocally accepts the point of view that a verbal root expresses an action. On the occasion of sūtra 5.1.118, for example, he asks the question *kaḥ punar dhātvarthaḥ* 'what does a root express?' and replies immediately: *kriyā* 'action'."

---

[22] See Section 8.

She is never wrong in her assumption that Patañjali accepts a verb meaning as *kriyā*. Patañjali himself explicitly says that a verb meaning is an action (*kriyā*). However, she never makes clear what he means by the term *kriyā* in saying so. As I believe it is intentional, she does not touch on Patañjali's interpretation of the term *bhāva* as signifying something brought into being ('*bhāva*' as a *karmasādhana*) in spite of mentioning its interpretations as existence (*bhavana*) and what comes into being ('*bhāva*' as a *kartṛsādhana*).[23] As shown, he characterizes the semantic *kriyā* as *bhāva* or what is brought into being.[24] Her studied neglect of this point shows that for her it is amiss that the two semantic definitions, *kriyā*-based and *bhāva*-based, are equivalent to each other. In this connection let me stress again that Patañjali's description of the verb meaning *kriyā* as *bhāva* forms the core of his semantics of verbs.

In the last place Rocher, presenting the interpretation of the sūtra in question by the *Kāśikāvṛtti*, concludes that Pāṇini and Pāṇinīyas accept the *kriyā*-based definition.

> Rocher [1969: 81]: "But the Kāsikā too, thinks it necessary to add a semantic definition of the root, which is the same as the

---

[23] To be precise, Rocher takes the term *bhāva* as *kartṛsādhana* to signify what exists. She [1969: 78] says: "Patañjali therefore proposes the definition that the root is the element that expresses the agent of the action 'exist'. It seems, however, difficult to accept such a definition, because it would also include elements which are not verbal roots: trees, for example, have an existence; they are agents of the action 'exist', and yet they are expressed by nominal stems, and not by verbal roots." She also directs our notice to the fact that the verb *bhū* has a double aspect: 'be' and 'come into being', remarking: "This double aspect of the root *bhū* makes *bhāva* a term which is not easy to translate. I have decided on 'existence' as the least misleading translation. It should be recalled, however, that 'existence' does not imply here anything static, but involves process, or transformation, as exemplified by the existence of living beings. The 'coming into being' is but the first of all processes involved." See Rocher [1969: 78; fn. 5]. Obviously she makes this remark with *Nirukta* 1.2 in mind (see Section 4, Part 4 [4.8.3]). However, it is to be noted that, as shown in Section 4, Part 3 [4.6.2.1] and Section 5 [5.2], Patañjali carefully distinguishes between the two meanings of the verb *bhū*: *sattā* (existence) and *janman* (birth).

[24] See Section 4, Part 3 [4.6.2.2].

> one in the Aṣṭādhyāyī and the Mahābhāṣya; i.e. roots express actions. However, the Kāśikā assumes that there is no reason to modify the sūtra so as to include this definition. Moreover, it presents a justification which is not only ingenious, but quite simple. Pāṇini borrowed the technical term *dhātu* from his predecessors. This means that the term has to be taken with the meaning which the pre-Pāṇinian grammarians gave it. And the latter did define the root as expressing an action."

Thus Rocher brings us back to the starting point of the argument on the semantic definition of the term *dhātu* in the *Mahābhāṣya*. We have to put the same question as Patañjali. The action (*kriyā*) as conceived of by pre-Pāṇinian grammarians—what is it? It is surprising that without giving a clear picture of the notions of *kriyā* and *bhāva* she can talk about them.

Appendix 2

Analyzed text of the *Mahābhāṣya* ad *A* 1.3.1

1. The text of the *Mahābhāṣya* ad *A*1.3.1 shall be given, divided into four parts according as the vārttikas of Kātyāyana are grouped under four heads. Under *A*1.3.1 Kātyāyana discusses the following four main subjects:

1) Formal definition of the term *dhātu*: the dhātupāṭha-based definition
2) Semantic definition of the term *dhātu*: *kriyāvacano dhātuḥ* (*kriyā*-based definition)
3) Semantic definition of the term *dhātu*: *bhāvavacano dhātuḥ* (*bhāva*-based definition)
4) Roles to be played by the dhātupāṭha[1]

2. I use mainly the Rohatak edition (R), referring to the Nirṇayasāgara Press edition: first and second (NSP[1]; NSP[2]) and Kielhorn's edition (K) as necessary. References are given to volumes, pages, and lines of Kielhorn [1980–85] = Abhyankar [1962–72].

3. In addition to being divided into four parts, the text is paragraphed: each paragraph, numbered, is given its very brief outline which shows its content.

---

[1] See Section 3.

Aṣṭādhyāyī **1.3.1** ***bhūvādayo dhātavaḥ*** //

I. Formal definition of the term *dhātu*: the dhātupāṭha-based definition

1.1. Preliminary to the discussion on the dhātupāṭha-based definition: justification of the interpretation of *A*1.3.1 as the dhātupāṭha-based definition (*pāṭhena dhātusaṃjñā*)

1.1.1. Segmentation of the compound *bhūvādi* into *bhū*, *v*, and *ādi*

[Bh. 1 (I.253.2–3)]
kuto 'yaṃ vakāraḥ / yadi tāvat saṃhitayā nirdeśaḥ kriyate bhvādaya iti bhavitavyam / athāsaṃhitayā bhū ādaya iti bhavitavyam /

1.1.2. Treatment of the sound -*v*- as being *maṅgalārtha*

[Bh. 2 (I.253.3–7)]
ata uttaraṃ paṭhati /
Ślokavārttika ab: ***bhūvādīnāṃ vakāro 'yaṃ maṅgalārthaḥ prayujyate /***
māṅgalika ācāryo mahataḥ śāstraughasya maṅgalārthaṃ vakāram āgamaṃ prayuṅkte / maṅgalādīni maṅgalamadhyāni maṅgalāntāni hi śāstrāṇi prathante vīrapuruṣāṇī ca bhavanty āyuṣmatpuruṣāṇi cādhyetāraś ca maṅgalayuktā yathā syur iti /

1.1.3. Indication of the dhātupāṭha by a bahuvrīhi compound with -*ādi*: the bahuvrīhi of *bhū* and *ādi* with the augment *v*

[Bh. 3 (I.253.7–12)]
athādigrahaṇaṃ kimartham / yadi tāvat paṭhyante nārtha ādigrahaṇena / anyatrāpi hy ayaṃ paṭhann ādigrahaṇaṃ na karoti /
kvānyatra /
mṛḍamṛdagudhakuṣakliśavadavasaḥ ktveti /
atha na paṭhyante natarām artha ādigrahaṇena / na hy apaṭhitāḥ śakyā ādigrahaṇena viśeṣayitum /
evaṃ tarhi siddhe sati yad ādigrahaṇaṃ karoti taj jñāpayaty ācāryo 'sti ca pāṭho bāhyaś ca sūtrād iti /

kim etasya jñāpane prayojanam /
pāṭhena dhātusaṃjñety etad upapannaṃ bhavati /

1.2. Difficulty 1: over-application of the term *dhātu* to non-verbs homophonous with verbs

1.2.1. vārttika 1 and its exposition

[Bh. 4 (I.253.13–16)]
Vt. 1: pāṭhena dhātusaṃjñāyāṃ samānaśabdapratiṣedhaḥ //
pāṭhena dhātusaṃjñāyāṃ samānaśabdānāṃ pratiṣedho vaktavyaḥ / yā iti dhātuḥ, yā ity ābantaḥ / vā iti dhātuḥ, vā iti nipātaḥ / nu iti dhātuḥ, nu iti pratyayaś ca nipātaś ca / div iti dhātuḥ, div iti prātipadikam /

1.2.2. Undesired occurrence of kṛtya affixes after non-verbs and its avoidance

[Bh. 5 (I.253.16–19)]
kiṃ ca syād yady eteṣām api dhātusaṃjñā syāt / dhātor iti tavyadādīnām utpattiḥ prasajyeta /
naiṣa doṣaḥ / sādhane tavyadādayo vidhīyante sādhanaṃ ca kriyāyāḥ / kriyābhāvāt sādhanābhāvaḥ / sādhanābhāvāt satyām api dhātusaṃjñāyāṃ tavyadādayo na bhaviṣyanti /

1.2.3. Undesired application of *A*6.4.140 to *yā* in *yāḥ paśya* and its avoidance

[Bh. 6 (I.253.19–20)]
iha tarhi—yāḥ paśya—āto dhātor iti lopaḥ prasajyeta /
naiṣa doṣaḥ / anāpa ityevaṃ saḥ /

1.2.4. Undesired prohibition on the application of *A*1.2.45 to the nipāta *vā* and its avoidance

[Bh. 7 (I.253.20–23)]
asya tarhi vāśabdasya nipātasyādhātur iti prātipadikasaṃjñāyāḥ pratiṣedhaḥ prasajyeta / aprātipadikatvāt svādyutpattir na syāt /
naiṣa doṣaḥ / nipātasyānarthakasya prātipadikatvaṃ coditaṃ tatrānarthagrahaṇaṃ na kariṣyate, nipātaḥ prātipadikam ity eva /

1.2.5. Undesired application of *A*6.4.77 to the string *trasnu* + *au* and its avoidance

[Bh. 8 (I.253.23–254.3)]
iha tarhi—trasnū iti aci śnudhātubhruvāṃ yvor iyaṅuvaṅāv ity uvaṅādeśaḥ prasajyeta /
naiṣa doṣaḥ / ācāryapravṛttir jñāpayati na pratyayasyovaṅādeśo bhavatīti / yad ayaṃ tatra śnugrahaṇaṃ karoti /

1.2.6. Undesired prohibition of the application of *A*1.2.45 to the nominal base *div* and its unavoidability: absolute necessity to lay a prohibition saying that non-verbs homophonous with verbs are not called *dhātu*

[Bh. 9 (I.254.3–9)]
asya tarhi divśabdasyādhātur iti prātipadikasaṃjñāyāḥ pratiṣedhaḥ prasajyeta / aprātipadikatvāt svādyutpattir na syāt /
naiṣa doṣaḥ / ācāryapravṛttir jñāpayaty utpadyante divśabdāt svādaya iti / yad ayaṃ divaḥ sāv auttvaṃ śāsti /
naitad asti jñāpakam / asti hy anyad etasya vacane prayojanam / kim /
divśabdo yat prātipadikaṃ tadartham etat syāt—akṣadyūr iti /
na vā atreṣyate /
aniṣṭaṃ ca prāpnotīṣṭaṃ ca na sidhyati /
evaṃ tarhi—ananubandhakagrahaṇe na sānubandhakasyety evam etasya na bhaviṣyati /
evam apy ananubandhako divśabo nāstīti kṛtvā sānubandhakasya grahaṇaṃ vijñāsyate /

1.3. Difficulty 2: specific mention of the extent of each unit

1.3.1. vārttika 2 and its exposition

[Bh. 10 (I.254.10–12)]
Vt. 2: parimāṇagrahaṇaṃ ca //
parimāṇagrahaṇaṃ ca kartavyam / iyān avadhir dhātusaṃjño bhavatīti vaktavyam / kuto hy etad bhūśabdo dhātusaṃjño bhaviṣyati na punar bhvedhaśabda[2] *iti /*

II. Semantic definition of the term *dhātu*: *kriyāvacano dhātuḥ* (*kriyā*-based definition)

2.1. Preliminary to the discussion on the *kriyā*-based definition: epistemological and ontological status of the action (*kriyā*) and a way to establish that verbs like *pac* denote actions

2.1.1. Introduction of the *kriyā*-based definition

[Bh. 11 (I.254.13)]
yadi punaḥ—kriyāvacano dhātur ity etal lakṣaṇaṃ kriyeta /

2.1.2. Ontological question about an action: Is an action distinct from a substance?

[Bh. 12 (I.254.13)]
kā punaḥ kriyā /

2.1.3. Explaining words with words: *kriyā*, *īhā*, *ceṣṭā*, *vyāpāra*

[Bh. 13 (I.254.13–14)]
īhā /
kā punar īhā /
ceṣṭā /
kā punaś ceṣṭā /
vyāpāraḥ /

---

[2] R, K: *bhvedhśabda*. I follow NSP[1,2]. See Section 4 Part 1, fn. 36.

2.1.4. Demand for showing the distinction between action and substance

[Bh. 14 (I.254.14–15)]
sarvathā bhavāñ chabdenaiva śabdān ācaṣṭe—na kiṃcid arthajātaṃ nidarśayaty evaṃjātīyikā kriyeti /

2.1.5. Epistemological status of an action: imperceptibility and being known through inference

[Bh. 15 (I.254.15–17)]
kriyā nāmeyam atyantāparidṛṣṭā / aśakyā kriyā piṇḍībhūtā nidarśayituṃ, yathā garbho nirluṭhitaḥ / sāsāv anumānagamyā /[3]

2.1.5.1. Question about that from which an action is inferred

[Bh. 16 (I.254.17)]
ko 'sāv anumānaḥ /

2.1.5.2. Three types of inference: inference of the distinction between action and substance; inference of an action from the use of finite verb forms; inference of an action from its result

[Bh. 17 (I.254.17–19)]
iha sarveṣu sādhaneṣu saṃnihiteṣu kadācit pacatīty etad bhavati, kadācin na bhavati /
yasmin saṃnihite pacatīty etad bhavati sā nūnaṃ kriyā /[4]
atha vā yayā devadatta iha bhūtvā pāṭaliputre bhavati sā nūnaṃ kriyā /

---

[3]We find the same statement in *MBh* ad *A*3.2.102 (II.114.10–11), 115 (II.120.9–10). In his *Pradīpa* on *A*1.3.1 Kaiyaṭa points out that we may have two readings: *garbho nirluṭhitaḥ* and *garbho 'nirluṭhitaḥ*. See Section 4. Part 2, fn. 6.

[4]Kaiyaṭa records in his *Pradīpa* that there is the following variant reading: *yasmin sādhane saṃnihite* instead of *yasmin saṃnihite*. R, K: *yasmin sādhane saṃnihite*. I follow NSP[1,2]. See Section 4, Part 2, fn. 15.

2.1.6. Proof of the verb *pac* denoting an action: the question-and-answeı *kiṃ karoti—pacati*

[Bh. 18 (I.254.20–21)]
kathaṃ punar jñāyate kriyāvacanāḥ pacādaya iti /
yad eteṣāṃ karotinā sāmānādhikaraṇyam / kiṃ karoti, pacati / kiṃ kariṣyati, pakṣyati / kim akārṣīt, apākṣīd iti /

2.2. Difficulty 1: over-application of the term *dhātu* to a verb-affix complex and a preverb-verb complex because of their being meaning-conveyers in actual usage

[Bh. 19 (I.254.21–26)]
tatra—
Vt. 3: kriyāvacana upasargapratyayapratiṣedhaḥ //
kriyāvacane dhātāv upasargapratyayayoḥ pratiṣedho vaktavyaḥ / pacati prapacati /
kiṃ punaḥ kāraṇaṃ prāpnoti /
Vt. 4: saṅghātenārthagateḥ //
saṅghātena hy artho gamyate saprakṛtikena sapratyayakena sopasargeṇa ca /

2.3. Difficulty 2: inapplicability to the verbs *as*, *bhū*, *vid*

[Bh. 20 (I.255.1–4)]
Vt. 5: astibhavatividyatīnāṃ ca dhātutvam //
astibhavatividyatīnāṃ ca[5] *dhātusaṃjñā vaktavyā /*
yathā hi bhavatā karotinā pacādīnāṃ sāmānādhikaraṇyaṃ nidarśitaṃ, na tathāstyādīnāṃ nidarśyate / na hi bhavati—kiṃ karoti, astīti /

2.4. Solution for difficulty 1: a verb-affix complex

2.4.1. Attribution of meaning difference to components of a complex

[Bh. 21 (I.255.5–10)]
Vt. 6A: pratyayārthasyāvyatirekāt prakṛtyantareṣu /

---

[5] NSP[1,2] and K lack *ca*.

pratyayārthasyāvyatirekāt prakṛtyantareṣu manyāmahe dhātur eva kriyām āheti /
pacati paṭhati / *prakṛtyartho 'nyaś cānyaś ca pratyayārthaḥ sa eva* /
Vt.* 6B: *dhātoś cārthābhedāt pratyayāntareṣu /
dhātoś cārthābhedāt pratyayāntareṣu manyāmahe dhātur eva kriyām āheti / *paktiḥ pacanaṃ pāka iti* /[6] *pratyayārtho 'nyaś cānyaś ca bhavati prakṛtyarthaḥ sa eva* /

2.4.2. Reasoning from *anvaya* and *vyatireka*: meaning assignment

[Bh. 22 (I.255.10–20)]
kathaṃ punar jñāyate—ayaṃ prakṛtyarthaḥ, ayaṃ pratyayārtha iti /
Vt.* 6C: *siddhan tv anvayavyatirekābhyām //
[*siddham etat* / *katham* /][7] *anvayāc ca vyatirekāc ca* /
ko 'sāv anvayo vyatireko vā / *iha pacatīty ukte kaścic chabdaḥ śrūyate pacchabdaś cakārāntaḥ, atiśabdaś ca pratyayaḥ* / *artho 'pi kaścid gamyate viklittiḥ kartṛtvam ekatvaṃ ca* /
paṭhatīty ukte kaścic chabdo hīyate, kaścid upajāyate, kaścid anvayī / *pacchabdo hīyate, paṭhśabda upajāyate, atiśabdo 'nvayī* / *artho 'pi kaścid dhīyate, kaścid upajāyate, kaścid anvayī* / *viklittir hīyate, paṭhikriyopajāyate, kartṛtvaṃ caikatvaṃ cānvayī* /
te manyāmahe—yaḥ śabdo hīyate tasyāsāv artho yo 'rtho hīyate, yaḥ śabda upajāyate tasyāsāv artho yo 'rtha upajāyate, yaḥ śabdo 'nvayī tasyāsāv artho yo 'rtho 'nvayī /

2.4.3. Limits of the *anvaya-vyatireka* method: synonyms and homonyms, and the negation of verbs and affixes following them being *sāmānyaśabdas* 'generic words'

[Bh. 23 (I.255.20–256.2)]
viṣama upanyāsaḥ / *bahavo hi śabdā ekārthā bhavanti* / *tad yathā—indraḥ śakraḥ puruhūtaḥ purandaraḥ* / *kanduḥ koṣṭhaḥ kusūla iti* / *ekaś ca śabdo bahvarthaḥ* / *tad yathā—akṣāḥ pādā māṣā iti* /

---

[6] R, NSP[1,2]: *paktiḥ pacanaṃ pāka iti*; K: *paktā pacanam pāka iti*. I have adopted the former reading in accordance with Nāgeśa's comment on this passage. See Section 3, fn. 18.

[7] Supplied in R. *MBh* on *vt.* 9 ad *A*1.2.45 reads: *siddhaṃ ceti* / *katham* / *anvayāc ca vyatirekāc ca*.

ataḥ kiṃ na sādhīyo 'rthavattā siddhā bhavati /
nāpi brūmo 'rthavattā na sidhyatīti / varṇitā hy arthavattānvayavyatirekābhyām eva / tatra kuta etad ayaṃ prakṛtyartho 'yaṃ pratyayārtha iti, na punaḥ prakṛtir evobhāv arthau brūyāt pratyaya eva vā / sāmānyaśabdā eta evaṃ syuḥ / sāmānyaśabdāś ca nāntareṇa prakaraṇaṃ viśeṣaṃ vā viśeṣeṣv avatiṣṭhante / yatas tu khalu niyogataḥ pacatīty ukte svabhāvataḥ kasmiṃścid viśeṣe pacatiśabdo vartate 'to manyāmahe—neme sāmānyaśabdā iti / na cet sāmānyaśabdāḥ prakṛtiḥ prakṛtyarthe vartate, pratyayaḥ pratyayārthe /

2.5. Solution for difficulty 1: a preverb-verb complex

2.5.1. *prapacati* (where a verb deviates from a preverb): establishment of the relation of the preverb *pra* to its meaning through the *anvaya-vyatireka* method, and *adhyeti/adhīte* (where a verb does not deviate from a preverb): establishment of the preverb *adhi* to its meaning through inference

[Bh. 24 (I.256.3–8)]
Vt. 7: kriyāviśeṣaka upasargaḥ //
pacatīti kriyā gamyate, tāṃ pro viśinaṣṭi / yady api tāvad atraitac chakyate vaktuṃ yatra dhātur upasargaṃ vyabhicarati / yatra na khalu taṃ vyabhicarati tatra katham adhyeti adhīta iti /
yady apy atra dhātur upasargaṃ na vyabhicarati upasargas tu dhātuṃ vyabhicarati / te manyāmahe—ya evāsyādher anyatrārthaḥ sa ihāpīti /
kaḥ punar anyatrādher arthaḥ /
adhir uparibhāve vartate /

2.5.2. *pratiṣṭhate* (where a meaning, totally separate from the one understood when a verb is used without a preverb, is understood when the verb is used with the preverb): establishment of the relation of the preverb *pra* to its meaning through familiarity and inference, and the polysemy of the verb

[Bh. 25 (I.256.8–16)]
iha tarhi vyaktam arthāntaraṃ gamyate—tiṣṭhati pratiṣṭhata iti / tiṣṭhatīti vrajikriyāyā nivṛttiḥ, pratiṣṭhata iti vrajikriyā gamyate / te

manyāmahe—upasargakṛtam etad yenātra vrajikriyā gamyata iti /
pro 'yaṃ dṛṣṭāpacāra ādikarmaṇi vartate / *na cedaṃ nāsti—bahvarthā api dhātavo bhavantīti* / *tad yathā—vapiḥ prakiraṇe dṛṣṭaś chedane cāpi vartate—keśaśmaśru vapatīti* / *īḍiḥ stuticodanāyācñāsu dṛṣṭaḥ preraṇe cāpi vartate—agnír vā́ itó vṛ́ṣṭim ī́ṭṭe marúto 'mútaś cyāvayantīti*[8] / *karotir abhūtaprādurbhāve dṛṣṭo nirmalīkaraṇe cāpi vartate—pṛṣṭhaṃ kuru pādau kuru* / *unmṛdāneti gamyate* / *nikṣepaṇe cāpi vartate—kaṭe kuru ghaṭe kuru aśmānam itaḥ kuru* / *sthāpayeti gamyate* /
evam ihāpi tiṣṭhatir eva vrajikriyām āha tiṣṭhatir eva vrajikriyāyā nivṛttim /

III. Semantic definition of the term *dhātu*: *bhāvavacano dhātuḥ* (*bhāva*-based definition)

3.1. Preliminary to the discussion on the *bhāva*-based definition: inquiry into the meaning of the term *bhāva*, looking into the evidence that verbs denote *bhāva*, and pursuit of the possibility of *A*1.3.1 being a semantic definition

3.1.1. Proposal of the *bhāva*-based definition as a solution for difficulty 2 (*Bh.* 20)

[Bh. 26 (I.256.16–18)]
ayaṃ tarhi doṣaḥ—astibhavatividyatīnāṃ dhātutvam iti /
yadi punar bhāvavacano dhātur ity etal lakṣaṇaṃ kriyeta /

3.1.2. Usage to establish that verbs like *pac* denote *bhāva*: *bhavati pacati, bhavati pakṣyati, bhavaty apākṣīt*; the relation of concurrence (*sāmānādhikaraṇya*)

[Bh. 27 (I.256.18–20)]
kathaṃ punar jñāyate—bhāvavacanāḥ pacādaya iti /
yad eteṣāṃ bhavatinā sāmānādhikaraṇyaṃ—bhavati pacati, bhavati pakṣyati, bhavaty apākṣīd iti /

---

[8] See Rau [1985: 9].

3.1.3. Interpretation of the term *bhāva* 1: existence (*bhavanaṃ bhāvaḥ*); inapplicability to verbs for non-existence

[Bh. 28 (I.256.20–23)]
kaḥ punar bhāvaḥ /
bhavateḥ svapadārtho bhavanaṃ bhāva iti /
yadi bhavateḥ svapadārtho bhavanaṃ bhāvo vipratiṣiddhānāṃ dhātusaṃjñā na prāpnoti—bhedaḥ chedaḥ / anyo hi bhāvo 'nyo 'bhāvaḥ / ātaś cānyo bhāvo 'nyo 'bhāva iti, yo hi yasya bhāvam icchati sa na tasyābhāvaṃ, yasya cābhāvaṃ na tasya bhāvam /

3.1.4. No usage to show the relation of concurrence in terms of the relation of universal and particular: *kriyāviśeṣa* and **bhāvaviśeṣa*

[Bh. 29 (I.256.23–27)]
pacādīnāṃ ca dhātusaṃjñā na prāpnoti / yathā hi bhavatā kriyāvacane dhātau karotinā pacādīnāṃ sāmānādhikaraṇyaṃ nidarśitaṃ, na tathā bhāvavacane dhātau nidarśyate /
karotiḥ pacādīnāṃ sarvān kālān sarvān puruṣān sarvāṇi vacanāny anuvartate, bhavatiḥ punar vartamānakālaṃ caikatvaṃ ca /

3.1.5. Analysis of the usage *bhavati pacati*, *bhavati pakṣyati*, *bhavaty apākṣīt*: the relation of what is to be accomplished and what does the accomplishing (*sādhyasādhanabhāva*)

[Bh. 30 (I.256.27–257.5)]
kā tarhīyaṃ vācoyuktiḥ—bhavati pacati, bhavati pakṣyati, bhavaty apākṣīd iti / eṣaiṣā vācoyuktiḥ—pacādayaḥ kriyā bhavatikriyāyāḥ kartryo bhavanti / yady api tāvad atraitac chakyate vaktuṃ yatrānyā cānyā ca kriyā / yatra khalu saiva kriyā tatra katham—bhaved api bhavet, syād api syād iti / atrāpy anyatvam asti / kutaḥ / kālabhedāt sādhanabhedāc ca / ekasyātra bhavater bhavatiḥ sādhanaṃ sarvakālaś ca pratyayaḥ / aparasya bāhyaṃ sādhanaṃ vartamānakālaś ca pratyayaḥ / yāvatātrāpy anyatvam asti, pacādayaś ca kriyāḥ bhavatikriyāyāḥ kartryo bhavantīti /

3.1.6. Interpretation of the term *bhāva* 2: what comes into being (*bhavatīti bhāvaḥ*); over-application to nominal bases

[Bh. 31 (I.257.5–8)]
astv ayaṃ kartṛsādhanaḥ—bhavatīti bhāva iti / kiṃ kṛtaṃ bhavati / vipratiṣiddhānāṃ dhātusaṃjñā siddhā bhavati / bhaved vipratiṣiddhānāṃ dhātusaṃjñā siddhā syāt, prātipadikānām api tu[9] *prāpnoti vṛkṣaḥ plakṣa iti / kiṃ kāraṇam / etāny api hi bhavanti /*

3.1.7. Interpretation of the term *bhāva* 3: what is brought into being (*bhāvyate yaḥ sa bhāva iti*); over-application to nominal bases (relative terms), and the introduction of the notion of *svabhāva*

[Bh. 32 (I.257.8–10)]
evaṃ tarhi karmasādhano bhaviṣyati—bhāvyate yaḥ sa bhāva iti / kriyā caiva hi bhāvyate svabhāvasiddhaṃ tu dravyam /
evam api bhavet keṣāṃcin na syād yāni na bhāvyante / ye tv ete sambandhiśabdās teṣāṃ prāpnoti—mātā pitā bhrāteti /

3.1.8. Demand of the device to avoid the over-application to nominal bases

[Bh. 33 (I.257.10–11)]
sarvathā vayaṃ prātipadikaparyudāsān na mucyāmahe /

3.1.9. Acceptance of the term *bhāva* as signifying what comes into being (*bhavatīti bhāvaḥ*) on the assumption that the dhātupāṭha plays the role of preventing the over-application to nominal bases, and a proposal of the interpretation of *A*1.3.1 as the *bhāva*-based definition: the ṣaṣṭhī tatpuruṣa of *bhū* and *vādi*

[Bh. 34 (I.257.11–15)]
paṭhiṣyati hy ācāryo bhūvādipāṭhaḥ prātipadikāṇapayatyādinivṛttyartha[10] *iti / yāvatā paṭhiṣyati pacādayaś ca kriyā bhavatikriyāyāḥ kartryo*

---

[9] K lacks *tu*.

[10] NSP[1.2]: *prātipadikāṇavayatyādinivṛttyarthaḥ*; K, R: *prātipadikāṇapayatyādinivṛttyarthaḥ*. The latter reading has been adopted.

bhavantīti astv ayaṃ kartṛsādhanaḥ, bhavatīti bhāva iti /
kiṃ vaktavyam etat / na hi / katham anucyamānaṃ gaṃsyate /
etenaivābhihitaṃ sūtreṇa bhūvādayo dhātava iti /
katham /
nedam ādigrahaṇam / vader ayam auṇādika iñ kartṛsādhanaḥ—bhuvaṃ vadantīti bhūvādaya iti /

3.2. Difficulty 1: over-application to svārthika affixes

[Bh. 35 (I.257.16–18)]
***Vt.* 8: *bhāvavacane tadarthapratyayapratiṣedhaḥ* //**
bhāvavacane dhātau tadarthasya pratyayasya pratiṣedho vaktavyaḥ / śiṣye iti / kiṃ ca syāt / aśitīty āttvaṃ prasajyeta / tad dhi dhātor vihitam /

3.3. Difficulty 2: mutual dependence of the occurrence of an affix after a base and the understanding of the base as denoting *bhāva*

[Bh. 36 (I.257.19–22)]
***Vt.* 9: *itaretarāśrayaṃ ca pratyaye bhāvavacanatvaṃ tasmāc ca pratyayaḥ* //**
itaretarāśrayaṃ ca bhavati / ketaretarāśrayatā / pratyaye bhāvavacanatvaṃ tasmāc ca pratyayaḥ / utpanne hi pratyaye bhāvavacanatvaṃ gamyate, sa ca tāvad bhāvavacanād utpādyaḥ / tad etad iretarāśrayaṃ bhavati / itaretarāśrayāṇi ca kāryāṇi na prakalpante /

3.4. Solution of difficulty 2 (*Bh.* 36) on the basis of the perenniality of speech

[Bh. 37 (I.257.23–25)]
***Vt.* 10: *siddhaṃ tu nityaśabdatvād anāśritya bhāvavacanatvaṃ pratyayaḥ* //**
siddham etat / katham / nityaśabdatvāt / nityāḥ śabdāḥ / nityeṣu ca śabdeṣv anāśritya bhāvavacanatvaṃ pratyaya utpadyate /

3.5. Solution of difficulty 1 (*Bh.* 35) by revision

[Bh. 38 (I.258.1–6)]
Vt.* 11: *prathamabhāvagrahaṇaṃ ca //
prathamabhāvagrahaṇaṃ ca kartavyam / prathamaṃ yo bhāvam āheti / kutaḥ punaḥ prāthamyam / kiṃ śabdata āhosvid arthataḥ / kiṃ cātaḥ / yadi śabdataḥ, sanādīnāṃ dhātusaṃjñā na prāpnoti—putrīyati vastrīyatīti / athārthataḥ, siddhā sanādīnāṃ dhātusaṃjñā, sa eva tu doṣaḥ bhāvavacane tadarthapratyayapratiṣedha iti / evaṃ tarhi nāpi śabdato nāpy arthataḥ[11] */ kiṃ tarhy*[12]*abhidhānataḥ / sumadhyame 'bhidhāne yaḥ prathamaṃ bhāvam āha /*

IV. Roles to be played by the dhātupāṭha

4.1. Preliminary to the discussion on roles to be played by the dhātupāṭha: getting over difficulty 2 (*Bh.* 20) of the *kriyā*-based definition to establish the dhātupāṭha's roles other than that of supplying items to be called *dhātu*, and interpretation of *A*1.3.1 as both indicating the dhātupāṭha and defining the term *dhātu* semantically

4.1.1. Equality of the *kriyā*-based definitions with the *bhāva*-based definition except for its inapplicability to the verbs *as*, *bhū*, *vid*

[Bh. 39 (I.258.7–8)]
iha ya eva bhāvavacane dhātau doṣās ta eva kriyāvacane 'pi / tatra ta eva parihārāḥ / tatredam aparihṛtam—astibhavatividyatīnāṃ dhātutvam iti /

4.1.2. Solution of difficulty 2 (*Bh.* 20)

4.1.2.1. Proposal of a new notion of *kriyā*: behavioral *kriyā* (*kārakāṇāṃ pravṛttiviśeṣaḥ kriyā*) and illustration of the thesis that the meaning of the verb *as* consists in behavioral *kriyā*

[Bh. 40 (I.258.8–13)]
tasya parihāraḥ / kāṃ punaḥ kriyāṃ bhavān matvāha—astibhavativi-

---

[11] K: *naivārthato nāpi śabdataḥ*. I have followed R, NSP[1,2].
[12] For the punctuation for *kiṃ tarhi*, see Section 4, Part 3, fn. 21.

dyatīnāṃ dhātusaṃjñā na prāpnoti / kiṃ yat tad devadattaḥ kaṃsapātryāṃ pāṇinaudanaṃ bhuṅkta iti /
na brūmaḥ kārakāṇi kriyeti / kiṃ tarhi[13] *kārakāṇāṃ pravṛttiviśeṣaḥ kriyā / anyathā ca kārakāṇi śuṣkaudane pravartante, anyathā ca māṃsaudane /*
yady evaṃ siddhāstibhavatividyatīnāṃ dhātusaṃjñā / anyathā hi kārakāṇy astau pravartante 'nyathā hi mriyatau /

4.1.2.2. The *Nirukta* in testimony of the thesis that the meaning of the verb *as* is an action, and proof of the thesis by the property of an action: exclusion of other actions

[Bh. 41 (I.258.13–18)]
ṣaḍ bhāvavikārā iti ha smāha bhagavān[14] *vārṣyāyaṇiḥ / jāyate 'sti vipariṇamate vardhate 'pakṣīyate vinaśyatīti /*
sarvathā sthita ity atra dhātusaṃjñā na prāpnoti / bāhyo hy etebhyas tiṣṭhatiḥ / evaṃ tarhi kriyāyāḥ kriyā nivartikā bhavati, dravyaṃ dravyasya nivartakam / evaṃ hi kaścit kaṃcit pṛcchati—kimavastho devadattasya vyādhir iti / sa āha—vardhata iti / apara āha—apakṣīyata iti / apara āha—sthita iti / sthita ity ukte vardhateś cāpakṣīyateś ca nivṛttir bhavati /

4.1.2.3. Proof of the above-stated thesis by the property of an action: association with time

[Bh. 42 (I.258.19–20)]
atha vā nāntareṇa kriyāṃ bhūtabhaviṣyadvartamānāḥ kālā vyajyante / astyādibhiś cāpi bhūtabhaviṣyadvartamānakālā vyajyante /

---

[13] For the punctuation for *kiṃ tarhi*, see Section 2. fn. 8.
[14] NSP[1,2] lacks *bhagavān*.

4.1.2.4. Denial of the disproof of the thesis in question by the non-occurrence of the question-and-answer *kiṃ karoti—asti*: a question-and-answer rule

[Bh. 43 (I.258.20–21)]
atha vā nānyat pṛṣṭenānyad ākhyeyam[15] / *tena na bhaviṣyati—kiṃ karoti, astīti* /

4.1.3. Interpretation of *A*1.3.1 as both indicating the dhātupāṭha and providing a semantic definition (*bhvādaya iti ca vādaya iti ca*)

4.1.3.1. Two approaches to *A*1.3.1: *vā* as a meaningful unit (the *kriyā*-based definition) or *bhū* as a meaningful unit (the *bhāva*-based definition)

[Bh. 44 (I.258.22–23)]
atha yady eva kriyāvacano dhātur ity eṣa pakṣo 'thāpi bhāvavacano dhātur iti, kiṃ gatam etad iyatā sūtreṇa, āhosvid anyatarasmin pakṣe bhūyaḥ sūtraṃ kartavyam /

4.1.3.2. Grammatical explanation of the bahuvrīhi *bhūvādi*: *bhūvau ādī yeṣām*: two *ādis* (*vyavasthā-ādi* and *prakāra-ādi*), and two ways of interpreting *A*1.3.1: *bhū ityevamādayo vā ityevaṃprakārāḥ* (*bhvādigaṇa* and the *kriyā*-based definition) and *vā ityevamādayo bhū ityevaṃprakārāḥ* (*vādigaṇa* and the *bhāva*-based definition)

[Bh. 45 (I.258.23–259.3)]
gatam ity āha / *katham* / *ayam ādiśabdo 'sty eva vyavasthāyāṃ vartate, tad yathā—devadattādīn samupaviṣṭān āha devadattādaya ānīyantām iti* / *ta utthāpyānīyante* / *asti prakāre vartate, tad yathā—devadattādaya āḍhyā abhirūpā darśanīyāḥ pakṣavantaḥ* / *devadattaprakārā iti gamyate* /
pratyekaṃ cādiśabdaḥ parisamāpyate—bhvādaya iti ca vādaya iti ca / *tad yadā tāvat kriyāvacano dhātur ity eṣa pakṣas tadā bhū ity*

[15] R, NSP[1]: *nānyat pṛṣṭe nānyad ākhyeyam.* K, NSP[2]: *nānyat pṛṣṭenānyad ākhyeyam.* The latter reading should be adopted.

atra ya ādiśabdaḥ sa vyavasthāyāṃ vartate, vā ity atra ya ādiśabdaḥ sa prakāre, bhū ityevamādayo vā ityevaṃprakārā iti /
yadā tu bhāvavacano dhātur ity eṣa pakṣas tadā vā ity atra ya ādiśabdaḥ sa vyavasthāyām, bhū ity atra ya ādiśabdaḥ sa prakāre, vā ityevamādayo bhū ityevaṃprakārā iti /

4.2. Roles to be played by the dhātupāṭha

4.2.1. Roles supplementary to a semantic definition: prevention of its over-application to nominal bases and corruptions, and citation of no instance of the over-application to nominal bases

[Bh. 46 (I.259.3–7)]
yadi tarhi lakṣaṇaṃ kriyate, nedānīṃ pāṭhaḥ kartavyaḥ /
kartavyaś ca /
kiṃ prayojanam /
Vt. 12: bhūvādipāṭhaḥ prātipadikāṇapayatyādinivṛttyarthaḥ[16] //
bhūvādipāṭhaḥ kartavyaḥ /
kiṃ prayojanam /
prātipadikāṇapayatyādinivṛttyarthaḥ[17] / *prātipadikanivṛttyartha āṇapayatyādinivṛttyarthaś*[18] *ca* /
ke punar āṇapayatyādayaḥ[19] /
āṇapayati[20] *vaṭṭati vaḍḍhatīti*[21] /

4.2.2. Roles presupposed by Pāṇini's grammar: to make known accentuations of base vowels and markers, and difficulty involved: restriction on verbs to be listed

[Bh. 47 (I.259.8–11)]
Vt. 13: svarānubandhajñāpanāya ca //
svarānubandhajñāpanāya ca pāṭhaḥ kartavyaḥ / *svarānubandhāṃś*

---

[16] NSP[1.2]: *prātipadikāṇavayatyādinivṛttyarthaḥ.*
[17] NSP[1.2]: *prātipadikāṇavayatyādinivṛttyarthaḥ.*
[18] NSP[1.2]: *āṇavayatyādinivṛttyarthaś.*
[19] NSP[1.2]: *āṇavayatyādayaḥ.*
[20] NSP[1.2]: *āṇavayati.*
[21] NSP[1.2]: *vaḍḍhayatīti.*

ca jñāsyāmīti / na hy antareṇa pāṭhaṃ svarā anubandhā vā śakyā vijñātum /
ye tv ete nyāyyavikaraṇā udāttā ananubandhakāḥ paṭhyanta eteṣāṃ[22] *pāṭhaḥ śakyo 'kartum /*

4.3. Misuse (*viparyāsa*): respect for the usage of the śiṣṭas and no absolute need of the dhātupāṭha

[Bh. 48 (I.259.11–14)]
eteṣām apy avaśyam āṇapayatyādinivṛttyarthaḥ[23] *pāṭhaḥ kartavyaḥ / na kartavyaḥ / śiṣṭaprayogād āṇapayatyādīnāṃ nivṛttir bhaviṣyati / sa cāvaśyaṃ śiṣṭaprayoga upāsyo ye 'pi paṭhyante teṣām api viparyāsanivṛttyarthaḥ / loke hi kṛṣyarthe kasiṃ prayuñjate, dṛśyarthe ca disim*[24] *//*

[22] NSP^{1,2}: *paṭhyante teṣām.*
[23] NSP^{1,2}: *āṇavayatyādinivṛttyarthaḥ.*
[24] K: *diśim.*

Bibliography

Abhyankar, Kashinath Vasudev

1960 *The Paribhāṣenduśekhara of Nāgojībhaṭṭa, edited and explained by F. Kielhorn. 2: translation and notes.* Poona: Bhandarkar Oriental Research Institute.

1962 *Tha Paribhāṣenduśekhara of Nāgojībhaṭṭa, edited critically with the commentary Tattvādarśa of MM. Vasudev Shastri Abhyankar.* 1. Poona: Bhandarkar Oriental Research Institute.

1962-72 *The Vyākaraṇa-mahābhāṣya of Patañjali, edited by F. Kielhorn, third edition, revised and furnished with additional readings, references and select critical notes by K. V. Abhyankar.* 3 vols. Poona: Bhandarkar Oriental Research Institute. 1: 1962; 2: 1965; 3: 1972.

1967 *Paribhāṣāsaṃgraha (a collection of original works on vyākaraṇa paribhāṣā), edited critically with an introduction and an index of paribhāṣās.* Bhandarkar Oriental Research Institute Series, 7. Poona: Bhandarkar Oriental Research Institute.

Abhyankar, Vasudev Shastri — Kashinath Vasudev Abhyankar

1938–54 *Śrīmad-bhagavat-patañjali-viracita-vyākaraṇa-mahābhāṣya, mūḷa āṇi marāṭhī bhāṣāntara; bhāṣāntara-kāra mahāmahopādhyāya Vāsudeva Śāstrī Abhyaṅkara, saṃpādaka Kāśīnātha Vāsudeva Abhyaṅkara.* Poona: Deccan Education Society.

Abhyankar, Kashinath Vasudev, and Ganesh Ambadas Joshi

1976 *Śrījaiminipraṇītaṃ Mīmāṃsādarśanam . . .* Ānandāśrama Sanskrit Series, 97. Pune: Ānandāśrama.

Aklujkar, Ashok

forthcoming

"Where do *lakṣaṇaika-cakṣuṣka* and *lakṣyaika-cakṣuṣka* apply?" *Journal of Indian Linguistics* (= *A. R. Kelkar Felicitation Volume*).

Aryendra Sharma, Khanderao Deshpande, and D. G. Padhye

1969-70 *Kāśikā, a commentary on Pāṇini's grammar by Vāmana and Jayāditya.* 2 vols. Sanskrit Academy Series, 17, 20. Hyderabad: Sanskrit Academy, Osmania University.

Aufrecht, Theodor

1859 *Ujjvaladatta's commentary on the uṇādisūtras, edited from a manuscript of the East India House.* Bonn: Marcus.

Bhadkamkar, H. M.

1985 *The Nirukta of Yāska (with Nighaṇṭu); edited with Durga's commentary; Vol. I.* Bombay Sanskrit and Prakrit Series, No. LXXIII. Reprint of 1918 edition. Poona: Bhandarkar Oriental Research Institute.

Bhāṇḍāri, Mādhava Śāstrī, Madan Mohan Pāṭhak, Nityānand Panta Parvatīya

1926 *Vaiyākaraṇa Siddhānta Laghu Mañjūsha by Mahāmahopādhyāya Śrī Nāgeśa Bhaṭṭa, with two commentaries, i.e., Kuñjikā of Durbalāchārya and Kalā of Bālam Bhaṭṭa.* Chowkhamba Sanskrit Series, 44. Benares: Chowkhamba. Reprint: Varanasi: Chowkhamba, 1989.

Bronkhorst, Johannes.

1981 "Meaning entries in Pāṇini's Dhātupāṭha." *Journal of Indian Philosophy* 9: 335-357.

1987 *Mahābhāṣyadīpikā of Bhartṛhari, Fascicule IV: Āhnika I.* Post-Graduate and Research Department Series, 28. Poona: Bhandarkar Oriental Research Institute.

Cardona, George

1970 Review of R. Rocher [1968], *Lingua* 25: 210-22.

1976 *Pāṇini: A Survey of Research.* Trends in Linguistics State-of-the-Art Reports, 6. The Hague: Mouton. Indian Edition, 1980: Delhi: Motilal Banarsidass.

1980 See Cardona [1976].

1981 "On reasoning from *anvaya* and *vyatireka* in early Advaita." In *Studies in Indian Philosophy: A Memorial Volume in Honour of Pandit Sukhlalji Sanghvi* (L. D. Series, 84), ed. Dalsukh Malvania and Nagin J. Shah, 79–104. Ahmedabad: L. D. Institute of Indology.

1983 *Linguistic Analysis and Some Indian Traditions* (Pandit Shripad Shastri Deodhar Memorial Lectures [First Series]). Bhandarkar Oriental Research Institute Post-graduate and Research Series, 20. Pune: Bhandarkar Oriental Research Institute.

1984 "On the Mahābhāṣya evidence for a Pāṇinīya Dhātupāṭha without meaning entries." In *Amṛtadhārā: Professor R. N. Dandekar Felicitation Volume*, ed. S. D. Joshi, 79–84. Delhi: Ajanta Publications.

1988 *Pāṇini: His Work and its Traditions, Volume 1: Background and Introduction.* Delhi: Motilal Banarsidass.

1991 "A path yet taken: Some Indian arguments concerning time." *Journal of the American Oriental Society* 111: 445-464.

1992 "Indian grammatical traditions and historical linguistics." In *Reconstructing Languages and Cultures* (Trends in Linguistics, Studies and Monographs, 58), ed. Edgar C. Polomé and Werner Winter, 239–259. Berlin, New York: Mouton de Gruyter.

1997 *Pānini: His Work and its Traditions, Part I: General Introduction and Background,* Second edition, revised and enlarged. Delhi: Motilal Banarsidass.

1998 "On *kiṁ tarhi* in the Mahābhāṣya." In *Mír Curad: Studies in Honor of Carvert Watkins,* ed. Jay Jasanoff, H. Craig Melchert, and Lisi Oliver, 63–73. Innsbruck: Institut für Sprachwissenschaft der Universität Innsbruck.

1999a "Approaching the Vākyapadīya." *Journal of the American Oriental Society* 119: 88-125.

1999b *Recent Research in Pāṇinian Studies.* Delhi: Motilal Banarsidass.

2002 "Indo-Aryan and historical linguistics: Observable change and grammarians' insights." *Journal of the Asiatic Society* 44.4: 1-48.

Chakravarti, Srish Chandra

1919 *The Dhātu-pradeepa by Maitreya-rakṣita; edited with annotations.* Savitarāya-smṛtirakṣaṇa-grantha-mālā, 2. Rajshahi: The Varendra Research Society.

Chaturvedi, Mithilesh

2001 *Vṛttisamuddeśa of Bhartṛhari's Vākyapadīya: A Study.* Delhi: Shivalik Prakashan.

Deshpande, Madhav Murlidhar

1991 "Prototypes in Pāṇinian syntax." *Journal of the American Oriental Society* 111: 465-480.

1993 "The changing notion of Śiṣṭa from Patañjali to Bhartṛhari." In *Proceedings of the First International Conference on Bhartṛhari, University of Poona, January 6-8, 1992* (*Asiatische Studien/Études Asiatiques* 47.1), ed. Saroja Bhate and Johannes Bronkhorst, 95–115. Bern: Peter Lang, 1993.

Dwarikadas Shastri

1964 *The Mādhavīya Dhātuvṛtti (a treatise on Sanskrit roots based on the dhātupāṭha of Pāṇini) by Sāyaṇācārya.* Prāchya Bhāratī Series, 1. Varanasi: Prāchya Bhāratī Prakāshana. Reprint: Varanasi: Tara Book Agency, 1987.

Filliozat, Pierre-Sylvain

1975-86 *Le Mahābhāṣya de Patañjali avec le Pradīpa de Kaiyaṭa et l'Uddyota de Nāgeśa.* Publications de l'Institut Français de'Indologie, 54, 1-4. Pondichéry: Institut Français de'Indologie. 1 (1975): adhyāya 1, pāda 1, āhnika 1-4; 2 (1976): adhyāya 1, pāda 1, āhnika 5-7; 3 (1976): adhyāya 1, pāda 1, āhnika 8-9; 4 (1980): adhyāya 1, pāda 2; 5 (1986): adhyāya 1, pāda 3.

Giridhara Śarmā Caturveda and Parameśvarānanda Śarmā Bhāskara

1958-61 *Śrī-bhaṭṭojī-dīkṣita-viracitā vaiyākaraṇa-siddhānta-kaumudī śrīmadvāsudeva-dīkṣita-praṇītayā bālamano-ramākhya-vyākhyayā śrīmaj-jñānendra-sarasvatī-viracitayā tattva-bodhiny-ākhya-vyākhyayā ca sanāthitā.* 4 vols. Varanasi: Motilal Banarsidass.

Honda, Yoshichika

1993 "Bhartṛhari's definition of *kriyā*." In *Proceedings of the First International Conference on Bhartṛhari, University of Poona, January 6-8, 1992* (*Asiatische Studien/Études Asiatiques* 47.1), ed. Saroja Bhate and Johannes Bronkhorst, 141–154. Bern: Peter Lang, 1993.

Jambūvijaya, Muni

1966-88 *Dvādaśāraṃ Nayacakram of Ācārya Śrī Mallavādi Kṣamāśramaṇa with the Commentary Nyāyāgamānusāriṇī of Śrī Siṃhasūri Gaṇi Vādi Kṣamāśramaṇa . . . Edited with Critical Notes by Muni Jambūvijayajī.* 3 vols. Śrī Ātmānand Jain Granthamālā Series, 94. Bhavnagar: Sri Jain Atmanand Sabha.

Joshi (Jośi), Bhārgavaśāstrī Bhikājī

1942 *Patañjali's Vyākaraṇa Mahābhāṣya with Kaiyaṭa's Pradīpa and Nāgeśa's Uddyota; vol. IV, edited with footnotes etc.* Bombay: Nirnaya-Sagar Press.

1945 *Patañjali's Vyākaraṇa Mahābhāṣya with Kaiyaṭa's Pradīpa and Nāgeśa's Uddyota; vol. V, edited with footnotes etc.* Bombay: Nirnaya-Sagar Press.

1951 *Śrīmad-bhagavat-patañjali-maharṣi-praṇīte vyākaraṇa-mahābhāṣye navāhnikam, aṣṭādhyāyī-prathamādhyāya-prathama-pāda-vyākhyānam, śrīmad-upādhyāya-kaiyaṭa-nirmita-pradīpa-prakāśitam, sarva-tantra-svatantra-śrīman-nāgeśabhaṭṭa-viracitoddyotodbhāsitam; . . . ṭippaṇa-pāṭha-bhedādi-pradarśana-puraskāreṇa pariṣkṛtam.* [vol. 1] Bombay: Nirnaya-Sagar Press.

Joshi/Roodbergen. Joshi, S. D. and J.A.F. Roodbergen

1969 *Patañjali's Vyākaraṇa-mahābhāṣya: Avyayībhāvatatpuruṣāhnika (P. 2.1.2-2.1.49); edited with translation and explanatory notes by S. D. Joshi in collaboration with J. A. F. Roodbergen.* Publications of the Centre of Advanced Study in Sanskrit-C 5. Poona: University of Poona.

1975 *Patañjali's Vyākaraṇa-mahābhāṣya: Kārakāhnika (P. 1.4.23-1.4.55): Introduction, Translation and Notes.* Publications of the Centre of Advanced Study in Sanskrit-C 10. Poona: University of Poona.

1980 *Patañjali's Vyākaraṇa-mahābhāṣya: Vibhaktyāhnika (P. 2.3.18-2.3.45); Introduction, Text, Translation and Notes.* Publications of the Centre of Advanced Study in Sanskrit-C 12. Pune: University of Poona.

1994 *The Aṣṭādhyāyī of Pāṇini with Translation and Explanatory Notes, Volume III (1.3.1–1.3.93).* Delhi: Sahitya Akademi.

Kapil Dev Shastri (Kapil Deo Shastri)

1963 "Significance of the word *prakāra* in the sūtras of the Aṣṭādhyāyī." *Vishveshvaranand Indological Journal* 1: 239-46.

1985 *Nāgeśa Bhaṭṭa's Vaiyākaraṇasiddhāntamañjūṣā.* Kurukshetra: Vishal Publications.

Katre, Sumitra Mangesh

1967 *Pāṇinian studies I.* Deccan College Building Centenary and Silver Jubilee Series, 52. Poona: Deccan College.

1981 *A Glossary of Grammatical Elements and Operations in the Aṣṭādhyāyī.* Mysore: Central Institute of Indian Languages.

Kielhorn, Lorenz Franz

1868 *The Paribhāṣenduśekhara of Nāgojībhaṭṭa, edited and explained by F. Kielhorn; part I: the Sanskrit text and various readings.* Bombay Sanskrit and Prakrit Series, 2, 7. Bombay: The Indu Prakash Press. Revised edition: see K. V. Abhyankar [1962].

1874 *The Paribhāṣenduśekhara of Nāgojībhaṭṭa, edited and explained by F. Kielhorn; part II: translation and notes.* Bombay Sanskrit and Prakrit Series, 9, 12. Bombay: Government Central Book Dept. New edition: see K. V. Abhyankar [1960].

1880-85 *The Vyākaraṇa-mahābhāshya of Patañjali.* 3 vols. Bombay Sanskrit and Prakrit Series, 18-22, 28-30. Bombay: Government Central Press. 1: 1880, 2: 1883, 3: 1885; reprint: Osnabrück: Zeller, 1970. 2nd edition: 1: 1892, 2: 1906, 3: 1909. 3rd edition: see K. V. Abhyankar [1962-72].

Kudāla, Śivadatta D.

1912 *Patañjali's Vyākaraṇa Mahābhāṣya with Kaiyaṭa's Pradīpa and Nāgeśa's Uddyota; edited with foot-notes, collected from Padamañjarī and Prātiśākhyas as well as supplied by the editor's own originality; vol. 2 (vidhiśesharūpam).* Bombay: Nirnaya-Sagar Press.

Liebich, Bruno

1930 *Kṣīrataraṅgiṇī, Kṣīrasvāmin's Kommentar zu Pāṇini's Dhātupāṭha, zum ersten Mal herausgegeben; mit fünf Anhängen. IndF Doppelheft* 8/9. Breslau: Marcus.

Miśra, Śrīnārāyaṇa

1985 *Kāśikavṛtti of Jayāditya-Vāmana, along with Commentaries Vivaraṇapañcikā–Nyāsa of Jinendrabuddhi and Padamañjarī of Haradatta Miśra.* 6 vols. Ratnabharati Series, 5–10. Varanasi: Ratna Publications.

Narasimha, M. S.

1973-83 *Mahābhāṣyapradīpavyākhyānāni: Commentaires sur le Mahābhāṣya de Patañjali et le Pradīpa de Kaiyaṭa.* Publications de l'Institut Français de'Indologie, 51, 1-10. Pondichéry: Institut Français de'Indologie. I (1973): adhyāya 1, pāda 1, āhnikas 1-4; II (1975): adhyāya 1, pāda 1, āhnikas 5-7; III (1976): adhyāya 1, pāda 1, āhnikas 8-9; IV (1977): adhyāya 1, pādas 2-4; V (1978): adhyāya 2; VI (1979): adhyāya 3; VII (1980): adhyāya 4; VIII (1981): adhyāya 5; IX (1982): adhyāya 6; X (1983): adhyāya 7-8.

Nene, Gopāla Shastri (Śāstrī)

1929 *The Śabda Kaustubha by Pandit Bhattoji Dīkshit, vol. II — fas. 5 to 10, from the second pāda of the 1st adhyāya to second pāda of 3rd adhyāya; and Sphoṭa Chandrikā by Pandit Srikrisna Mauni.* Benares: Chowkhamba.

1987 *Laghuśabdenduśekhara by Nāgojibhaṭṭa with a Commentary Chandrakalā by Bhairava Miśra, Edited by Narahari Śāstrī Peṇḍse. Re-edited by Gopāla Śāstrī Nene.* 2 vols. The Kashi Sanskrit Series, 5. Varanasi: Chaukhambha Sanskrit Sansthan.

Nene, Gopāla Śāstrī and Mukund Śāstrī Puṇtamkar

1933 *The Śabda Kaustubha by Śrī Bhaṭṭoji Dīkshita, vol. I, fas. I to IV, first pāda of the first adhyāya complete.* Benares: Chowkhamba.

Ogawa, Hideyo

1995 "An action (*kriyā*) and its cognition: Grammarians' approach." *Journal of Indian and Buddhist Studies* 44.1: 5-10.

2000a "Bhartṛhari on the non-distinction between reality and unreality." *Studies in the History of Indian Thought (Indo-shisōshi Kenkyū)* 12: 5-27.

2000b "Bhartṛhari on *pravṛtti* as the first *kāraka*." In *On the Understanding of Other Cultures (Proceedings of the International Conference on Sanskrit and Related Studies to Commemorate the Centenary of the Birth of Stanisław Schayer (1899-1941), Warsaw University, Poland, October 7-10, 1999)* (*Studia Indologiczne* 7), ed. Piotr Balcerowicz and Marek Mejor, 343–368. Warsaw: Oriental Institute, Warsaw University.

2001 "Bhartṛhari on *A.* 1.1.68", *Journal of Indian Philosophy* 29: 531-543.

Palsule, Gajanan Balakrishna

1957 "A survey of pre-Pāṇinian grammatical thought in the matter of the verbal root." *Indian Linguistics* 18: 116-39.

1961 *The Sanskrit dhātupāṭhas, a critical study.* Poona: University of Poona.

1985 *Mahābhāṣyadīpikā of Bhartṛhari, Fascicule I: Āhnika III, Critically Edited.* Bhandarkar Oriental Research Institute Postgraduate and Research Series, 22. Pune: Bhandarkar Oriental Research Institute.

Pañcholi, Bālakṛṣṇa

1969 *Vaiyākaraṇabhūṣaṇasāra of Śrī Kauṇḍabhaṭṭa, edited with 'Prabhā' Commentary by Pt. Śrī Bālakṛṣṇa Pañcholi and with 'Darpaṇa' Commentary by Śrī Harivallabha Śāstrī.* The Kashi Sanskrit Series, 188. Varanasi: The Chowkhamba Sanskrit Series Office.

Pischel, Richard

1900 *Grammatik der Prakrit-Sprachen.* Grundriss der indo-arischen Philologie und Altertumskunde I.8. Strassburg: Trübner. Translation: *Comparative grammar of the Prākṛt languages by R. Pischel; translated from the German by Subhadra Jhā* (Delhi: Motilal Banarsidass, 1965).

Raghunātha (Kāśinātha) Śāstrī and Śivadatta D. Kudāla

1937 *Patañjali's Vyākaraṇa Mahābhāṣya with Kaiyaṭa's Pradīpa and Nāgeśa's Uddyota; edited with foot notes collected from Chhāyā, Padamañjarī and Śabdakaustubha as well as supplied by the editors' own originality, vol. III.* Bombay: Nirnaya-Sagar Press.

Raghunātha Śarmā (Sharmā)

1963 *Vākyapadīyam, Part I (Brahmakāṇḍam). with the commentary Ambākartrī by Pt. Raghunātha Sharmā.* Sarasvatī Bhavana Grantha-mālā, 91. Varanasi: Vārāṇaseya Saṃskṛta Viśvavidyālaya.

1968 *Vākyapadīyam. part II (Vākyakāṇḍam). with the commentary Ambākartrī by Pt. Raghunātha Sharmā.* Sarasvatī Bhavana Grantha-mālā, 91. Varanasi: Vārāṇaseya Saṃskṛta Viśvavidyālaya.

1974 *Vākyapadīyam. part III (Pada-kāṇḍa, Jāti, Dravya and Sambandha Samuddeśa) with the commentary Prakāśa by Helārāja and Ambākartrī by Pt. Raghunātha Śarmā.* Sarasvatī Bhavana Grantha-mālā, 91. Varanasi: Vārāṇaseya Saṃskṛta Viśvavidyālaya.

1976 *Vākyapadīyam, Part I (Brahmakāṇḍam) with the Commentary Svopajñavṛtti by Harivṛṣabha and Ambākartrī by Pt. Raghunātha Śarmā.* Sarasvatī Bhavana Grantha-mālā, 91. Varanasi: Sampurnanand Sanskrit University. Reissue of Raghunātha Śarmā [1963].

1977 *Vākyapadīyam, Part III(Padakāṇḍa, Vṛttisamuddeśa) with the Commentary Prakāśa by Helārāja and Ambākartrī by Pt. Raghunātha Śarmā.* Sarasvatī Bhavana Grantha-mālā, 91. Varanasi: Sampurnanand Sanskrit University.

1979 *Vākyapadīyam, Part III, vol. 2 (Bhūyodravya, Guṇa, Dik, Sādhana, Kriyā, Kāla, Puruṣa, Saṅkhyā, Upagraha and Liṅga Samuddeśa) with the Commentary Prakāśa by Helārāja and Ambākartrī by Pt. Raghunātha Śarmā.* Sarasvatī Bhavana Grantha-mālā, 91. Varanasi: Sampurnanand Sanskrit University.

1980 *Vākyapadīyam, Part II (Vākyakāṇḍam) by Bhartṛhari with the Commentary of Puṇyarāja and Ambākartrī by Pt. Raghunātha Śarmā.* Sarasvatī Bhavana Grantha-mālā, 91. Varanasi: Sampurnanand Sanskrit University. Reissue of Raghunātha Śarmā [1968].

Rau, Wilhelm.

1977 *Bhartṛharis Vākyapadīya: Die Mūlakārikās nach den Handschriften herausgegeben und mit einem Pāda-Index versehen.* Abhandlungen für die Kunde des Morgenlandes XLII, 4. Wiesbaden: Franz Steiner Verlag.

1985 *Die vedischen Zitate im Vyākaraṇa-Mahābhāṣya.* Akademie der Wissenschaften und der Literatur, Mainz Jahrgang 1985, Nr. 4. Stuttgart: Franz Steiner Verlag.

2002 *Bhartṛharis Vākyapadīya: Versuch einer vollständigen deutschen Übersetzung nach der kritischen Edition der Mūla-Kārikās, hrsg. von Oskar von Hinüber.* Akademie der Wissenschaften und der Literatur, Abhandlung der Geistes- und Sozialwissenschaftlichen Klasse, Einzelveröffentlichung Nr. 8. Akademie der Wissenschaften und der Literatur, Mainz. Stuttgart: Franz Steiner Verlag.

Rocher, Rosane

1968 *La théorie des voix du verbe dans l'école pāṇinéenne (le 14e āhnika).* Université Libre de Bruxelles, Travaux de la faculté de philosophie et lettres, 35. Bruxelles: Presses Universitaires de Bruxelles.

1969 "The concept of verbal root in Indian grammar (a propos of Pāṇini 1.3.1)." *Foundations of Language* 5: 73-82.

Sarup, Lakshman

1927a *The Nighanṭu and the Nirukta, the oldest Indian treatise on etymology, philology and semantics; critically edited from original manuscripts and translated for the first time into English, with introduction, exegetical and critical notes, three indexes and eight appendices; Sanskrit text, with an appendix showing the relation of the Nirukta with other Sanskrit works.* Lahore: University of the Panjab. Reprint: Delhi: Motilal Banarsidass, 1967.

1927b *Fragments from the commentaries of Skandasvāmin and Maheśvara on the Nirukta; edited for the first time from the original palm leaf and paper manuscripts written in Malayalam and Devanāgarī characters with an introduction and critical notes.* Lahore: University of the Panjab. Reprint with additions and corrections by Acharya V. P. Limaye (Panini Vaidika Granthamala, 11): New Delhi: Panini, 1982.

1934 *Commentary of Skandasvāmin and Maheśvara on the Nirukta; vols. III and IV: chapters VII-XIII; critically edited for the first time from original manuscripts with an introduction, indices and appendices.* Lahore: University of the Panjab. Reprint with additions and corrections by Acharya V. P. Limaye (Panini Vaidika Granthamala, 11): New Delhi: Panini, 1982.

Sitaram Shastri

1960 *Bṛhat-śabdenduśekhara by Nāgeśa Bhaṭṭa.* 3 vols. Sarasvatī Bhavana Grantha-mālā, 87. Varanasi: Vārāṇaseya Saṃskrta Viśvavidyālaya.

Sivadatta D. Kudāla and Raghunātha Śāstrī

1935 *Patañjali's Vyākaraṇa Mahābhāṣya with Kaiyaṭa's Pradīpa and Nāgeśa's Uddyota (Vol. 2 Vidhiśeṣarūpa), edited with foot-notes, collected from Padamañjari and Prātiśākhyas as well as supplied by the editors' own originality.* [The second edition of Kudāla [1912]] Bombay: Nirnaya-Sagar Press.

Subrahmanya Sastri, P. S.

1951-62 *Lectures on the Mahābhāṣya.* 6 vols. 2 (āhnikas 4-6): (Annamalai University Sanskrit Series, 11) Annamalainagar: Annamalai University, 1951; 1^2(āhnikas 1-3), 6 (āhnikas 23-28): Thiruvaiyaru: The author, 1960, 1962; 3 (āhnikas 7-9), 4 (āhnikas 10-14), 5 (āhnikas 15-22): Tiruchirapalli: The author, 1955, 1956, 1957.

Subramania Iyer, K. A.

1950-51 "The conception of action among the vaiyākaranas." *Journal of the Gangānātha Jhā Research Institute* 8: 165-88.

1963 *Vākyapadīya of Bhartṛhari with the Commentary of Helārāja, Kāṇḍa III, Part 1.* Deccan College Monograph Series, 21. Poona: Deccan College.

1965 *The Vākyapadīya of Bhartṛhari with the Vṛtti: Chapter I, English Translation.* Deccan College Building Centenary and Silver Jubilee Series, 26. Poona: Deccan College.

1966 *Vākyapadīya of Bhartṛhari with the Commentaries Vṛtti and Paddhati of Vṛṣabhadeva.* Deccan College Monograph Series, 32. Poona: Deccan College.

1969 *Bhartṛhari: A study of the Vākyapadīya in the light of ancient commentaries.* Deccan College Building Centenary and Silver Jubilee Series, 68. Poona: Deccan College.

1971 *The Vākyapadīya of Bhartṛhari, chapter III, part 1: English translation.* Deccan College Building Centenary and Silver Jubilee Series, 71. Poona: Deccan College.

1973 *Vākyapadīya of Bhartṛhari with the Commentary of Helārāja, Kāṇḍa III, Part II.* Poona: Deccan College.

1974 *The Vākyapadīya of Bhartṛhari, chapter III, part ii; English translation with Exegetical Notes.* Delhi: Motilal Banarsidass.

1977 *The Vākyapadīya of Bhartṛhari, Kāṇḍa II: English Translation with Exegetical Notes.* Delhi: Motilal Banarsidass.

1983 *The Vākyapadīya of Bhartṛhari (An Ancient Treatise on the Philosophy of Sanskrit Grammar), Containing the Ṭīkā of Puṇyarāja and the Ancient Vṛtti, Kāṇḍa II, with a Foreword by Ashok Aklujkar.* Delhi: Motilal Banarsidass.

Śukla, Kālikā Prasāda

1977 *Vaiyākaraṇasiddhāntamañjūṣā by Nāgeśa Bhaṭṭa.* M. M. Śivakumāraśāstrī-Granthamālā, 3. Varanasi: Sampurnanand Sanskrit University.

Tripāṭhī, Rāmaprasāda

1986 *Ṛgvedaprātiśākhyam of Maharṣi Śaunaka, with the Commentary of 'Uvaṭācārya'.* Sarasvatī Bhavana Grantha-mālā, 121. Varanasi: Sampurnanand Sanskrit University.

Vedavrata

1962–63 *Śrībhagavat-patañjali-viracitaṃ Vyākaraṇa-Mahābhāṣyam (Śrī-kaiyaṭa-kṛta-pradīpena nāgojībhaṭṭa-kṛtena-bhāṣya-pradīpoddyotena ca vibhūṣitam).* 5 vols. Gurukul Jhajjar (Rohatak): Hairyāṇā-Sāhitya-Saṃsthānam.

Vindhyeśvarī Prasāda Dvivedī — Gaṇapati Śāstrī Mokate

1917 *Śabdakaustubha by Paṇḍit Bhaṭṭoji Dīkshita, vol. III.* Chowkhamba Sanskrit Series, 234–235. Benares: Chowkhamba.

Yudhiṣṭhira Mīmāṃsaka

1957/8 *Kṣīra-taraṅgiṇī, kṣīrasvāmi-viracitā pāṇinīya-dhātu-pāṭhasya paścimottara-śākhāyā vyākhyā.* Rāma Lāl Kapūr Trust Series, 25. Amritsar: Rāma Lāl Kapūr Trust.

1972 *Mahābhāṣyam patañjalimuni-viracitam hindī-vyākhyā-sahitam dvitīyo bhāgaḥ (1/2-4).* Delhi: Srī Pyārelāl Drākṣādevī Trust.

1974 *Mahābhāṣyam patañjalimuni-viracitam hindī-vyākhyā-sahitam tṛtīyo bhāgaḥ (dvitīyo 'dhyāyaḥ).* Delhi: Śrī Pyārelāl Drākṣādevī Trust.

1979 *Mahābhāṣyam patañjalimuni-viracitam hindī-vyākhyā-sahitam prathamo bhāgaḥ (prathamādhyāyasya prathamaḥ pādaḥ).* Delhi: Śrī Pyārelāl Drāksādevī Trust.

Index